Classic reference books at affordable prices!

SCROGGIE'S BIBLE HANDBOOK, *W. Graham Scroggie*
One of the world's greatest Bible teachers of this century, W. Graham Scroggie wrote in a style that both laymen and clergy could enjoy. *Scroggie's Bible Handbook* is a testimony to that fact. This book is an in-depth study, examining each book of the Bible. As he probes God's Word book by book, Scroggie points out words and themes that provide enriching bypaths for further study.

Let *Scroggie's Bible Handbook* be the start of your quest for more knowledge of God's wonderful Word.

THE CRISES OF THE CHRIST, *G. Campbell Morgan*
Many books have been published about the life of our Savior, but *The Crises of the Christ,* first published in 1903, stands out among the rest —a book offering a rare insight into the pivotal events in Christ's life. Examining His life as the accomplishment of a Divine work, the author divides it into seven turning points, the crises: the Birth, the Baptism, the Temptation, the Transfiguration, the Death, the Resurrection, and the Ascension.

Let this renowned classic inspire you as it has thousands of others over the years.

The Quotable Matthew Henry

Matthew Henry

William T. Summers, Compiler

Fleming H. Revell Company
Old Tappan, New Jersey

First published 1982 as
A Topical Index to Matthew Henry's
A Commentary on the Whole Bible
© Evangelical Press
16–18 High Street, Welwyn, Hertfordshire, AL6 9EQ, England
Typeset in Great Britain by Inset, Hertford Heath.

Library of Congress Cataloging-in-Publication Data

Henry, Matthew, 1662–1714.
    [Commentary on the whole Bible. Selections]
    The quotable Matthew Henry / William T. Summers, compiler.
        p.   cm.
    Topically arranged excerpts from: Commentary on the whole Bible.
    Originally published: A topical index to Matthew Henry's A
commentary on the whole Bible. Welwyn, England: Evangelical Press,
1982.
    ISBN 0-8007-5334-8
    1. Bible—Indexes. 2. Bible—Commentaries. I. Summers,
William T. II. Title.
    BS432.H44   1990
    220.7—dc20   89-48222
                                                                CIP

Published by Fleming H. Revell Company
Printed in the United States of America

Preface

I suppose the usefulness of such a book as this dawned on me very slowly. At first I began reading through Matthew Henry's commentary purely for my own spiritual benefit, marking passages that were specially valuable for future reference. When I had been reading and meditating for some years (cf. Spurgeon's advice to his son: 'Read it all before you get married', and to his students: 'Read it in the first year of your ministry'), the thought occurred to me to collect the numerous pithy sayings under topical headings for help in the preparation of sermons. Perhaps a year or so later, as the value of such a scheme became more obvious the idea came to me of sharing the fruitfulness of 'the great Mr. Henry', as George Whitefield described him.

Here then indeed we have 'fruit from Matthew Henry'. As you read, remember his own words in a letter to Mr. Thoresby: 'Every page, Sir, is a child of prayer.'

Matthew Henry himself had no thoughts of publication when he began to write his 'notes'. He tells us, 'It has long been my practice, what little time I had to spare in my study, from my constant preparations for the pulpit, to spend it in drawing up expositions upon some parts of the New Testament, not so much for my own use, as purely for my own entertainment, because I knew not how to employ my thoughts and time more to my satisfaction.'

This was some time before his commentary appeared, although it was hardly surprising, when we consider his father's regular exposition of Scripture in family prayers, and his requirement that his children write out later what they had heard. Matthew kept these notes and 'made judicious use' of them in his own work. Add to this his own practice of preaching through the Bible regularly, and we see his commentary in the making. He would begin on Sunday morning at nine o'clock, starting at Genesis chapter 1, until, Sunday by Sunday, he eventually completed the Old Testament. On Sunday afternoons he had the same method, only then he preached through the New Testament.

It was the substance of this preaching which he incorporated into his *Exposition of the Old and New Testament,* and which George Whitefield read through (unabridged) four times on his knees! In Whitefield's days the commentary cost about sixteen weeks of a working man's wages, but he bought it, and read it, and preached it. What more can I say, than that I hope you will all go and do likewise.

William T. Summers
1982

List of Subjects

Fear
Fellowship
Fickleness of Man
Fighting the Right
  Enemy
Final Perseverance
Forbearance
Forgetfulness
Forgiveness
Fortitude
Free Will
Friendship

Generosity
Gentleness
God
God: His Attributes
God: His Dominion
God: His Faithful-
  ness
God: His Goodness
God: His Grace
God: His Mercy
God: His Omni-
  potence
God: His Omni-
  presence
God: His Omni-
  science
God: His Patience
God: His Righteous-
  ness
God: His Sovereignty
God: His Transcend-
  ence
God: His Ways
God: His Wrath
Godly Fear
Good Works
Gospel: Above
  Reason
Gossip
Gratitude
Greed
Growth
Grumbling
Guidance

Happiness
Hardness of Heart

Harvest
Heart Religion
Heart Searching
Heaven
Heavenly-Mindedness
Hell
Heresy
Holiness
Holy Spirit
Honour
Honouring God
Hope
Hospitality
Human Responsi-
  bility
Humility
Husbands and Wives
Hymn Singing
Hypocrisy
Hypocrites

Idolatry
Ignorance
Immutability
Impatience
Impenitence
Imprecatory Psalms
Influence
Ingratitude
Injustice
Inner Resources
Interpreting Provi-
  dences

Jealousy
Joy
Judging Others
Judgment
Judicial Blindness
Justice
Justification

Kindness
Knowing God
Knowledge

Large-Heartedness
Law
Law and Grace
Law and Order

Leaving a Will
Legalism
Lessons from Nature
Liberality
Liberty
Lies
Listening to Sermons
Living in the Light
  of Eternity
Living Sacrifice
Loneliness
Longsuffering
Lord's Supper
Love
Love of Ease
Love to God
Lowering of
  Standards
Loyalty
Lukewarmness
Luxurious Living

Man Helpless Before
  God's Judgments
Manifestations
Marks of Grace
Marriage
Material Prosperity
Means of Grace
Meditation
Meekness
Mercy
Methods
Ministers
Ministers (Desire for)
Miracles
Money
Mortification
Motives
Mourning
Music

National Punish-
  ments
New Year

Obedience
Obstinacy
Old Age
Omissions

The Quotable Matthew Henry

Accountability

In Zerubbabel's time the vessels were delivered by number, here by weight, that all might be forthcoming and it might easily appear if any were missing, to intimate that such as are entrusted with the holy things (as all the stewards of the mysteries of God are) are concerned to remember, both in receiving their trust and in discharging it, that they must shortly give a *very particular account* of it, that they may be faithful to it and so give up their account with joy.

Ezra 8

When he spake to the father of the child and to the people, he charged it upon their unbelief; when he spake to his disciples, he charged it upon theirs; for the truth was, there were faults on both sides; but we are more concerned to hear of our own faults than of other people's, and to impute what is amiss to ourselves than to others. When the preaching of the word seems not to be so successful as sometimes it has been, the people are apt to lay all the fault upon the ministers, and the ministers upon the people; whereas, it is more becoming for each to own his own faultiness, and to say, 'It is owing to me.'

Matthew 17

Adoration

'His glory is above the heavens', that is, above the angels; he is above what they are, for their brightness is nothing to his — above what they do, for they are under his command and do his pleasure — and above what even they can speak him to be. He is exalted above all blessing and praise, not only all ours, but all theirs. We must therefore say, with holy admiration, 'Who is like unto the Lord our God?'

Psalm 113

Whenever we enter into communion with God it becomes us to have a due sense of the vast distance and disproportion that there are between us and the holy angels, and of the infinite distance, and no proportion at all, between us and the holy God, and to acknowledge that we cannot 'order our speech by reason of darkness'. How shall we that are dust and ashes speak to the Lord of Glory?

Daniel 10

In thanking God, we fasten upon his favours to us; in praising and adoring God, we fasten upon his perfections in himself.

Romans 16

Adultery

Sin lessens men, thrusts them down from their excellency. Seventh commandment sins especially leave an indelible stain upon men's names and families, a reproach which time will not wipe away. Reuben's seed to the last bore the disgrace of Reuben's sin.

1 Chronicles 5

The representing of those sins which are most provoking to God and most ruining to a people by the sin of whoredom plainly intimates what an

exceedingly sinful sin uncleanness is, how offensive, how destructive. Doubtless it is itself one
of the worst of sins, for the
worst of other sins are compared
to it here and often elsewhere,
which should increase our detestation and dread of all manner
of fleshly lusts, all appearances
of them and approaches to
them, as warring against the
soul, infatuating sinners, be-
witching them, alienating their
minds from God and all that is
good, debauching conscience,
rendering them odious in the
eyes of the pure and holy God,
and drowning them at last in
destruction and perdition.

Ezekiel 23

In the enumeration of these
commandments, the apostle puts
the seventh before the sixth,
and mentions this first, 'Thou
shalt not commit adultery'; for
though this commonly goes
under the name of love (pity it
is that so good a word should
be so abused) yet it is really as
great a violation of it as killing
and stealing is, which shows
that true brotherly love is love
to the souls of our brethren in
the first place. He that tempts
others to sin, and defiles their
minds and consciences, though
he may pretend the most
passionate love (Prov. 7:15, 18),
does really hate them, just as
the devil does, who wars against
the soul.

Romans 13

Afflictions

Those who in the day of their
mirth had cried to Baal and
Ashtaroth, now that they are in
trouble, cry to the Lord
from whom they had revolted,
whose justice brought them
into this trouble, and whose
power and favour could alone
help them out of it. Affliction
makes those cry to God with
importunity who, before, would
scarcely speak to him.

Judges 3

Weeping must never hinder
worship.

2 Samuel 12

Those that acknowledge God
righteous in afflicting them
shall find him gracious. Those
that humble themselves before
him shall find favour with
him. So ready is the God of
mercy to take the first occasion
to show mercy. If we have
humbled hearts under humbling
providences, the affliction has
done its work.

2 Chronicles 12

Those are wicked and vile
indeed that are made worse by
their afflictions instead of being
made better by them, who in
their distress trespass yet more,
have their corruptions exasperated by that which should
mollify them and their hearts
more fully set in them to do
evil.

2 Chronicles 28

Then he knew (that is, he
believed and considered) that
the Lord he was God. He might
have known it at a less expense
if he would have given due attention and credit to the word
written and preached but it was
better to pay thus dearly for the
knowledge of God than to perish
in ignorance and unbelief. Had

he been a prince in the palace of Babylon it is probable he would have been confirmed in his idolatry but being a captive in the prisons of Babylon he was convinced of it and re-claimed from it . . . Afflictions are continued no longer than till they have done their work.

2 Chronicles 33

If the cries of the oppressed be not heard, the fault is not in God; he is ready to hear and help them. But the fault is in themselves; they ask and have not, but it is because they ask amiss. (James 4.3.) They cry out by reason of the arm of the Mighty, but it is a com-plaining cry, a wailing cry, not a penitent praying cry, the cry of nature and passion, not of grace. See (Hos. 7:14.) They have not cried unto Me with their heart when they howled upon their beds. How then can we expect that they should be answered and relieved?

They do not enquire after God, nor seek to acquaint them-selves with him, under their affliction (v. 10). But none saith, Where is God my Maker? Afflictions are sent to direct and quicken us to enquire early after God (Ps. 78:34.) But many that groan under great oppress-ions never mind God, nor take notice of his hand in their troubles; if they did, they would bear their troubles more patiently and be more benefited by them. Of the many that are afflicted and oppressed, few get the good they might get by their affliction. It should drive them to God, but how seldom is this the case.

Yet this is not all: they are proud still, and therefore they do not seek unto God (Ps. 10.4) or, if they do cry unto him, therefore he does not give answer, for he hears only the desire of the humble (Ps. 10.17) and delivers those by his provi-dence whom he has first by his grace prpeared and made fit for deliverance. The case is plain then, if we cry to God for the removal of the oppress-ion and affliction we are under, and it is not removed, the reason is not because the Lord's hand is shortened or his ear heavy, but because the affliction has not done its work; we are not sufficiently humbled, and therefore we must thank our-selves that it is continued.

Job 35

God's eye is upon our souls when we are in trouble, to see whether they be humbled for sin, submissive to the will of God, and bettered by the afflic-tion. If the soul, when cast down under affliction, has been lifted up to him in true devo-tion, he knows it.

Psalm 31

Before he prays 'Remove thy stroke from me' (v. 10) he prays 'Deliver me from all my offences, from the guilt I have contracted, the punishment I have deserved, and the power of corruption by which I have been enslaved.' (v. 8). When God forgives our sins, he delivers us from them.

Psalm 39

Sometimes God makes his people's troubles contribute to the increase of their greatness, and their sun shines the brighter for having been under a cloud. If he make them contribute to the increase of their goodness, that will prove in the end the increase of their greatness, their glory; and if he comfort them on every side, according to the time and degree wherein he has afflicted them on every side, they will have no reason to complain. When our Lord Jesus was quickened again, and brought back from the depths of the earth, his greatness was increased, and he entered on the joy set before him.

Psalm 71

It is observable that Heman, who became eminently wise and good, was afflicted and ready to die, and suffered God's terrors, from his youth up. Thus many have found it was good for them to bear the yoke in their youth, that sorrow has been much better for them than laughter would have been, and that being much afflicted, and often ready to die, when they were young, they have, by the grace of God, got such an habitual seriousness and weanedness from the world as have been of great use to them all their days. Sometimes those whom God designs for eminent services are prepared for them by exercises of this kind.

Psalm 88

Their being related to Christ shall not excuse them from being called to an account. But observe what affliction is to God's people. 1. It is but a rod, not an axe, not a sword; it is for correction, not for destruction. This denotes gentleness in the affliction; it is the rod of men,

such a rod as men use in the correcting of their children; and it denotes a design of good in and by the affliction, such a rod as yields the peaceable fruit of righteousness. 2. It is a rod in the hand of God (I will visit them), he who is wise, and knows what he does, gracious, and will do what is best. 3. It is a rod which they shall never feel the smart of but when there is great need: 'If they break my law, then I will visit their transgression with the rod', but not else. Then it is requisite that God's honour be vindicated, and that they be humbled and reduced.

Psalm 89

Prosperity is the unhappy occasion of much iniquity; it makes people conceited of themselves, indulgent of the flesh, forgetful of God, in love with the world, and deaf to the reproofs of the word. See (30:6.) It is good for us, when we are afflicted, to remember how and wherein we went astray before we were afflicted, that we may answer the end of the affliction.

It has been the advantage of God's people to be afflicted. David could speak experimentally: 'It was good for me'; many a good lesson he had learnt by his afflictions, and many a good duty he had been brought to which otherwise would have been unlearnt and undone. Therefore God visited him with affliction, that he might learn God's statutes.

Psalm 119

As the fining-pot is for silver, both to prove it and to improve it, so the Lord tries the hearts; he searches whether they are standard or no, and those that are he refines and makes purer, (Jer. 17:10.) God tries the heart by affliction (Ps. 66:10, 11), and often chooses his people in that furnace (Isa. 68:10), and makes them choice.

Proverbs 16

We have reason to account those happy afflictions which part between us and our sins, and by sensible convictions of the vanity of the world, that great idol, cool our affections to it and lower our expectations from it.

Isaiah 17

The benefit we often have by afflictions. They bring us to God, quicken us to our duty, and show us our dependence upon him. Those that before seldom looked at God now visit him; they come frequently, they become friendly, and make their court to him. Before prayer came drop by drop, but now they pour out a prayer; it comes now like water from a fountain, not like water from a still. They poured out a secret speech; so the margin.

Isaiah 26

Though God will debate with them, yet it shall be in measure, and the affliction shall be mitigated, moderated, and proportioned to their strength, not to their deserts (v. 8.) He will deal out afflictions to them as the wise physician prescribes medicines to his patients, just such a quantity of each ingredient . . . Therefore, because the affliction is mitigated and moderated, and

the rough wind stayed, therefore we may conclude that he designs their reformation, not their destruction; and, because he deals thus gently with us, we should therefore study to answer his ends in afflicting us.

Isaiah 27

He was not sensible of the displeasure of God that he was under. He felt the smart of the rod, but had no regard at all to the hand; the more he was crossed in his worldly pursuits the more eager he was in them. He either would not see his error or if he saw it would not amend it. Covetousness was the way of his heart; it was what he was inclined to and intent upon, and he would not be reclaimed, but in his distress he trespasses yet more (2 Chron. 28:22.) See the strength of the corruption of men's hearts, and sinfulness of sin, which will take its course in despite of God himself and all the flames of his wrath. See also how insufficient afflictions of themselves are to reform men, unless God's grace work with them.

Isaiah 57

It is an instance of their sottishness that, though they are God's people, and therefore should readily understand his mind upon every intimation of it, yet they know not the judgment of the Lord; they apprehend not the meaning either of a mercy or an affliction, nor how to accommodate themselves to either, nor to answer God's intention in either. They know not how to improve the seasons of grace that God affords them when he sends them his prophets, nor how to make use of the rebukes they are under when his voice cries in the city. They discern not the signs of the times (Matt. 16:3), nor are aware how God is dealing with them.

Jeremiah 8

They have grown so very corrupt that there is no other way with them but to put them into the furnace; what other course can I take with them? (Isa. 5:4, 5.) It is the daughter of my people, and I must do something to vindicate my own honour, which will be reflected upon if I connive at their wickedness. I must do something to reduce and reform them. A parent corrects his own children because they are his own. Note, when God afflicts his people, it is with a gracious design to mollify and reform them; it is but when need is and when he knows it is the best method he can use.

Jeremiah 9

When I am in affliction I should say, 'This is an evil, and I will bear it, because it is the will of God that I should, because his wisdom has appointed this for me and his grace will make it work for good to me.' This is receiving evil at the hand of God (Job 2:10.)

Jeremiah 10

Here is an account of the temptation he was in under this affliction; his feet were almost gone, as the psalmist's (Ps. 73:2.) And this is that which is most to be dreaded in affliction, being driven by it to sin (Neh. 6:13.) He was tempted to quarrel with God for making him a prophet.

Jeremiah 20

Even this disgraceful uncomfortable captivity God intended for their benefit; and we are sure that his intentions are never frustrated: 'I have sent them into the land of the Chaldeans for their good'. It seemed to be every way for their hurt, not only as it was the ruin of their estates, honours and liberties, separated them from their relations and friends, and put them under the power of their enemies and oppressors, but as it sunk their spirits, discouraged their faith, deprived them of the benefit of God's oracles and ordinances, and exposed them to temptations; yet it was designed for their good, and proved so, in the issue, as to many of them. 'Out of the eater came forth meat'. By their afflictions they were convinced of sin, humbled under the hand of God, weaned from the world, made serious, taught to pray, and turned from their iniquity; particularly they were cured of their inclination to idolatry; and thus it was 'good for them that they were afflicted', (Ps. 119: 67, 61.)

Jeremiah 24

They were now sent into a miserable thraldom for mocking the messengers of the Lord and misusing his prophets. This was the sin for which God now contended with them; and yet in their distress they trespass yet more against the Lord, (2 Chron. 28:22.) This very sin they are notoriously guilty of in their captivity, which shows that afflictions will not of themselves cure men of their sins, unless the grace of God work with them, but will rather exasperate the corruptions they are intended to mortify; so true is that of Solomon (Prov. 27: 22), 'Though thou shouldst bray a fool in a mortar, yet will not his foolishness depart from him.'

Jeremiah 29

When God afflicts his people, yet he does not forget them; when he casts them out of their land, yet he does not cast them out of sight, nor out of mind. Even then when God is speaking against us, yet he is acting for us, and designing our good in all; and this is our comfort in affliction, that 'the Lord thinks upon us', though we have forgotten him. 'I remember Him still', and therefore 'my bowels are troubled for Him', as Joseph's yearned towards his brethren, even when he spoke roughly to them. When Israel's afflictions extorted a penitent confession and submission it is said that his soul was grieved for the misery of Israel (Judg. 10:16), for he always afflicts with the greatest tenderness.

Jeremiah 31

He never afflicts us but when we give him cause to do it. He does not dispense his frowns as he does his favours, from his mere good pleasure. If he show us kindness, it is because so it seems good unto him; but, if he write bitter things against us, it is because we both deserve them and need them. He does not afflict with pleasure. He delights not in the death of sinners, or the disquiet of saints, but punishes with a kind of reluctance. He comes out of his place to punish, for his place is the mercy-seat. He

delights not in the misery of any of his creatures, but, as it respects his own people, he is so far from it that in all their afflictions he is afflicted and his soul is grieved for the misery of Israel. He retains his kindness for his people even when he afflicts them. If he does not willingly grieve the children of men, much less his own children. However it be, yet God is good to them (Ps. 73:1), and they may by faith see love in his heart even then whey see frowns in his face and a rod in his hand.

Lamentations 3

See the benefit of affliction; by the account Jeremiah gives of the princes and great men now at Jerusalem it appears that they were very corrupt and wicked, and defiled themselves with things offered to idols, while these young gentlemen that were in captivity would not defile themselves, no, not with their portion of the king's meat. How much better is it with those that retain their integrity in the depths of affliction than with those that retain their iniquity in the heights of prosperity.

Daniel 1

'Some of those of understanding shall fall', but it shall be for the good of the church and for their own spiritual benefit. It shall be to try them, and to purge, and to make them white. They needed these afflictions themselves. The best have their spots which must be washed off, their dross, which must be purged out; and their troubles, particularly their share in the public troubles, help to do this; being sanctified to them by the grace of God, they are means of mortifying their corruptions, weaning them from the world, and awakening them to greater seriousness and diligence in religion.

Daniel 11

Though God may suffer his people to fall into sin, yet he will not suffer them to lie still in it, but will take a course effectually to show them their error, and to bring them to themselves and to their right mind again. We have reason to hope that Jonah, after this, was well reconciled to the sparing of Nineveh, and was as well pleased with it as ever he had been displeased.

Jonah 4

It is a great mercy to be deprived of those things in which we have reposed a confidence in competition with God, which we have made our arm, and after which we have gone a whoring from God.

Micah 5

Hear the rod when it has come, and is actually upon you, and you are sensible of the smart of it; hear what it says to you, what convictions, what counsels, what cautions, it speaks to you. Note, every rod has a voice, and it is the voice of God that is to be heard in the rod of God, and it is well for those that understand the language of it, which if we would do we must have an eye to 'Him that appointed it.' Note, every rod is appointed, of what kind it shall be, where it shall light, and

how long it shall lie. God in every affliction 'performs the thing that is appointed for us' (Job 23:14), and to him therefore we must have an eye, to Him we must have an ear; we must hear what He says to us by the affliction. 'Hear it, and know it for thy good' (Job 5:6.)

Micah 6

It should seem, because God had punished them with scarcity of bread, they made that a pretence for robbing him — that now, being impoverished, they could not afford to bring their tithes and offerings, but must save them, that they might have bread for their families. Note, it argues great perverseness in sin when men make those afflictions excuses for sin which are sent to part between them and their sins. When they had but little they should have done the more good with that little, and that would have been the way to make it more; but it is ill with the patient when that which should cure the disease serves only to palliate it, and prevent its being searched into.

Malachi 3

Outward afflictions, wants and burdens, are the great arguments Satan uses to make the people of God question their sonship; as if afflictions could not consist with, when really they proceed from, God's fatherly love.

Matthew 4

Paul knew as much of it as any man, and he calls it a 'light affliction' (2 Cor. 4:17.) God's presence (Isa. 43:2), Christ's sympathy (Isa. 43:9), (Dan. 3:

25), and especially the Spirit's aids and comforts (2 Cor. 1:5), make suffering for Christ light and easy. As afflictions abound, and are prolonged, consolations abound, and are prolonged too. Let this therefore reconcile us to the difficulties, and help us over the discouragements we may meet with, both in doing work and suffering work; though we may lose *for* Christ, we shall not lose *by Him*.

Matthew 11

If water have a sediment at the bottom, though it may be clear while it stands still, yet, when shaken, it grows muddy; so it is with our affections: but pure water in a clean glass, though ever so much stirred, continues clear; and so it was with Christ.

Mark 14

Afflictions, when they are sanctified by divine grace, prove happy means of turning sinners from the error of their ways. By them the ear is opened to discipline and the heart disposed to receive instruction; and they are sensible proofs both of the vanity of the world and of the mischievousness of sin.

Luke 15

What a blessed change was here in this house, occasioned by the sickness of the child! This should reconcile us to afflictions; we know not what good may follow from them.

John 4

Afflictions cannot make us miserable, if it be not our own fault. A blessing may arise from them, and we may be blessed in them. They are so far from taking away a good man's felicity that they really increase it.

James 1

Affluence

This denotes that Israel was near to ruin, and that their luxury and sensuality were the cause of it. They were as the 'evil figs' that could not be eaten, they were so evil. It intimates sin to be the daughter of plenty and destruction the daughter of the abuse of plenty.

Hosea 1

How basely their plenty was abused by them. They robbed God of the honour of his gifts. . . . They served and honoured His enemies with them . . . It is a very great dishonour to the God of heaven to make those gifts of his providence the food and fuel of our lusts which he gave us for our support in his service, and to be oil to the wheels of our obedience.

Hosea 2

Ambition

Surely he was fond of a crown indeed who, at this time, would run such a hazard as a traitor did, for the crown of Israel now that it had lost the choicest of its flowers and jewels, was lined more than ever with thorns, had of late been fatal to all the heads that had worn it, was forfeited to divine justice and now ready to be laid in the dust, a crown which a wise man would not have taken up in the street, yet Hoshea not only ventured upon it but ventured for it and it cost him dear.

2 Kings 15

Most people bring themselves into inconvenience, because they do not know when they are well off, but gain harm and loss by aiming against advice to better themselves.

Acts 27

Angels

That which comes out of the fire, of a fiery amber colour, when it comes to be distinctly viewed, is the likeness of four living creatures; not the living creatures themselves (angels are spirits, and cannot be seen), but the likeness of them, such a hieroglyphic, or representation, as God saw fit to make use of for the leading of the prophet, and us with him, into some acquaintance with the world of angels (a matter purely of divine revelation), so far as is requisite to possess us with an awful sense of the greatness of that God who has angels for his attendants, and the goodness of that God who has appointed them to be attendants on his people.

Ezekiel 1

We must acknowledge the hand of God in the strengthening of those that are friends to the church for the service they are to do it, and confirming them in their good resolutions; herein he uses the ministry of angels more than we are aware of. And the many instances we have known of God's care of his church formerly encourage us to depend upon him in further straits and difficulties.

Daniel 11

God has a variety of work and employment for his holy angels. Sometimes they are to sound the trumpet of divine Providence, and give fair warning to a careless world; sometimes they are to pour out the vials of God's anger upon impenitent sinners; and sometimes to discover things of a heavenly nature to those that are 'the heirs of salvation'. They readily execute every commission they receive from God; and, when this world shall be at an end, yet the angels shall be employed by the great God in proper pleasant work to all eternity.

Revelation 21

Anger

Anger is a sin that is its own punishment. Fretful passionate people tear and torment themselves. *He teareth his soul* (so the word is); every sin wounds the soul, tears that, wrongs that (Prov. 8: 36), unbridled passion particularly.

Job 18

He is a revenger, and 'he is furious'; he 'has fury' (so the word is), not as man has it, in whom it is an ungoverned passion (so he has said, 'Fury is not in me'), (Isa. 27:4), but he has it in such a way as becomes the righteous God, to put an edge upon his justice and to make it appear more terrible to those who otherwise would stand in no awe of it.

10

He is 'Lord of anger' (so the Hebrew phrase is for that which we read, 'He is furious'); he has anger, but he has it at command and under government. Our anger is often lord over us, as theirs that have 'no rule over their own spirits', but God is always 'Lord of His anger' and 'weighs a path to it', (Ps. 78:50.)

Nahum 1

Anger is a natural passion; there are cases in which it is lawful and laudable; but it is then sinful when we are angry without cause. The word signifies — without cause, without any good effect, without moderation; so that the anger is then sinful, (1) When it is without any just provocation given; either for no cause, or no great and proportionable cause; when we are angry at children or servants for that which could not be helped, which was only a piece of forgetfulness or mistake, that we ourselves might easily have been guilty of, and for which we should not have been angry at ourselves; when we are angry upon groundless surmises, or for trivial affronts not worth speaking of, (2) When it is without any good end aimed at, merely to show our authority, then it is vain, it is to do hurt; whereas if we are at any time angry, it should be to awaken the offender to repentance, and prevent his doing so again; to clear ourselves (2 Cor. 7:11), and to give warning to others. (3) When it exceeds due bounds; when we are hardy and headstrong in our anger, violent and vehement, outrageous and mischievous, and when we seek the hurt of those we are displeased at. This is a breach of the sixth commandment, for he that is thus angry would kill if he could and durst; he has taken the first step towards it: Cain's killing his brother began in anger; he is a murderer in the account of God, who knows his heart, whence murders proceed, (Ch. 15:19.)

Matthew 5

Anxiety

When he saw an extraordinary crop upon his ground, instead of thanking God for it, or rejoicing in the opportunity it would give him of doing the more good, he afflicts himself with this thought, 'What shall I do, because I have no room where to bestow my fruits?' He speaks as one at a loss, and full of perplexity. What shall I do now? The poorest beggar in the country, that did not know where to get a meal's meat, could not have said a more anxious word. Disquieting care is the common fruit of an abundance of this world, and the common fault of those that have abundance.

Luke 12

It is the duty and interest of Christians to live without care. There is a care of diligence which is our duty, and consists in a wise forecast and due concern; but there is a care of diffidence and distrust which is our sin and folly; and which only perplexes and distracts the mind. 'Be careful for nothing', so as by your care to distrust God, and unfit yourselves for his service.

Philippians 4

Apathy

Their wickedness was so great that they had reason to fear Divine vengeance every day. It was a sign that the Israelites, through their sloth and cowardice were not now such a terror to the Canaanites as they were when they first came among them else the city of Laish which probably knew itself to be assigned to them, would not have been so very secure. Though they were an open and inland town, they lived secure.

Judges 18

It is sad to think what a deep sleep the world is cast into, what a spirit of slumber has seized the generality of mankind, that are under God's wrath and Satan's power, and yet secure and unconcerned! They sit still and are at rest, (Luke 17:26.)

Zechariah 1

The 'spirit of slumber', that is, an indisposedness to mind either their duty or interest. They are under the power of a prevailing unconcernedness, like people that are slumbering and sleeping; not affected with any thing that is said or done. They were resolved to continue as they were, and would not stir.

Romans 11

Apostasy

See the method of apostasy; men first cast off that which is good; then those omissions make way for commissions; and frequent actual transgressions of God's law bring men at length to an habitual renunciation of his covenant. When men cast off praying, and hearing, and sabbath-sanctifications, and other things that are good, they are in the high road to a total forsaking of God.

Hosea 8

The sin here mentioned is a total and final apostasy, when men with a full and fixed will and resolution despise and reject Christ, the only Saviour — despise and resist the Spirit, the only sanctifier — and despise and renounce the gospel, the only way of salvation, and the words of eternal life; and all this after they have known, owned, and professed, the Christian religion, and continue to do so obstinately and maliciously.

Hebrews 10

Appreciating God's Mercies

Now, in the days of affliction and misery, when everything was black and dismal, she remembers all her pleasant things that she had in the days of old, and now knows how to value them better than formerly, when she had the full enjoyment of them. God often makes us know the worth of mercies by the want of them; and adversity is borne with the greatest difficulty by those that have fallen into it from the height of prosperity. This cut David to the heart, when he was banished from God's ordinances, that he could remember when he went with the multitude to the house of God (Ps. 42:4.)

Lamentations 1

Assurance

God would not at first give him full assurances of his being reconciled to him lest if the comfort of a pardon were too easily obtained they should be emboldened to do the like again and should not be made sensible enough of the evil of sin. Comforts are suspended that convictions may be the deeper impressed.

Exodus 32

The earnest is part of payment, and it secures the full sum: so is the gift of the Holy Ghost; all his influences and operations, both as a sanctifier and a comforter, are heaven begun, glory in the seed and bud. The Spirit's illumination is an earnest of everlasting light; sanctification is an earnest of perfect holiness; and his comforts are earnests of everlasting joys.

Ephesians 1

Christ is in this gospel covenant a surety for us to God and for God to us, to see that the articles be performed on both parts. He, as surety, has united the divine and human nature together in his own person, and therein given assurance of reconciliation; and he has, as surety, united God and man together in the bond of the everlasting covenant. He pleads with men to keep their covenant with God, and he pleads with God that he will fulfil his promises to men, which he is always ready to do in a way suitable to his majesty and glory, that is, through a *Mediator*.

Hebrews 7

The hidden manna, the influences and comforts of the Spirit of Christ in communion with him, coming down from heaven into the soul, from time to time, for its support, to let it taste something how saints and angels live in heaven. This is hidden from the rest of the world.

The new name is the name of adoption: adopted persons took the name of the family into which they were adopted. None can read the evidence of a man's adoption but himself; he cannot always read it, but if he persevere he shall have both the evidence of sonship and the inheritance.

Revelation 2

Atheism

No man will say, 'There is no God' till he is so hardened in sin that it has become his interest that there should be none to call him to account.

Psalm 14

Atonement

Atonement must be made for the sins of the last reign. They thought it not enough to lament and forsake those sins but they brought a sin offering. Even our repentance and reformation will not obtain pardon but in and through Christ who was made sin (that is a sin-offering) for us. No peace but through his blood, no, not for penitence.

2 Chronicles 29

He did not die for any sin of his own, even in the judgment of the judge himself, and therefore he died as a sacrifice for our sins, and that, even in the judgment of the prosecutors themselves, 'one man should die for the people' (Ch. 11:50.) This is he that 'did no violence, neither was any deceit in his mouth' (Isa. 53:9), who was to 'be cut off, but not for himself', (Dan. 9:26.)

John 18

Had he not been God, he could not have been our righteousness; the transcendent excellence of the divine nature put such a value upon, and such a virtue into, his sufferings, that they became sufficient to satisfy for the sins of the world, and to bring in a righteousness which will be effectual to all that believe.

Philippians 3

Backsliding

God's judgments upon others, who have really revolted from God while they have kept up a profession of nearness to him, should be a warning to us not to trust in lying words. It is good to consult precedents, and make use of them. Remember Lot's wife; remember Shiloh and the seven churches of Asia; and know that the ark and candlestick are moveable things (Rev. 2:5; Matt. 21:43.)

Jeremiah 7

When men turn from their righteousness they soon learn to commit iniquity. When they grow careless and remiss in the duties of God's worship, neglect them, or are negligent in them, they become an easy prey to the tempter. Omissions make way for commissions.

Ezekiel 3

They slumbered, and then they slept. Note, one degree of carelessness and remissness makes way for another. Those that allow themselves in slumbering, will scarcely keep themselves from sleeping; therefore dread the beginning of spiritual decays — attend to the first symptoms of disease.

Matthew 25

Soon after men began to call upon the name of the Lord all flesh corrupted their way — soon after the covenant with Noah the Babel-builders bade defiance to heaven — soon after the covenant with Abraham his seed degenerated in Egypt — soon after the Israelites were planted in Canaan, when the first generation was worn off, they forsook God and served Baal — soon after God's covenant with David his seed revolted, and served other gods — soon after the return out of captivity there was a general decay of piety, as appears by the story of Ezra and Nehemiah.

2 Thessalonians 2

Balance in Doctrine

It is sad to see how much one part of religion is opposed, under colour of zeal for another part. There was a perfect harmony between Christ and Moses; Moses prepared for Christ, and Christ perfected Moses, so that they might be disciples of Moses, and become the disciples of Christ too; and yet they here put them in opposition, nor could they have persecuted Christ but under the shelter of the abused name of Moses. Thus those who gainsay the doctrine of free grace value themselves as promoters of man's duty, 'We are Moses' disciples'; while, on the other hand, those that cancel the obligation of the law value themselves as the assertors of free grace, and as if none were the disciples of Jesus but they; whereas, if we rightly understand the matter, we shall see God's grace and man's duty meet together and kiss and befriend each other.

John 9

Balance in Religion

Those who read David's psalms, especially those towards the latter end, would be tempted to think that religion is all rapture and consists in nothing but the ecstasies and transports of devotion; and doubtless there is a time for them, and if there be a heaven upon earth it is in them; but, while we are on earth, we cannot be wholly taken up with them; we have a life to live in the flesh, must have a conversation in the world, and into that we must now be taught to carry our religion, which is a rational thing, and very serviceable to the government of human life, and tends as much to make us discreet as to make us devout, to make the face shine before men, in a prudent, honest, useful conversation, as to make the heart burn towards God in holy and pious affections.

Proverbs 1

Baptism

Baptism is a sacrament, that is, it is an oath; super sacramentum dicere, is to say upon oath. It is an oath of abjuration, by which we renounce the world and the flesh, as rivals with God for the throne in our hearts; and an oath of allegiance, by which we resign and give up ourselves to God, to be his, our own selves, our whole selves, body, soul and spirit, to be governed by his will, and made happy in his favour; we become his men, so the form of homage in our law runs. Therefore baptism is applied to the person, as livery and seisin is given of the premises, because it is the person that is dedicated to God.

Matthew 28

'Those who are baptised into Christ have put on Christ'; for thence it appears that under the gospel baptism comes in the room of circumcision, and that those who by baptism are devoted to Christ, and do sincerely believe in him, are to all intents and purposes as much admitted into the privileges of the Christian state as the Jews were by circumcision into those of the legal (Phil. 3:3), and therefore there was no reason why the use of that should still be continued.

Galatians 3

Bearing Fruit

It is observable here concerning this vine that it is praised for its shadow, its boughs, and its branches, but not a word of its fruit, for 'Israel was an empty vine' (Hos. 10:1.) God came looking for grapes, but, behold, wild grapes (Isa. 5:2.) And, if a vine do not bring forth fruit, no tree so useless, so worthless, (Ezek. 15:2, 6.)

Psalm 80

We then bear fruit, when we practise according to the word; when the temper of our minds and the tenor of our lives are conformable to the gospel we have received, and we do as we are taught.

Matthew 13

Fruit is the thing that God expects and requires from those that enjoy the Gospel: fruit according to the seed; a temper of mind, and a course of life, agreeable to the Gospel; Christian graces daily exercised, Christian duties duly performed. This is fruit, and it will abound to our account.

Mark 4

If a man be really a good man, if he have a principle of grace in his heart, and the prevailing bent and bias of the soul be towards God and heaven, though perhaps he may not abound in fruit, and though he may be sometimes like a tree in winter, yet he does not bring forth corrupt fruit; though he may not do you all the good he should, yet he will not in any material instance do you hurt.

If the fruit be good, you may conclude that the tree is so; if the conversation be holy, heavenly, and regular, though you cannot infallibly know the heart, yet you may charitably hope that it is upright with God; for every tree is known by its fruit.

Luke 6

The in-dwelling of the word, and Spirit, and grace of God in us, is best tried by its effects, particularly by our receiving what he sends, the commands, the messengers, the providences he sends, especially Christ whom he hath sent.

John 5

Beatific Vision

The greatest and best of men cannot bear the immediate discoveries of the divine glory; no man can see it and live; it is next to death to see a glimpse of it, as Daniel here; but glorified saints see Christ as he is and can bear the sight.

Daniel 10

The face of Moses shone but as the moon, with a borrowed reflected light, but Christ's shone as the sun, with an innate inherent light, which was the more sensibly glorious, because it suddenly broke out, as it were, from behind a black cloud.

'His raiment was white as the light.' All his body was altered, as his face was; so that beams of light, darting from every part through his clothes, made them white and glittering. The shining of the face of Moses was so weak, that it could easily be concealed by a thin veil; but such was the glory of Christ's body, that his clothes were enlightened by it.

Matthew 17

Gracious souls reckon it good to be in communion with Christ, good to be near him, good to be in the mount with him though it be a cold and solitary place; it is good to be here retired from the world, and alone with Christ: and if it is good to be with Christ transfigured only upon a mountain with Moses and Elias, how good will it be to be with Christ glorified in heaven with all the saints?

Mark 9

Being Different

The Tempter suggests that the worshipping of these gods was the common practice of the world and if they limited their adorations to an invisible Deity they were singular and like nobody for these gods were the gods of the people round about them and indeed of all the nations of the earth. This suggestion draws many away from religion and godliness for it is an unfashionable thing and they make their court to the world and the flesh because these are the gods of the people that are round about them.

Deuteronomy 13

By these (fringes) they were distinguishable from other people so that it might be said upon the first sight 'there goes an Israelite' which taught them not to be ashamed of their country nor

the peculiarities of their religion; how much so-ever their neighbours looked upon them and it with contempt.

Deuteronomy 21

In court, city, and country, Baal had the ascendant; and the generality of the people, more or less, paid their respect to Baal. The best evidence of integrity is a freedom from the present prevailing corruptions of the times and places that we live in, to swim against the stream when it is strong.

Romans 11

Bible

The Ark had the Tables of the Law in it and nothing more welcome to faithful Israelites than the Word of God; to them it is a savour of life unto life but to uncircumcised Philistines that persist in enmity to God, nothing more dreadful nor unwelcome, to them it is a savour of death unto death.

1 Samuel 5

The testimony of the Lord (which witnesses for him to us), is sure, incontestably and inviolably sure, what we may give credit to, may rely upon, and may be confident it will not deceive us. It is a sure discovery of divine truth, a sure direction in the way of duty. It is a sure fountain of living comforts and a sure foundation of lasting hopes.

Psalm 19

It must be not only a 'light to our eyes' to gratify them, and fill our heads with speculations, but 'a light to our feet and to our path', to direct us in the right ordering of our conversation, both in the choice of our way in general and in the particular steps we take in that way, that we may not take a false way nor a false step in the right way. We are then truly sensible of God's goodness to us in giving us such a lamp and light when we make it a guide to our feet, our path.

Psalm 119

The church had long enjoyed the benefit of prophets, extraordinary messengers from God, and now they had a whole book of their prophecies put together, and it was a finished piece; but they must not think that hereby the 'law of Moses' was superseded, and had become as an almanac out of date, as if now they were advanced to a higher form and might forget that. No; the prophets do but confirm and apply the law, and press the observance of that; and therefore still 'Remember the law'.

Malachi 4

He is himself the eternal Word, and could have produced the mind of God without having recourse to the writings of Moses; but he put honour upon the Scripture, and, to set us an example, he appealed to what was written in the Law; and he says this to Satan, taking it for granted that he knew well enough what was written.

Matthew 4

It is observable that though Peter was 'filled with the Holy Ghost, and spoke with tongues as the Spirit gave him utterance', yet he did not set aside the scriptures, nor think himself above them; nay, much of his discourse is quotation out of the Old Testament, to which he appeals, and with which he proves what he says. Christ's scholars never learn above their Bible; and the Spirit is given not to supersede the scriptures, but to enable us to understand and improve the scriptures.

Acts 2

This sanction is like a flaming sword, to guard the canon of the scripture from profane hands. Such a fence as this God set about the law (Deut. 4:2), and the whole Old Testament (Mal. 4:4), and now in the most solemn manner about the whole Bible, assuring us that it is a book of the most sacred nature, divine authority, and of the last importance, and therefore the peculiar care of the great God.

Revelation 22

Bible (Apparent Contradiction in)

By this event two predictions that seemed to contradict one another were both fulfilled. Jeremiah prophesied that Zedekiah should be brought to Babylon (Jer. 32:5). Ezekiel prophesied that he should not see Babylon (Ezek. 12: 13). He was brought thither but his eyes being put out he did not see it.

2 Kings 25

When we know not how to reconcile one word of God with another we may yet be sure that both are true, both

18

are pure, both shall be made good, and not one iota or tittle of either shall fall to the ground. When Jeremiah was ordered to buy the field in Anathoth he was willing to hope that God was about to revoke the sentence of his wrath and to order the Chaldeans to raise the siege. 'No', says God, 'the execution of the sentence shall go on; Jerusalem shall be laid in ruins'. Note, assurances of future mercy must not be interpreted as securities from present troubles.

Jeremiah 32

Bible (Right Use of)

It is all one to him to save by many or by few. This is a truth easily granted in general, that it is all alike to Omnipotence what the instruments are by which it works and yet it is not so easy to apply it to a particular case.

1 Samuel 14

In singing this, and praying it over, we must give glory to Christ as the eternal Son of God and our rightful Lord, and must take comfort from this promise and plead it with God, that the kingdom of Christ shall be enlarged and established and shall triumph over all opposition.

Psalm 2

Good men are afraid of sin, and are in care to prevent it; and the most effectual way to prevent it is to hide God's word in our hearts, that we may answer every temptation, as our Master did, with, 'It is written'; may

oppose God's precepts to the dominion of sin, his promises to its allurements, and his threatenings to its menaces.

Psalm 119

This was a word that the prophets much used, and used it seriously, to show what a weight the word of God was upon their spirits, of what importance it was, and how pressingly it should come upon those that heard it. The words of the false prophets had nothing ponderous in them, but God's words had; those were as chaff, these as wheat. Now the profane scoffers took this word, and made a jest and a byword of it; they made people merry with it, that so, when the prophets used it, they might not make people serious with it. Note, it has been the artifice of Satan, in all ages, to obstruct the efficacy of sacred things by turning them into matter of sport and ridicule; the mocking of God's messengers was the baffling of his messages.

Jeremiah 23

The Christians to whom James wrote were apt to speak very hard things of one another, because of their differences about indifferent things (such as the observance of meats and days, as appears from Rom. 14); now, says the apostle, he who censures and condemns his brother for not agreeing with him in those things which the law of God has left indifferent thereby censures and condemns the law, as if it had done ill in leaving them indifferent. He who quarrels with his brother, and condemns him for the sake of any thing not determined in the word of God, does thereby reflect on that word of God, as if it were not a perfect rule.

James 4

Birds of a Feather

They will then be bound in bundles (v. 30). Sinners of the same sort will be bundled together in the great day: a bundle of atheists, a bundle of epicures, a bundle of persecutors, and a great bundle of hypocrites. Those who have been associates in sin, will be so in shame and sorrow; and it will be an aggravation of their misery, as the society of glorified saints will add to their bliss. Let us pray, as David, 'Lord, gather not my soul with sinners' (Ps. 26:9), but let it be bound in 'the bundle of life, with the Lord our God' (1 Sam. 25:29).

Matthew 13

Blasphemy

God himself is out of the sinner's reach, and not capable of receiving any real injury; and therefore enmity to God spits its venom at his name, and so shows its ill-will.

John 10

Boasting

Justly, were those denied the honour of the service who would not give God the honour of the success.

Judges 7

Brevity of Life

If we would use this as a plea with God for mercy ('Are not my days few? Lord, pity me'), we should use it as a plea with ourselves, to quicken us to duty: 'Are not my days few? Then it concerns me to redeem time, to improve opportunities, what my hand finds to do to do it with all my might, that I may be ready for the days of eternity, which shall be many.'

Job 10

It is an excellent art rightly to number our days, so as not to be out in our calculation, as he was who counted upon many years to come, when, that night, his soul was required of him. We must live under a constant apprehension of the shortness and uncertainty of life and the near approach of death and eternity. We must so number our days as to compare our work with them, and mind it accordingly with a double diligence, as those that have no time to trifle.

We number our days to good purpose when our hearts are inclined and engaged to true wisdom, that is, to the practice of serious godliness. This is a thing to which it is necessary that we apply our hearts, and the matter requires and deserves a close application, to which frequent thoughts of the uncertainty of our continuance here, and the certainty of our removal hence, will very much contribute.

Psalm 90

He took to him flesh, and for some days tabernacled therein; he became a mortal man, and reckoned his life by days, herein setting us an example how we should reckon ours. Were we to reckon our lives by days, it would be a means to quicken us to do the work of every day in its day.

Hebrews 5

Broken Reeds

We cannot expect too little from the creature nor too much from the Creator. It is no new thing even for brethren to *deal deceitfully* (Jer. 9, 4—5; Mic. 7, 5); let us therefore put our confidence in the rock of ages, not in broken reeds — in the fountain of life, not in broken cisterns. God will outdo our hopes as much as men come short of them.

Job 6

What folly is it to trust to that, and boast of that, which will not enable us so much as for one hour to respite the execution of the sentence of death upon a parent, a child, or a friend that is to us as our own soul!

Psalm 49

The sin here condemned; it is trusting in man, putting that confidence in the wisdom and power, the kindness and faithfulness of men, which should be placed in those attributes of God only.

Jeremiah 17

It is rare to find even those that have shared with us in our joys willing to share with us in our griefs too. The canker-worms will continue upon the field while there is anything to be had, but they are gone when all is gone. Those that men have got by they do not care to lose by. Nineveh's merchants bid her farewell in her distress. Riches themselves are as the canker-worms, which on a sudden 'fly away as the eagle towards heaven' (Prov. 23:5).

Nahum 3

Brotherly Love

Christ delights even in the saints on earth, notwithstanding their weaknesses and manifold infirmities, which is a good reason why we should.

Psalm 16

David had often expressed the great love he had to God; here he expresses the great love he had to the people of God; observe, why he loved them; not so much because they were his best friends, most firm to his interest and most forward to serve him, but because they were such as feared God and kept his precepts. Our love to the saints is then sincere when we love them for the sake of what we see of God in them and the service they do to him.

Psalm 119

'I will keep the passover with my disciples'. Note, wherever Christ is welcome, he expects that his disciples should be welcome too. When we take God for our God, we take his people for our people.

Matthew 26

It is the true honour of Christ's disciples to excel in brotherly love. Nothing will be more effectual than this to recommend them to the esteem and respect of others. See what a powerful attractive it was (Acts 2:46, 46). Tertullian speaks of it as the glory of the primitive church that the Christians were known by their affection to one another. Their adversaries took notice of it, and said, 'See how these Christians love one another', Apol. cap. 39. If the followers of Christ do not love one another, they not only cast an unjust reproach upon their profession, but give just cause to suspect their own sincerity. O Jesus! are these thy Christians, these passionate, malicious, spiteful, ill-natured people? 'Is this thy son's coat?' When our brethren stand in need of help from us, and we have an opportunity of being serviceable to them, when they differ in opinion and practice from us, or are any ways rivals with or provoking to us, and so we have an occasion to condescend and forgive, in such cases as this it will be known whether we have this badge of Christ's disciples.

John 13

'This is my commandment' (v. 12), as if this were the most necessary of all the commandments. As under the law the prohibition of idolatry was the commandment more insisted on than any other, foreseeing the people's addictedness to that sin, so Christ, foreseeing the addictedness of the Christian church to uncharitableness, has laid most stress upon this precept.

John 15

That in consideration of their agreement and communion in one creed and one covenant, one Spirit and one Bible — in consideration of what they have in one God and one Christ, and of what they hope for in one heaven, they may be of one mind and one mouth. Worldly glory sets men at variance; for if some be advanced others are eclipsed, and therefore, while the disciples dreamed of a temporal kingdom, they were ever and anon quarrelling; but spiritual honours being conferred alike upon all Christ's subjects, they being all 'made to our God kings and priests', there is no occasion for contest nor emulation. *The more Christians are taken up with the glory Christ has given them, the less desirous they will be of vain-glory, and consequently, the less disposed to quarrel.*

John 17

We cannot forget how often, while their Master was with them, there were 'strifes among them, who should be the greatest'; but now all these strifes were at an end, we hear no more of them. What they had received already of the Holy Ghost, when Christ breathed on them, had in a good measure rectified the mistakes upon which those contests were grounded, and had disposed them to holy love. They had prayed more together of late than usual (ch. 1:14), and this made them love one another better.

Acts 2

Every member of the body is to preserve its own rank, and

do its own office; and all are to minister to one another, and promote the good of the body in general, without envying, or despising, or neglecting, or ill-using, any one particular member. How blessed a constitution were the Christian church, if all the members did their duty.

1 Corinthians 12

It wishes ill to none, *much less* will it hurt or wrong any, *and least of all* make this the matter of its delight, rejoice in doing harm and mischief. *Nor will it rejoice at the faults and failings of others, and triumph over them, either out of pride or ill-will, because it will set off its own excellences or gratify its spite.* The sins of others are rather the grief of a charitable spirit than its sport or delight; they will touch it to the quick, and stir all its compassion, but can give it no entertainment. It is the very height of malice to take pleasure in the misery of a fellow-creature. And is not falling into sin the greatest calamity that can befall one? How inconsistent is it with Christian charity, to rejoice at such fall!

How well-natured and amiable a thing is Christian charity? How lovely a mind is that which is tinctured throughout with such benevolence, and has it diffused over its whole frame! Happy the man who has this heavenly fire glowing in his heart, flowing out of his mouth, and diffusing its warmth over all with whom he has to do! How lovely a thing would Christianity appear to the world, if those who profess it were more actuated and animated by this divine principle, and paid a due regard to a command on which its blessed author laid a chief stress! 'A new commandment give I to you, that you love one another, as I have loved you, that you also love one another', (John 13:34). By this shall all men know that you are my disciples' (v. 35). Blessed Jesus! How few of thy professed disciples are to be distinguished and marked out by this characteristic!

1 Corinthians 13

Though one party among them had declared for Apollos against Paul (if that passage is to be understood literally, vide ch. 4: 6), yet Paul did not hinder Apollos from going to Corinth in his own absence, nay, he pressed him to go thither. He had no suspicions of Apollos, as if he would lessen Paul's interest and respect among them, to the advancement of his own. Note, Faithful ministers are not apt to entertain jealousies of each other, nor suspect of such selfish designs. True charity and brotherly love think no evil. And where should these reign, if not in the breasts of the ministers of Christ?

1 Corinthians 16

This is the law of Christ's kingdom, the lesson of his school, the livery of his family.

There is no greater enemy to Christian love than pride and passion. If we do things in contradiction to our brethren, this is doing them through strife; if we do them through ostentation of ourselves, this is doing them through vain-glory: both are destructive of Christian love and kindle un-christian heats. Christ came to slay all enmities; therefore let there not be among Christians a spirit of opposition. Christ came to humble us, and therefore let there not be among us a spirit of pride. We must 'esteem others in lowliness of mind better than ourselves', be severe upon our own faults and charitable in our judgment of others, be quick in observing our own defects and infirmities, but ready to overlook and make favourable allowances for the defects of others.

Philippians 2

Now, in conformity to the example of his great Master, instead of upbraiding them for their neglect, he makes an excuse for them: 'Wherein you were also careful, but you lacked opportunity'. How could they lack opportunity, if they had been resolved upon it? They might have sent a messenger on purpose. But the apostle is willing to suppose, in favour of them, that they would have done it if a fair opportunity had offered. How contrary is this to the behaviour of many to their friends, by whom neglects which really are excusable are resented very heinously, when Paul excused that which he had reason enough to resent.

Philippians 4

It is happy where there is such mutual love between minister and people. This tends to promote religion, and the success of the gospel. The world hates them, and therefore they should love one another.

1 Thessalonians 3

This brotherly love was in danger of being lost, and that in a time of persecution, when it would be most necessary; it was in danger of being lost by those disputes that were among them concerning the respect they ought still to have to the ceremonies of the Mosaic law. Disputes about religion too often produce a decay of Christian affection; but this must be guarded against, and all proper means used to preserve brotherly love.

Hebrews 13

The precept of love must be as old as human nature; but it might admit divers enactions, enforcements, and motives. In the state of innocence, had human nature then been propagated, men must have loved one another as being of one blood, made to dwell on the earth, as being God's offspring, and bearing his image. In the state of sin and promised recovery, they must love one another as related to God their Maker, as related to each other by blood, and as partners in the same hope. When the Hebrews were peculiarly incorporated, they must accordingly love each other, as being the privileged people, whose were the covenants and the adoption, and of whose race the Messiah and head of the church must spring; and the law of love must be conveyed with new obligations to the new Israel of God, to the gospel church.

1 John 2

Calling Upon God

This calling upon God supposes knowledge of him, faith in him, desire towards him, dependence on him, and, as an evidence of the sincerity of all this, a conscientious obedience to him; for, without that, crying 'Lord, Lord', will not stand us in any stead. Note, it is the praying remnant that shall be the saved remnant. And it will aggravate the ruin of those who perish that they might have been saved on such easy terms.

Joel 2

Calmness in Trouble

The fixedness of the heart is a sovereign remedy against the disquieting fear of evil tidings. If we keep our thoughts composed, and ourselves masters of them, our wills resigned to the holy will of God, our temper sedate, and our spirits even, under all the unevenness of Providence, we are well fortified against the agitations of the timorous.

Psalm 112

Carnal Reasoning

Let the house of Israel hear and receive this word from the God of Israel: 'Learn not the way of the heathen', do not approve of it, no, nor think indifferently concerning it, much less imitate it or accustom yourselves to it. Let not any of their customs steal in among you (as they are apt to do insensibly) nor mingle themselves with your religion. Note, it ill becomes those that are taught of God to 'learn the way of the heathen', and to think of worshipping the true God with such rites and ceremonies as they used in the worship of their false gods. See (Deut. 12: 29–31).

Jeremiah 10

They said, 'Let God give us our plenty again, as formerly, and try us whether we will not then bring Him His tithes and offerings, as we did formerly.' 'No,' says God, 'do you first bring in all your tithes as they become due, and all the arrears of what is past, and try Me, whether I will not then restore you your plenty.' Note, those that will deal with God must deal upon trust; and we may all venture to do so, for, though many have been losers for him, never any were losers by him in the end. It is fit that we should venture first, for 'His reward is with Him', but 'His work is before Him'; we must first do the work which is our part, and then try him and trust him for the reward.

Malachi 3

God forbid, that thou shouldst suffer and be killed; we cannot bear the thoughts of it. 'Master, spare thyself': so it might be read — Be merciful to thyself, and then no one else can be cruel to thee; pity thyself, and then this shall not be to thee. He would have Christ to dread suffering as much as he did; but we mistake, if we measure Christ's love and patience by our own. He intimates, likewise, the improbability of the thing, humanly speaking; 'This shall not be unto thee'.

Matthew 16

He knew not that the thing was necessary for the glory of God, the destruction of Satan, and the salvation of man, that the Captain of our salvation must be made perfect through sufferings, and so must bring many sons to glory. Note, the wisdom of man is perfect folly, when it pretends to give measures to the divine counsels. The cross of Christ, the greatest instance of God's power and wisdom, was to some a stumbling-block, and to others foolishness.

It seems policy to shun trouble, but if with that we shun duty, it is fleshly wisdom (2 Cor. 1: 12), and it will be folly in the end.

Mark 8

Casting Pearls Before Swine

Profane scoffers are not to be humoured, nor pearls cast before swine. David prudently kept silence even from good when the wicked were before him, who, he knew, would ridicule what he said and make a jest of it (Ps. 39:1, 2).

Psalm 137

Though they are not forbidden to invite those simple ones to Wisdom's house, yet they are advised not to pursue the invitation by reproving and rebuking them. 'Reprove not a scorner, cast not these pearls before swine.' (Matt. 7:6). Thus Christ said of the Pharisees, 'Let them

alone' (Matt. 15:14). 'Do not reprove them.'
1. In justice to them, for those have forfeited the favour of further means who scorn the means they have had. Those that are thus filthy, let them be filthy still; those that are joined to idols, let them alone; lo, we turn to the Gentiles.
2. In prudence to yourselves; because, if you reprove them, you lose your labour, and so get to yourselves shame for the disappointment.

Proverbs 9

Christ doth not forbid him to tell it to others, but he must not tell it to any in the town. Slighting Christ's favours is forfeiting them; and Christ will make those know the worth of their privileges by the want of them, that would not know them otherwise. Bethsaida, in the day of her visitation, would not know the things that belonged to her peace, and now they are hid from her eyes. They will not see, and therefore shall not see.

Mark 8

They did not deserve to be told; for it was plain that they contended not for truth, but victory.

Mark 11

Gospel light is justly taken away from those that endeavour to extinguish it. Christ will withdraw from those that drive him from them, will hide his face from those that spit in it, and justly shut up his bowels from those who spurn at them.

John 7

They forfeit all the benefit of further instructions and means of knowledge and conviction: they that have been told once, and would not hear, why should they be told it again? (Jer. 51:9). See (Matt. 10:14). They hereby receive the grace of God in vain. This is implied in that, 'Will you be his disciples?' No, you resolve, you will not; why then would you hear it again, only that you may be his accusers and persecutors?

John 9

Chastisements

This was one of the judgments which God had threatened to bring upon them for their sins, (Lev. 26; 19, 20). He has many arrows in his quiver. In the days of the judges they were oppressed by their enemies; and, when by that judgment they were not reformed, God tried this, for when he *judges he will overcome*. When the land had rest, yet it had not plenty; even in Bethlehem, which signifies the house of bread, there was scarcity. A fruitful land is turned into barrenness, to correct and restrain the luxury and wantonness of those that dwell therein.

Ruth 1

Many are chastised that do not bear chastisement, do not bear it well, and so, in effect, do not bear it at all. Penitents, if sincere, will take all well that God does, and will bear chastisement as a medicinal operation intended for good. A good man is willing to know the worst of himself, and particularly, under affliction, desires to be told wherefore God contends with him and what God designs in correcting him.

Job 33

When the teachings of the Word and Spirit go along with the rebukes of Providence they then both manifest men to be blessed and help to make them so; for then they are marks of adoption and means of sanctification. When we are chastened we must pray to be taught, and look into the Law as the best expositor of Providence. It is not the chastening itself that does good, but the teaching that goes along with it and is the exposition of it.

Psalm 94

They looked upon him as having wounded them with the wound of an enemy and with the chastisement of a cruel one (v. 14), as if he had designed their ruin, and neither mitigated the correction nor had any mercy in reserve for them. It did indeed seem as if God had dealt thus severely with them, as if he had turned to be their enemy and had fought against them (Isa. 63:10). Job complains that God had become cruel to him and multiplied his wounds. When troubles are great and long we have need carefully to watch over our own hearts, that we entertain not such hard thoughts as these of God and his providence. His are the chastisements of a merciful one, not of a cruel one, whatever they may appear.

Jeremiah 30

It is a great mercy to have the Word of God brought to us, and a great duty to attend to it diligently, when we are in affliction. The word of instruction and the rod of correction may be of great service to us, in concert and concurrence with each other, the word to explain the rod and the rod to enforce the word: both together give wisdom. It is happy for a man, when he is sick and in pain, to have a messenger with him, an interpreter, one among a thousand, if he have but his ear open to discipline (Job 23:23).

Ezekiel 1

Choosing Where to Live

No secular advantages whatsoever should draw us thither or detain us there where we are in danger of making a shipwreck of faith and a good conscience ... they loved their work better than their maintenance in that they left their suburbs and possessions in the country where they might have lived at ease upon their own) because they were restrained from serving God there and cast themselves upon God's providence and the charity of their brethren in coming to a place where they might have the free enjoyment of God's ordinances according to his institution. Poverty in the way of duty is to be chosen rather than plenty in the way of sin. Better live upon alms or die in a prison with a good conscience than roll in wealth and pleasure with a prostituted one . . . That is best for us which is best for our souls and in all choices, advantages for

religion must take place of all outward conveniences. Where God's faithful priests are His faithful people should be.

2 Chronicles 11

Choosing Where to Work

Though he was himself a great apostle, yet he chose to work with Aquila and Priscilla, because he found them to be very intelligent in the things of God, as appears afterwards (v. 26), and he owns that they had been his 'helpers in Christ Jesus' (Rom. 16:3). This is an example to those who are going to service to seek for those services in which they may have the best help for their souls. Choose to work with those that are likely to be helpers in Christ Jesus.

Acts 18

All that care which disquiets the mind, and distracts it in the worship of God, is evil; for God must 'be attended upon without distraction' (v. 35). The whole mind should be engaged when God is worshipped. The work ceases while it diverts to any thing else, or is hurried and drawn hither and thither by foreign affairs and concerns. Those who are engaged in divine worship should attend to this very thing, should make it their whole business. But how is this possible when the mind is swallowed up of the cares of this life? Note, it is the wisdom of a Christian so to order his outward affairs, and choose such a condition in life, as to be without distracting cares, that he may attend upon the Lord with a mind at leisure and disengaged. This is the general maxim by which the apostle would have Christians govern themselves. In the application of it Christian prudence must direct. *That condition of life is best for every man which is best for his soul, and keeps him most clear of the cares and snares of the world.*

1 Corinthians 7

Choosing the Right Friends

We commonly study to approve ourselves to those with whom we choose to associate; we value ourselves upon their good word and covet to stand right in their opinion. As we choose our people we choose our praise, and govern ourselves accordingly; we are therefore concerned to make the first choice well, and not to mingle with those whom we cannot please without displeasing God.

John 18

Christ

The judge that condemned him (as if his trial were only like the scrutiny that was made concerning the sacrifices whether they were without blemish or not) pronounces him innocent.

Exodus 12

The Son can be angry, though a Lamb; he is the lion of the tribe of Judah, and the wrath of this King, this King of kings, will be as the roaring of a lion, and will drive even mighty men and chief captains to seek in vain for shelter in rocks and mountains (Rev. 6:16). If the Son be angry, who shall intercede for us? There remains no more sacrifice, no other name by which we can be saved. Unbelief is a sin against the remedy.

Psalm 2

Never did any tradesman court customers that he hoped to get by as Christ courts us to that which we only are to be the gainers by.

Isaiah 55

We are foolishness, ignorant and blind in the things of God, with all our boasted knowledge; and he is made wisdom to us. We are guilty, obnoxious to justice; and he is made righteousness, our great atonement and sacrifice. We are depraved and corrupt; and he is made sanctification, the spring of our spiritual life; from him, the head, it is communicated to all the members of his mystical body by his Holy Spirit. We are in bonds, and he is made redemption to us, our Saviour and deliverer.

1 Corinthians 1

Christ: His Blood

Cleansed lepers are as welcome to the blood and oil as consecrated priests. When the leper was sprinkled, the water must have blood in it; when he was annointed the oil must have blood under it; to signify that all the graces and comforts of the Spirit, all his purifying dignifying influences are owing to the death of Christ. It is by

29

his blood alone that we are sanctified.

Leviticus 14

Egypt shall be sacrificed rather than Israel continue in slavery, when the time has come for their release. The Ethiopians had invaded them in Asa's time; but they shall be destroyed rather than Israel shall be disturbed. And if this was reckoned so great a thing, to give Egypt for their ransom, what reason have we to admire God's love to us in giving his own Son to be a ransom for us! (1 John 4:10). What are Ethiopia and Seba, all their lives and all their treasures, compared with the blood of Christ?

Isaiah 43

Christ: His Deity

As God, he is Jehovah, the incommunicable name of God, denoting his eternity and self-existence. As Mediator, he is our righteousness. By making satisfaction to the justice of God for the sin of man, he has brought in an everlasting righteousness, and so made it over to us in the covenant of grace that, upon our believing consent to that covenant, it becomes ours. his being 'Jehovah our Righteousness' implies that he is so our righteousness as no creature could be. He is a sovereign, all-sufficient, eternal righteousness.

Jeremiah 23

Religious worship is due to God only, and must not be given to any creature; it is a flower of the crown which cannot be alienated, a branch of God's glory which he will not give to another, and which he would not give to his own Son, by obliging all men to honour the Son, even as they honour the Father, if he had not been God, equal to him and one with him. Christ quotes this law concerning religious worship, and quotes it with application to himself.

Matthew 4

In these verses he explains, and afterwards confirms, his commission, as Mediator and plenipotentiary in the treaty between God and man. And, as the honours he is hereby entitled to are such as it is not fit for any creature to receive, so the work he is hereby entrusted with is such as it is not possible for any creature to go through with, and therefore he is God, equal with the Father.

John 5

Some said, he is a good man. This was a truth, but it was far short of being the whole truth. He was not only a good man, but more than a man, he was the Son of God. Many who have no ill thoughts of Christ have yet low thoughts of him, and scarcely honour him, even when they speak well of him, because they do not say enough.

John 7

We cannot say, 'He that knows a man knows an angel', or, 'He that knows a creature knows the Creator'; but he that knows Christ knows the Father.

John 8

He is, in person, the Son of God, the only-begotten Son of God, and as such, he must have the same nature. This personal distinction always supposes one and the same nature. Every son of man is man; were not the nature the same, the generation would be monstrous.

Hebrews 1

Christ: His Incarnation

By the light of nature, we see God as God above us; by the light of the law, we see him as a God against us; but by the light of the Gospel, we see him as Immanuel, God with us, in our own nature, and (which is more), in our interest. Herein the Redeemer commended his love. With Christ's name, Immanuel, we may compare the name given to the gospel church (Ezek. 48:35), Jehovah Shammah — The Lord is there; the Lord of hosts is with us.

Nor is it improper to say that prophecy which foretold that he should be called Immanuel was fulfilled, in the design and intention of it, when he was called Jesus: for if he had not been Immanuel — God with us, he could not have been Jesus — a Saviour; and herein consists the salvation he wrought out, in the bringing of God and man together; this was what he designed, to bring God to be with us, which is our great happiness, and to bring us to be with God, which is our great duty.

Matthew 1

The bitings of the fiery serpents were cured by a serpent of brass, which had the shape, though free from the venom, of the serpents that bit them. It was great condescension that he who was God should be made in the likeness of flesh; but much greater that he who was holy should be made in the likeness of sinful flesh.

Romans 8

Christ: His Lordship

Christ, who is ordained to offer sacrifices for us, is authorized to give law to us. He will not save us unless we be willing that he should govern us. God has prepared him a throne 'in the heavens'; and, if we would have any benefit by that, we must prepare him a throne in our hearts, and be willing and glad that he should 'sit and rule upon that throne'; and to him every thought within us must be brought into obedience.

Zechariah 6

All the works of creation being put under his feet, all the affairs of redemption are put into his hand; he is Lord of all. Angels are his servants; devils are his captives. He has power over all flesh, the heathen given him for his inheritance. The kingdom of providence is committed to his administration. He has power to settle the terms of the covenant of peace as the great plenipotentiary, to govern his church as the great lawgiver, to dispense divine favours as the great almoner, and to call all to account as the great Judge. Both the golden sceptre and the iron rod are given into his hand.

John 3

Christ: His Love

There is a spiritual manifestation of Christ and his love made
to all believers. When he en-
lightens their minds to know
his love, and the dimensions
of it (Eph. 3:18, 19), enlivens
their graces, and draws them
into exercise, and thus enlarges
their comforts in himself —
when he clears up the evidence
of their interest in him, and
gives them tokens of his love,
experiences of his tenderness,
and earnests of his kingdom
and glory — then he manifests
himself to them; and Christ is
manifested to none but those
to whom he is pleased to manifest himself.

John 14

As the Father loved him, who
was most worthy, he loved
them, who were most unworthy.
The Father loved him as his
Son, and he loves them as his
children. 'The Father gave all
things into his hand'; so, with
himself, 'he freely giveth us all
things'. The Father loved him
as Mediator, as head of the
church, and the great trustee
of divine grace and favour,
which he had not for himself
only, but for the benefit of
those for whom he was en-
trusted; and, says he, 'I have
been a faithful trustee. As the
Father has committed his love
to me, so I transmit it to you'.
Therefore the Father was well
pleased with him, that he might
be well pleased with us in him;
and loved him, that in him, as
beloved, he might 'make us
accepted' (Eph. 1:6).

John 15

The carnal mind is not only an
enemy to God, but enmity
itself (ch. 8:7; Col. 1:21). This
enmity is a mutual enmity, God
loathing the sinner, and the
sinner loathing God (Zech. 11:8).
And that for such as these
Christ should die is such a
mystery, such a paradox, such
an unprecedented instance of
love, that it may well be our
business to eternity to adore
and wonder at it. This is a commendation of love indeed. Justly
might he who had thus loved us
make it one of the laws of his
kingdom that we should love
our enemies.

Romans 5

When Paul was whipped, and
beaten, and imprisoned, and
stoned, did Christ love him ever
the less? Were his favours inter-
mitted? His smiles any whit
suspended? His visits more shy?
By no means, but the contrary.
These things separate us from
the love of other friends. When
Paul was brought before Nero
all men forsook him, but then
the Lord stood by him (2 Tim.
4:16, 17). Whatever persecuting
enemies may rob us of, they
cannot intercept his love-tokens,
they cannot interrupt nor exclude his visits; and therefore,
let them do their worst, they
cannot make a true believer
miserable.

Romans 8

The love of God is the spring
and fountain of all the good we
have or hope for: our election,
vocation, justification, and salvation, are all owing to the love of
God in Christ Jesus.

2 Thessalonians 2

Christ: His Sufferings

See what abuses were put upon Him:

1. He was reproached as a bad man, as a blasphemer, a sabbath-breaker, a wine-bibber, a false prophet, an enemy to Caesar, a confederate with the prince of the devils.

2. He was despised of the people as a mean contemptible man, not worth taking notice of, his country in no repute, his relations poor mechanics, his followers none of the rulers, or the Pharisees, but the mob.

3. He was ridiculed as a foolish man, and one that not only deceived others, but himself too. Those that saw him hanging on the cross laughed him to scorn. So far were they from pitying him, that they added to his afflictions, with all the gestures and expressions of insolence upbraiding him with his fall.

Our Lord Jesus, having undertaken to satisfy for the dishonour we had done to God by our sins, did it by submitting to the lowest possible instance of ignominy and disgrace.

Psalm 22

The most unspotted innocency, and the most unparalleled excellency, will not always be a fence against the reproach of tongues; nay, a man's best gifts and best actions, which are both well intended and well calculated for edification, may be made the matter of his reproach. The best of our actions may become the worst of our accusations, as David's fasting (Ps. 69:10).

Matthew 11

There was a struggle between the work he had taken upon him, which required sufferings, and the nature he had taken upon him, which dreaded them; between these two he here pauses with 'What shall I say?' He looked, and there was 'none to help', which put him to a stand. Calvin observes this as a great instance of Christ's humiliation, that he should speak thus like one at a loss.

'Father, glorify thy name', to the same purport with 'Father, thy will be done'; for God's will is for his own glory. This expresses more than barely a submission to the will of God; it is a consecration of his sufferings to the glory of God. It was a mediatorial word, and was spoken by him as our surety, who had undertaken to satisfy divine justice for our sin. The wrong which by sin we have done to God is in his glory, his declarative glory; for in nothing else are we capable of doing him injury. We were never able to make him satisfaction for this wrong done him, nor any creature for us; nothing therefore remained but that God should get him honour upon us in our utter ruin. Here therefore our Lord Jesus interposed, undertook to satisfy God's injured honour, and he did it by his humiliation; he denied himself in, and divested himself of, the honours due to the Son of God incarnate, and submitted to the greatest reproach. Now here he makes a tender of this satisfaction as an equivalent: 'Father, glorify thy name'; let thy justice be honoured upon the sacrifice, not upon the sinner; let the debt be levied upon me, I am solvent, the principal is not. Thus he 'restored that which he took not away'.

John 12

He had something in view under all his sufferings, which was pleasant to him; he rejoiced to see that by his sufferings he should make satisfaction to the injured justice of God and give security to his honour and government, that he should make peace between God and man, that he should seal the covenant of grace and be the Mediator of it, that he should open a way of salvation to the chief of sinners, and that he should effectually save all those whom the Father had given him, and himself be the first-born among many brethren. This was the joy that was set before him.

Hebrews 12

Christ: His Work

These prayers for David are prophecies concerning Christ the son of David, and in Him they were abundantly answered; He undertook the work of our redemption, and made war upon the powers of darkness. In the day of trouble, when his soul was exceedingly sorrowful, the Lord heard him, heard him in that he feared (Heb. 5:7), 'sent him help out of the sanctuary', sent an angel from heaven to strengthen him, took cognizance of his offering when he made his soul an offering for sin, and accepted his burnt-sacrifice, turned it to ashes, the fire that should have fastened upon the sinner, fastening upon the sacrifice, with which God was well pleased. And He granted him

according to his own heart, made him to see of the travail of his soul, to his satisfaction, prospered his good pleasure in his hand, fulfilled all his petitions for himself and us; for him the Father heareth always and his intercession is ever prevailing.

Psalm 20

Christ: Our Example

It is well for us, that Christ has more love and tenderness in Him than the best of His disciples have. And let us learn of Him not to discountenance any willing well-meaning souls in their enquiries after Christ, though they are but weak. If He do not break the bruised reed, we should not. Those that seek unto Christ, must not think it strange if they meet with opposition and rebuke, even from good men, who think they know the mind of Christ better than they do.

Matthew 19

Christ's answer to this address (v. 22, 23), directed not to the mother, but to the sons that set her on. Though others be our mouth in prayer, the answer will be given to us according as we stand affected. Christ's answer is very mild; they were overtaken in the fault of ambition, but Christ restored them with the spirit of meekness.

The check that Christ gave them, which was very gentle, rather by way of instruction what they should be, than by way of reprehension for what they were. He had reproved this very sin before (Ch. 18:3), and told them they must be humble as little children; yet they relapsed into it, and yet he reproved them for it thus mildly.

He called them unto Him, which intimates great tenderness and familiarity. He did not, in anger, bid them get out of His presence, but called them, in love, to come into His presence: for therefore he is fit to teach, and we are invited to learn of Him, because He is meek and lowly in heart.

He never took state upon him, was not waited on at table; he once washed his disciples' feet, but we never read that they washed his feet. He came to minister help to all that were in distress; he made himself a servant to the sick and diseased; was as ready to their requests as ever any servant was at the beck of their master, and took as much pains to serve them; he attended continually to this very thing, and denied himself both food and rest to attend to it.

When we are ever so much in haste about any business, yet we should be willing to stand still to do good.

Matthew 20

It was much to the honour of Christ and his doctrine, that he did not interpose as a Judge or a Divider in matters of this nature, but left them as he found them, for his kingdom is not of this world; and in this he hath given an example to his ministers, who deal in sacred things, not to meddle with disputes about things secular, not to wade far into controversies

relating to them, but to leave that to those whose proper business it is. Ministers that would mind their business, and please their master, must not entangle themselves in the affairs of this life.

Matthew 22

They took it for granted that their Master would eat the passover, though he was at this time persecuted by the chief priests, and his life sought; they knew that he would not be put by his duty, either by frightenings without or fears within. Those do not follow Christ's example who make it an excuse for their not attending on the Lord's supper, our gospel passover, that they have many troubles and many enemies, are full of care and fear; for, if so, they have the more need of that ordinance, to help to silence their fears, and comfort them under their troubles, to help them in forgiving their enemies, and casting all their cares on God.

Matthew 26

And herein he is an example to children and young people, who should learn of Christ to delight in the company of those they may get good by, and choose to sit in the midst of the doctors rather than in the midst of the players. Let them begin at twelve years old, and sooner, to enquire after knowledge, and to associate with those that are able to instruct them; it is a hopeful and promising presage in youth, to be desirous of instruction. Many a youth at Christ's age now would have been playing with the children in the temple, but he was sitting with the doctors in the temple.

Luke 2

Christ's disciples had been very defective in their duty. We find them guilty of many mistakes and weaknesses: they were very dull and very forgetful, and often blundered, yet their Master passes all by and forgets it; he does not upbraid them with their infirmities, but gives them this memorable testimonial, 'You are they who have continued with me.' Thus does he praise at parting, to show how willing he is to make the best of those whose hearts he knows to be upright with him.

Luke 22

He does not pray to be glorified with the princes and great men of the earth: no; *he that knew both worlds, and might choose which he would have his preferment in, chose it in the glory of the other world,* as far exceeding all the glory of this. He had despised 'the kingdoms of this world and the glory of them', when Satan offered them to him, and therefore might the more boldly claim the glories of the other world. 'Let the same mind be in us'. Lord, give the glories of this world to whom thou wilt give them, but let me have my portion of glory in the world to come.

John 17

Christ had the Spirit given him without measure (John 3:34). But the saints have it by measure (see Eph. 4:7). Christ, who had gifts without measure, was meek and lowly; and shall we, that are stinted, be proud and self-conceited?

Romans 12

Christ: Our Sin-Bearer

The law appointed only one goat for a sin-offering as on the day of atonement (Lev. 16; 15) and on such extraordinary occasions as this (Num. 15; 24) but they here offered seven, (v. 21) because the sins of the congregation had been very great and long continued in. Seven is a number of perfection; our great sin-offering is but one yet that one perfects for ever those that are sanctified.

2 Chronicles 29

God could have taken away the sin by taking away the sinner, as he took away the sin of the old world; but he has found out a way of abolishing the sin, and yet sparing the sinner.

John 1

Thousands of sheep had been offered in sacrifice for their shepherds, as sin-offerings, but here, by a surprising reverse, the shepherd is sacrificed for the sheep. When David, the shepherd of Israel, was himself guilty, and the destroying angel drew his sword against the flock for his sake, with good reason did he plead, 'These sheep, what evil have they done? Let thy hand be against me,' (2 Sam. 24:17). But the Son of David was sinless and spotless; and his sheep, what evil have they not done? Yet he saith, 'Let thine hand be against me.'

John 10

Surely Adam could not propagate so strong a poison but Jesus Christ could propagate as strong an antidote, and much stronger. . . *The stream of grace and righteousness is deeper and broader than the stream of guilt*; for this righteousness does not only take away the guilt of that one offence, but of many other offences, even of all. God in Christ forgives all trespasses, (Col. 2:13).

Romans 5

Christian Freedom

To prevent these mistakes, the apostle tells the Christians that they were free, but from what? Not from duty or obedience to God's law, which requires subjection to the civil magistrate. They were free spiritually from the bondage of sin and Satan, and the ceremonial law; but they must not make their Christian liberty a cloak or covering for any wickedness, or for the neglect of any duty towards God or towards their superiors, but must still remember they were 'the servants of God'. Learn, all the servants of Christ are free men (John 8:36); they are free from Satan's dominion, the law's condemnation, the wrath of God, the uneasiness of duty, and the terrors of death.

1 Peter 2

Christian Life

He goes on his way with a humble boldness, being well armed against the temptations of Satan, the troubles of the world, and the reproaches of men. He knows what ground he stands on, what guide he follows, what guard he is surrounded with, and what glory he is going to, and therefore proceeds with assurance and great peace (Isa. 32:17; 33:15, 16).

Proverbs 10

Good principles fixed in the head will produce good resolutions in the heart and good practices in the life.

Isaiah 26

Here the apostle proceeds to more particular exhortations. Two he enlarges upon in this chapter: — to unity and love, purity and holiness, which Christians should very much study. We do not 'walk worthy of the vocation wherewith we are called' if we be not faithful friends to all Christians, and sworn enemies to all sin.

Ephesians 4

Christmas

When men by their sins have caused the life and substance of ordinances to cease it is just with God by His judgments to cause the remaining show and shadow of them to cease. He will take away the supports of their carnal mirth. They loved the new-moons and the sabbaths only for the sake of the good cheer that was stirring then, not for the sake of any religious exercises then performed; these they had dropped long ago; and now God will take away their provisions for these solemnities (v. 12).

Hosea 2

Church

It is built firmly; the mountains are rocky, and on a rock the church is built. The world is founded upon the seas (24:2), which are continually ebbing and flowing, and are a very weak foundation. Babel was built in a plain, where the ground was rotten. But the church is built on the everlasting mountains and the perpetual hills; for sooner shall the mountains depart, and the hills be removed, than the covenant of God's peace shall be disannulled, and on that the church is built (Isa. 54:10). The foundation is upon the holy mountains. Holiness is the strength and stability of the church: it is this that will support it and keep it from sinking; not so much that it is built upon mountains as that it is built upon holy mountains — upon the promise of God, for the confirming of which he has sworn by His holiness, upon the sanctification of the Spirit, which will secure the happiness of all the saints.

Psalm 87

The church of God is a spiritual house. The foundation is Christ, (Eph. 2:20). The builders are ministers (1 Cor. 3:10). The inhabitant is God (Eph. 2:22). It is a house for its strength, beauty, variety of parts, and usefulness of the whole. It is spiritual in its foundation, Christ Jesus — in the materials of it, spiritual persons — in its furniture, the graces of the Spirit — in its connection, being held together by the Spirit of God and by one common faith — and in its use, which is spiritual work, to offer up spiritual sacrifices. This house is daily built up, every part of it improving, and the whole supplied in every age by the addition of new particular members.

1 Peter 2

Church's Weakness

But God saith 'They are too many' and when diminished to a third part, 'they are yet too many' which may help us to understand those providences which sometimes seem to weaken the Church and its interests. Its friends are too many, too mighty, too wise, for God to work deliverances by. God is taking a course to lessen them that He may be exalted in His own strength.

Judges 7

Israel's ground would never have been footing for Philistine armies if Israel had been faithful to their God. The Philistines, it is probable, had heard that Samuel had fallen out with Saul and forsaken him and no longer assisted and advised him, and that Saul had grown melancholy and unfit for business and this news encouraged them to make this attempt for the retrieving of the credit they had lately lost. The enemies of the Church are watchful to take all advantages and they never have greater advantages than when her protectors have provoked God's Spirit and prophets leave them.

1 Samuel 17

Clothing

The purity of the heart will show itself in the modesty of the dress, which becomes women professing godliness.

Proverbs 7

As to fine clothing; this teaches us not to care for it at all, not to covet it, nor to be proud of it, not to make the putting on of apparel our adorning, for after all our care in this the lilies will far outdo us; we cannot dress so fine as they do, why then should we attempt to vie with them? Their adorning will soon perish, and so will ours; they fade — are today, and tomorrow are cast, as other rubbish, into the oven; and the clothes we are proud of are wearing out, the gloss is soon gone, the colour fades, the shape goes out of fashion, or in a while the garment itself is worn out; such is man in all his pomp (Isa. 40:6, 7).

Matthew 6

The outward adorning of the body is very often sensual and excessive; for instance, when it is immoderate, and above your degree and station in the world, when you are proud of it and puffed up with it, when you dress with design to allure and tempt others, when your apparel is too rich, curious, or super-fluous, when your fashions are fantastical, imitating the levity and vanity of the worst people, and when they are immodest and wanton.

1 Peter 3

Comfort

. . . I cannot find one wise man among you, that knows how to *explain* the difficulties of God's providence or how to *apply* the consolations of his promises. Those do not go wisely about the work of comforting the afflicted who fetch their comforts from the possi-bility of their recovery and enlargement in this world; though that is not to be des-paired of, it is at the best un-certain; and if it should fail, as perhaps it may, the comforts built upon it will fail too. It is therefore our wisdom to com-fort ourselves, and others, in distress, with that which will not fail, the promise of God, his love and grace, and a well-grounded hope of eternal life.

Job 17

None can relieve the distresses of the outward condition with-out God. If the Lord do not help thee, whence shall I? (2 Kings 6:27). Nor can any relieve the distresses of the mind against God and his terrors. If he impress the sense of his wrath upon a guilty con-science, all the comforts the creature can administer are ineffectual. As vinegar upon nitre, so are songs to a heavy heart. The irresistibleness of God's operations must be acknowledged in his dealings both with communities and with particular persons: what he does cannot be controlled, whether it be done against a nation in its public capacity or against a man only in his private affairs.

Job 34

There are two words with which we may comfort ourselves and

one another in reference to the mismanagements of power among men: one is 'Hallelujah, the Lord God omnipotent reigneth' (Rev. 14:6); the other is 'surely I come quickly' (Rev. 22:20).

Psalm 82

Those are blessed who have the liberty of ordinances and the privileges of God's house. But, though we should be debarred from them, yet we are not therefore debarred from blessedness if we trust in God. If we cannot go to the House of the Lord, we may go by faith to the Lord of the House, and in him we shall be happy and may be easy.

Psalm 84

Instead of enquiring after that which would comfort you, you pore upon that which looks melancholy, and 'sorrow has filled your heart' . . . That they were too intent, and pored too much, upon the occasions of their grief: 'Sorrow has filled their hearts'. Christ had said enough to fill them with joy (ch. 15:11); but by looking at that only which made against them, and overlooking that which made for them, they were so full of sorrow that there was no room left for joy. Note, it is the common fault and folly of melancholy Christians to dwell only upon the dark side of the cloud, to meditate nothing but terror, and turn a deaf ear to the 'voice of joy and gladness'.

John 16

Commandments

Nay, though first-table duties have in them more of the essence of religion, yet second-table duties have in them more of the evidence of it. Our light burns in love to God, but it shines in love to our neighbour.

Taking the law in its spiritual sense, as Christ expounded it, no doubt, in many things he had offended against all these commands. Had he been acquainted with the extent and spiritual meaning of the law, instead of saying, 'All these have I kept; what lack I yet?', he would have said, with shame and sorrow, 'All these have I broken, what shall I do to get my sins pardoned?'

Matthew 19

Common Grace

How much are we beholden to the restraining grace of God for the preserving any thing of the honour and decency of the human nature! For, were it not for this, man, who was made but little lower than the angels, would make himself a great deal lower than the devils.

Romans 1

Common Sense

We must so depend on God's providence as to make use of our own prudence. Help thyself and God will help thee. God answers our prayers by teaching us to order our affairs with discretion.

Everything is beautiful in its season. Even the business of religion and the comforts of communion with God must sometimes give way to the necessary affairs of this life.

Genesis 32

Though God's promise would have secured him anywhere yet he would use means for his own preservation.

1 Kings 11

The rules of a strict discipline must not be made too strict, but so as to admit of a dispensation when the necessity of a case calls for it, which therefore, in making vows of that nature, it is wisdom to provide expressly for, that the way may be made the more clear, and we may not afterwards be forced to say, It was an error (Eccles. 5:6). Commands of that nature are to be understood with such limitations. These Rechabites would have tempted God, and not trusted Him, if they had not used proper means for their own safety in a time of common calamity, notwithstanding, the law and custom of their family.

Jeremiah 35

We are not called to suffer while we may avoid it without sin; and therefore, though we may not, for our own preservation, change our religion, yet we may change our place. Christ secured himself, not by a miracle, but in a way common to men, for the direction and encouragement of his suffering people.

John 4

Communion with God

To hear God's praises sweetly sung as David had appointed would cheer his spirits and settle his mind and help to put him into a right frame both to speak to him and to hear from him. We find a company of prophets prophesying with a psaltery and tabret before them. (1 Sam. 10: 5). Those that desire communion with God must keep their spirits quiet and serene. Elisha being refreshed and having the tumults of his spirits laid by this divine music, the Hand of the Lord came upon him.

2 Kings 3

The sedateness of his mind was evinced by the Spirit's coming upon him; for the Spirit chooses to move upon the still waters. Let no unkindness, no, not of a child or a friend, ever be laid so much to heart as to disfit us for communion with God.

Even our sorrow for sin must not hinder either our joy in God or our hope in God.

Psalm 3

By this we may now know that God accepts our spiritual sacrifices, if by his Spirit he kindles in our souls a holy fire of pious and divine affection and with that makes our hearts burn within us.

Psalm 20

The opening of his hand will satisfy the desire of other living things (145:16), but it is only the shining of his face that will satisfy the desire of a living soul. (4:6, 7).

Psalm 27

He longed, he fainted, he cried out, importunate to be restored to his place in God's courts, and almost impatient of delay. Yet it was not so much the courts of the Lord that he coveted, but he cried out, in prayer, for the living God himself. O that I might know him, and be again taken into communion with him! (1 John 1:3). Ordinances are empty things if we meet not with God in the ordinances.

Psalm 84

Let our disappointments in the creature turn our eyes to the Creator; let us have recourse to the word of God's grace and consult that, to the throne of his grace and solicit that. In the word and prayer there is a balm for every wound.

Ecclesiastes 5

Raptures and transports of joy are not the daily bread of God's children, however they may upon special occasions be feasted with them. We must not deny but that we have truly communion with God (1 John 1:3) though we have it not always so sensibly as at some times. And, though the mysteries of the kingdom of heaven may sometimes be looked into, yet ordinarily it is plain preaching that is most for edification.

Ezekiel 3

It is not wisdom to raise our expectations high in this world, for the most valuable of our glories and joys here are vanishing, even those of near communion with God are so, not a continual feast, but a running banquet. If sometimes we are favoured with special manifestations of divine grace, glimpses and pledges of future glory, yet they are withdrawn presently; two heavens are too much for those to expect that never deserve one.

Matthew 17

Composure of Spirit

He kept his temper and was not ruffled nor discomposed by any of the slights that were put upon him or the mischievous things that were said or done against him (v. 13, 14): 'I, as a deaf man, heard not.' I took no notice of the affronts put upon me, did not resent them, nor was put into disorder by them, much less did I meditate revenge or study to return the injury. Note, the less notice we take of the unkindness and injuries that are done us, the more we consult the quiet of our own minds.

Psalm 38

Wisdom teaches us not to be quick-sighted, or quick-scented, in apprehending and resenting affronts, but to wink at many of the injuries that are done to us, and act as if we did not see them (v. 21): 'Take no heed to all words that are spoken; set not thy heart to them.' Vex not thyself at men's peevish reflections upon thee, or suspicions of thee, but be as a deaf man that hears not (Ps. 38:13, 14). Be not solicitious or inquisitive to know what people say of thee; if they speak well of thee, it will feed thy pride, if ill, it will stir up thy passion. See therefore that thou approve thyself to God and thy own conscience, and then heed not what men say of thee.

Ecclesiastes 7

When he says, I will take my rest, it is not as if he were weary of governing the world, or as if he either needed or desired to retire from it and repose himself; but it intimates that the great God has a perfect, undisturbed, enjoyment of himself, in the midst of all the agitations and changes of this world (the Lord sits even upon the floods unshaken); the Eternal Mind is always easy.

Isaiah 19

Compromise

Heaven and Hell can never be reconciled, not light and darkness; No more can Satan and a sanctified soul, for these are contrary one to the other.

Genesis 3

Perhaps he might have this excuse for gratifying the king herein, that by this means he might keep him at the temple at Jerusalem and prevent his totally deserting it for the high places and the groves. Let us oblige him in this, thinks Urijah and then he will bring all his sacrifices to us for by this craft we get our living but whatever pretence he had, it was a most base wicked thing for him that was a priest, a chief priest, to make this altar.

2 Kings 16

They know they must obey God rather than man; they must rather suffer than sin, and must not do evil that good may come. And therefore none of these things move them; they are resolved rather to die in their integrity than live in their iniquity. While their brethren, who yet remained in their own land, were worshipping images by choice, they in Babylon would not be brought to it by constraint, but, as if they were good by 'antiperistasis', were most zealous against idolatry in an idolatrous country. And truly, all things considered, the saving of them from this sinful compliance was as great a miracle in the kingdom of grace as the saving of them out of the fiery furnace was in the kingdom of nature. These were those who formerly resolved not to defile themselves with the king's meat, and now they as bravely resolve not to defile themselves with his gods. Note, a steadfast, self-denying adherence to God and duty in less instances will qualify and prepare us for the like in greater.

Daniel 3

They were divided between God and their idols. They had a remaining affection in their hearts for God, but a reigning affection for their idols. They halted between God and Baal, that was the dividing of their heart. But God is the sovereign of the heart and he will by no means endure a rival; he will either have all or none. Satan, like the pretended mother, says, 'Let it be neither mine nor thine, but divide it'; but, if this be yielded to, God says, Nay, 'let him take it all.'

Hosea 10

Those that think to divide their affections and adorations between God and idols will not only come short of acceptance with God, but will have their doom with the worst of idolaters; for what communion can there be between light and darkness, Christ and Belial, God and mammon? She whose own the child is not pleads for the dividing of it, for, if Satan have half, he will have all; but the true mother says, 'Divide it not', for, if God have but half, he will have none.

Zephaniah 1

Concern for Others

It is probable that they were for entertaining themselves with the sight of the sepulchre and discourse with the angels. It was good to be here, but they have other work appointed them; this is a day of good tidings, and though they have the first taste of it, yet they must not have the monopoly of it, must not hold their peace, any more than those lepers (2 Kings 7:9). They must go tell the disciples. Note, public usefulness to others must be preferred before the pleasure of secret communion with God ourselves; for it is more blessed to give than to receive.

Matthew 28

When it is well with us, we are apt to be mindless of others, and in the fulness of our enjoyments to forget the necessities of our brethren; it was a weakness in Peter to prefer private communion with God before public usefulness. Paul is willing to abide in the flesh, rather than depart to the mountain of glory (though that be far better), when he sees it needful for the church (Phil. 1: 24, 25).

Mark 9

Seeing Paul while he was a prisoner employed himself in such prayers to God on behalf of the Ephesians, we should learn that no particular sufferings of our own should make us so solicitous about ourselves as to neglect the cases of others in our supplications and addresses to God.

Ephesians 3

As those who are grown Christians must be willing to hear the plainest truths preached for the sake of the weak, so the weak must be willing to hear the more difficult and mysterious truths preached for the sake of those who are strong.

Hebrews 6

Confidence in God

He sits there, as one easy and at rest, out of the reach of all their impotent menaces and attempts. There he sits as Judge in all the affairs of the children of men, perfectly secure of the full accomplishment of all his own purposes and designs, in spite of all opposition (29:10). The perfect repose of the eternal mind may be our comfort under all the disquietments of our mind. We are tossed on earth, and in the sea, but he sits in the heavens, where he has prepared his throne for judgment.

Those attempts of the kingdom of Satan which in our eyes are formidable, in his are despicable.
Psalm 2

If, in the worst times, God's people can lift up their heads with joy, knowing that all shall work for them to good, they will own it is God that is the lifter up of their head, that gives them both cause to rejoice and hearts to rejoice.
Psalm 3

We need not look upon those enemies with fear whom God looks upon with contempt.
Psalm 53

But particular notice must be taken of this, that the first prophecy against Egypt was just at the time when the king of Egypt was coming to relieve Jerusalem and raise the siege (Jer. 37:5), but did not answer the expectations of the Jews from them. Note, it is good to foresee the failing of all our creature-confidences, then when we are most in temptation to depend upon them, that we may cease from man.
Ezekiel 29

Conscience

We must never be over-awed either by majesty or multitude to do a sinful thing and go against our consciences.
Joshua 9

Even those that do the greatest wrong yet have such a conviction in their consciences that they would seem to do right.
Judges 11

David was ashamed of it and willing it should be forgotten because there fell wrath for it against Israel. A good man cannot, in the reflection, please himself with that which he knows God is displeased with, cannot make use of that nor take comfort in that which is obtained by sin.
1 Chronicles 27

The fear of God restrained him from oppressing the people. Those that truly fear God will not dare to do any thing cruel or unjust. It was purely that which restrained him. He was thus generous, not that he might have praise of men, or serve a turn by his interest in the people, but purely for conscience' sake, because of the fear of God.
Nehemiah 5

Sense of guilt quite dispirits men, upon the approach of any threatening trouble. What can those hope to do for themselves who have made God their enemy?
Jeremiah 6

Our only confidence in trouble will be that, having through grace in some measure done our duty, we shall find God a God all-sufficient to us. We may glory in this, that, wherever we are, we have an acquaintance with and an interest in a God that exercises lovingkindness, and judgment, and righteousness in the earth, that is not only just to all his creatures and will do no wrong to any of them, but kind to all his children and will protect them and provide for them. 'For in these things I delight'. God delights to show kindness and to execute judgment himself, and is pleased with those who herein are followers of him as dear children. Those that have such knowledge of the glory of God as to be changed into the same image, and to partake of his holiness, find it to be their perfection and glory; and the God they thus faithfully conform to they may cheerfully confide in, in their greatest straits.

Jeremiah 9

Why is he in such a fright? He perceives not what is written, and how does he know but it may be some happy presage of deliverance to him and to his kingdom? But the business was 'his thoughts troubled him'; his own guilty conscience flew in his face, and told him that he had no reason to expect any good news from heaven, and that the hand of an angel could write nothing but terror to him. He that knew himself liable to the justice of God immediately concluded this to be an arrest in his name, a summons to appear before him. Note, God can soon awaken the most secure and make the heart of the stoutest sinner to tremble; and there needs no more to do it than to let loose his own thoughts upon him; they will soon play the tyrant, and give him trouble enough.

Daniel 5

How he was filled with causeless fears merely from the guilt of his own conscience. Thus blood cries, not only from the earth on which it was shed, but from the heart of him that shed it, and makes him Magor-missabib — a terror round about, a terror to himself. A guilty conscience suggests everything that is frightful, and, like a whirlpool, gathers all to itself that comes near it. Thus the wicked flee when none pursue (Prov. 28:1); are in great fear, where no fear is, (Ps. 14:5).

Matthew 14

The reflections and reproaches of the sinner's own conscience are the 'worm that dieth not'; which will cleave to the damned soul as the worms do to the dead body, and prey upon it, and never leave it till it is quite devoured. 'Son, remember', will set this worm a gnawing; and how terribly will it bite with that word, 'How have I hated instruction!' (Prov. 5:12, 23). The soul that is food to this worm, dies not; the worm is bred in it, and one with it, and therefore neither doth that die. Damned sinners will be to eternity accusing, condemning, and upbraiding themselves with their own follies.

The wrath of God fastening upon a guilty and polluted conscience, is the fire that is not quenched; for it is the wrath of the living God, the eternal God, into whose hands it is a fearful thing to fall. There are no operations of the Spirit of grace upon the souls of damned sinners, and therefore there is nothing to alter the nature of the fuel, which must remain for ever combustible; nor is there any application of the merit of Christ to them, and therefore there is nothing to appease or quench the violence of the fire.

Mark 9

When men will not be persuaded to do what they should do, it is no marvel that they are ever and anon at a loss what to do.

Acts 4

He who does a thing which he believes to be unlawful, however the thing be in itself, to him it is a sin. This arises from that unchangeable law of our creation, which is, that our wills, in all their choices, should follow the dictates of our understandings. This is the order of nature, which order is broken if the understanding tell us that such a thing is a sin, and yet we will do it. This is a will to do evil; for, if it appears to us to be sin, there is the same pravity and corruption of the will in the doing of it as if really it were a sin; and therefore we ought not to do it.

He that will venture to do that which his own conscience suggests to him to be unlawful, when it is not so in itself, will by a like temptation be brought to do that which his conscience tells him is unlawful when it is really so.

Romans 14

Consistency

Those that cast off the duties of religion in their prosperity cannot expect the comforts of it when they come to be in distress; justly, are they then sent to 'the gods whom they have served' (Juds. 10, v. 14).

Deuteronomy 4

If God's goodness to us be like the morning light, which shines more and more to the perfect day, let not ours to him be like the morning cloud and the early dew that passeth away.

Psalm 23

Contentment

As we may go anywhere in comfort when God's Presence goes with us, so we can stay anywhere contentedly if that blessing rest upon us.

Genesis 26

It is much easier to bring ourselves to the external services of religion and observe all the formalities of devotion than to live a life of dependence upon and submission to the Divine Providence in the course of our life.

Numbers 14

Let Zebulun rejoice in his going out; let him thank God for the gains and make the best of the losses and inconveniences of his merchandise and not despise the meanness nor envy the quietness of Issachar's tents. Let Issachar rejoice in his tents; let him be well pleased with his retirements and content with the small profits of his country seats and not grudge that he has not Zebulun's pleasure of travelling and profit of trading.

Every business has both its conveniences and inconveniences and, therefore, whatever Providence has made our business we ought to bring our minds to it.

Deuteronomy 33

It is an evidence of a discontented, distrustful, unstable spirit, to be weary of the place in which God hath set us, and to be for leaving it immediately whenever we meet with any uneasiness or inconvenience in it.

Ruth 1

How little God affects external pomp and splendour in his service. His Ark was content with a tabernacle and he never so much as mentioned the building of a house for it; no, not when he had fixed his people in great and goodly cities which they builded not (Deut. 6, 10.) he commanded the judges to feed his people but never bid them build him a house. We may well be content awhile with mean accommodations; God's Ark was so.

1 Chronicles 17

Solomon knew how to set bounds to his desires. He was not one of those that enlarged them endlessly and can never be satisfied but knew when to draw in, for he finished all he desired and then he desired no more. He did not sit down and fret that he had not more cities to build as Alexander did that he had no more worlds to conquer (Hab. 2; 5.)

2 Chronicles 8

The consideration of the mercies we receive from God, both past and present, should make us receive our afflictions with a suitable disposition of spirit.

Job 2

His own covetous mind keeps him from being truly rich. He is not rich that has not enough, and he has not enough that does not think he has. It is contentment only that is great gain.

Job 15

That heart must needs wander that walks after the eyes; for then it looks no further than the things that are seen, whereas it ought to be in heaven, whither the eyes cannot reach: it should follow the dictates of religion and right reason: if it follow the eye, it will be misled to that for which God will bring men into judgment (Eccl. 11, 9).

Job 31

Natural desires are at rest when that which is desired is obtained, but corrupt desires are insatiable. Nature is content with little, grace with less, but lust with nothing.

Only as his friends, when he came naked into the world, in pity to him, helped him with swaddling-clothes, so, when he goes out, they help him with grave-clothes, and that is all. See (Job 1:21; Ps. 49:17). This is urged as a reason why we should be content with such things as we have (1 Tim. 6:7). In respect of the body we must go as we came, the dust shall return to the earth as it was.

Ecclesiastes 5

Even a poor man, who has business, and is discreet, diligent, and dexterous, in the management of it, may get as comfortably through this world as he that is loaded with an overgrown estate. Consider what the poor has less than the rich, if he but knows to walk before the living, knows how to conduct himself decently, and do his duty to all, how to get an honest livelihood by his labour, how to spend his time well and improve his opportunities. What has he? Why, he is better beloved and more respected among his neighbours, and has a better interest than many a rich man that is griping and haughty. What has he? Why he has as much of the comfort of this life, has food and raiment, and is therewith content, and so is as truly rich as he that has abundance.

He is much happier that is always content, though he has ever so little, than he that is always coveting, though he has ever so much.

Ecclesiastes 6

Then I commended joy, a holy security and serenity of mind, arising from a confidence in God, and his power, providence and promise, because a man has no better thing under the sun (though a good man has much better things *above* the sun) than to eat and drink, that is soberly and thankfully to make use of the things of this life according as his rank is, and to be cheerful, whatever happens, for that shall abide with him of his labour. That is all the fruit he has for himself of the pains

that he takes in the business of the world; let him therefore take it, and much good may it do him; and let him not deny himself that, out of a peevish discontent because the world does not go as he would have it.

Ecclesiastes 8

The frowns of the world would not disquiet us as they do if we did not foolishly flatter ourselves with the hopes of its smiles and court and covet them too much. It is our over-fondness for the good things of this present time that makes us impatient under its evil tidings.

Jeremiah 45

We could better be without mines of gold than fields of corn; the products of the earth, which may easily be gathered from the surface of it, are much greater blessings to mankind than its treasures, which are with so much difficulty and hazard dug out of its bowels. If God give us daily bread, we have reason to be thankful, and no reason to complain, though silver and gold we have none.

Ezekiel 7

Nature is content with little, grace with less, but lust with nothing.

Matthew 15

God is the sovereign King, the righteous Judge, and to him it belongs to administer justice; for, being a God of infinite knowledge, by him actions are weighed in unerring balances; and, being a God of infinite purity, he hates sin and cannot endure to look upon iniquity.

Romans 12

We must bring our minds to our present condition, and this is the sure way to contentment; and those who cannot do it would not be contented though God should raise their condition to their minds, for the mind would rise with the condition. Haman was the great court-favourite, and yet not contented — Ahab on the throne, and yet not contented — Adam in paradise, and yet not contented; yea, the angels in heaven, and yet not contented; but Paul, though abased and empty, had 'learned in every state, in any state, therewith to be content.'

Hebrews 13

Conversation

Make known His deeds, that others may join with you in praising him. Talk of all his wondrous works, as we talk of things that we are full of, and much affected with, and desire to fill others with. God's wondrous works ought to be the subject of our familiar discourses with our families and friends, and we should talk of them 'as we sit in the house and as we go by the way' (Deut. 6:7), not merely for entertainment, but for the exciting of devotion and the encouraging of our own and others' faith and hope in God. Even sacred things may be the matter of common talk, provided it be with due reverence.

Psalm 105

The more we see of the righteousness of God's commandments, the more industrious we should be to bring others acquainted with them, that they may be ruled by them. We should always make the Word of God the governor of our discourse, so as never to transgress it by sinful speaking or sinful silence; and we should often make it the subject-matter of our discourse, that it may feed many and minister grace to the hearers.

Psalm 119

Conversion

The proselytes of other nations, all that had separated themselves from the people of the lands, their gods and their worship, unto the law of God, and the observance of that law. See what conversion is; it is separating ourselves from the course and custom of this world, and devoting ourselves to the conduct of the word of God.

Nehemiah 10

Conversion begins in serious consideration (Ezek. 18:28, Luke 15:17). Consideration must end in a sound conversion. To what purpose have we thought on our ways if we do not turn our feet with all speed to God's testimonies?

Psalm 119

Observe, what is required to denominate a man a true convert, how he must be qualified that he may be entitled to this act of indemnity. The first step towards conversion is consideration (v. 28): 'Because he considers and turns.'

Ezekiel 18

The understanding is opened to receive the divine light, the will opened to receive the divine law, and the affections opened to receive the divine love. When the heart is thus opened to Christ, the ear is opened to his word, the lips opened in prayer, the hand opened in charity, and the steps enlarged in all manner of gospel obedience.

Acts 16

He did not reason himself into Christianity by a chain of arguments, but was brought into the highest degree of an assurance of it, immediately from the highest degree of prejudice against it, by which it appeared that he was made a Christian and a preacher by a supernatural power; so that his conversion in such a miraculous way was not only to himself, but to others also, a convincing proof of the truth of Christianity.

Acts 26

Walk by new rules, towards new ends, from new principles. Make a new choice of the way. Choose new paths to walk in, new leaders to walk after, new companions to walk with. Old things should pass away, and all things become new. The man is what he was not, does what he did not.

Romans 6

This Rahab believed the report she had heard of God's powerful presence with Israel; but that which proved her faith sincere, was, that, to the hazard of her life, she 'received the messengers, and sent them out another way'.

. . . Rahab must prefer the honour of God and the good of his people before the preservation of her own country. Her former acquaintance must be discarded, her former course of life entirely abandoned, and she must give signal proof and evidence of this before she can be in a justified state.

James 2

He that is said to 'err from the truth' in (v. 19) is described as 'erring in his way' in (v. 20), and we cannot be said to convert any merely by altering their opinions, unless we can bring them to correct and amend their ways. This is conversion — to turn a sinner from the error of his ways, and not to turn him from one party to another, or merely from one notion and way of thinking to another.

James 5

Conviction

The servant knew before that he was so much in debt, and yet was under no concern about it, till he was called to an account. Sinners are commonly careless about the pardon of their sins, till they come under the arrests of some awakening word, some startling providence, or approaching death, and then, 'Wherewith shall I come before the Lord?' (Miceh 6:6). How easily, how quickly, can God bring the proudest sinner to his feet; Ahab to his sackcloth, Manasseh to his prayers, Pharaoh to his confessions, Judas to his restitution, Simon Magus to his supplication, Belshazzar and Felix to their tremblings. The stoutest heart will fail, when God sets the sins in order before it. This servant doth not deny the debt, nor seek evasions, nor go about to abscond.

Matthew 18

What he had said concerning his grace and eternal life he found had made little impression upon her, because she had not been convinced of sin; therefore, waiving the discourse about the living water, he sets himself to awaken her conscience, to open the wound of guilt, and then she would more easily apprehend the remedy by grace. And this is the method of dealing with souls; they must first be made weary and heavy-laden under the burden of sin, and then brought to Christ for rest; first pricked to the heart, and then healed. This is the course of spiritual physic; and if we proceed not in this order we begin at the wrong end.

John 4

The scribes and Pharisees had the wound opened, and now they should have been desirous to have it searched, and then it might have been healed, but this was the thing they dreaded and declined. It is folly for those that are under convictions to get away from Jesus Christ, as these here did, for he is the only one that can heal the wounds of conscience, and speak peace to us.

John 8

The Spirit convinces of the fact of sin, that we have done so and so; of the fault of sin, that we have done ill in doing so; of the folly of sin, that we have acted against right reason, and our true interest; of the filth of sin, that by it we are become odious to God; of the fountain of sin, the corrupt nature; and, lastly, of the fruit of sin, that the end thereof is death. The Spirit demonstrates the depravity and degeneracy of the whole world, that all the world is guilty before God.

John 16

Correction

There is little hope of those who are made worse by that which should make them better, whose corruptions are excited and exasperated by those rebukes both of the word and of the providence of God which were designed for the suppressing and subduing of them.

. . . I have given thee medicine, but it has done thee no good. I have used the means of cleansing thee, but they have been ineffectual; the intention of them has not been answered. Note, it is sad to think how many there are on whom ordinances and providences are all lost.

Ezekiel 24

Counterfeits

There is a kind of peace in the palace of an unconverted soul, while the devil, as a strong man armed, keeps it. The sinner has a good opinion of himself, is very secure and merry, has no doubt concerning the goodness of his state nor any dread of the judgment to come; he flatters himself in his own eyes, and cries peace to himself. Before Christ appeared, all was quiet, because all went one way; but the preaching of the Gospel disturbed the peace of the devil's palace.

Luke 11

Courage

The way of access to the enemies' camp is described as being peculiarly difficult and their natural entrenchments impregnable yet this does not discourage him; the strength and sharpness of the rocks do but harden and whet his resolutions. Great and generous souls are animated by opposition and take pleasure in breaking through it.

1 Samuel 14

The boldness of the attacks which profane people make upon religion should sharpen the courage and resolution of its friends and advocates. It is time to stir when proclamation is made in the gate of the camp, who is on the Lord's side? When vice is daring it is no time for virtue, through fear to hide itself.

Job 17

When Jeremiah delivered God's message he spoke as one having authority, with the greatest boldness; but, when he presented his own request, he spoke as one under authority, with the greatest submissiveness: 'Hear me, I pray thee, O my Lord the king! Let my supplication, I pray thee, be accepted before thee.' Here is not a word

of complaint of the princes that unjustly committed him, no offer to bring an action of false imprisonment against them, but all in a way of modest supplication to the king, to teach us that even when we act with the courage that becomes the faithful servants of God, yet we must conduct ourselves with the humility and modesty that become dutiful subjects to the government God hath set over us. A lion in God's cause must be a lamb in his own.

Jeremiah 37

Though at first he came to Jesus by night, for fear of being known, and still continued in his post; yet, when there was occasion, he boldly appeared in defence of Christ, and opposed the whole council that were set against him. Thus many believers who at first were timorous, and ready to flee at the shaking of a leaf, have at length, by divine grace, grown courageous, and able to laugh at the shaking of a spear. Let none justify the disguising of their faith by the example of Nicodemus, unless, like him, they be ready upon the first occasion openly to appear in the cause of Christ, though they stand alone in it; for so Nicodemus did here, and ch. 19:39.

John 7

Though they knew the prisoners would hear them, yet they sang aloud, as those that were not ashamed of their Master, nor of his service. Shall those that would sing psalms in their families plead, in excuse for their omission of the duty, that they are afraid their neighbours should hear them, when those that sing profane songs roar them out, and care not who hears them?

Acts 16

Covetousness

Nothing is more violent than anger. O the force of strong wrath! And yet a handsome present, prudently managed, will turn away some men's wrath when it seemed implacable, and disarm the keenest and most passionate resentments. Covetousness is commonly a master-sin and has the command of other lusts. Money commands all things. Thus Jacob pacified Esau and Abigail David.

It is not having silver and gold, horses and chariots, that is a provocation to God, but: 1. Desiring them insatiably, so that there is no end of the treasures, no end of the chariots, no bounds or limits set to the desire of them. Those shall never have enough in God (who alone is all-sufficient) that never know when they have enough of this world, which at the best is insufficient. 2. Depending upon them, as if we could not be safe, and easy, and happy, without them, and could not but be so with them.

Isaiah 2

Those have the spirit of Edomites who desire the death of others because they hope to get by it, or are pleased with their failing because they expect to come into their business. When we see the vanity of the world in the disappointments, losses,

and crosses, that others meet with, in it, instead of showing ourselves, upon such an occasion, greedy of it, we should rather be made thereby to sit more loose to it, and both take our affections off it and lower our expectations from it.

Ezekiel 35

His sin is his punishment, his ambition is his perpetual uneasiness. Though the home be a palace, yet to a discontented mind it is a prison.

Those that will not be content with their allotments shall not have the comfort of their achievements.

Habakkuk 2

If he had had but two mites in all the world, and had been commanded to give them to the poor, or but one handful of meal in the barrel, and a little oil in the cruse, and had been bidden to make a cake of that for a poor prophet, the trial, one would think, had been much greater, and yet those trials have been overcome (Luke 21:4; 1 Kings 17:14); which shows that the love of the world draws stronger than the most pressing necessities.

Matthew 19

'What will ye give me?' Why, what did he want? Neither bread to eat, nor raiment to put on; neither necessaries nor conveniences. Was not he welcome, wherever his Master was? Did he not fare as he fared? Had he not been but just now nobly entertained at a supper in Bethany, in the house of Simon the leper, and a little before at another, where no less a person than Martha herself waited at table? And yet this covetous wretch could not be content, but comes basely cringing to the priests with, 'What will ye give me?' Note, it is not the lack of money, but the love of money, that is the root of all evil, and particularly of apostasy from Christ; witness Demas (2 Tim. 4: 10). Satan tempted our Saviour with this bait, 'All these things will I give thee' (Ch. 4:9); but Judas offered himself to be tempted with it.

Matthew 26

That is, an inordinate love of present good and outward enjoyments, which proceeds from too high a value in the mind, puts upon too eager a pursuit, hinders the proper use and enjoyment of them, and creates anxious fear and immoderate sorrow for the loss of them. Observe, covetousness is spiritual idolatry: it is the giving of that love and regard to worldly wealth which are due to God only, and carries a greater degree of malignity in it, and is more highly provoking to God, than is commonly thought. And it is very observable that among all the instances of sin which good men are recorded in the scripture to have fallen into (and there is scarcely any but some or other, in one or other part of their life, have fallen into) there is no instance in all the scripture of any good man charged with covetousness.

Colossians 3

Criticism

We should be afraid of censuring the devotion of others though it may not agree with our sentiments because for aught that we know the heart might be upright in it and who are we that we should despise those whom God has accepted? If we can prove ourselves to God in all we do in religion and do it as before the Lord, we need not value the censures and reproaches of men.

2 Samuel 6

Christ's ministers must not think it strange if they be censured and quarrelled with, not only by their professed enemies, but by their professing friends; not only for their follies and infirmities, but for their good actions seasonably and well done; but, if we have proved our own work, we may have rejoicing in ourselves, as Peter had, whatever reflections we may have from our brethren. Those that are zealous and courageous in the service of Christ must expect to be censured by those who, under pretence of being cautious, are cold and indifferent. Those who are of catholic, generous, charitable principles, must expect to be censured by such as are conceited and strait-laced, who say, 'Stand by thyself, I am holier than thou'.

Acts 11

God sees not as man sees; and he is their master, and not we. In judging and censuring our brethren, we meddle with that which does not belong to us: we have work enough to do at home; and, if we must needs be judging, let us exercise our faculty upon our own hearts and ways.

We have reason to think, because in other things he conducts himself like a good Christian, that in this also his eye is single, and that 'he regardeth it unto the Lord'; and God will accept of his honest intention, though he be under a mistake about the observance of days; for the sincerity and uprightness of the heart were never rejected for the weakness and infirmity of the head: so good a master do we serve.

Romans 14

We should be very careful how we censure others, when we have to do with a Judge from whom we cannot conceal ourselves. Others do not lie open to our notice, but we lie all open to his: and, when he shall come to judge, 'every man shall have praise of God.'

... But how fearful should they be of loading any with reproaches now whom their common Judge shall hereafter commend.

1 Corinthians 4

Crucifixion

And now let us pause awhile, and with an eye of faith look upon Jesus. Was ever sorrow like unto his sorrow? See him who was clothed with glory stripped of it all, and clothed with shame — him who was the 'praise of angels' made a 're-proach of men' — him who had been with eternal delight and joy in the bosom of the Father now in the extremities of pain and agony. See him bleeding, see him struggling, see him dying, see him and love him, love him

and live to him, and study what we shall render.

John 19

Curiosity

The practical instructions Christ had given them concerning brotherly love he overlooks, and asks no questions upon them, but fastens upon that concerning which Christ purposely kept them in the dark. Note, it is a common fault among us to be more inquisitive concerning things secret, which belong to God only, than concerning things 'revealed, which belong to us and our children', more desirous to have our curiosity gratified than our consciences directed, to know what is done in heaven than what we may do to get thither. It is easy to observe it in the converse of Christians, how soon a discourse of that which is plain and edify-ing is dropped, and no more said to it, the subject is ex-hausted; which in a matter of doubtful disputation runs into an endless strife of words.

John 13

Darkness

Darkness was one of the plagues of Egypt, and it is opposed to lustre and honour, and so fore-bodes the contempt and scorn to which the antichristian inter-est should be exposed. Darkness is opposed to wisdom and pene-tration, and forebodes the con-fusion and folly which the idolaters should discover at that time. It is opposed to pleasure and joy, and so signifies their anguish and vexation of spirit, when their calamities thus came upon them.

Revelation 16

Day of Judgment

For damned sinners in hell shall not be allowed their light, being cast into utter darkness, and glorified saints in heaven shall not need their light, for God himself will be their everlasting light (Isa. 60:19). Those that fall under the wrath of God in that day of wrath shall be cut off from all comfort and joy, signified by the darkening not only of sun and moon, but of the stars also.

When God comes to pull down and destroy his enemies, and make them all his footstool, though heaven and earth should stand up in defence of them and undertake their protection, it shall be all in vain. Even they shall shake before him and be an insufficient shelter to those whom he comes forth to contend with. Note, as blessings out of Zion are the sweetest blessings, and enough to make heaven and earth sing, so terrors out of Zion are the sorest terrors, and enough to make heaven and earth shake.

Joel 3

If we look to the end of all these things, the period of the world, and the posture of souls then, we shall thence form a very different idea of the present state of things. If we see things as they will appear then, we shall see them as they should appear now.

Matthew 16

Death

When it drew towards night, and the shadows of the evening were stretched out, *they began to think (as it behoves us to do when we observe the day of our life hastening towards a period) where they must lodge.*

Judges 19

He had the unhappiness to die in the midst of his days but to balance that, the happiness not to outlive his reputation as the last three of his predecessors did.

2 Chronicles 27

Let discontented people declaim ever so much against life, they will be loth to part with it when it comes to the point. When the old man in the fable, being tired with his burden, threw it down with discontent for Death, and Death came to him and asked him what he would have with him, he then answered 'Nothing, but to help me up with my burden.'

If the miseries of this life can prevail, contrary to nature, to make death itself desirable, shall not much more the hopes and prospects of a better life, to which death is our passage, make it so, and set us quite above the fear of it? It may be a sin to long for death, but I am sure it is no sin to long for heaven.

Job 3

He is said to be carried away, and hurled out of his place as with a storm, and with an east wind, violent, and noisy, and very dreadful. Death to a godly man, is like a fair gale of wind to convey him to the heavenly country, but, to a wicked man, it is an east wind, a storm, a tempest, that hurries him away in confusion and amazement, to destruction...

Those who will not be persuaded now to fly to the arms of divine grace, which are stretched out to receive them, will not be able to flee from the arms of divine wrath, which will shortly be stretched out to destroy them.

Job 27

It is death indeed that is before us; but,
1. It is but the shadow of death; there is no substantial evil in it; the shadow of a serpent will not sting nor the shadow of a sword kill.
2. It is the valley of the shadow, deep indeed, and dark and dirty; but the valleys are fruitful, and so is death itself fruitful of comforts to God's people.
3. It is but a walk in this valley, a gentle pleasant walk. The wicked are chased out of the world, and their souls are required; but the saints take a walk to another world as cheerfully as they take their leave of this.
4. It is a walk through it. They shall not be lost in this valley, but get safely to the mountain of spices on the other side of it.

Psalm 23

While a saint can ask proud death, 'Where is thy sting?' Death will ask the proud sinner, 'Where is thy wealth, thy pomp?', and the more he was fattened with prosperity the more sweetly will death feed on him.

The greatest and wealthiest cannot therefore be the happiest, because they are never the better for their living in this world; as they came naked into it, they shall go naked out of it. But those have something to show in the other world for their living in this world who can say, through grace, that though they came corrupt, and sinful, and spiritually naked, into it, they go renewed, and sanctified, and well clothed with the righteousness of Christ, out of it. Those that are rich in the graces and comforts of the Spirit have something which, when they die, they shall carry away with them, something which death cannot strip them of, nay, which death will be the improvement of; but, as for worldly possessions, as we brought nothing into the world (what we have we had from others), so it is certain that we shall carry nothing out, but leave it to others. (1 Tim. 6:7).

Psalm 49

We are too apt to look upon death as no more than a debt owing to nature; whereas it is not so; if the nature of man had continued in its primitive purity and rectitude, there would have been no such debt owing to it. It is a debt to the justice of God, a debt to the law. 'Sin entered into the world and death by sin.'

Psalm 90

Between the death of a godly and wicked man there is a

great difference, but not between the death of a wise man and a fool; the fool is buried and forgotten (Ch. 8: 10), and no one remembered the poor man that by his wisdom delivered the city (Ch. 9: 15); so that to both the grave is a land of forgetfulness; and wise and learned men, when they have been awhile there out of sight, grow out of mind, a new generation arises that knew them not.

Ecclesiastes 2

When the soul is required it must be resigned, and it is to no purpose to dispute it, either by arms or arguments, by ourselves or by any friend: There is no man that has power over his own spirit to retain it, when it is summoned to return to God who gave it. It cannot fly anywhere out of the jurisdiction of death, nor find any place where its writs do not run. It cannot abscond so as to escape death's eye, though it is hidden from the eyes of all living. A man has no power to adjourn the day of his death, nor can he by prayers or bribes obtain a reprieve; no bail will be taken, no essoine (excuse), protection, or imparlance (conference), allowed.

Death is a battle that must be fought, there is no sending to that war (so some read it), no substituting another to muster for us, no champion admitted to fight for us; we must ourselves engage, and are concerned to provide accordingly, as for a battle.

Ecclesiastes 8

And should it not awaken us to get ready for death, to consider that the thing itself is certain, and the time fixed in the counsel of God, but that we are kept in the dark and uncertainty about it in order that we may be always ready? We cannot be so sure that we shall live forty days as Nineveh now was that it should stand forty days ...We should be alarmed if we were sure not to live a month, and yet we are careless, though we are not sure to live a day.

Jonah 3

Death cuts off a good man, as a choice imp is cut off to be grafted in a better stock; but it cuts off a wicked man, as a withered branch is cut off for the fire — cuts him off from this world, which he set his heart so much upon, and was, as it were, one with. Or, as we read it, shall cut him asunder, that is, part body and soul, send the body to the grave to be a prey for devils, and there is the sinner cut asunder. The soul and body of a godly man at death part fairly, the one cheerfully lifted up to God, the other left to the dust; but the soul and body of a wicked man at death are cut asunder, torn asunder, for to them death is the king of terrors (Job. 18: 14). The wicked servant divided himself between God and the world, Christ and Belial, his profession and his lusts, justly therefore will he thus be divided.

Matthew 24

Death is the rending of the veil of flesh which interposes between us and the holy of holies; the death of Christ was so, the death of true Christians is so.

It is the most melancholy circumstance in the funerals of our Christian friends, when we have laid their bodies in the dark and silent grave, to go home, and leave them behind; but alas, it is not we that go home, and leave them behind, no, it is they that are gone to the better home, and have left us behind.

Matthew 27

It is better to die, and go along with our Christian friends to that world which is enriched by their removal to it, than stay behind in a world that is impoverished by their departure out of it. The more of our friends are translated hence, the fewer cords we have to bind us to this earth, and the more to draw our hearts heavenwards. How pleasantly does the good man speak of dying, as if it were but undressing and going to bed!

John 11

The most that death does to our Christian friends is to take them out of our sight, not out of being, not out of bliss, not out of all relation to us, only out of sight, and then not out of mind.

John 16

It should be a pleasure to those that have their home in the other world to think of being 'no more in this world'; for when we have done what we have to do in this world, and are made meet for that, what

is there here that should court our stay? When we receive a sentence of death within ourselves, with what a holy triumph should we say, 'Now I am no more in this world', this dark deceitful world, this poor empty world, this tempting defiling world; no more vexed with its thorns and briars, no more endangered by its nets and snares; now I shall wander no more in this howling wilderness, be tossed no more on this stormy sea; 'now I am no more in this world', but can cheerfully quit it, and give it a final farewell.

John 17

It is altogether owing to the grace of God in Christ that sin is pardoned and death disarmed. The law puts arms into the hand of death, to destroy the sinner; but pardon of sin takes away this power from the law, and deprives death of its strength and sting.

1 Corinthians 15

Death is a great loss to a carnal worldly man; for he loses all his comforts and all his hopes: but to a good Christian it is gain, for it is the end of all his weakness and misery and the perfection of his comforts and accomplishment of his hopes; it delivers him from all the evils of life, and brings him to the possession of the chief good.

Philippians 1

As the death of the body consists in its separation from the soul, so the death of the soul consists in its separation from God and the divine favour. As the death of the body is the corruption and putrefaction of it, so sin is the corruption or depravation of the soul. As a man who is dead is unable to help himself by any power of his own, so an habitual sinner is morally impotent: *though he has a natural power, or the power of a reasonable creature, he has not a spiritual power*, till he has the divine life or a renewed nature.

Colossians 2

Christ became man, and died, to deliver them from those perplexities of soul, by letting them know that death is not only a conquered enemy, but a reconciled friend, not sent to hurt the soul, *or* separate it from the love of God, but to put an end to all their grievances and complaints, and to give them a passage to eternal life and blessedness.

Hebrews 2

It is a great work, and it is a work that can be but once done, and therefore had need to be well done. This is matter of comfort to the godly, that they shall die well and die but once; but it is matter of terror to the wicked, who die in their sins, that they cannot return again to do that great work better.

Hebrews 9

Death of Infants

Godly parents have great reason to hope concerning their children that die in infancy, that it is well with their souls in the other world for the promise is to us and our children which shall be performed to those who do not put a bar in their own door as infants do not.

2 Samuel 12

Debts

Do not spend that upon yourselves, much less heap it up for yourselves, which you owe to others. The 'wicked borroweth and payeth not again', (Ps. 37:21). Many that are very sensible of the trouble think little of the sin of being in debt.

Romans 13

Deception

A secret emnity to Christ and his gospel is often gilded over with a pretended affection to Caesar and his power. The Jews hated the Roman government and yet, to serve a turn, could cry 'We have no king but Caesar'.

Ezra 4

Though Philip had very lately been deceived in Simon Magus, and had admitted him to baptism, though he afterwards appeared to be no true convert, yet he did not therefore scruple to baptize the eunuch upon his profession of faith immediately, without putting him upon a longer trial than usual. If some hypocrites crowd into the church, who afterwards prove a grief and scandal to us, yet we must not therefore make the door of admission any straiter than Christ has made it; they shall answer for their apostasy, and not we.

Acts 8

Defending Our Rights

He renounced his right, rather than by claiming it he would hinder his success. He denied himself, for fear of giving offence; but asserted his right lest his self-denial should prove prejudicial to the ministry. Note, he is likely to plead most effectually for the rights of others who shows a generous disregard to his own. It is plain, in this case, that justice, and not self-love, is the principle by which he is actuated.

1 Corinthians 9

Defending Ourselves

As to his offences against God, he prays, Lord, enter not into judgment with me (143:2), remember not my transgressions (25:7), in which he appeals to God's mercy; but, as to his offences against Saul, he appeals to God's justice and begs of him to judge for him as 43:1. Or thus, he cannot justify himself against the charge of sin; he owns his iniquity is great and he is undone if God, in his infinite mercy, do not forgive him; but he can justify himself against the charge of hypocrisy.

Psalm 26

Christ's answer is so framed, as that it might sufficiently justify the practice of his own disciples, and yet not condemn the institution of John, or the practice of his disciples. When the Pharisees fomented this dispute, they hoped Christ would cast blame, either on his own disciples, or on John's, but he did neither. Note, when at any time we are unjustly censured, our care must be only to clear ourselves, not to recriminate, or throw dirt upon others; and such a variety may there be of circumstances, as may justify us in our practice, without condemning those that practice otherwise.

Matthew 9

Depression

Though they had just now obtained a glorious victory over the Canaanites and were going on conquering and to conquer, yet they speak very discontentedly of all God had done for them and distrustfully of what he would do.

Numbers 21

Heman was a very wise man, and a very good man, a man of God, and a singer too, and one may therefore suppose him to have been a man of a cheerful spirit, and yet now a man of a sorrowful spirit, troubled in mind, and upon the brink of despair. Inward trouble is the sorest trouble, and that which sometimes, the best of God's saints and servants have been severely exercised with. The spirit of man, of the greatest men, will not always sustain his infirmity, but will droop and sink under it.

Psalm 88

Desires

Men's characters appear in their choices and desires. 'What wouldst thou have?' tries a man as much as 'What wouldst thou do?' Thus God tried whether

Solomon was one of the children of this world that say 'Who will show us any good?' or of the children of Light that say 'Lord, lift up the light of thy countenance upon us.' As we choose we shall have and that is likely to be our portion to which we give the preference, whether the wealth and pleasures of this world or spiritual riches and delights.

2 Chronicles 1

Then our desire must be towards him and our delight in him (the word signifies both); we must delight in what we have of God and desire what we yet further hope for. Our desires must not only be offered up to God, but they must all terminate in him, desiring nothing more than God, but still more and more of him. This includes all our prayers, 'Lord, give us Thyself', as that includes all the promises, 'I will be to them a God.'

Psalm 73

Determination

Nothing could be said more fine, more brave, than this. She seems to have had another spirit, and another speech, now that her sister had gone, and it is an instance of the grace of God inclining the soul to the resolute choice of the better part. Draw me thus, and we will run after thee. Her mother's dissuasions made her the more resolute; as when Joshua said to the people, You cannot serve the Lord, they said it with the more vehemence, 'Nay but we will' . . . Our relations they may be, but they cannot be our

friends, that would dissuade us from and discourage us in the service of God and the work of religion.

Ruth 1

Christ has hereby taught us to go on with resolution in the way of our duty, how violent soever the opposition is, that we meet with in it. We must deny ourselves sometimes in our ease, pleasure, and convenience, rather than give offence even to those who causelessly take it; but we must not deny ourselves the satisfaction of serving God, and doing good, though offence may unjustly be taken at it. None could be more tender of giving offence than Christ; yet, rather than send this poor man away uncured, he would venture offending all the scribes and Pharisees that compassed him about.

Mark 3

Thus the enemies of religion are made more resolute and active by being baffled; and shall its friends be disheartened with every disappointment, who know its cause is righteous and will at last be victorious?

John 12

Devotion to God

Yet, if it had been true, as they said here, that since they returned to the service of the true God, the God of Israel, they had been in want and trouble, was that a reason why they should revolt from him again? That was as much as to say that they served not him, but their own bellies. Those who know God, and put their trust in him, will serve him, though he starve them, though he slay them, though they never see a good day with him in this world, being well assured that they shall not lose by him in the end.

Jeremiah 44

Since in him and upon him we live, we ought to live to him; since in him we move, we ought to move towards him; and since in him we have our being, and from him we receive all the supports and comforts of our being, we ought to consecrate our being to him, and to apply to him for a new being, a better being, an eternal well-being.

Acts 17

Diligence

He sought the law of the Lord; that is, he made it his business to enquire into it, searched the Scriptures and sought the knowledge of God, of his mind and will in the Scriptures which is to be found there but not without seeking.

Ezra 7

If valuable things were too easily obtained men would never learn to take pains . . . What is for necessity is had with a little labour from the surface of the earth; but what is for ornament must be dug with a great deal of pains out of the bowels of it. To be fed is cheap, but to be fine is chargeable . . .

Go to the miners then, thou sluggard in religion; consider their ways, and be wise. Let their courage, diligence, and constancy in seeking the wealth that perisheth shame us out of slothfulness and faint-heartedness in labouring for the true riches. How much better is it to get wisdom than gold! How much easier and safer! Yet gold is sought for, but grace neglected. Will the hopes of *precious things* out of the earth (so they call them, though really they are paltry and perishing) be such a spur to industry, and shall not the certain prospect of truly precious things in heaven be much more so? . . .

It is better to get wisdom than gold. Gold is another's, wisdom our own; gold is for the body and time, wisdom for the soul and eternity. Let that which is most precious in God's account be so in ours. See (Prov. 3, 14), etc. . .

Such is the degeneracy of human nature that there is no true wisdom to be found with any but those who are born again, and who, through grace, partake of the divine nature. As for others, even the most ingenious and industrious, they can tell us no tidings of this lost wisdom . . .

Men can more easily break through the difficulties they meet with in getting worldly wealth than through those they meet with in getting heavenly wisdom, and they will take more pains to learn how to live in this world than how to live for ever in a better world.

Job 28

He had said, 'The hand of the diligent makes rich', as a means; but, here he ascribes it to 'the blessing of the Lord'; but that blessing is upon the hand of the diligent. It is thus in spiritual riches. Diligence in getting them is our duty, but God's blessing and grace must have all the glory of that which is acquired, (Deut. 8:17, 18).

Proverbs 10

This reason is further illustrated by the rule God observes in dispensing his gifts; he bestows them on those who improve them, but takes them away from those who bury them. It is a rule among men, that they will rather entrust their money with those who have increased their estates by their industry, than with those who have diminished them by their slothfulness.

Matthew 13

The work of religion is vineyard work, pruning, dressing, digging, watering, fencing, weeding. We have each of us our own vineyard to keep, our own soul; and it is God's, and to be kept and dressed for him. In this work we must not be slothful, not loiterers, but labourers, working, and working out our own salvation. Work for God will not admit of trifling. A man may go idle to hell; but he that will go to heaven, must be busy.

Matthew 20

The endowments of the mind — reason, wit, learning, must be used in subserviency to religion; the enjoyments of the world — estate, credit, interest, power, preferment, must be improved for the honour of Christ. The ordinances of the Gospel, and our opportunities of attending them, bibles, ministers, sabbaths, sacraments, must be improved for the end for which they were instituted, and communion with God kept up by them, and the gifts and graces of the Spirit must be exercised; and this is trading with our talents.

Matthew 25

Disasters

He cast off God himself for he sacrificed to the gods of Damascus not because he loved them, for he thought they smote him, but because he feared them thinking they helped his enemies and that if he could bring them into his interest they would help him. Foolish man! It was his own God that smote him and strengthened the Syrians against him, not the gods of Damascus. Had he sacrificed to him and him only he would have helped him. But no marvel that men's affections and devotions are misplaced when they mistake the author of their trouble and their help.

2 Chronicles 28

Discerning God's Hand

See how God can raise up friends for his people in distress where they little thought of them, and animate men for his service even beyond expectation.

Jeremiah 38

Those whom Christ designs for the greatest honours are commonly first laid low. Those who are designed to excel in knowledge and grace are commonly laid low first, in a sense of their own ignorance and sinfulness. Those whom God will employ are first struck with a sense of their unworthiness to be employed.

Acts 9

Discernment

See what a distinction is put between sins of presumption and sins of infirmity. Alexander the coppersmith, who maliciously withstood Paul, he prays against: 'The Lord reward him according to his works'; but respecting these Christians, who through weakness shrunk from Paul in time of trial, he says, 'The Lord lay it not to their charge'.

2 Timothy 4

Discipleship

As long as we live we must be scholars in Christ's school, and sit at his feet; but we should aim to be head-scholars, and to get into the highest form.

Psalm 119

All the disciples and followers of Jesus Christ must deny themselves. It is the fundamental law of admission into Christ's school, and the first and great lesson to be learned in this school, to deny ourselves; it is both the strait gate, and the narrow way; it is necessary in order to our learning all the other good lessons that are there taught.

Matthew 16

Discipline

Sinners must be put to shame that those who will not be restrained by the shamefulness of their sin before God and their consciences may be restrained by the shamefulness of the punishment before men.

Judges 18

Discontent

It is an evidence of a discontented, distrustful, unstable spirit, to be weary of the place in which God hath set us, and to be for leaving it immediately whenever we meet with any uneasiness or inconvenience in it.

Ruth 1

God had given them meat for their hunger, in the manna, wholesome pleasant food and in abundance; he had given them meat for their faith out of the heads of leviathan which he 'broke in pieces' (74:14). But all this would not serve; they must have meat for their lust, dainties and varieties to gratify a luxurious appetite. Nothing is more provoking to God than our quarrelling with our allotment and indulging the desires of the flesh.

Psalm 78

Have nothing to do, he does not say, with those that change, for there may be cause to change for the better; but those that are given to change, that affect change for change-sake, out of a peevish discontent with that which is, and a fondness for novelty, or a desire to fish in troubled waters: 'Meddle not with those that are given to change', either in religion or the civil government; 'come not into their secret'; join not with them in their cabals, nor enter into the mystery of their iniquity. Those that are of a restless, factious, turbulent spirit, commonly pull mischief upon their own head ere they are aware.

Proverbs 24

Those destroy themselves who are not pleased with what God does for them, but think they can do better for themselves. Well, in both these requests, Providence humoured them, gave them Saul first, and afterwards Jeroboam. And what the better were they for them? Saul was 'given in anger' (given in 'thunder') (1 Sam. 12:18, 19) and soon after was 'taken away in wrath', upon Mount Gilboa. The kingly government of the ten tribes was given in anger, not only against Solomon for his defection, but against the ten tribes that desired it, for their discontent and disaffection to the house of David; and God was now about to take that away in wrath by the power of the king of Assyria. . . First, God often gives in anger what we sinfully and inordinately desire, gives it with a curse, and with it gives us up to our own hearts' lusts. Thus he gave Israel quails. Secondly, what we inordinately desire we are commonly disappointed in, and it cannot save us, as we expected it should.

Hosea 13

A good method of religious services, which we have found beneficial to ourselves and others, ought not to be altered without good reason, and therefore not without mature deliberation.

Zechariah 7

Discouragements

Observe here the encouragement of God to Joshua to proceed 'Fear not, neither be thou dismayed'. This intimates that the sin of Achan and the consequences of it had been a very great discouragement to Joshua and made his heart almost ready to fail. Corruptions within the church weaken the hands and damp the spirits of her guides and helpers more than oppositions from without. Treacherous Israelites are to be dreaded more than malicious Canaanites.

Joshua 8

This was a great trial of David's faith whether he would go on in a dependence upon the word of God when so many of his men failed him. When we are disappointed and discouraged in our expectations from second causes, then to go on with cheerfulness confiding in the Divine power, this is giving glory to God by believing against hope in hope.

1 Samuel 30

It was their infirmity to mingle thus tears with the common joys and so to cause a damp upon them. They despised the day of small things and were unthankful for the good they enjoyed because it was not so much as their ancestors had though it was much more than they deserved. In the harmony of public joys let not us be jarring strings.

Ezra 3

At the very time when the adversaries said, Let us cause the work to cease, Judah said, 'Let us even let it fall, for we are not able to go forward with it,' (v. 10). They represent the labourers as tired, and the remaining difficulties, even of that first part of their work, the removing of the rubbish, as insuperable, and therefore they think it advisable to desist for the present. Can Judah, that warlike valiant tribe, sneak thus? Active leading men have many times as much ado to grapple with the fears of their friends as with the terrors of their enemies.

Nehemiah 4

If we stand thus magnifying every little difficulty and making the worst of it, starting objections and fancying hardship and danger where there is none, we shall never go on, much less go through with our work, nor make anything of it. If the husbandman should decline, or leave off, sowing for the sake of every flying cloud, and reaping for the sake of every blast of wind, he would make but an ill account of his husbandry at the year's end. The duties of religion are as necessary as sowing and reaping, and will turn as much to our own advantage. The discouragements we meet with in these duties are but as winds and clouds, which will do us no harm, and which those that put on a little courage and resolution will despise and easily break through. Note, those that will be deterred and driven off by small and seeming difficulties from great and real duties will never bring anything to pass in religion, for there will always arise some wind, some cloud or other, at least in our imagination, to discourage us. Winds and clouds are in God's hands, are designed to try us, and our christianity obliges us to endure hardness.

Ecclesiastes 11

As long as we see ourselves in the way of God and duty it is weakness and folly, when we meet with difficulties and discouragements in it, to wish we had never set out in it.

It is a strong temptation to poor ministers to resolve that they will preach no more when they see their preaching slighted and wholly ineffectual. But let people dread putting their ministers into this temptation. Let not their labour be in vain with us, lest we provoke them to say that they will take no more pains with us, and provoke God to say, 'They shall take no more'. Yet let not ministers hearken to this temptation, but go on in their duty, notwithstanding their discouragements, for this is the more thankworthy.

Jeremiah 20

Those that engage in any great and good work must expect to meet with hindrance and opposition from friends and foes, from within and from without.

Matthew 16

Discretion

He left Judea, because he was likely to be persecuted there even to the death; such was the rage of the Pharisees against him, and such their impious policy to devour the man-child in his infancy. To escape their designs, Christ quitted the country, and went where what he did would be less provoking than just under their eye. For, His hour was not yet come, (John 7:30).

John 4

He prudently argues from the principles of their own law, and an incontestable rule of justice, that no man is to be condemned unheard. Had he urged the excellency of Christ's doctrine or the evidence of his miracles, or repeated to them his divine discourse with him (ch. 3), it had been but to cast pearls before swine, who would trample them under their feet, and would turn again and rend him.

John 7

Disobedience

Never was people so perverse and so desperately resolved in everything to work contrary to God. God bade them go and they would not; He forbade them and they would. Thus is the carnal mind enmity to God.

Numbers 14

Our first parents ate the forbidden fruit in hopes of getting thereby the knowledge of good and evil but it was a miserable knowledge they got. Of good by the loss of it and of evil by the sense of it.

Deuteronomy 30

Their multiplying of altars dedicated to the God of Israel would introduce altars dedicated to other gods. Note, it is a great sin to corrupt the worship of God, and it will be charged as sin upon those that do it, how plausible soever their pretensions may be. And the way of this, as other sins, is down-hill; those that once deviate from the fixed rule of God's commands will wander endlessly.

Hosea 8

'They spread abroad His fame'. This was more an act of zeal than of prudence; and though it may be excused as honestly meant for the honour of Christ, yet it cannot be justified, being done against a particular charge. Whenever we profess to direct our intention to the glory of God, we must see to it that the action be according to the will of God.

Matthew 9

Kings have sceptres put into their hand, marks of dominion, as the crown is of dignity; to imitate this, they put a reed in his right hand. Those who despise the authority of the Lord Jesus, as not to be observed and obeyed, who regard not either the precepts of his word, or the threatenings of his wrath, do, in effect, put a reed in his hand; nay, and, as these here, smite him on the head with it, such is the indignity they do him.

Mark 15

69

Distrust

The many experiences we have had of the goodness of God to us aggravate our distrust of Him. Has he not helped us in six troubles and have we any reason to suspect Him in the seventh. See how deceitful our hearts are? We trust in God when we have nothing else to trust to when need drives us to Him but when we have other things to stay on we are apt to stay too much on them and to lean to our own understanding as long as that has anything to offer but a believing confidence will be in God only when a smiling world courts it most.

2 Chronicles 16

Division

The conquerors gave no quarter so they put to the sword 500,000 chosen men, more, it is said, than ever we read of in any history to have been killed in one battle but the battle was the Lord's who would thus chastise the idolatry of Israel and own the house of David. But see the sad effect of division. It was the blood of Israel that was shed like water by Israelites while the heathen, their neighbours, to whom the name of Israel had formerly been a terror, cried 'Aha, so would we have it.'

2 Chronicles 13

The objection which the disciples of John made against Christ's disciples, for not fasting so often as they did; which they are charged with, as another instance of the looseness of their profession, besides that of eating with publicans and sinners; and it is therefore suggested to them, that they should change that profession for another more strict. It appears by the other evangelists (Mark 2:18 and Luke 5:33) that the disciples of the Pharisees joined with them, and we have reason to suspect that they instigated them, making use of John's disciples as their spokesmen, because they, being more in favour with Christ and his disciples, could do it more plausibly. Note it is no new thing for bad men to set good men together by the ears: if the people of God differ in their sentiments, designing men will take that occasion to sow discord, and to incense them one against another, and alienate them one from another, and so make an easy prey of them. If the disciples of John and of Jesus clash, we have reason to suspect the Pharisees have been at work underhand, blowing the coals. Now the complaint is, 'Why do we and the Pharisees fast often, but thy disciples fast not?' It is pity the duties of religion, which ought to be the confirmations of holy love, should be made the occasions of strife and contention.

Matthew 9

In the best-ordered church in the world there will be something amiss, some mal-administration or other, some grievances, or at least some complaints; those are the best that have the least and the fewest.

Acts 6

So liable are the best things in the world to be corrupted, and the gospel and its institutions, which are at perfect harmony with themselves and one another, to be made the engines of variance, discord, and contention. This is no reproach to our religion, but a very melancholy evidence of the corruption and depravity of human nature. Note, How far will pride carry Christians in opposition to one another! Even so far as to set Christ and his own apostles at variance, and make them rivals and competitors.

1 Corinthians 1

Ministers should avoid, as much as may be, what will occasion disputes; and would do well to insist on the great and practical points of religion, about which there can be no disputes; for even disputes about great and necessary truths draw off the mind from the main design of Christianity, and eat out the vitals of religion.

1 Timothy 1

Divine Patience

We are not only so disobedient that we have need of 'precept upon precept' to bring us to our duty, but so distrustful that we have need of promise upon promise to bring us to our comfort.

Jeremiah 33

Doubts

To resolve that our hearts shall not reproach us while we still hold fast our integrity is to baffle the designs of the evil spirit (who tempts good Christians to question their adoption, 'if thou be the Son of God') and to concur with the operations of the good Spirit, who witnesses to their adoption.

Job 27

A child of God startles at the very thought of despairing of help in God; you cannot vex him with anything so much as if you offer to persuade him that there is no help for him in God. David comes to God, and tells him what his enemies said of him, as Hezekiah spread Rabshakeh's blasphemous letter before the Lord. 'They say, there is no help for me in thee; but Lord, if it be so, I am undone. They say to my soul, there is no salvation,' (for so the word is) 'for him in God; but Lord, do thou say unto my soul, I am thy salvation, and that shall satisfy me, and in due time silence them.'

Psalm 3

The souls of good men are often straitened by doubts and fears, cramped and fettered through the weakness of faith and the prevalency of corruption; and it is then their duty and interest to apply themselves to God, and beg of Him to set them at liberty and to enlarge their hearts, that they may run the way of His commandments.

Psalm 142

The leper was confident of Christ's power, but put an 'if' upon his will (Matt. 8:2); 'If thou wilt, thou canst.' This poor man referred himself to his good will, but put an 'if' upon his power, because his disciples,

71

who cast out devils in his name, had been non-plussed in this case. Thus Christ suffers in his honour by the difficulties and follies of his disciples.

Mark 9

Duty

Though, as a faithful prophet, he foresaw and foretold the destruction of Jerusalem, yet, as a faithful Israelite, he prayed earnestly for the preservation of it, in obedience to that command, 'Pray for the peace of Jerusalem'. Though the will of God's purpose is the rule of prophecy and patience, the will of his precept is the rule of prayer and practice. God himself, though he has determined, does not desire, the death of sinners.

Jeremiah 28

A great difference should be made between plain and positive duty, and the improvement of a present opportunity of doing or getting good. Many a thing which is good for us to do, yet cannot be said to be, by express and indispensable commandment, our duty at this or that time.

2 Corinthians 8

Earnestness

They did not seek the Lord while He might be found and now He would not be found. Oh, if men would but be as earnest for Heaven while their day of Grace lasts as they will be when it is over, would be as solicitous to provide themselves

with oil while the Bridegroom tarries as they will be when the Bridegroom comes, how well were it for them.

Numbers 14

When diseased sinners come to this that they are content to do anything, to submit to anything, to part with anything, for a cure, then, and not till then, there begin to be some hopes of them. Then they will take Christ on His own terms when they are made willing to have Christ upon any terms.

2 Kings 5

Those that were sick of these bodily diseases took the pains to come far and had the patience to wait long for a cure; any of us would have done the same, and we ought to do so but Oh that men were as wise for their souls, and as solicitous to get their spiritual diseases healed!

John 5

Effectual Call

The call and offer of the Gospel are like Cyrus's proclamation; deliverance is preached to the captives (Luke 4, 18). Those that are bound under the unrighteous dominion of sin and bound over to the righteous judgment of God may be made free by Jesus Christ. Whoever will, by repentance and faith, return to God, his duty to God, his happiness in God, Jesus Christ has opened the way for him and let him go up out of the slavery of sin into the glorious liberty of the children of God. The offer is general to all. Christ makes it in pursuance of the grant which the Father has made him of all power in heaven and in earth (a much greater dominion than that given to Cyrus, v. 2) and of the charge given him to build God a house, to set him up a church in the world, a kingdom among men. Many that hear this joyful sound choose to sit still in Babylon, are in love with their sins and will not venture upon the difficulties of a holy life. But some there are that break through the discouragements and resolve to build the house of God, to make heaven of their religion whatever it cost them and they are those whose spirit God has raised above the world and the flesh and whom he has made willing in the day of his power. Thus will the heavenly Canaan be replenished though many perish in Babylon and the gospel offer will not be made in vain.

Ezra 1

Comparing them together, it is intimated that we are brought to Christ by the force of his call to us, not of our promises to him; it is not of him that willeth, nor of him that runneth, but of God that showeth mercy; He calls whom he will (Rom. 9: 16). And further, note, though chosen vessels may make excuses, and delay their compliance with divine calls a great while, yet Christ will at length answer their excuses, conquer their unwillingness, and bring them to his feet; when Christ calls, he will overcome, and make the call effectual (1 Sam. 3:10). His excuse is laid aside as insufficient; 'Let the dead bury their dead'.

Matthew 8

The Gospel command is like this recorded here; and the command is rational and just; though our hands are withered, and we cannot of ourselves stretch them forth, we must attempt it, must, as well as we can, lift them up to God in prayer, lay hold on Christ and eternal life, and employ them in good works; and if we do our endeavour, power goes along with the word of Christ, he effects the cure. Though our hands be withered yet if we will not offer to stretch them out, it is our own fault that we are not healed; but if we do, and are healed, Christ and his power and grace must have all the glory.

Mark 3

Election

The not being included among the elect is not the proper cause of infidelity, but merely the accidental cause. But faith is the gift of God, and the effect of predestination.

John 10

The original of the brotherhood that is between Christians and the relation wherein they stand one to another is election. And it is a good reason why we should 'love one another', because we are all beloved of God, and were beloved of him in his counsels when there was not any thing in us to merit his love. The election of these Thessalonians was known to the apostles, and therefore might be known to themselves, and that by the fruits and effects thereof — their sincere faith, and hope, and love, by the successful preaching of the gospel among them.

1 Thessalonians 1

Emotion and Health

Wrath kills the foolish man, his own wrath, and therefore he is foolish for indulging it; it is a fire in his bones, in his blood, enough to put him into a fever. *Envy* is the rottenness of the bones, and so *slays the silly one* that frets himself with it.

Job 5

It is a common principle, every one for himself. Now, if this be rightly understood, it will be a reason for the cherishing of gracious dispositions in ourselves and the crucifying of corrupt ones. We are friends or enemies to ourselves, even in respect of present comfort, according as we are or are not governed by religious principles.

A cruel, froward, ill-natured man troubles his own flesh, and so his sin becomes his punishment . . . He is vexatious to his nearest relations, that are, and should be, to him as his own flesh (Eph. 5:29). Envy, and malice, and greediness of the world, are the rottenness of the bones and the consumption of the flesh.

Proverbs 11

The foregoing verse showed how much our reputation, this how much our health, depends upon the good government of our passions and the preserving of the temper of the mind. A healing spirit, made up of love and meekness, a hearty, friendly, cheerful disposition, is the life of the flesh; it contributes to a good constitution of body; people grow fat with good humour. A fretful, envious, discontented spirit, is its own punishment; it consumes the flesh, preys upon the animal spirits, makes the countenance pale, and is the rottenness of the bones.

Proverbs 14

He has so little regard to himself as to abandon his own life, and to think it no harm to indulge his passion even to death, to kill himself with fretting. We read of 'wrath that kills the foolish man', and 'envy that slays the silly one' (Job 5:2), and foolish silly ones indeed those are that cut their own throats with their own passions, that fret themselves into consumptions and other weaknesses, and put themselves into fevers with their own intemperate heats.

Jonah 4

Emptiness of Life

Solomon had shown the vanity of pleasure, gaiety, and fine works, of honour, power, and royal dignity; and there is many a covetous worldling that will agree with him, and speak as slightly as he does of these things; but money, he thinks, is a substantial thing, and if he can but have enough of that he is happy. This is the mistake which Solomon attacks, and attempts to rectify, in these verses; he shows that there is as much vanity in great riches, and the lust of the eye about them, as there is in the lusts of the flesh and the pride of life, and a man can make himself no more happy by hoarding an estate than by spending it.

Ecclesiastes 5

Encouragement

Mutual helpfulness is brotherly duty . . . Christ's soldiers should thus strengthen one another's hands in their spiritual warfare. The strong must succour and help the weak. Those that through grace are conquerors over temptation must counsel and comfort and pray for those that are tempted. . . The members of the natural body help one another (1 Cor. 12, 21).

2 Samuel 10

By what the prophet said he perceived that his former attempts for reformation were well pleasing to God and, therefore, he revived them and did what was then left undone. It is good when commendations thus quicken us to our duty and when the more we are praised for doing well, the more vigorous we are in well doing.

2 Chronicles 19

Two solemn farewells we find our Lord Jesus giving to his church, and his parting word at both of them is very encouraging; one was here, when he closed up his personal converse with them, and then his parting word was, 'Lo, I am with you always; I leave you, and yet still I am with you'; the other was, when he closed up the canon of the scripture by the pen of his beloved disciple, and then his parting word was, 'Surely, I come quickly; I leave you awhile, but I will be with you again shortly' (Rev. 22:20). By this it appears that he did not part in anger, but in love, and that it is his will we should keep up both our communion with him and our expectation of him.

Matthew 28

For bloody persecutors, when they perceive themselves applauded for that which every one ought to cry shame upon them for, are encouraged to go on, and have their hands strengthened and their hearts hardened, and the checks of their own consciences smothered; nay, it is as strong a temptation to them to do the like as it was here to Herod, 'because he saw it pleased the Jews.'

Acts 12

Such faithful souls can hear their own praises without being puffed up; the commendation of what is good in us is designed, not for our pride, but for our encouragement to continue therein, and should be accordingly improved.

3 John

Endurance

Good men, by setting their sorrow continually before them, have been ready to halt, who, by setting God always before them, have kept their standing.

Psalm 38

Entreaty Precedes Judgment

The generality of them slighted the call and turned a deaf ear to it. The messengers went from city to city; some to one and some to another and used pressing entreaties with the people to come up to Jerusalem to keep the Passover but they were so far from complying with the message that they abused those that brought it, laughed them to scorn and mocked them. Not only refused but refused with disdain. Tell them of the God of Abraham! they knew him not. They had other gods to serve, Baal and Ashtaroth. Tell them of the Sanctuary! their high places were as good. Tell them of God's mercy and wrath! they neither dreaded the one nor desired the other. No marvel that the king's messengers were thus despitefully used by this apostate race, when God's messengers were so, his servants the prophets, who produced credentials from Him. The destruction of the ten tribes was now at hand. It was but two or three years after this that the king of Assyria laid siege to Samaria which ended in the captivity of those tribes. Just before this they had not only a king of their own that permitted them to return to God's Sanctuary but a king of Judah that earnestly invited them to do it. Had they generally accepted this invitation it might have prevented their ruin but their contempt of it hastened and aggravated it and left them inexcusable.

2 Chronicles 30

Envy

To be secretly pleased with the death or decay of others, when we are likely to get by it, with their fall when we may thrive upon it, is a sin which most easily besets us, but is not thought to be such a bad thing, and so provoking to God, as really it is. We are apt to say, when those who stand in our light, in our way, are removed, when they break or fall into disgrace, 'We shall be replenished now that they are laid waste.' But this comes from a selfish covetous principle, and a desire to be placed alone in the midst of the earth, as if we grudged that any should live by us. This comes from a want of that love to our neighbour as to ourselves which the law of God so expressly requires, and from that inordinate love of the world as our happiness which the love of God so expressly forbids.

Ezekiel 26

Though the acts and instances of strife and envy are very common, yet none are willing to own the principles, or to acknowledge themselves envious and contentious.

Romans 13

'You are envious' at each other's gifts. In ch. 13:4, the same word is thus translated. You quarrel and contend about them. This they certainly did. And this behaviour the apostle here reprehends, and labours to rectify. 'Only of pride cometh contention'. These contests in the church of Corinth sprang from this original. It was a quarrel about precedency (as most quarrels among Christians are, with whatever pretences they are gilded over); and it is no wonder that a quarrel about precedency should extinguish charity. When all would stand in the first rank, no wonder if they jostle, or throw down, or thrust back, their brethren. Gifts may be valued for their use, but they are mischievous when made the fuel of pride and contention. This therefore the apostle endeavours to prevent.

1 Corinthians 12

It is not grieved at the good of others; neither at their gifts nor at their good qualities, their honours nor their estates. If we love our neighbour we shall be so far from envying his welfare, or being displeased with it, that we shall share in it and rejoice at it. His bliss and sanctification will be an addition to ours, instead of impairing or lessening it. This is the proper effect of kindness and benevolence: envy is the effect of ill-will. The prosperity of those to whom we wish well can never grieve us; and the mind which is bent on doing good to all can never wish ill to any.

1 Corinthians 13

Eternal Life

Christ died to bring us to God. To know him as our Creator, and to love him, obey him, submit to him, and trust in him, as our owner, ruler, and benefactor — to devote ourselves to him as our sovereign Lord, depend upon him as our chief good, and direct all to his praise as our highest end — 'this is life eternal'.

If man had continued innocent, the knowledge of the only true God would have been life eternal to him; but now that he is fallen there must be something more; now that we are under guilt, to know God is to know him as a righteous Judge, whose curse we are under; and nothing is more killing than to know this. We are therefore concerned to know Christ as our Redeemer, by whom alone we can now have access to God; it is life eternal to believe in Christ.

John 17

Evangelism

Not the Levites only but every Israelite must, in his place, help to make known to the sons of men, God's mighty acts. (Ps. 145, 12).

Joshua 4

The purity and love of the primitive Christians, their heavenly-mindedness, contempt of the world, and patient sufferings, were the brightness of the church's rising, which drew many into it.

Isaiah 60

The knowledge they have, they must communicate for the good of others; not put it under a bushel, but spread it. The talent must not be buried in a napkin, but traded with. The disciples of Christ must not muffle themselves up in privacy and obscurity, under pretence of contemplation, modesty, or self-preservation, but, as they have received the gift, must minister the same (Luke 12:3).

Matthew 5

Christ has many ways of gaining the heart, and by the grant of a temporal mercy may make way for better things.

Those who can do little else towards the conviction and conversion of others may and should bring them to those means of grace which they themselves have found effectual.

John 4

Those who have experienced special instances of God's power and goodness, in temporal or spiritual things, should be ready upon all occasions to communicate their experiences, for the glory of God and the instruction and encouragement of others. See David's collection of his experiences, his own and others', (Ps. 34: 4—6). It is a debt we owe to our benefactor, and to our brethren. God's favours are lost upon us, when they are lost with us, and go no further.

John 9

It is our duty not only to hold fast, but to hold forth the word of life; not only to hold it fast for our own benefit, but to hold it forth for the benefit of others, to hold it forth as the candlestick holds forth the candle, which makes it appear to advantage all around, or as the luminaries of the heavens, which shed their influence far and wide.

Philippians 2

The bad temper and example of imprudent parents often prove a great hindrance to their children and a stumbling-block in their way; see (Eph. 6:4). And it is by the tenderness of parents, and dutifulness of children, that God ordinarily furnishes his church with a seed to serve him, and propagates religion from age to age.

Colossians 3

Evil Spirits

Had it been the true Samuel when Saul desired to be told what he should do he would have told him to repent and make his peace with God and recall David from his banishment and would then have told him that he might hope in this way to find mercy with God but instead of that he represents his case as helpless and hopeless serving him as he did Judas to whom he was first a tempter and then a tormentor, persuading him first to sell his master and then to hang himself.

1 Samuel 28

Excuses

See what a hard thing it is to convince the children of disobedience of their sin and to strip them of their fig-leaves.

1 Samuel 15

This servant thought that his account would pass well enough, because he could say, 'There thou hast that is thine. Lord, I was no spendthrift of my estate, no prodigal of my time, no profaner of my sabbaths, no opposer of good ministers and good preaching; Lord, I never ridiculed my bible, nor set my wits to work to banter religion, nor abused my power to persecute any good man; I never drowned my parts, nor wasted God's good creatures in drunkenness and gluttony, nor ever to my knowledge did I injure any body'. Many that are called Christians, build great hopes for heaven upon their being able to make such an account; yet all this amounts to no more than 'there thou hast that is thine'; as if no more were required, or could be expected.

Matthew 25

Those who lay the blame of their sins either upon their constitution or upon their condition in the world, or who pretend they are under a fatal necessity of sinning, wrong God, as if he were the author of sin. . . In other scriptures the devil is called 'the tempter', and other things may sometimes concur to tempt us; but neither the devil nor any other person or thing is to be blamed so as to excuse ourselves; for the true original of evil and temptation is in our own hearts.

James 1

Experience

There is many a profitable good lesson to be learned by experience. We are very unapt scholars if we have not learned by experience the evil of sin, the treachery of our own hearts, the vanity of the world, the goodness of God, the gains of godliness and the like.

Genesis 30

Experimental Religion

The graciousness of our Redeemer is best discovered by an experimental taste of it. There must be an immediate application of the object to the organ of taste; we cannot taste at a distance, as we may see, and hear, and smell. To taste the graciousness of Christ experimentally supposes our being united to him by faith, and then we may taste his goodness in all his providences, in all our spiritual concerns, in all our fears and temptations, in his word and worship every day.

1 Peter 2

Externals

David in his Psalms often called the tabernacle a temple as (Ps. 5:7, 27:4, 29:9, 65:4, 138:2) because it answered the intention of a temple though it was made but of curtains. Wise and good men value not the show while they have the substance.

2 Samuel 7

He teaches us several good lessons, as, not to admire bodily bulk, or beauty, or strength, nor to value persons or think the better of them for such advantages, but to judge of men by their wisdom and conduct, their industry and application to business, which are characters that deserve respect.

Proverbs 30

It is intimated, that the people, as long as they had the fruits of the earth brought in their season, presented to the Lord his dues out of them, and brought the offerings to the altar and tithes to those that served at the altar. Note, a people may be filling up the measure of their iniquity apace, and yet may keep up a course of external performances in religion.

Joel 1

Even good men are apt to be too much enamoured with outward pomp and gaiety, and to overvalue it, even in the things of God; whereas we should be, as Christ was, dead to it, and look upon it with contempt.

They forgot how many providences, concerning Solomon's temple, had manifested how little God cared for that outward glory which they had so much admired, when the people were wicked (2 Chron. 7:21). This house, which is high, sin will bring low. Christ had lately looked upon the precious souls, and wept for them (Luke 19:41). The disciples look upon the pompous buildings, and are ready to weep for them. In this, as in other things, his thoughts are not like ours. It was weakness, and meanness of spirit, in the disciples, to be so fond of the fine buildings; it was a childish thing.

They would have Christ look upon them, and be as much in love with them as they were; he would have them look upon them, and be as dead to them as he was.

Matthew 24

The holy place was at first but a tabernacle, mean and movable, showing itself to be short-lived, and not designed to continue always. Why might not this holy place, though built of stones, be decently brought to its end, and give place to its betters, as well as that though framed of curtains? As it was no dishonour, but an honour to God, that the tabernacle gave way to the temple, so it is now that the material temple gives way to the spiritual one, and so it will be when, at last, the spiritual temple shall give way to the eternal one.

Acts 7

Faith

A lively active faith can take encouragement from the least intimation of the divine favour, a merciful hint of providence will encourage those who make diligent search.

Exodus 2

She believed, upon the report she had heard of the wonders wrought for Israel, that their God was the only true God and that their declared design upon Canaan would undoubtedly take effect and in this faith she sided with them, protected them and courted their favour. Had she said 'I believe God is yours and Canaan yours but I dare not show you any kindness' her faith had been dead and inactive and would not have justified her.

Joshua 2

He pitched near a famous well that his army might not be

distressed for want of water and gained the higher ground which possibly might be of some advantage to him, for the Midianites were beneath him in the valley. Faith in God's promises must not slacken but rather quicken our endeavours. When we are sure God goes before us, then we must bestir ourselves. (2 Sam. 5:24).

Judges 7

Learn to reason as Manoah's wife did. If God had designed me to perish under his wrath he would not have given me such distinguishing tokens of his favour. Oh, woman, great is thy faith.

Judges 13

See the power of God who kills and makes alive again. See the power of prayer. As it has the key of the clouds so it has the key of death. See the power of faith. That fixed law of nature (that death is a way whence there is no return) shall rather be dispensed with than that this believing Shunamite shall be disappointed.

2 Kings 4

An active faith can give thanks for a promise though it be not yet performed knowing that God's bonds are as good as ready money. God has spoken in His holiness, I will rejoice (Ps. 60:5).

2 Chronicles 20

Nehemiah walled the city in faith, and with an eye to that promise of the replenishing of it which God had lately made by the prophet (Zech. 8, v. 3) etc. Though the people were now few, he believed they would be multiplied, and therefore, built the walls so as to make room for them; had he not depended upon this he might have thought walls without a city as great a reproach as a city without walls.

Nehemiah 7

'If thou shouldst decline the service, enlargement and deliverance will arise to the Jews from another place.' This was the language of a strong faith, which staggered not at the promise when the danger was most threatening, but against hope believed in hope. Instruments may fail, but God's covenant will not.

Esther 4

With what constancy he depends upon him: Though he slay me, yet will I trust in him (v. 15). This is a high expression of faith, and what we should all labour to come up to — to trust in God, though he slay us, that is, we must be well pleased with God as a friend even when he seems to come forth against us as an enemy (ch. 23:8—10). We must believe that all shall work for good to us even when all seems to make against us (Jer. 24:5). We must proceed and persevere in the way of our duty, though it cost us all that is dear to us in this world, even life itself (Heb. 11:35). We must depend upon the performance of the promise when all the ways leading to it are shut up (Rom. 4:18). We must rejoice in God when we have nothing else to rejoice in, and cleave to him, yea, though we cannot for the present find comfort in him. In a dying hour we must derive from him living comforts; and this is to trust in him though he slay us.

Job 13

'My eyes fail while I wait for my God'; he had almost looked his eyes out in expectation of deliverance. Yet his pleading this with God is an indication that he is resolved not to give up believing and praying. His throat is dried, but his heart is not; his eyes fail, but his faith does not. Thus our Lord Jesus, on the cross, cried out, 'Why hast Thou forsaken me?' yet, at the same time, he kept hold of his relation to him: 'My God, My God.'

Psalm 69

If fear and melancholy ask such peevish questions, let faith answer them from the Scripture: 'Will the Lord cast us off for ever?' God forbid (Rom. 11:1), no, 'The Lord will not cast off His people' (94:14). 'Will He be favourable no more?' Yes He will, 'for though He cause grief, yet will He have compassion.' (Lam. 3:32). 'Is His mercy clean gone for ever?' No, 'His mercy endures for ever'; as it is 'from everlasting' it is 'to everlasting' (103:17). 'Doth His promise fail for evermore?' No, 'it is impossible for God to lie' (Heb. 6:18). 'Hath God forgotten to be gracious?' No, 'He cannot deny Himself' and His own name which He hath proclaimed 'gracious and merciful' (Exod. 34:6). 'Has He in anger shut up His tender mercies?' No, they are 'new every morning' (Lam. 3:23); and therefore 'How shall I give thee up Ephraim?' (Hos. 11:8, 9).

Psalm 77

So full is he of the comfort of God's presence with him, the divine protection he is under, and the divine promise he has to depend upon, that in a transport of joy he stirs up himself and others to give God the glory of it: Sing unto the Lord, praise you the Lord. Here appears a great change with him since he began this discourse; the clouds are blown over, his complaints all silenced and turned into thanksgivings. He has now an entire confidence in that God whom he was distrusting (v. 7); he stirs up himself to praise that name which he was resolving no more to make mention of (v. 9). It was the lively exercise of faith that made this happy change, that turned his sighs into songs and his tremblings into triumphs.

Jeremiah 20

The prophet did himself lift up his eyes and see the four horns, and saw them so formidable that he began to despair of the safety of every good man, and the success of every good work; but 'the Lord' then 'showed him four carpenters', or 'smiths' who were empowered to cut off these horns, (vs. 20, 21). With an eye of sense we see the power of the enemies of the church; look which way we will, the world shows us that. But it is with an eye of faith that we see it safe, notwithstanding; it is the Lord that shows us that, as he opened the eyes of the prophet's servant to see the angelic guards round about his master (2 Kings 6:17).

Zechariah 1

It was a great honour which Christ put upon this Centurion, when he gave him a blank, as it were; 'Be it done as thou believest'. What could he have more? Yet what was said to him is said to us all, 'Believe, and ye shall receive, only believe'. See here the power of Christ, and the power of faith. As Christ can do what he will, so an active believer may have what he will from Christ; the oil of grace multiplies, and stays not till the vessels of faith fail.

Matthew 8

Still it is put to us, 'Believe we that Christ is able to do for us', by the power of his merit and intercession in heaven, of his Spirit and grace in the heart, and of his providence and dominion in the world? To believe the power of Christ is not only to assure ourselves of it, but to commit ourselves to it, and encourage ourselves in it.

Though he had kept them in suspense awhile, and had not helped them at first, they honestly imputed that to his wisdom, not to his weakness, and were still confident of his ability.

Matthew 9

He rebuked him, for as many as he loves and saves, he reproves and chides; 'O thou of little faith, wherefore didst thou doubt?' Note, 1. Faith may be true, and yet weak; at first like a grain of mustard seed Peter had faith enough to bring him upon the water, yet, because not enough to carry him through, Christ tells him he had but little. 2. Our discouraging doubts and fears are all owing to the weakness of our faith. Therefore we doubt, because we are but of little faith. It is the business of faith to resolve doubts, the doubts of sense, in a stormy day, so as even then to keep the head above water. Could we but believe more, we should doubt less. . . Our doubts and fears would soon vanish before a strict enquiry into the cause of them; for, all things considered, there is no good reason why Christ's disciples should be of a doubtful mind, no, not in a stormy day, because he is ready to them, 'a very present help'.

Matthew 14

Christ treated her thus, to try her; he knows what is in the heart, knew the strength of her faith, and how well able she was, by his grace, to break through such discouragements; he therefore met her with them, 'that the trial of her faith might be found unto praise, and honour, and glory,' (1 Pet. 1:6, 7). This was like God's tempting Abraham (Gen. 22:1), like the angel's wrestling with Jacob, only to put him upon wrestling (Gen. 32:24). Many of the methods of Christ's providence, and especially of his grace, in dealing with his people, which are dark and perplexing, may be explained with the key of this story, which is for that end left upon record, to teach us that there may be love in Christ's heart while there are frowns in his face, and to encourage us, therefore, 'though he slay us, yet to trust in him'.

It is her faith that he commends. There were several graces that shone bright in her conduct of this affair — wisdom, humility, meekness, patience, perseverance in prayer; but these were the product of her faith, and therefore Christ fastens upon that as most commendable; because of all graces faith honours Christ most, therefore of all graces Christ honours faith most.

Matthew 15

Faith in general is a firm assent to, a compliance with, and a confidence in, all divine revelation. The faith here required, is that which had for its object that particular revelation by which Christ gave his disciples power to work miracles in his name, for the confirmation of the doctrine they preached. It was a faith in this revelation that they were defective in.

Matthew 17

Now those to whom Christ said this immediately, did not live to see this dismal day, none of all the twelve but John only; they needed not to be hidden in the mountains (Christ hid them in heaven), but they left the direction to their successors in profession, who pursued it, and it was of use to them; for when the Christians in Jerusalem and Judea saw the ruin coming on, they all retired to a town called Pella, on the other side of Jordan, where they were safe; so that of the many thousands that perished in the destruction of Jerusalem, there was not so much as one Christian. See (Euseb. Eccl. Hist. lib 3 cap 5). Thus the prudent man foresees the evil, and hides himself (Prov. 22:3; Heb. 11:7). This warning was not kept private. St. Matthew's gospel was published long before that destruction, so that others might have taken the advantage of it; but their perishing through their unbelief of this, was a figure of their eternal perishing through their unbelief of the warnings Christ gave concerning the wrath to come.

Matthew 24

He believes it with application, not only in general, 'Thou canst do everything' (as John 11:22), but, 'Thou canst make me clean'. Note, what we believe of the power of Christ we must bring home to our particular case; 'Thou canst do this for me'.

Mark 1

It justifies us (Rom. 5:1), and so removes mountains of guilt, and casts them into the depths of the sea, never to rise up in judgment against us (Mic. 7:19). It purifies the heart (Acts 15:9), and so removes mountains of corruption, and makes them plains before the grace of God (Zech. 4:7). It is by faith that the world is conquered, Satan's fiery darts are quenched, a soul is crucified with Christ, and yet lives; by faith we set the Lord always before us, and see him that is invisible, and have him present to our minds; and this is effectual to remove mountains, for at the presence of the

Lord, at the presence of the God of Jacob, the mountains were not only moved, but *re*moved, (Ps. 114:4–7).

Mark 11

First, to be a Christian indeed is to believe on Christ's name; it is to assent to the Gospel discovery, and consent to the Gospel proposal, concerning him. His name is the Word of God; the King of kings, the Lord our righteousness; Jesus a Saviour.

Now to believe on his name is to acknowledge that he is what these great names bespeak him to be, and to acquiesce in it, that he may be so for us.

Secondly, believing in Christ's name is receiving him as a gift from God. We must receive his doctrine as true and good; receive his law as just and holy; receive his offers as kind and advantageous; and we must receive the image of his grace, and impressions of his love, as the governing principle of our affections and actions.

John 1

A good opinion of Christ is far short of a lively faith in Christ; many give Christ a good word that give him no more. These here said, 'This is the prophet, and this is the Christ', but could not persuade themselves to leave all and follow him; and so this their testimony to Christ was but a testimony against themselves.

John 7

He did not wind himself into the affections of the people, nor wheedle them by sly insinuations, nor impose upon their credulity by bold assertions, but with the greatest fairness imaginable quitted all demands of their faith, further than he produced warrants for these demands. Christ is no hard master, who expects to reap in assents where he has not sown in arguments. None shall perish for the disbelief of that which was not proposed to them with sufficient motives of credibility, Infinite Wisdom itself being judge.

. . . Believe your own eyes, your own reason; the thing speaks itself plainly enough. *As* the invisible things of the Creator are clearly seen *by* his works of creation and common providence (Rom. 1:20), *so* the invisible things of the Redeemer were seen *by* his miracles, and by all his works both of power and mercy; so that those who were not convinced by these works were 'without excuse'.

John 10

The crosses and comforts of this present time would not make such an impression upon us as they do if we did but believe the things of eternity as we ought.

John 11

What it is to believe; it is to 'know surely', to know 'that it is so of a truth'. The disciples were very weak and defective in knowledge; yet Christ, who knew them better than they knew themselves, passes his word for them that they did believe. We may know surely that which we neither do nor can know fully; may 'know the certainty of the things which are not seen', though we cannot particularly describe the nature of them. 'We walk by faith', which knows surely, 'not' yet 'by sight', which knows clearly.

John 17

We should have said 'Let his ignominious death be private, and his glorious resurrection public'. But God's thoughts are not as ours; and he ordered it that his death should be public before the sun, by the same token that the sun blushed and hid his face upon it. But the demonstrations of his resurrection should be reserved as a favour for his particular friends, and by them be published to the world, that those might be blessed who have not seen, and yet have believed.

He consented to him as his Lord and his God. *In faith there must be the consent of the will to gospel terms, as well as the assent of the understanding to gospel truths.* We must accept of Christ to be that to us which the Father hath appointed him.

John 20

'His feet and ankle bones received strength', which they had not done if he had not attempted to rise, and been helped up; he does his part, and Peter does his, and yet it is Christ that does all: it is he that puts strength into him. As the bread was multiplied in the breaking, and the water turned into wine in the pouring out, so strength was given to the cripple's feet in his stirring them and using them.

Acts 3

If with God saying and doing are not two things, then with us believing and enjoying should not.

Acts 27

From faith engrafting us into Christ, to faith deriving virtue from him as our root; both implied in the next words, 'The just shall live by faith'. 'Just by faith', there is faith justifying us; 'live by faith', there is faith maintaining us; and so 'there is a righteousness from faith to faith.' Faith is all in all, both in the beginning and progress of a Christian life. It is not from faith to works, as if faith put us into a justified state, and then works preserved and maintained us in it, but it is all along from faith to faith.

Romans 1

An 'anointed Saviour', so Jesus Christ signifies. Justifying faith respects Christ as a Saviour in all his three anointed offices, as prophet, priest, and king — trusting in him, accepting of him, and adhering to him, in all these.

Romans 3

When God intends some special blessing, some child of promise, for his people, he commonly puts a sentence of death upon the blessing itself, and upon all the ways that lead to it. Joseph must be enslaved and imprisoned before he be advanced.

Romans 4

Moving mountains is a great achievement in the account of men; but one dram of charity is, in God's account, of much greater worth than all the faith of this sort in the world. Those may do many wondrous works in Christ's name whom yet he will disown, and bid depart from him, as workers of iniquity (Matt. 7:22, 23). Saving faith is ever in conjunction with charity, but the faith of miracles may be without it.

1 Corinthians 13

The design of it is to show that those only are just or righteous who do truly live, *who are freed from death and wrath*, and *restored into a state of life in the favour of God*; and that it is only through faith that persons become righteous, and as such obtain this life and happiness — that they are accepted of God, and enabled to live to him now, and are entitled to an eternal life in the enjoyment of him hereafter.

Galatians 3

There must be a sound believing of the great truths of Christianity, and a resolute cleaving to them, in times of trial. That faith which is spoken of here as tried by afflictions consists in a belief of the power, and word, and promise of God.

James 1

Thus we see that our persons are justified before God by faith, but our faith is justified before men by works.

James 2

Gold is the most valuable, pure, useful, and durable, of all the metals; so is faith among the Christian virtues; it lasts till it brings the soul to heaven, and then it issues in the glorious fruition of God for ever. The trial of faith is much more precious than the trial of gold; in both there is purification, a separation of the dross, and a discovery of the soundness and goodness of the things. Gold does not increase and multiply by trial in the fire, it rather grows less; but 'faith' is established, improved, and multiplied, by the oppositions and afflictions that it meets with. 'Gold' must perish at last — 'gold that perisheth'; but 'faith' never will. 'I have prayed for thee, that thy faith fail not', (Luke 22:32).

The faith of a Christian is properly conversant about things revealed, but not seen. Sense converses with things sensible and present; reason is a higher guide, which by sure deductions can infer the operation of causes, and the certainty of events; but faith ascends further still, and assures us of abundance of particulars that sense and reason could never have found out, upon the credit of revelation; it is 'the evidence of things not seen'.

1 Peter 1

To believe on the name of his Son Jesus Christ is, 1) *To discern* what he is, according to his name, to have an intellectual view of his person and office, as the Son of God, and the anointed Saviour of the world. 'That every one that seeth the Son, and believeth on him, may have everlasting life' (John 6:40). 2) *To approve* him in judgment and conscience, in conviction and consciousness of our case, as one wisely and wonderfully prepared and adapted for the whole work of eternal salvation.

3) *To consent* to him, and acquiesce in him, as our Redeemer and recoverer unto God. 4) To *trust* to him, and rely upon him, for the full and final discharge of his saving office. 'Those that know thy name will put their trust in thee' (Ps. 9:10).

1 John 3

Faithfulness

Let not Jeremiah himself distrust the truth of what he had delivered in God's name because it met with such a daring opposition and contradiction. If what we have spoken be the truth of God, we must not unsay it because men gainsay it; for great is the truth and will prevail. It will stand, therefore let us stand to it, and not fear that men's unbelief or blasphemy will make it of no effect.

Jeremiah 28

Jeremiah's life and comfort are in Zedekiah's hand, and he has now a petition to present to him for his favour, and yet, having this opportunity, he tells him plainly that there is a word from the Lord, but no word of comfort for him or his people: 'Thou shalt be delivered into the hand of the king of Babylon. If Jeremiah had consulted with flesh and blood, he would have given him a plausible answer, and, though he would not have told him a lie, yet he might have chosen whether he would tell him the worst at this time; what occasion was there for it, when he had so often told it him before? But Jeremiah was one

that had 'obtained mercy of the Lord to be faithful', and would not, to obtain mercy of man, be unfaithful to God or to his prince; he therefore tells him the truth, the whole truth.

Jeremiah 37

If ministers, who are reprovers by office, connive at sin and indulge sinners, either show them not their wickedness or show them not the fatal consequences of it, for fear of displeasing them and getting their ill-will, they hereby make themselves partakers of their guilt and are rebellious like them. If people will not do their duty in reforming, yet let ministers do theirs in reproving.

Ezekiel 2

It appears by his contest with Amaziah the priest of Bethel that he met with opposition in his work, but was a man of undaunted resolution in it, faithful and bold in reproving sin and denouncing the judgments of God for it, and pressing in his exhortations to repentance and reformation.

Amos (Intro.)

It is observable that he who had but two talents, gave up his account as cheerfully as he who had five; for our comfort, in the day of account, will be according to our faithfulness, not according to our usefulness; our sincerity, not our success; according to the uprightness of our hearts, not according to the degree of our opportunities.

Matthew 25

False Hopes

That which they thought would have been their shelter was made their prison first and then their grave. So shall we be disappointed in that which we flee to from God.

Joshua 10

The Elamites were famous archers, but, 'Behold I will break the bow of Elam' (v. 35), will ruin their artillery, and then the chief of their might is gone. God often orders it so that that which we most trust to first fails us, and that which was the chief of our might proves the least of our help.

Jeremiah 49

Her deceivers have created her as much vexation as her destroyers. The staff that breaks under us may do us as great a mischief as the staff that beats us (Ezek. 29: 6, 7).

Lamentations 1

Those who neglect God, and seek to creatures for help, will certainly be disappointed; those who depend upon them for support will find them, not 'foundations', but 'broken reeds'; those who depend upon them for supply will find them, not 'fountains', but 'broken cisterns'; those who depend upon them for comfort and a cure will find them 'miserable comforters' and 'physicians of no value.'

Hosea 5

Many are much affected with the word for the present, who yet receive no abiding benefit by it. The motions of soul they have, answerable to what they hear, are but a mere flash, like the crackling of thorns under a pot. We read of hypocrites, that they delight to know God's ways (Isa. 58:2); of Herod, that he heard John gladly (Ch. 6:20); of others, that they rejoiced in his light (John 5:35); of those to whom Ezekiel was a lovely song (Ezek. 33:32); and those represented here by the stony ground, received the word with gladness, and yet came to nothing.

Mark 4

False Humility

Here was a show of humility and modesty. Peter herein seemed to have, and no doubt he really had, a great respect for his Master, as he had (Luke 5:8). Thus many are beguiled of their reward in a voluntary humility (Col. 2:18, 23), such a self-denial as Christ neither appoints nor accepts; for, under this show of humility there was a real contradiction to the will of the Lord Jesus: 'I will wash thy feet', saith Christ; 'But thou never shalt', saith Peter, 'It is not a fitting thing'; so making himself wiser than Christ. It is not humility, but infidelity, to put away the offers of the gospel, as if too rich to be made to us or too good news to be true.

John 13

False Repentance

We are greatly confounded, ashamed of ourselves and our poverty; for that is it that they complain of, that is it that they blush at the thoughts of, rather than of their sin: We are confounded because we have forsaken the land (forced so to do by the enemy), not because we have forsaken the Lord, being drawn aside of our own lust and enticed — because our dwellings have cast us out, not because our God has cast us off. Thus unhumbled hearts lament their calamity, but not their iniquity, the procuring cause of it.

Jeremiah 9

Those that will not take the direction of God's grace how to get clear of their sins would yet be glad of the directions of his providence how to get clear of their troubles. . . All their care is to get rid of their trouble, not to make their peace with God and be reconciled to him — 'That our enemy may go up from us', not, 'That our God may return to us'. Thus Pharaoh (Exod. 10:17). 'Entreat the Lord that He may take away this death'. All their hope is that God had done wondrous works formerly in the deliverance of Jerusalem when Sennacherib besieged it, at the prayer of Isaiah — so we are told (2 32:20, 21), and who can tell but he may destroy these besiegers (as he did those) at the prayer of Jeremiah? But they did not consider how different the character of Zedekiah and his people was from that of Hezekiah and his people; those were days of general reformation and piety, these of general corruption and apostasy. Jerusalem is now the reverse of what it was then.

Note, it is folly to think that God should do for us while we hold fast our iniquity as he did for those that held fast their integrity.

Jeremiah 21

Fashion

He let it grow till it was a burden to him and was heavy on him nor would he cut it as long as he could bear it. As pride feels no cold so it feels no heat and that which feeds and gratifies it is uncomplained of though very uneasy.

2 Samuel 14

Many of these things, we may suppose, were very odd and ridiculous, and, if they had not been in fashion, would have been hooted at. They were fitter to be toys for children to play with than ornaments for grown people to go to Mount Zion in.

Isaiah 3

Fasting

Hereby we own ourselves unworthy of our necessary food, and that we have forfeited it and deserve to be wholly deprived of it, we punish ourselves and mortify the body, which has been the occasion of sin, we keep it in a frame fit to serve the soul in serving God, and, by the appetite's craving food, the desires of the soul towards that which is better than life, and all the supports of it, are excited. This was in a special manner seasonable now that God was depriving them of their 'meat and drink'; for hereby they accommodated themselves to the affliction they were under. When God says 'You shall fast', it is time to say 'We will fast'.

Joel 1

In this chapter we have, 1. A case of conscience proposed to the prophet by the children of the captivity concerning fasting, whether they should continue their solemn fasts which they had religiously observed during the seventy years of their captivity (vs. 1—3. 2). The answer to this question, which is given in this and the next chapter; and this answer was given, not all at once, but by piece-meal, and, it should seem, at several times, for here are four distinct discourses which have all of them reference to this case, each of them prefaced with 'the word of the Lord came', in this chapter (vs. 4—8, and ch. 8:1, 18). The method of them is very observable. In this chapter, 1. The prophet sharply reproves them for the mismanagements of their fasts (vs. 4—7. 2). He exhorts them to reform their lives, which would be the best way of fasting, and to take heed of those sins which brought those judgments upon them which they kept these fasts in memory of (vs. 8—14). And then in the next chapter, having searched the wound, he binds it up, and heals it, with gracious assurances of great mercy God had yet in store for them, by which he would turn their fasts into feasts.

Those that make fasting a cloak for sin, as Jezebel's fast, or by it make their court to men for their applause, as the Pharisees, or that rest in outward expressions of humiliation while their hearts are unhumbled, as Ahab, do they 'fast to God, even to Him?' 'Is this the fast that God has chosen?' (Isa. 58:5). If the solemnities of our fasting, though frequent, long, and severe, do not serve to put an edge upon devout affections, to quicken prayer, to increase godly sorrow, and to alter the temper of our minds and the course of our lives for the better, they do not at all answer the intention, and God will not accept them as performed to him, even to him.

Zechariah 7

Fear

It alludes to a tempestuous sea, such as the wicked are compared to (Isa. 57:20). The 'heathen rage' (Ps. 2:1) and think to ruin the church, to overwhelm it like a deluge, to sink it like a ship at sea. The church is said to be 'tossed with tempests' (Isa. 54:11), and the 'floods of ungodly men make the saints afraid' (Ps. 18:4). We may apply it to the tumults that are sometimes in our own bosoms, through prevailing passions and frights, which put the soul into disorder, and are ready to overthrow its graces and comforts; but, if the Lord reign there, even the winds and seas shall obey him.

Psalm 93

When without are fightings, within are fears, and those fears greater tyrants and oppressors than Saul himself and not so easily outrun. It is sometimes the lot of the best men to have their spirits for a time almost overwhelmed and their hearts desolate, and doubtless it is their infirmity. David was not only a great saint, but a great soldier, and yet even he was sometimes ready to faint in a day of adversity. Howl, fir trees, if the cedars be shaken.

Psalm 143

'Magor-Missabib' — 'Terror round about' or, 'Fear on every side'. God Himself shall give him this name, whose calling him so will make him so. It seems to be a proverbial expression, bespeaking a man not only in distress but in despair, not only in danger on every side (that a man may be and yet by faith may be in no terror, as David) (Ps. 3:6, 27:3), but in fear on every side, and that a man may be when there appears no danger. 'The wicked flee when no man pursues', are in 'great fear where no fear is'.

Jeremiah 20

Thou saidst, Fear not. This was the language of God's prophets preaching to them not to fear (Isa. 41:10, 13, 14), of his providence preventing those things which they were afraid of, and of his grace quieting their minds, and making them easy, by the witness of his Spirit with their spirits that they were his people still, though in distress, and therefore ought not to fear.

Lamentations 3

That which shall make them think themselves safe is their confidence in the wisdom, power, and goodness of God: 'They shall know that I am the Lord'. All our disquieting fears arise from our ignorance of God and mistakes concerning him. Their experience of his particular care concerning them encourages their confidence in him.

. . . They shall argue, he that has delivered does and will, therefore will we dwell safely. This is explained, and applied to our gospel-state (Luke 1:74). That we, being delivered out of the hand of our enemies, might serve Him without fear,' as those may do that serve him in faith.

Ezekiel 34

Fellowship

Had Eve kept close to the side out of which she was lately taken, she would have been less exposed. There are many temptations to which solitude gives greater disadvantage; but the communion of saints contributes much to their strength and safety.

Genesis 3

The strongest should not despise but desire the assistance even of those who are weaker. Judah was the most considerable of the tribes and Simeon the least considerable and yet Judah begs Simeon's friendship and prays an aid from him. The head cannot say to the foot 'I have no need of thee' if we are members one of another.

Those that crave assistance must be ready to give assistance. Come with me into my lot and then I will go with thee into thine. It becomes Israelites to help one another against Canaanites.

Judges 1

David, though a strong believer, needed the help of his friends for the perfecting of what was lacking in his faith.

1 Samuel 23

It had been suggested that the ways of God are melancholy unpleasant ways, solitary and sorrowful; and therefore then those that feared God studied to evince the contrary by their cheerfulness in mutual love and converse, that they might 'put to silence the ignorance of foolish men'. When seducers were busy to deceive and to possess unwary souls with prejudices against religion, those that feared God were industrious to arm themselves and one another against the contagion by mutual instructions, excitements, and encouragements, and to strengthen one another's hands. As evil communication corrupts good minds and manners, so good communication confirms them.

Malachi 3

His being led into the wilderness gave some advantage to the tempter; for there he had him alone, no friend with him, by whose prayers and advice he might be assisted in the hour of temptation. Woe to him that is alone! He might give Satan advantage, who knew his own strength; we may not, who know our own weakness.

Luke 4

When we shall sit down with Abraham, and Isaac, and Jacob, with all the saints, and none but saints, and saints made perfect, we shall have enough of that society, and be quite filled with that company.

Romans 15

Fickleness of Man

Absalom's faction, like a snowball, strangely gathered in its motion. He speaks of it as one amazed, and well he might, that a people he had so many ways obliged should almost generally revolt from him, rebel against him, and choose for their head such a foolish and giddy man as Absalom was. How slippery and deceitful are the many! And how little fidelity and constancy are to be found among men! David had had the hearts of his subjects as much as ever any king had, and yet now, of a sudden, he had lost them. As people must not trust too much in princes, so princes must not build too much upon their interest in the people. Christ, the Son of David, had many enemies. When a great multitude came to sieze him, when the crowd cried 'Crucify him, Crucify him,' how were those then increased that troubled him! Even good people must not think it strange if the stream be against them and the powers that threaten them grow more and more formidable.

Psalm 3

Though they that cried thus, perhaps, were not the same persons that the other day cried Hosanna, yet see what a change was made upon the mind of the populace in a little time: when he rode in triumph into Jerusalem, so general were the acclamations of praise, that one would have thought he had no enemies; but now when he was led in triumph to Pilate's judgment-seat, so general were the outcries of enmity, that one would think he had no friends.

Matthew 27

How uncertain the respects of people are, how apt they are to change their minds, and how easily they are drawn into contempt of those for whom they once had the greatest esteem and affection, so that they are ready to pluck out the eyes of those for whom they would before have plucked out their own! We should therefore labour to be accepted of God, 'for it is a small thing to be judged of man's judgment', (1 Cor. 4:3).

Galatians 4

Fighting the Right Enemy

This conquest of his own passion was in some respects more honourable than his conquest of Goliath. He that hath rule over his own spirit is better than the mighty. It was no time for David to quarrel with his brother when the Philistines were upon them. The more threatening the Church's enemies are, the more forbearing her friends should be with one another.

1 Samuel 17

Those that differed in communion, while they agreed to fight against Satan under the banner of Christ, ought to look upon one another as on the same side, notwithstanding that difference. He that is not against us is on our part. As to the great controversy between Christ and Beelzebub, he had said, 'He that is not with me is against me', (Matt. 12:30). He that will not own Christ, owns Satan. But as to those that own Christ, though not in the same circumstances, that follow him, though not with us, we must reckon that though these differ from us, they are not against us, and therefore are on our part, and we must not be any hindrance to their usefulness.

Mark 9

Final Perseverance

He that did so well for us in that helpless useless state will not leave us when he has reared us and nursed us up into some capacity of serving Him.

Psalm 22

He will gather them in mercy out of the countries whither they were scattered, to be monuments of mercy, as the incorrigible were gathered to be vessels of wrath (v. 41). Not one of God's jewels shall be lost in the lumber of this world.

Ezekiel 20

The accomplishment of the divine promise (v. 25). She brought forth her firstborn son. The circumstances of it are more largely related (Luke 2:1) etc. Note, that which is conceived of the Holy Ghost never proves abortive, but will certainly be brought forth in its season. What is the will of the flesh, and of the will of man, often miscarries; but, if Christ be formed in the soul, God himself has begun the good work which he will perform; what is conceived in grace will no doubt be brought forth in glory.

Matthew 1

It is the unspeakable comfort of all believers that Christ himself has committed them to the care of God. Those cannot but be safe whom the almighty God keeps, and he cannot but keep those whom the Son of his love commits to him, in the virtue of which we may by faith 'commit the keeping of our souls to God', (1 Peter 4:19; 2 Tim. 1:12).

John 17

These indeed may fall frequently and foully, but yet they will not totally nor finally from God; the purpose and the power of God, the purchase and the prayer of Christ, the promise of the gospel, the everlasting covenant that God has made with them, ordered in all things and sure, the indwelling of the Spirit, and the immortal seed of the word, these are their security.

Hebrews 6

Forbearance

The apostle, as a wise physician, prescribes proper remedies for the disease, which are made up of rules and reasons. Such gentle methods does he take, with such cords of a man does he draw them together; not by excommunicating, suspending, and silencing either side, but by persuading them both to a mutual forbearance.

Romans 14

Forgetfulness

As their understandings were dull, so their memories were treacherous; though one would think such astonishing events should never have been forgotten, yet they remembered them not, at least, 'they remembered not the multitude of God's mercies' in them. Therefore God is distrusted because his favours are not remembered.

Psalm 106

Christ's disciples are often to be blamed for the shallowness of their understandings, and the slipperiness of their memories. 'Have ye forgot those repeated instances of merciful and miraculous supplies; five thousand fed with five loaves, and four thousand with seven loaves, and yet they had enough and to spare? Remember how many baskets ye took up?' These baskets were intended for memorials, by which to keep the mercy in remembrance, as the pot of manna which was preserved in the ark (Exod. 16:32).

That meat for their bodies was intended to be meat for their faith (Ps. 24:14).

We are therefore perplexed with present cares and distrusts, because we do not duly remember our former experiences of divine power and goodness.

Matthew 16

Forgiveness

This fire did consume (or, as the word is, 'eat up') the present sacrifice. And two ways this was a testimony of acceptance:—
(1) It signified the turning away of God's wrath from them. God's wrath is a consuming fire; this fire might justly have fastened upon the people, and consumed them for their sins; but its fastening upon the sacrifice, and consuming that, signified God's acceptance of that as an atonement for the sinner.
(2) It signified God's entering into a covenant and communion with them: they ate their part of the sacrifice, and the fire of the Lord ate up his part; and thus he did, as it were, sup with them, and they with him. (Rev. 3, 20).

Leviticus 9

David had severely revenged the abuses done to his ambassadors by the Ammonites (Ch. 12; 31), but easily passes by the abuse done to himself by an Israelite.

2 Samuel 19

His sin is not again recorded because it was repented of and pardoned and so became as if it had never been. Scriptures' silence sometimes speaks. I am willing to believe that its silence here concerning the sin of Solomon is an intimation that none of the sins he committed were mentioned against him (Ezek. 33:16). When God pardons sin, he casts it behind his back and remembers it no more.

2 Chronicles 9

He had begged (v. 7) for the pardon of the sins of his youth, and (v. 11) for the pardon of some one particular iniquity that was remarkably great, which, some think, was his sin in the matter of Uriah. But here he prays, Lord, forgive all, take away all iniquity. It is observable that, as to his affliction, he asks for no more than God's regard to it: 'Look upon my affliction and my pain, and do with it as thou pleasest.' But, as to his sin, he asks for no less than a full pardon: Forgive all my sins. When at any time we are in trouble we should be more concerned about our sins, to get them pardoned, than about our afflictions, to get them removed.

Psalm 25

Deliverances from trouble are granted in love, and are mercies indeed, when they are grounded upon the pardon of sin and flow from that; we should therefore be more earnest with God in prayer for the removal of our sins than for the removal of our afflictions, and the pardon of them is the foundation and sweetness of our deliverances.

Psalm 79

Not only the punishments of their iniquity shall be taken off, but the offences which it gave to God shall be forgotten, and he will be reconciled to them. Their sin shall be before him as if it had never been; it shall be blotted out as a cloud, crossed out as a debt, shall be cast behind his back; nay, it shall be cast into the depth of the sea, shall be no longer sealed up among God's treasures, nor in any danger of appearing again or rising up against them. This denotes how fully God forgives sin; he remembers it no more. Note, deliverances out of trouble are then comforts indeed when they are the fruits of the forgiveness of sin (Isa. 38:17).

Jeremiah 50

Now that it has become his grief it shall not be his ruin. Now that there is a settled separation between him and sin there shall no longer be a separation between him and God. Nay, he shall not be so much as upbraided with them (v. 16): 'None of his sins that he has committed shall be mentioned unto him', either as a clog to his pardon or an allay to the comfort of it, or as any blemish and diminution to the glory that is prepared for him.

Ezekiel 33

One would have expected that though his life was spared, yet he would be laid under a disability and incapacity ever to serve the government again in the character of a prophet! But, behold! the word of the Lord comes to him again, to show that when God forgives he forgets, and whom he forgives he gives a new heart and a new spirit to; he receives those into his family again, and restores them to their former estate, that had been prodigal children and disobedient servants. Note, God's making use of us is the best evidence of his being at peace with us. Hereby it will appear that our sins are pardoned, and we have the good-will of God towards us.

Jonah 3

He should have been more conformable to the example of his master's tenderness, having himself experienced it, so much to his advantage. Note, the comfortable sense of pardoning mercy tends much to the disposing of our hearts to forgive our brethren. It was in the close of the day of atonement that the jubilee trumpet sounded a release of debts (Lev. 25:9); for we must have compassion on our brethren, as God has on us.

Matthew 18

He would have thought it sufficient, and been very thankful, if his father had but taken notice of him, and bid him go to the kitchen, and get his dinner with his servants; but God does for those who return to their duty, and cast themselves upon his mercy, abundantly above what they are able to ask or think.

Luke 15

Fortitude

We are men, and not brutes, reasonable creatures, who should act with reason, who should look upward and look forward, and both ways may fetch considerations enough to silence our complaints. We are men, and not children that cry for everything that hurts them. We are men, and not gods, subjects, not lords; we are not our own masters, not our own carvers; we are bound and must obey, must submit. We are men, and not angels, and therefore cannot expect to be free from troubles as they are; we are not inhabitants of that world where there is no sorrow, but this where there is nothing but sorrow. We are men, and not devils, are not in that deplorable, helpless, hopeless, state that they are in, but have something to comfort ourselves with which they have not.

Lamentations 3

Free Will

Were ever men that pretended to reason or religion, guilty of such prodigious madness, such horrid wickedness! This was it that Peter charged so home upon them (Acts 3:14); 'Ye *desired* a murderer to be granted to you'; yet multitudes who choose the world, rather than God, for their ruler and portion, thus choose their own delusions.

Matthew 27

Friendship

We may in some particular instance befriend a stranger; but we espouse all the interests of a friend, and concern ourselves in all his cares: *thus* Christ takes believers to be his friends. He visits them and converses with them as his friends, bears with them and makes the best of them, is afflicted in their afflictions, and takes pleasure in their prosperity; he pleads for them in heaven and takes care of all their interests there.

John 15

Generosity

The noble generosity of these Canaanites shames and con-

demns the closeness and selfishness and ill humour of many who call themselves Israelites.

Genesis 23

What is given to the poor, or done for them, God will place it to account as lent to him, lent upon interest (so the word signifies); he takes it kindly, as if it were done to himself, and he would have us to take the comfort of it and to be as well pleased as ever any usurer was when he had let out a sum of money into good hands. A very recompense shall be made for it: he will pay him again, in temporal, spiritual, and eternal blessings. Almsgiving is the surest and safest way of thriving.

Proverbs 19

Calvin observes how generous the maker of the feast was, though he seems to have been but of small substance, to invite four or five strangers more than he thought of, because they were followers of Christ, which shows, saith he, that there is more of freedom, and liberality, and true friendship, in the conversation of some meaner persons than among many of higher rank.

John 2

Gentleness

The necessary censures of those who have offended ought to be managed without noise. The words of the wise are heard in quiet. Christ himself shall not strive nor cry. Christian love and Christian prudence will hide a multidue of sins, and great ones, as far as may be done without having fellowship with them.

Matthew 1

Receive affronts and injuries, as a stone is received into a heap of wool, which gives way to it, and so it does not rebound back, nor go any further.

Romans 12

God

What God requires of us he himself works in us or it is not done. He that commands faith, holiness and love, creates them by the power of his grace going along with his word, that he might have all the praise. Lord, give what thou commandest and then command what thou pleasest.

Genesis 1

Abraham was obliged, both in duty and gratitude, to part with Isaac and parted with him to a Friend; but God was under no obligation to us for we were enemies.

Genesis 22

We are never straitened in God, in his power and bounty and the riches of his grace. All our straitness is in ourselves. It is our faith that fails, not his promise. He gives above what we ask. Were there more vessels there is enough in God to fill them, enough for all, enough for each. Was this pot of oil exhausted as long as there were any vessels to be filled from it? and shall we fear lest the golden oil which flows from the very root and fatness of the good olive should fail, as long as

there are any lamps to be supplied from it. (Zech. 4; 12).

2 Kings 4

It is common for great men to take little notice of their inferiors. The king knew not whether Mordecai was preferred or no till his servants informed him. High spirits take a pride in being careless and unconcerned about those that are below them and ignorant of their state. The great God takes cognizance of the meanest of his servants, knows what dignity is done them and what disgrace.

Esther 6

Job had complained of the prosperity and power of tyrants and oppressors, and was ready to charge God with maladministration for suffering it; but he ought not to find fault, except he could mend. If God, and he only, has power enough to humble and bring down proud men, no doubt he has wisdom enough to know when and how to do it, and it is not for us to prescribe to him or to teach him how to govern the world. Unless we had an arm like God we must not think to take his work out of his hands.

Job 40

To the end of time, nay, to eternity, thou shalt be known and honoured. A good man loves God better than himself, and therefore can balance his own sorrow and death with the pleasing thought of the unchangeable blessedness of the Eternal Mind.

Psalm 102

We must declare, 'Great is the Lord', his presence infinite, his power irresistible, his brightness insupportable, his majesty awful, his dominion boundless, and his sovereignty incontestable; and therefore there is no dispute, but 'great is the Lord' and, if great, then 'greatly to be praised', with all that is within us, to the utmost of our power, and with all the circumstances of solemnity imaginable. His greatness indeed cannot be comprehended, for it is unsearchable; who can conceive or express how great God is? But then it is so much the more to be praised. When we cannot, by searching, find the bottom, we must sit down at the brink, and adore the depth (Rom. 11:33).

Psalm 145

The reasons of divine grace are sometimes represented in scripture as strange and surprising (as *Isa. 57:17, 18; Hos. 2:13, 14);* so here, that is given as an inducement to Christ to stoop; which should rather have been a reason for his taking state; *for God's thoughts are not as ours.* Compare with this those passages which preface the most signal instances of condescending grace with the displays of divine glory, (as *Ps. 68: 4, 5; Isa. 57: 15; 66: 1, 2).*

John 13

In this method we must pray, first for grace, and then for glory (Ps. 84: 11); for in this method God gives. Far be it from the only wise God to come under the imputation either of that 'foolish builder who without a foundation built upon the sand', as he would if he should glorify any whom he has not first sanctified; or of that 'foolish builder who began to build and was not able to finish', as he would if he should sanctify any, and not glorify them.

John 17

It appears that he hates sin, when nothing less than the blood of Christ would satisfy for it. Finding sin, though but imputed, upon his own Son, he did not spare him, because he had made himself sin for us (2 Cor. 5:21). The iniquities of us all being laid upon him, though he was the Son of his love, yet it pleased the Lord to bruise him (Isa. 53:10).

Romans 3

God: His Attributes

Behold here the goodness and severity of God. Mercy here shines brightly in the pleasure God takes in doing good. He rejoices in it, yet justice here appears no less illustrious in the pleasure he takes in destroying the impenitent, not as it is making his creatures miserable, but as it is the asserting of his own honour and the securing of the ends of his government. See what a malignant, mischievous thing sin is which (as I may say) makes it necessary for the God of infinite goodness to rejoice in the destruction of his own creatures.

Deuteronomy 28

We cannot add to his greatness for it is infinite but we must acknowledge it and give him the glory of it. Now, when Moses would set forth the greatness of God he does it, not by explaining his eternity and immensity or describing the brightness of his glory in the upper world, but by showing the faithfulness of his word, the perfection of his works and the wisdom and the equity of all the administrations of his government for in these his glory shines most clearly to us.

Deuteronomy 32

They considered that God's Sovereignty is incontestable, his justice inflexible, his power irresistible and, therefore, resolved to try what his mercy was and found it was not in vain to cast themselves upon it.

Joshua 9

God is unsearchable. The ages of his eternity cannot be numbered, nor the spaces of his immensity measured; the depths of his wisdom cannot be fathomed, nor the reaches of his power bounded; the brightness of his glory can never be described, nor the treasures of his goodness reckoned up. This is a good reason why we should always speak of God with humility and caution and never prescribe to him nor quarrel with him, why we should be thankful for what he has revealed of himself and long to be where we shall see him as he is (1 Cor. 13, 9—10).

Job 11

His excellencies in themselves are amiable and lovely. He is the most beautiful Being; but considering man's distance from God by nature, and his defection and degeneracy by sin, his excellencies are dreadful. His power, holiness, justice, yea , and his goodness too, are dreadful excellencies. . . the consideration of our own meanness and mortality, should make us afraid of offending God, and furnishes a good reason why we should not despise and trample upon our brethren.

Job 13

There is enough in this one plain unquestionable truth, That God is greater than man, if duly improved, for ever to put to silence and to shame all our complaints of his providence and our exceptions against his dealings with us. He is not only more wise and powerful than we are, and therefore it is to no purpose to contend with him who will be too hard for us, but more holy, just and good, for these are the transcendent glories and excellencies of the divine nature; in these God is greater than man, and therefore it is absurd and unreasonable to find fault with him, for he is certainly in the right.

Job 33

Those that through grace know much of God, yet know little, yea nothing, in comparison with what is to be known, and what will be known, when that which is perfect shall come and the veil shall be rent. When we would speak of God we speak confusedly and with great uncertainty, and are soon at a loss and run aground, not for want of matter, but for want of words. As we must always begin with fear and trembling, lest we speak amiss (*De Deo etiam vera dicere periculosum est* — even while affirming what is true concerning God we incur risk), so we must conclude with shame and blushing, for having spoken no better.

Job 37

Now by this he proves himself to be God. Does he thus hate proud men? Then he is holy. Will he thus punish them? Then he is the just Judge of the world. Can he thus humble them? Then he is the Lord Almighty. When he had abased proud Pharaoh, and hidden him in the sand of the Red Sea, Jethro thence inferred that doubtless the Lord is greater than all gods, for wherein the proud enemies of his Israel dealt proudly he was above them, he was too hard for them (Exod. 18:11. See Rev. 19:1, 2).

Job 40

From the excellency of the work we may easily infer the infinite perfection of its great author. From the brightness of the heavens we may collect that the Creator is light; their vastness of extent bespeaks his immensity, their height his transcendency and sovereignty, their influence upon this earth his dominion, and providence, and universal beneficence: all declare his almighty power, by which they were at first made, and continue to this day according to the ordinances that were then settled.

Psalm 19

He knew something of the beauty of the Lord, the infinite and transcendent amiableness of the divine being and perfections; his holiness is his beauty (110: 3); his goodness is his beauty (Zech. 9:17). The harmony of all his attributes is the beauty of his nature. With an eye of faith and holy love we with pleasure behold this beauty, and observe more and more in it that is amiable, that is admirable. When with fixedness of thought, and a holy flame of devout affections, we contemplate God's glorious excellencies, and entertain ourselves with the tokens of his peculiar favour to us, this is that view of the beauty of the Lord which David here covets, and it is to be had in his ordinances, for there he manifests himself.

Psalm 27

'However it be, yet Thou art good.' He here acknowledges: 1. The transcendent perfections of the divine nature. Among men we have often reason to complain. There is no truth nor mercy (Hos. 4:1), no judgment nor justice (Isa. 5:7). But all these may be found in God without the least alloy. Whatever is missing, or amiss, in the world, we are sure there is nothing missing, nothing amiss in him that governs it. He is a God of inexhaustible goodness.

Psalm 36

He would praise his power and his mercy; both should be the subject matter of his song. Power, without mercy, is to be dreaded; mercy without power, is not what a man can expect much benefit from; but God's power by which he is able to help us, and his mercy by which he is inclined to help us, will justly be the everlasting praise of all the saints.

Psalm 59

Job, when he was entering into such a temptation, fixed for his principle the omniscience of God: 'Times are not hidden from the Almighty' (Job 24:1). Jeremiah's principle is the justice of God: 'Righteous art Thou O God, when I plead with Thee', (Jer. 12:1). Habakkuk's principle is the holiness of God: 'Thou art of purer eyes than to behold iniquity' (Hab. 1:13). The psalmist's here, is the goodness of God. These are truths which cannot be shaken and which we must resolve to live and die by. Though we may not be able to reconcile all the disposals of Providence with them, we must believe they are reconcilable. Note, good thoughts of God will fortify us against many of Satan's temptations. Truly God is good.

Psalm 73

Therefore all nations shall worship before thee, because as King of nations thou art great, thy sovereignty absolute and incontestable, thy majesty terrible and insupportable, thy power universal and irresistible, thy riches vast and inexhaustible, thy dominion boundless and unquestionable.

Psalm 86

'Mercy and truth shall go before thy face', to prepare thy way, as harbingers to make room for thee — mercy in promising, truth

in performing — truth in being as good as thy word, mercy in being better. How praiseworthy are these in great men, much more in the great God, in whom they are in perfection!

Psalm 89

As he is what he is, so he is what he should be, and in every thing acts as becomes him: there is nothing wanting, nothing amiss, in God; his will is the eternal rule of equity, and he is righteous, for he does all according to it.

Psalm 119

Divine truths look fully as well when they are prayed over as when they are preached over, and much better than when they are disputed over. When we speak of God to him himself, we shall find ourselves concerned to speak with the utmost degree of both sincerity and reverence, which will be likely to make the impressions the deeper.

Psalm 139

The Lord is gracious to those that serve him; he is full of compassion to those that need him, slow to anger to those that have offended him, and of great mercy to all that seek him and sue to him. He is ready to give, and ready to forgive, more ready than we are to ask, than we are to repent.

Psalm 145

Here is God's sufficiency for the saints: his name is a strong tower for them, in which they may take rest when they are weary and take sanctuary when they are pursued, where they may be lifted up above their enemies and fortified against them. There is enough in God, and in the discoveries which he has made of himself to us, to make us easy at all times. The wealth laid up in this tower is enough to enrich them, to be a continual feast and a continuing treasure to them. The strength of this tower is enough to protect them; the Name of the Lord is all that whereby he has made himself known as God, and our God, not only his titles and attributes, but his covenant and all the promises of it; these make up a tower, a strong tower, impenetrable, impregnable, for all God's people.

Proverbs 18

Take notice of the vastness of the heavens and the unmeasurable extent of the firmament; he must needs be a great God who manages such a great world as this is; the heavens above cannot be measured (v. 37), and yet God fills them.

Jeremiah 31

Though we cannot see into the fire, cannot by searching find out God to perfection, yet we see the brightness that is round about it, in the reflection of this fire from the thick cloud. Moses might see God's back parts, but not his face. We have some light concerning the nature of God, from the brightness which encompasses it, though we have not an insight into it, by reason of the cloud spread upon it. Nothing is more easy than to determine that God is, nothing more difficult than to describe what he is. When God displays

his wrath as fire, yet there is a brightness about it; for his holiness and justice appear very illustrious in the punishment of sin and sinners: even about the devouring fire there is a brightness which glorified saints will for ever admire.

Ezekiel 1

His righteousness is conspicuous as the great mountains, and the brightness of it fills the court; but his judgments are a great deep, which we cannot fathom, a cloud which we cannot see through. The brightness discovers enough to awe and direct our consciences, but the cloud forbids us to expect the gratifying of our curiosity; for we cannot order our speech by reason of darkness. Thus (Hab. 3:4) he had rays coming out of his hand, and yet there was the hiding of his power. Nothing is more clear than that God is, nothing more dark than *what* he is. God covers himself with light, and yet, as to us, makes darkness his pavilion.

Ezekiel 10

By him all goodness is to be measured; that is good which is like him, and agreeable to his mind. We in our language call him God, because he is good. In this, as in other things, our Lord Jesus was the Brightness of his glory (and his goodness is his glory), and the express image of his person, and therefore fitly called 'good Master'.

Matthew 19

The Word had a being before the world had a beginning. He that was in the beginning never

began, and therefore was ever —
without beginning of time.

John 1

Power to effect, without wisdom to contrive, and wisdom
to contrive without power to
effect, are alike vain and fruitless; but both together, and both
infinite, make a perfect being.

Romans 16

God: His Dominion

Next to the Being of God there
is nothing that we are more
concerned to believe and consider than God's dominion, that
Jehovah is God, and that this
God reigns (v. 1), not only that
he is King of right, and is the
owner and proprietor of all
persons and things, but that
he is King in fact, and does
direct and dispose of all the
creatures and all their actions
according to the counsel of his
own will.

Psalm 93

His dominion endures throughout all generations, for he himself is eternal, and his counsels
are unchangeable and uniform;
and Satan, who has set up a
kingdom in opposition to him,
is conquered and in a chain.

Psalm 145

God: His Faithfulness

God had promised to drive out
the nations before them (Ex. 33:
2; Ex. 34:11) and to bring
them down (Deut. 9:3) and
now it was done. There failed
not one word of the promise.
Our successes and enjoyments
are then doubly sweet and
comfortable to us when we see
them flowing to us from the
promise (this is according to
what the Lord said). As our
obedience is acceptable to God
when it has an eye to the precept and if we make conscience
of our duty we need not question the performance of the
promise.

Joshua 11

The better God is known the
more he is trusted. Those who
know him to be a God of
infinite wisdom will trust him
further than they can see him.
(Job 35:14); those who know
him to be a God of almighty
power will trust him when
creature-confidence fails and
they have nothing else to trust
to (2 Chron. 20:12); and those
who know him to be a God of
infinite grace and goodness will
trust him though he slay them
(Job 13:15). Those who know
him to be a God of inviolable
truth and faithfulness will
rejoice in his word of promise,
and rest upon that, though the
performance be deferred and
intermediate providences seem
to contradict it. Those who
know him to be the Father of
spirits, and an everlasting Father,
will trust him with their souls
as their main care and trust in
him at all times, even to the
end.

Psalm 9

This is plainly taught us, that,
as sure as we may be that,
'though the sun will set tonight,
it will rise again tomorrow
morning, whether we live to see
it or no', so sure we may be that
though the kingdom of the

Redeemer in the world may for a time be clouded and eclipsed by corruptions and persecutions, yet it will shine forth again, and recover its lustre, in the time appointed.

Jeremiah 33

God: His Goodness

All who have any knowledge of God and dealings with him will own that he does good, and therefore will conclude that he is good. The streams of God's goodness are so numerous, and run so full, so strong, to all the creatures, that we must conclude the fountain that is in himself to be inexhaustible. We cannot conceive how much good our God does every day, much less can we conceive how good he is. Let us acknowledge it with admiration and with holy love and thankfulness.

Psalm 119

See what is the most powerful inducement to an evangelical repentance, and that is a sense of the mercy of God; when God settles them in the midst of plenty, 'then shall they loathe themselves for their iniquities'. Note, the goodness of God should overcome our badness and 'lead us to repentance'. The more we see of God's readiness to receive us into favour upon our repentance, the more reason we shall see to be ashamed of ourselves that we could ever sin against so much love. That heart is hard indeed that will not be thus melted.

Ezekiel 36

If guilt and wrath be communicated, much more shall grace and love; for it is agreeable to the idea we have of the divine goodness to suppose that he should be more ready to save upon an imputed righteousness than to condemn upon an imputed guilt.

Romans 5

God: His Grace

Outward judgments, though they may terrify and restrain men, cannot of themselves sanctify and renew them; the grace of God must work with these judgments. Man's nature was as sinful after the deluge as it had been before.

Genesis 8

God's grace shall never be wanting to those who sincerely desire to know and do their duty . . . The increase of gold lowers the value of it, but the increase of grace advances its price. The more men have of that, the more they value it.

2 Chronicles 1

One of the quarrels God had with the Jews, when he sent them into captivity, was for mocking his messengers and misusing his prophets; and yet, when they were suffering for this sin, he favoured them with this forfeited mercy. It were ill with us if God did not sometimes graciously thrust upon us those means of grace and salvation which we have foolishly thrust from us. In their captivity they were destitute of ordinary helps for their souls, and therefore God raised them up these extraordinary ones; for God's children, if they be hindered in their education one way, shall have it made up another way.

Ezekiel 1

'He died for the ungodly'; *not only helpless creatures, and therefore likely to perish, but guilty sinful creatures, and therefore deserving to perish*; not only mean and worthless, but vile and obnoxious, unworthy of such favour with the holy God.

Romans 5

The Gentiles did neither will it, nor run for it, for they 'sat in darkness' (Matt. 4:16). In darkness, therefore not willing what they knew not; 'sitting' in darkness, a contented posture, therefore not running to meet it, but anticipated with these invaluable blessings of goodness. Such is the method of God's grace towards all that partake of it, for he is found of those that sought him not (Isa. 65:1).

Romans 9

God: His Mercy

Adam was sent to a place of toil, not to a place of torment. He was sent to the ground, not to the grave, to the workhouse, not to the dungeon, to hold the plough, not to drag the chain.

Genesis 3

If he should put to death Shimei who cursed him, those would expect the same fate who had taken up arms and actually levied war against him which would drive them from him, while he was endeavouring to draw them to him. Acts of severity are seldom acts of policy. The throne is established by mercy.

2 Samuel 19

Those that repent, and do their first works, shall rejoice, and recover their first comforts. God's mercies to his people have been ever of old (Ps. 25:6); and therefore they may hope, even then when he seems to have forsaken and forgotten them, that the mercy which was from everlasting will be to everlasting.

Lamentations 5

It is true God has determined to punish sinners; his justice calls for their punishment, and, pursuant to that, impenitent sinners will lie for ever under his wrath and curse; that is the will of his decree, his consequent will, but it is not his antecedent will, the will of his delight. Though the righteousness of his government requires that sinners die, yet the goodness of his nature objects against it. 'How shall I give thee up, Ephraim?' It is spoken here comparatively; he has not pleasure in the ruin of sinners, for he would rather they should turn from their ways and live; he is better pleased when his mercy is glorified in their salvation than when his justice is glorified in their damnation.

Ezekiel 18

Can it be imagined that a God of infinite love and mercy should limit and confine his favours to that little perverse people of the Jews, leaving all the rest of the children of men in a condition eternally desperate? This would by no means agree with the idea we have of the divine goodness, for his 'tender mercies are over all his works.'

Romans 3

God: His Omnipotence

Though the opposition given to the salvation of God's people have all imaginable disadvantages yet God can and will conquer it. Let the banks of Jordan be filled to the brink, filled till they run over, it is as easy to Omnipotence to divide them and dry them up as if they were ever so narrow, ever so shallow. It is all one with the Lord. The God of nature, when He pleases, can change the course of nature and alter its properties, can turn fluids into solids, waters into standing rock as, on the contrary, rocks into waters, to serve his own purposes (see Ps. 114, v. 8). What cannot God do? What will He not do for the perfecting of His people's salvation?

Joshua 3

Giants are dwarfs to Omnipotence.

Joshua 11

Let us by faith see God on His throne, on His throne of glory, infinitely transcending the splendour and majesty of earthly princes — on His throne of government, giving law, giving motion, and giving aim, to all the creatures — on His throne of judgment rendering to every man according to his works — and on His throne of grace, to which His people may come boldly for mercy and grace; we shall then see no reason to be discouraged by the pride and power of oppressors, or any of the afflictions that attend the righteous.

Psalm 11

All things were made by the word of the Lord and by the breath of His mouth. Christ is the Word, the Spirit is the breath, so that God the Father made the world as He rules it and redeems it, by His Son and Spirit. He spoke and He commanded (v. 9), and that was enough; there needed no more. With men, saying and doing are two things, but it is not so with God. By the Word and Spirit of God as the world was made, so was man, that little world. God said, let us make man, and He breathed into him the breath of life. By the Word and Spirit the church is built, that new world, and grace wrought in the soul, that new man, that new creation. What cannot that power do which with a word made a world!

Psalm 33

The command God has of the most ungovernable creatures (v. 9): 'Thou rulest the raging of the sea' than which nothing is more frightful or threatening, nor more out of the power of man to give check to; it can swell no higher, roll no further, beat no harder, continue no longer, nor do any more hurt, than God suffers it.

Psalm 89

God Himself glories in this instance of His power (Job 38:8), and uses it as an argument with us to fear Him (Jer. 5:22). This, if duly considered, would keep the world in awe of the Lord and His goodness, that the waters of the sea would soon cover the earth if God did not restrain them.

Psalm 104

He is with me to support me and bear me up under the burden which now presses me down. He is with me to make the word I preach answer the end he designs, though not the end I desire. He is with me as a mighty terrible one, to strike a terror upon them, and so to overcome them. Even that in God which is terrible is really comfortable to his servants that trust in him, for it shall be turned against those that seek to terrify his people. God's being a mighty God bespeaks him a terrible God to all those that take up arms against him or any one that, like Jeremiah, was commissioned by him. How terrible will the wrath of God be to those that think to daunt all about them and will themselves be daunted by nothing. The most formidable enemies that act against us appear despicable when we see the Lord for us as a mighty terrible one. (Neh. 4:14). Jeremiah speaks now with a good assurance: If the Lord be with me, my persecutors shall stumble.

Jeremiah 20

I am the God of all flesh, that is, of all mankind, here called flesh because weak and unable to contend with God (Ps. 56: 4), and because wicked and corrupt and unapt to comply with God. God is the creator of all, and makes what use he pleases of all. He that is the God of Israel is the God of all flesh and of the spirits of all flesh, and, if Israel were cast off, could raise up a people to his name out of some other nation. If he be the God of all flesh, he may well ask, 'Is anything too hard for me?' What cannot he do from whom all the powers of men are derived, on whom they depend, and by whom all their actions are directed and governed? Whatever he designs to do, whether in wrath or in mercy, nothing can hinder him nor defeat his designs.

Jeremiah 32

The king saw 'the part of the hand that wrote', but saw not the person whose hand it was, which made the thing more frightful. Note, what we see of God, the part of the hand that writes in the book of the creatures and the book of the scriptures (Lo, these are parts of his ways, Job. 26:14), may serve to possess us with awful thoughts concerning that of God which we do not see. If this be 'the finger of God', what is His arm made bare? And what is He?

Daniel 5

God can bring great things to pass without much ado. He needs not great power and many people to effect His purposes; a handful will serve if He pleases. He can without any difficulty ruin any king and kingdom and make no more of it than we do of rooting up a tree that cumbers the ground.

Ezekiel 17

They could not but know that God is almighty, but they would not apply that doctrine to this matter, but gave up the truth to the objections of the impossibility of it, which would all have been answered, if they had but stuck to the doctrine of God's omnipotence, to which nothing is impossible. This therefore which God hath spoken once, we are concerned to hear twice, to hear and believe, to hear and apply — that 'power belongs to God', (Ps. 62:11; Rom. 4:19—21). The same power that made soul and body, and preserved them while they were together, can preserve the body safe, and the soul active, when they are parted, and can unite them together again; for 'behold, the Lord's arm is not shortened'. The power of God, seen in the return of the spring (Ps. 104:30), in the reviving of the corn (John 12:24), in the restoring of an abject people to their prosperity (Ezek. 37:12—14), in the raising of so many to life, miraculously, both in the Old Testament and in the New, and especially in the resurrection of Christ (Eph. 1:19, 20), are all earnests of our resurrection by the same power (Phil. 3:21): 'according to the mighty working whereby he is able to subdue all things to himself.'

Mark 12

The Spirit is the 'arm of the Lord' (Isa. 53:1). His greatest and most mighty works were wrought by His Spirit; but, if the Spirit in this work is said to be the finger of the Lord, it perhaps may intimate how easily Christ did and could conquer Satan, even with the finger of God, the exerting of the divine power in a less and lower degree than in many other instances. He needed not make bare his everlasting arm; that roaring lion, when He pleases, is crushed, like a moth, with a touch of a finger.

Luke 11

God: His Omnipresence

There is no escaping God's avenging eye, no going out of the reach of His hand; rocks and mountains will be no better shelter at last than fig-leaves were at first.

Psalm 21

No place can either include Him or exclude Him.

Jeremiah 23

God: His Omniscience

By publishing among the nations the number of his people, he thought to appear the more formidable and doubted not that if he should have any wars he should overpower his enemies with the multitudes of his forces, trusting in an arm of flesh more than he should have done who had written so much of trusting in God only. God judges not of sin as we do. What appears to us harmless or, at least, but a small offence may be a great sin in the eye of God who sees men's principles and is a discerner of the thoughts and intents of the heart, but His judgment we are sure is according to truth.

2 Samuel 24

If we be ever so industrious to justify ourselves before men and to preserve our credit with them — if we keep our hands ever so clean from the pollutions of gross sin, which fall under the eye of the world — yet God, who knows our hearts, can charge us with so much secret sin as will for ever take off our pretensions to purity and innocency, and make us see ourselves odious in the sight of the holy God. Paul, while a Pharisee, made his hands very clean; but when the commandment came and discovered to him his heart-sins, and made him know lust, that plunged him in the ditch.

Job 9

1. He is sure that God does not discover things, nor judge of them, as men do: He has not *eyes of flesh* (v. 4), for he is a Spirit. Eyes of flesh cannot see in the dark, but darkness hides not from God. Eyes of flesh are but in one place at a time, and can see but a little way; but the *eyes of the Lord are in every place, and run to and fro through the whole earth.* Many things are hidden from eyes of flesh, the most curious and piercing; *there is a path which even the vulture's eye has not seen:* but nothing is, or can be, hidden from the eye of God, to which all things are naked and open. *Eyes* of flesh see the outward appearance only, and may be imposed upon by a deceptio vista — *an illusion of the senses*; but God sees every thing truly. His sight cannot be deceived for he tries the heart, and is a witness to the thoughts and intents of that. *Eyes* of flesh discover things gradually, and when we gain the sight of one thing, we lose the sight of another; but God sees every thing at one view. Eyes of flesh are soon tired, must be closed every night that they may be refreshed, and will shortly be darkened by age and shut up by death; but the keeper of Israel neither slumbers nor sleeps, nor does his sight ever decay. *God sees not as man sees,* that is, he does not judge as man judges, at the best secundum allegata et probata — according to what is alleged and proved, as the thing appears rather than as it is, and too often according to the bias of the affections, passions, prejudices, and interest; but we are sure that the judgment of God is according to truth, and that he knows the truth, not by information, but by his own inspection. Men discover secret things by search, and examination of witnesses, comparing evidence and giving conjectures upon it, wheedling or forcing the parties concerned to confess; but God needs not any of these ways of discovery. *He sees not as man sees.*

2. He is sure that as God is not short-sighted, like man, so he is not short-lived (v. 5): *'Are thy days as the days of man,* few and evil? Do they roll on in succession, or are they subject to change, like the days of man? No, by no means.' Men grow wiser by experience and more

knowing by daily observation; with them truth is the daughter of time, and therefore they must take time for their searches, and, if one experiment fail, must try another. But it is not so with God; to him nothing is past, nothing future, but everything present.

Job 10

This knowledge is hidden in God, as the apostle speaks, (Eph. 3, 9.) Known unto God are all his works, though they are not known to us (Acts 15, 18). There are good reasons for what he does, though we cannot assign them (v. 23); God understands the way thereof. Men sometimes do they know not what, but God never does. Men do what they did not design to do; new occurrences put them upon new counsels, and oblige them to take new measures. But God does all according to the purpose which he purposed in himself, and which he never alters. Men sometimes do that which they cannot give a good reason for, but in every will of God there is a counsel: he knows both what he does and why he does it, the whole series of events and the order and place of every occurrence. This knowledge he has in perfection, but keeps to himself.

Job 28

It is a great truth that God's eyes are upon all the ways of men (Prov. 5, 20, 21); but Job here mentions it with application to himself and his own actions: Doth not he see my ways? O God! thou hast searched me and known me. God sees what rule we walk by,

what company we walk with, what end we walk towards, and therefore what ways we walk in. . . 'He not only sees, but takes notice; he counts all my steps, all my false steps in the way of duty, all my by-steps into the way of sin.' God takes a more exact notice of us than we do of ourselves; for who ever counted his own steps? Yet God counts them. Let us therefore walk circumspectly.

Job 31

He knows things truly and not by their colours — thoroughly, and not by piecemeal. To His knowledge there is nothing distant, but all near — nothing future, but all present — nothing hid, but all open. We ought to acknowledge this in all His wondrous works, and it is sufficient to satisfy us in those wondrous works which we know not the meaning of that they are the works of one that knows what He does.

Job 37

They please themselves with an atheistical conceit that God Himself takes no notice of their wicked practices: They say, 'Who shall see them?' A practical disbelief of God's omniscience is at the bottom of all the wickedness of the wicked.

Psalm 64

The gods of the heathen had eyes and saw not, ears and heard not; our God has no eyes nor ears, as we have, and yet we must conclude He both sees and hears, because we have our sight and hearing from Him, and are accountable to Him for our use of them.

The flowing of the streams is a certain sign of the fulness of the fountain. If all knowledge is from God, no doubt all knowledge is in God.   *Psalm 94*

The wise God is never put upon new counsels, nor obliged to take new measures, either in His laws or in His providences.
                         Psalm 111

He does not cast an eye upon men's ways now and then, but they are always actually in his view and under his inspection; and darest thou sin against God in His sight, and do that wickedness under His eye which thou durst not do in the presence of a man like thyself?
                         Proverbs 5

Those that do so shall find it remembered to their praise, as (according to our reading) it is here remembered to the praise of the land of Tema that they did bring water to the thirsty and relieved even those that were on the falling side.
                         Isaiah 21

There is the work of the heart as well as the work of the hands. As thoughts are words to God, so designs are works in His account.
                         Isaiah 32

'I the Lord search the heart'. This is true of all that is in the heart, all the thoughts of it, the quickest, and those that are most carelessly overlooked by ourselves — all the intents of it, the closest, and those that are most artfully disguised, and industriously concealed from others. Men may be imposed upon, but God cannot. He not only searches the heart with a piercing eye, but he tries the reins, to pass a judgment upon what he discovers, to give everything its true character and due weight. He tries it, as the gold is tried whether it be standard or no, as the prisoner is tried whether he be guilty or no.

God knows more evil of us than we do of ourselves, which is a good reason why we should not flatter ourselves, but always stand in awe of the judgment of God.
                         Jeremiah 17

The fixing of the time during which the captivity should last would be of great use, not only for the confirmation of the prophecy, when the event (which in this particular could by no human sagacity be foreseen) should exactly answer the prediction, but for the comfort of the people of God in their calamity and the encouragement of faith and prayer. Daniel, who was himself a prophet, had an eye to it (Dan. 9:2). Nay, God himself had an eye to it (2 Chron. 36: 22); for therefore He stirred up the spirit of Cyrus, that the word spoken by the mouth of Jeremiah might be accomplished. 'Known unto God are all His works from the beginning of the world', which appears by this, that, when he has thought fit, some of them have been made known to His servants the prophets and by them to His church.
                         Jeremiah 25

Ebed-melech gained his point, and soon brought Jeremiah the

good news; and it is observable how particularly the manner of his drawing him out of the dungeon is related (for God is not unrighteous to forget any work or labour of love which is shown to his people or ministers, no, nor any circumstance of it) (Heb. 6:10.)

Jeremiah 38

Sinners that are resolved to go on in sin are well enough pleased with gods that 'neither see, nor hear, nor know', for then they may sin securely; but they will find, to their confusion, that though those are the gods they choose those are not the gods they must be judged by, but One to whom 'all things are naked and open'.

Daniel 5

Christ not only foresaw that Judas would betray him though he only in heart designed it, but he foresaw that Peter would deny him though he did not design it, but the contrary. He knows not only the wickedness of sinners, but the weakness of saints.

John 13

'He chargeth his angels with folly' (Job 4:18), and much more the wisest among the children of men. 'His understanding is infinite' (Ps. 147:5). There can be no more comparison between his wisdom and ours than between his power and being and ours. There is no common measure by which to compare finite and infinite. And much more is the wisdom of man foolishness with God when set in competition with his.

1 Corinthians 3

He, by his omniscience, cuts up the sacrifice we bring to him, that it may be presented to the Father. Now as the high priest inspected the sacrificed beasts, cut them up to the back-bone to see whether they were sound at heart, so all things are thus dissected, and lie open to the piercing eye of our great high priest. And he who now tries our sacrifices will at length, as Judge, try our state

Hebrews 4

Foreknowledge may be taken in two ways: First, for mere prescience, foresight, or understanding, that such a thing will be, before it comes to pass. Thus a mathematician certainly foreknows that at such a time there will be an eclipse. This sort of foreknowledge is in God, who at one commanding view sees all things that ever were, or are, or ever will be. But such a prescience is not the cause why any thing is so or so, though in the event it certainly will be so, as the mathematician who foresees an eclipse does not thereby cause that eclipse to be. Secondly, foreknowledge sometimes signifies counsel, appointment, and approbation. (Acts 2:23), 'Him being delivered by the determinate counsel and foreknowledge of God.' The death of Christ was not only foreseen, but fore-ordained, as v. 20. Take it thus here; so the sense is, 'elect according to the counsel, ordination, and free grace of God.'

1 Peter 1

God: His Patience

He came into the garden, not

descending immediately from heaven in their view, as afterwards on Mount Sinai . . . but he came into the garden, as one who was still willing to be familiar with them. He came walking, not running, not riding upon the wings of the wind, but walking deliberately as one slow to anger, teaching us, when we are ever so much provoked not to be hot nor hasty, but to speak and act considerately and not rashly. He came in the cool of the day, not in the night when all fears are doubly fearful, nor in the heat of the day, for he came not in the heat of his anger. Nor did he come suddenly upon them; but they heard his Voice at some distance, giving them notice of his coming and probably it was a still, small voice like that in which he came enquiring after Elijah. Some think they heard him discoursing with himself concerning the sin of Adam and the judgment now to be passed upon him; perhaps, as he did concerning Israel (Hosea 11: 8, 9) — 'How shall I give them up?' Or, rather, they heard him calling for them and coming toward them.

Genesis 3

As he went to meet the younger son, so now he goes to court the elder, did not send a servant out with a kind message to him, but went himself. Now, this is designed to represent to us the goodness of God; how strangely gentle and winning he has been towards those that were strangely froward and provoking. He reasoned with Cain, 'Why art thou wroth?' He bore

Israel's manner in the wilderness (Acts 13:18). How mildly did God reason with Elijah, when he was upon the fret (1 Kings 19:46), and especially with Jonah, whose case was very parallel with this here, for he was there disquieted at the repentance of Ninevah, and the mercy shown to it, as the elder brother here.

Luke 15

God: His Righteousness

To be just is to render to all their due; now we do not render to God his due, nor are we just to him, if we do not acknowledge his equity and kindness in all the dispensations of his providence towards us, that he is righteous in all his ways and that, however it be, yet he is good.

Job 33

The law revealed that righteousness of God by which all sinners stand condemned, but the Gospel reveals that by which all believers stand acquitted.

Isaiah 56

He fell on his face, and cried, not in fear for himself (he was one of those that were marked), but in compassion to his fellow-creatures. Those that sigh and cry for the sins of sinners cannot but sigh and cry for their miseries too; yet the day is coming when all this concern will be entirely swallowed up in a full satisfaction in this, that God is glorified; and those that now fall on their faces, and cry, Ah! Lord God, will lift up their heads, and sing, Hallelujah (Rev. 19:1, 3).

Ezekiel 9

God sometimes makes sin to be its own punishment, and yet is not the author of sin; and there needs no more to make men miserable than to give them up to their own vile appetites and passions. Let them be put into the hand of their own counsels, and they will ruin themselves and make themselves desolate. And thus God makes them know that he is the Lord, and that he is a righteous God, which they themselves will be compelled to own when they see how much their wilful transgressions contribute to their own desolations. Note, those who will not acknowledge God as the Lord their ruler shall be made to acknowledge him as the Lord their judge when it is too late.

Ezekiel 20

God: His Sovereignty

The policies of the Church's enemies aim to defeat the promises of the Church's God but in vain God's counsels shall stand . . . Hell and earth cannot diminish those whom heaven will increase.

Exodus 1

The dust of the land became lice. Out of any part of the creation God can fetch a scourge with which to correct those that rebel against him. He has many arrows in his quiver, even the dust of the earth obeys him. Fear not then thou worm, Jacob, for God can use

thee as a threshing instrument if he pleases. (Isa. 41; 15).

Exodus 8

It is fit that God, who by his Providence, gives us all we have, should, by his law, direct the using of it.

Deuteronomy 26

Abimelech intended hereby to punish the Shechemites for their slighting him now but God intended to punish them for their serving him formerly in the murder of Gideon's sons, thus when God makes use of men as instruments in his hand to do his work he means one thing and they another (Isa. 10:6, 7). They design to maintain their honour but God to maintain his.

Judges 9

If any good appear to be in our own hearts or in the hearts of others, we must own it was God that put it there and bless him for it, for it is he that worketh in us both to will and to do that which is good. When princes and magistrates act for the suppression of vice and the encouragement of religion, we must thank God that put it into their hearts to do so as much as if they had granted us some particular favour.

Ezra 7

If he make a change in nations, in families, in the posture of our affairs — if he *shut up* in prison, or in the net of affliction (Ps. 66:11) — If he seize any creature as a hunter his prey, he will gather it (so bishop Patrick) and who shall force him to restore? Or if he *gather together* as tares for the fire, or *if he gather to himself man's spirit and breath (ch. 34: 14), then who can hinder him?* Who can either arrest the sentence or oppose the execution? Who can control his power or arraign his wisdom and justice? If he that made all out of nothing think fit to reduce all to nothing, or to their first chaos again — if he that separated between light and darkness, dry land and sea, at first, please to gather them together again — if he that made unmakes, *who can turn him away,* alter his mind or stay his hand, impede or impeach his proceedings.

Job 11

When Jacob by a fraud got the blessing the design of God's grace was served; when Ahab was drawn by a false prophecy into an expedition that was his ruin the design of God's justice was served; and in both *the deceived and the deceiver* were at his disposal. See (Ezek. 14:9f). God would not suffer the sin of the deciever, nor the misery of the deceived, if he knew not how to set bounds to both and bring glory to himself out of both. Hallelujah, the Lord God omnipotent thus reigns; and it is well he does, for otherwise there is so little wisdom and so little honesty in the world that it would all have been in confusion and ruin long ago.

Job 12

What his soul desires or designs *even that he does,* and nothing can stand in his way or put him upon new counsels. Men desire many things which they may not do, or cannot do, or dare not do.

But God has an incontestable sovereignty; his will is so perfectly pure and right that it is highly fit he should pursue all its determinations. And he has an uncontrollable power. *None can stay his hand. Whatever* the Lord pleased that did he (Ps. 135:6), and always will, for it is always best.

Job 23

We are here told what God designed in doing all this for Cyrus. What Cyrus aimed at in undertaking his wars we may easily guess, but what God aimed at in giving him such wonderful success in his wars we are here told.

Isaiah 45

It is good to see how the counsel and decree of God are pursued and executed in the devices and designs of men, even theirs that know him not (Isa. 10:6, 7). . . It was not that they might fulfil God's counsels, but that they might fill their own treasures, that they were thus eager; yet God thereby served his own purposes.

Jeremiah 6

God has both an incontestable authority and an irresistible ability to form and fashion kingdoms and nations as he pleases, so as to serve his own purposes.

Jeremiah 18

God has the sovereign command of all the hosts of men, even of those that know him not, that own him not, and they are all made to serve his purposes. He directs their marches, their counter-marches, their retreats, their returns, as it pleases him; and furious armies, like stormy winds, in all their motions are fulfilling his word. His word.

Jeremiah 37

'Even so Father, for so it seemed good in Thy sight'. Christ here subscribes to the will of his Father in this matter; 'Even so'. Let God take what way he pleases to glorify himself, and make use of what instruments he pleases for the carrying on of his own work; his grace is his own, and he may give or withhold it as he pleases. We can give no reason why Peter, a fisherman, should be made an apostle, and not Nicodemus, a Pharisee, and a ruler of the Jews, though he also believed in Christ; but 'so it seemed good in God's sight'. Christ said this in the hearing of his disciples, to show them that it was not for any merit of their own that they were thus dignified and distinguished, but purely from God's good pleasure; he made them to differ.

Matthew 11

There are those to whom this knowledge is not given, and a man can receive nothing unless it be given him from above (John 3:27); and be it remembered that God is debtor to no man; his grace is his own; he gives or withholds it at pleasure (Rom. 11:35); the difference must be resolved into God's sovereignty, as before (Ch. 11: 25, 26).

Matthew 13

When his friends were afraid to appear in defence of him, God made even those that were strangers and enemies, to speak in his favour; when Peter denied him, Judas confessed him; when the chief priests pronounced him guilty of death, Pilate declared he found no fault in him; when the women that loved him stood afar off, Pilate's wife, who knew little of him, showed a concern for him. Note, God will not leave himself without witnesses to the truth and equity of his cause, even when it seems to be most spitefully run down by its enemies, and most shamefully deserted by its friends.

Matthew 27

God has wicked men in a chain, and, whatever mischief they would do, they can do no more . than God will suffer them to do. The malice of persecutors is impotent even when it is most impetuous, and, when Satan fills their hearts, yet God ties their hands.

John 7

He is the prince of the kings of the earth; from him they have their authority; by him their power is limited and their wrath restrained; by him their counsels are over-ruled, and to him they are accountable. *This is good news to the church.*

Revelation 1

God: His Transcendence

Sin is said to be against God because so the sinner intends it and so God takes it, and it is an injury to his honour; yet it cannot do anything against him. The malice of sinners is impotent malice: it cannot destroy his being or perfections, cannot dethrone him from his power and dominion, cannot diminish his wealth and possessions, cannot disturb his peace and repose, cannot defeat his counsels and designs, nor can it derogate from his essential glory.

Job 35

The streams of being, power and perfection should lead us to the fountain. God is great, infinitely so — great in power, for he is omnipotent and independent — great in wealth, for he is self-sufficient and all-sufficient — great in himself — great in all his works — great, and therefore greatly to be praised — great, and therefore we know him not. We know that he is, but not what he is. We know what he is not, but not what he is. We know in part, but not in perfection. This comes in here as a reason why we must not arraign his proceedings, nor find fault with what he does, because it is speaking evil of the things that we understand not and answering a matter before we hear it... This is a good reason why we should not prescribe to him, nor quarrel with him, because, as he is, such are his operations, quite out of our reach.

Job 36

God: His Ways

Jephthah lay under three disadvantages — he was the son of a harlot ... he had been driven from his country by his brethren ... he had in his exile headed a rabble ... One would not have thought that this abandoned youth was intended to be Israel's deliverer and judge but God often humbles those whom he designs to exalt and make that stone the head of the corner which the builders refused, so Joseph, Moses and David, the three most eminent of the shepherds of Israel, were all thrust out by men before they were called of God to their great offices.

Judges 11

Even the infirmities and mistakes of those whom God employs are overruled by infinite wisdom and made serviceable to his purposes.

1 Samuel 3

It was in the fifth year of the captivity that Ezekiel was raised up among them, and not before. So long God left them without any prophet, till they began to lament after the Lord and to complain, that they saw not their signs and there was none to tell them how long (Ps. 74:9), and then they would know how to value a prophet and God's discoveries of himself to them by him would be the more acceptable and comfortable.

Ezekiel 1

God: His Wrath

Whatever men may think to the contrary, the executions of providence will fully answer the predictions of the word, and God will appear as terrible against sin and sinners as the scripture makes him; nor shall

119

the unbelief of men make either his promises or his threatenings of no effect or of less effect than they were thought to be of. The contempt of the prophecies is here the sin charged upon them, as the procuring cause of this judgment.

Jeremiah 19

As to the body of the people, it shall not be a correction in love, but he will execute judgments in anger, and in fury, and in furious rebukes (v. 15), strange expressions to come from a God who has said, 'Fury is not in Me', and who has declared himself gracious, and merciful, and slow to anger. But they are designed to show the malignity of sin, and the offence it gives to the just and holy God. That must needs be a very evil thing which provokes him to such resentments, and against his own people too, that had been so high in his favour.

Ezekiel 5

I will send my anger upon thee. Observe, God is Lord of his anger; it does not break out but when he pleases, nor fasten upon any but as he directs it and gives it commission.

Ezekiel 7

The wrath of God is not like our wrath, a heat and passion; no, fury is not in him (Isa. 27:4): but it is a righteous judgment, his will to punish sin, because he hates it as contrary to his nature.

Romans 2

Godly Fear

Happy is the man who always keeps up in his mind a holy awe and reverence of God, his glory, goodness and government, who is always afraid of offending God and incurring his displeasure, who keeps conscience tender and has a dread of the appearance of evil, who is always jealous of himself, distrustful of his own sufficiency, and lives in expectation of troubles and changes, so that, whenever they come, they are no surprise to him. He who keeps up such a fear as this will live a life of faith and watchfulness, and therefore happy is he, blessed and holy.

Proverbs 28

Good Works

'Art thou come hither to torment us — to cast us out from these men, and to restrain us from doing the hurt we would do?' Note, to be turned out, and tied up, from doing mischief, is a torment to the devil, all whose comfort and satisfaction are man's misery and destruction. Should we not then count it our heaven to be doing well, and reckon that our torment, whether within, or without, that hinders us from well-doing?

Matthew 8

Gospel: Above Reason

He was to the Greeks foolishness. They laughed at the story of a crucified Saviour, and despised the apostles' way of telling it. They sought for wisdom. They were men of wit and reading, men that had cultivated arts and sciences, and had, for some ages, been in a manner the very mint of knowledge and learning. There was nothing in the plain doctrine of the cross to suit their taste, nor humour their vanity, nor gratify a curious and wrangling temper: they entertained it therefore with scorn and contempt. What, hope to be saved by one that could not save himself! And trust in one who was condemned and crucified as a malefactor, a man of mean birth and poor condition in life, and cut off by so vile and opprobrious a death!

The thing preached was foolishness in the eyes of worldly-wise men. Our living through one who died, our being blessed by one who was made a curse, our being justified by one who was himself condemned, was all folly and inconsistency to men blinded with self-conceit and wedded to their own prejudices and the boasted discoveries of their reason and philosophy.

1 Corinthians 1

Gossip

Now, as the relating of the sin David fell into is an instance of the impartiality and fidelity of the sacred writers, so the avoiding of the repetition of it here when there was a fair occasion given to speak of it again, is designed to teach us that though there may be a just occasion to speak of the faults and miscarriages of others, yet we should not take delight in the repetition of them.

1 Chronicles 20

The good names of the greatest lie much at the mercy even of the meanest.

Ecclesiastes 7

Neither the innocence of the dove, no, nor the prudence of the serpent to help it, can secure men from unjust censure and false accusation.

Jeremiah 20

Gratitude

Let those who have good done to them look upon it as a just debt they owe to their protectors and benefactors to bless them and give witness to them, to use their interest on earth for their honour and in heaven for their comfort, to praise them, and pray for them. Those are ungrateful indeed who grudge these small returns.

Job 29

Greed

Though the subterraneous wealth is thus hard to obtain, yet men will have it. He that loves silver is not satisfied with silver, and yet is not satisfied without it; but those that have much must needs have more. . . See how foolish man adds to his own burden. He is sentenced to eat bread in the sweat of his face; but, as if that were not enough, he will get gold and silver at the peril of his life, though the more is gotten the less valuable it is. In Solomon's time silver was as stones.

Job 28

It is a sin, when corn is dear and scarce, to withhold it, in hopes that it will still grow dearer, so to keep up and advance the market, when it is already so high that the poor suffer by it; and at such a time it is the duty of those that have stocks of corn by them to consider the poor, and to be willing to sell at the market-price, to be content with moderate profit, and not aim to make a gain of God's judgments. It is a noble and extensive piece of charity for those that have stores wherewithal to do it to help to keep the markets low when the price of our commodities grows excessive.

Proverbs 11

It was folly for him to hoard up what he had, and then to think it well bestowed. There will I bestow it all; as if none must be bestowed upon the poor, none upon his family, none upon the Levite and the stranger, the fatherless and the widow, but all in the great barn.

Luke 12

If the preaching of the gospel ruin the craft of the silversmiths (ch. 19:24) much more the craft of the soothsayers; and therefore here is a great outcry raised, when Satan's power to deceive is broken: the priests hated the gospel because it turned men from the blind service of dumb idols, and so the hope of their gains was gone. The power of Christ, which appeared in dispossessing the woman, and the great kindness done to her in delivering her out of Satan's hand, made no impression upon them when they apprehended that they should hereby lose money.

Acts 16

Growth

Where God gives true grace he will give more grace. God's trees shall grow higher, like the cedars, the tall cedars in Lebanon; they shall grow nearer heaven, and with a holy ambition shall aspire towards the upper world; they shall grow stronger, like the cedars, and fitter for use.

Psalm 92

Grumbling

When we murmur against those who are instruments of any uneasiness to us whether justly or unjustly, we should do well to consider how much we reflect upon God by it. Men are but God's hand. Those that quarrel with the reproofs and convictions of the word and are angry with their ministers when they are touched in a tender part know not what they do for therein they strive with their Maker. Let this for ever stop the mouth of murmuring for it is daring impiety to murmur at God, because he is God and gross absurdity to murmur at men because they are but men.

Exodus 16

When we consider how their camp was guided, guarded, graced, etc . . . we may ask 'What could have been done more for a people to make them easy?' and yet they complained. Those that are of a fretful, discontented spirit will always find something or other to quarrel with though the circumstances of their outward condition be ever so favourable. . . We read of their murmurings several times when they came first out of Egypt (Ex. 15; 16; 17), but we don't read of any plagues inflicted on them for their murmurings as there were now; for now they had had great experience of God's care of them and, therefore, now to distrust him was so much the more inexcusable.

Numbers 11

They tempted God — tempted his Power whether he could help them in their straits; his goodness whether he would and his faithfulness whether his promises would be performed. They tempted his justice whether he would resent their provocation and punish them or not. They tempted him and in effect challenged him.

Numbers 14

Those resist the Prince who resist those that are commissioned by him for alas, says Moses, 'What is Aaron that you murmur against him?' If murmurers and complainers would consider that the instruments they quarrel with are but instruments whom God employs and they are but what he makes them and never more nor less, better nor worse, they would not be so bold and free in their censures and reproaches as they are.

Numbers 16

The words signify, Groan not one against another, that is 'Do not make one another uneasy by your murmuring groans at what befalls you, nor by your distrustful groans as to what may further come upon you, nor by your revengeful groans against the instruments of your sufferings, nor by your envious groans at those who may be free from your calamities: do not make yourselves uneasy and make one another uneasy by thus groaning to and grieving one another.'

James 5

Guidance

They did not stir a step till Joshua ordered them to move and Joshua did not order them out of Jordan till God directed him to do so. (v. 15—17). . . How low a condition soever God may at any time bring his priests or people to, let them patiently wait till, by his Providence, he shall call them up out of it as the priests here were called to come up out of Jordan and let them not be weary of waiting while they have the tokens of God's Presence with them, even the ark of the Covenant, in the depth of their adversity.

Joshua 4

God will, some way or other, direct the steps of those who acknowledge him in all their ways and seek unto him for direction with full purpose of heart to follow it.

1 Samuel 14

To those who understand aright, who depart from evil (for that is understanding), the knowledge of God and of his will is easy.

Proverbs 14

If men devise their way, so as to make God's glory their end and his will their rule, they may expect that he will direct their steps by his Spirit and grace, so that they shall not miss their way nor come short of their end.

Proverbs 16

'You shall have more knowledge on a sudden than hitherto you have had by diligent attendance.' They had asked some ignorant questions (ch. 9:2), some ambitious questions (Matt. 18:1), some distrustful ones (Matt. 19:27), some impertinent ones (ch. 21:21), some curious ones (Acts 1:6); but, after the Spirit was poured out, nothing of all this. In the story 'of the apostles' Acts' we seldom find them asking questions, as David, 'Shall I do this?' Or, 'Shall I go thither?' For they were constantly under a divine guidance. In that weighty case of preaching the 'gospel to the gentiles', Peter went, 'nothing doubting' (Acts 10:20). Asking questions supposes us at a loss, or at least at a stand, and the best of us have need to ask questions; but we should aim at such a full assurance of understanding that we may not hesitate, but be constantly led in a plain path both of truth and duty.

John 16

Those are best able to prove what is the good, and acceptable, and perfect will of God, who are transformed by the renewing of their mind.

A good wit can dispute and distinguish about the will of God; while an honest, humble heart, that has spiritual senses exercised, and is delivered into the mould of the word, loves it, and practises it, and has the relish and savour of it.

Romans 12

Happiness

Faint desires of happiness without a right choice at the end and a right use of the means deceive many into their own ruin. Multitudes go to hell with their mouths full of good desires.

Genesis 27

This was he, who having tasted of these enjoyments, wrote a whole book to show the vanity of all worldly things and the vexation of spirit that attends them, their insufficiency to make us happy and the folly of setting our hearts upon them, and to recommend to us the practice of serious godliness as that which is the whole of man, and will do infinitely more towards the making of us easy and happy than all the wealth and power that he was master of, and which through the grace of God, is within our reach, when the thousandth part of Solomon's greatness is a thousand times more than we can ever be so vain as to promise ourselves in this world.

1 Kings 10

When it is said, 'Blessed are the undefiled in the way, blessed is the man that walketh not in the counsel of the wicked' etc., the design is to show the characters of those that are blessed; but when it is said, 'Blessed are those whose iniquities are forgiven', the design is to show what that blessedness is, and what is the ground and foundation of it. Pardoned people are the only blessed people.

Romans 4

Observe, what a growing increasing happiness the happiness of the saints is: 'Not only so'. One would think such peace, such grace, such glory, and such a joy in hope of it, were more than such poor undeserving creatures as we are could pretend to; and yet it is 'not only so'.

Romans 5

Our establishment in the ways of God is a likely means in order to comfort; whereas, if we are wavering in faith, and of a doubtful mind, or if we are halting and faltering in our duty, no wonder if we are strangers to the pleasures and joys of religion. What is it that lies at the bottom of all our uneasiness, but our unsteadiness in religion?

2 Thessalonians 2

Hardness of Heart

Josiah was sincere in what he did but the generality of the people were averse to it and hankered after their idols still so that the reformation, though well designed and well prosecuted by the prince, had little or no effect upon the people. It was with reluctancy that they parted with their idols. Still they were in heart joined to them and wished for them again.

2 Chronicles 34

See how wretchedly the hearts of sinners are hardened by the deceitfulness of sin. Persecution was one of the sins for which God was now contending with them, and yet Zedekiah persists in it even now that he was in the depth of distress. No providences, no afflictions, will of themselves part between men and their sins, unless the grace of God work with them. Nay, some are made worse by those very judgments that should make them better.

Jeremiah 32

Those who are not acquainted with the divine speech have reason to fear that they are strangers to the divine nature. Christ spoke the words of God (Ch. 3:34) in the dialect of the kingdom of God; and yet they, who pretended to belong to the kingdom, understood not the idioms and properties of it, but like strangers, and rude ones too, ridiculed it. And the reason why they did not understand Christ's speech made the matter much worse: 'Even because you cannot hear my word', that is, 'You cannot persuade yourselves to hear it attentively, impartially, and without prejudice, as it should be heard.' The meaning of this 'cannot' is an obstinate 'will not'; as the Jews could not hear Stephen (Acts 7:57) nor Paul (Acts 22:22). *Note*, the rooted antipathy of men's corrupt hearts to the doctrine of Christ is the true reason of their ignorance of it, and of their errors and mistakes about it. They do not like it nor love it, and therefore they will not understand it; like Peter, who pretended he 'knew not what the damsel said' (Matt. 26:70), when in truth he knew not what to say to it.

John 8

Harvest

Harvest time is busy time; all hands must be then at work; every one must work for himself, that he may reap of the graces and comforts of the Gospel: ministers must work for God, to gather in souls to him. Harvest time is opportunity, a short and limited time, which will not last always; and harvest work is work that must be done then or not at all so the time of enjoyment of the Gospel is a particular season, which must be improved for its proper purposes; for, once past, it cannot be recalled.

John 4

Heart Religion

Now the burning of this fat is supposed to signify the offering up of our good affections to God in all our prayers and praises. God must have the inwards for we must pour out our souls and lift up our hearts in prayer and must bless his name with all that is within us. It is required that we be inward with God in everything wherein we

have to do with him. The fat denotes the best and choicest which must always be devoted to God who has made for us a feast of fat things.

Leviticus 3

We must not think that doing much in religion will be accepted if we do not do it well and after the manner that God has appointed.

Numbers 29

The Spirit of the Lord had departed from him yet he kept up his observance of the holy feasts. There may be the remains of external devotion where there is nothing but the ruins of real virtue.

1 Samuel 20

David who pitched a tent for the Ark and continued steadfast to it did far better than Solomon who built a temple for it and yet in his latter end turned his back upon it. The Church's poorest times were its purest.

1 Chronicles 16

Those who have the New Jerusalem in their eye must have the ways that lead to it in their heart, must mind them, their eyes must look straight forward in them, must ponder the paths of them, must keep close to them, and be afraid of turning aside to the right hand or to the left. If we make God's promise our strength, we must make God's word our rule, and walk by it.

Psalm 84

We make nothing of our religious performances if we do

not make heart-work of them if that which is within us, nay, if all that is within us, be not engaged in them. The work requires the inward man, the whole man, and all little enough.

Psalm 103

Some of the psalms of praise are very short, others very long, to teach us that, in our devotions, we should be more observant how our hearts work than how the time passes and neither overstretch ourselves by coveting to be long nor over-stint ourselves by coveting to be short, but either the one or the other as we find in our hearts to pray.

Psalm 105

For who hath engaged his heart, made a covenant with it, and brought it into bonds, to approach unto me? How few are there that do so! None can do it but by the special grace of God causing them to draw near. Note, whenever we approach God in any holy ordinance we must engage our hearts to do it; the heart must be prepared for the duty, employed in it, and kept closely to it. The heart is the main thing that God looks at and requires; but it is deceitful, and will start aside if a great deal of care and pains be not taken to engage it, to bind this sacrifice with cords.

Jeremiah 30

Perhaps this is mentioned here to show a difference between the God whom they deserted and the gods whom they went over to. The true God aimed at nothing but that they should be good men, and live good lives for their own good, and the ceremony of honouring him with sacrifices was one of the smallest matters of his law; whereas the false gods required that only; let their priests and altars be regaled with sacrifices and offerings, and the people might live as they listed. What fools were those then that left a God who aimed at giving his worshippers a new nature, for gods who aimed at nothing but making themselves a new name!

Hosea 6

Heart Searching

What we have done amiss we should be very desirous to come to the knowledge of. 'That which I see not teach Thou me and show me wherein I have erred' are prayers we should put up to God every day that though through ignorance we fall into sin, we may not through ignorance lie still in it.

Leviticus 4

Heaven

What a new world did Israel now come into. Most of them were born and had lived all their days in a vast howling wilderness where they knew not what either fields or cities were, had no houses to dwell in and neither sowed nor reaped and now, of a sudden, to become masters of a country so well built, so well husbanded, this made them amends for their long waiting and yet it was but the earnest of a great deal more.

Deuteronomy 2

The clusters of grapes that meet us in this wilderness should make us long for the full vintage in Canaan. If a day in his courts be so sweet, what then will an eternity within the veil be! If this be heaven, O that I were there!

Song of Solomon 8

The far better half is to think of going to the Father, to sit down in the *immediate, uninterrupted, and everlasting enjoyment of him*. Those who love God cannot but be pleased to think of coming to him, though it be through the valley of the shadow of death. When we go, to be 'absent from the body', it is to be 'present with the Lord', like children fetched home from school to their father's house. Now come I to thee whom I have chosen and served, and whom my soul thirsteth after; to thee the fountain of light and life, the crown and centre of bliss and joy; now my longings shall be satisfied, my hopes accomplished, my happiness completed, for 'now I come to thee'.

John 17

In our present state we come short, not only in the enjoyment, but in the knowledge of that glory (1 Cor. 2:9; 1 John 3:2): it shall be revealed. It surpasses all that we have yet seen and known: present vouchsafements are sweet and precious, very precious, very sweet; but there is something to come, something behind the curtain, that will outshine all. 'Shall be revealed in us'; not only revealed to us, to be seen, but revealed in us, to be enjoyed.

Romans 8

Do we look for such a happiness, and should we not set our affections upon that world, and live above this? What is there here to make us fond of it? What is there not there to draw our hearts to it? Our head is there, our home is there, our treasure is there, and we hope to be there for ever.

Colossians 3

They are happy in their employment, for they serve God continually, and that without weakness, drowsiness, or weariness. Heaven is a state of service, though not of suffering; it is a state of rest, but not of sloth; it is a praising delightful rest.

Revelation 7

Heavenly-Mindedness

Jesus Christ was not of this world; he never had been of it, and least of all now that he was upon the point of leaving it. This intimates, First, his state; he was none of the world's favourites nor darlings, none of its princes nor grandees; worldly possessions he had none, not even 'where to lay his head'; nor worldly power, he was no judge nor divider. Secondly, his spirit; he was perfectly dead to the world, the prince of this world had nothing in him, the things of this world were nothing to him; not honour, for he 'made himself of no reputation'; not riches, for 'for our sakes he became poor', not pleasures, for he 'acquainted himself with grief'. See (ch. 8: 23).

John 17

Hell

The damnation of Hell (as our Saviour calls it) is the fire of God's anger fastening upon the guilty conscience of a sinner to its inexpressible and everlasting torment.

Deuteronomy 32

The fire of God's wrath will consume them (v. 9); they shall not only be cast into a furnace of fire (Matt. 13:42), but he shall make them themselves as a fiery oven or furnace; they shall be their own tormentors; the reflections and terrors of their own consciences will be their hell. Those that might have had Christ to rule and save them, but rejected him and fought against him, shall find that even the remembrance of that will be enough to make them, to eternity, a fiery oven to themselves: it is the worm that dies not.

Psalm 21

There it was that they sacrificed some of their children, and dedicated others to Moloch, and there they should fall as victims to divine justice.

Jeremiah 7

The sin is so heinous, and the ruin proportionably so great, that he had better undergo the sorest punishments inflicted on the worst of malefactors, which can only kill the body. Note, 1. Hell is worse than the depth of the sea; for it is a bottomless pit, and it is a burning lake. The depth of the sea is only killing, but hell is tormenting. We meet with one that had comfort in the depth of the sea, it was Jonah (Ch. 2:2, 4, 9); but never had any the least grain or glimpse of comfort in hell, nor will have to eternity. 2. The irresistible irrevocable doom of the great Judge will sink sooner and surer, and bind faster, than a millstone hanged about the neck.

Matthew 18

Though we cannot make a full satisfaction for it, it will be continually demanded, 'till the last mite be paid', which will not be to all eternity. Christ's sufferings were short, yet the value of them made them fully satisfactory. In the sufferings of damned sinners, what is wanting in value must be made up in an endless duration.

Luke 12

He desires a drop of water to cool his tongue. He does not say, 'Father Abraham, send for me to thy bosom, to lie where Lazarus lies.' Unsanctified souls do not, cannot, truly desire the happiness of heaven; nay, he does not say, 'Father Abraham, order me a release from this misery, help me out of this pit', for he utterly despaired of this; but he asks as small a thing as could be asked, a drop of water to cool his tongue for one moment.

Luke 16

Heresy

How great an evil real heresy is, not lightly therefore to be charged upon any, though greatly to be taken heed of by all. Such a one is 'subverted' or perverted — a metaphor from a building so ruined as to render it difficult if not impossible to repair and raise it up again. Real heretics have seldom been recovered to the true faith: *not so much defect of judgment, as perverseness of the will,* being in the case, through pride, or ambition, or self-willedness, or covetousness, or such like corruption, which therefore must be taken heed of.

Titus 3

Holiness

Though David, as a good magistrate, was a terror to evil-doers, yet there were many such, even about court, intruding near his person; these he here abdicates, and resolves to have no conversation with them. Note, those that resolve to keep the commandments of God must have no society with evil-doers; for bad company is a great hindrance to a holy life. We must not choose wicked people for our companions, nor be intimate with them; we must not do as they do nor do as they would have us do (Ps. 1:1; Eph. 5:11).

Psalm 119

The heart must be pure, in opposition to mixture — an honest heart that aims well; and pure, in opposition to pollution and defilement; as wine unmixed, as water unmuddied. The heart must be kept pure from fleshly lusts, all unchaste thoughts and desires; and from worldly lusts; covetousness is called filthy lucre; from all filthiness of flesh and spirit, all that which comes out of the heart, and defiles the man.

Matthew 5

On the whole, the sacrifice of our Redeemer is the strongest argument with a gracious heart for purity and sincerity. How sincere a regard did he show to our welfare, in dying for us! And how terrible a proof was his death of the detestable nature of sin, and God's displeasure against it! Heinous evil, that could not be expiated but with the blood of the Son of God! And shall a Christian love the murderer of his Lord? God forbid.

1 Corinthians 5

Holy Spirit

The best knowledge of the Spirit of truth is that which is got by experience: 'You know him, for he dwelleth with you'. Christ had dwelt with them, and by their acquaintance with him they could not but know 'the Spirit of truth'. They had themselves been endued with the Spirit in some measure. What enabled them to leave all to follow Christ, and to continue with him in his temptations? What enabled them to preach the Gospel, and work miracles, but the Spirit dwelling in them? *The experiences of the saints are the explications of the promises; paradoxes to others are axioms* to them. Those that have an experimental acquaintance with the Spirit have a comfortable assurance of his continuance. He 'dwelleth with you, and shall be in you', for lodging. Those that know him know how to value him, invite him and bid him welcome; and therefore he shall be in them, as the light in the air, as the sap in the tree, as the soul in the body. Their communion with him shall be intimate, and their union with him inseparable. The gift of the Holy Ghost is a peculiar gift, bestowed upon the disciples of Christ in a distinguishing way — them, and not the world; it is to them 'hidden manna' and the 'white stone'. No comforts comparable to those which make no show, make no noise. This is the favour God bears to his chosen; it is the 'heritage of those that fear his name.'

John 14

Honour

Those that honour God he will honour and when he will magnify a man as he had said he would magnify Joshua (ch. 3: 7), he will do it effectually, yet it was not for Joshua's sake only that he was thus magnified but to put him in a capacity of doing so much the more service to Israel for hereupon they feared him as they feared Moses. See here what is the best and surest way to command the respect of inferiors and to gain their reverence and observance, not by blustering and threatening and carrying it with a high hand but by holiness and love and all possible indications of a

constant regard to their welfare, and to God's will and honour. Those are (respected) in the best manner, and to the best purpose, who make it to appear that God is with them and that they set him before them; those that are sanctified are truly magnified and are worthy of double honour. Favourites of heaven should be looked on with awe.

Joshua 4

What was the honour of their fine clothes, compared with that of his wisdom, and grace, and holiness, his courage and constancy in suffering for Christ! His bonds in so good a cause were more glorious than their chains of gold, and his guards than their equipage. Who would be fond of worldly pomp that here sees so bad a woman loaded with it and so good a man loaded with the reverse of it.

Acts 25

Honouring God

They assumed too much of the glory of this work of wonder to themselves. 'Must we fetch water?' as if it were done by some power or worthiness of theirs. Therefore, it is charged upon them that they did not sanctify God, that is, they did not give him that glory of this miracle which was due unto his Name.

Numbers 20

If we give not to God the glory of our successes even the Philistines will rise up in judgment against us and condemn us for when they had obtained a victory over Saul they sent tidings to their idols. Poor idols that knew not what was done a few miles off till the tidings were brought to them, nor then either.

1 Chronicles 10

Though weak faith shall not be rejected, the bruised reed not broken, the smoking flax not quenched, yet strong faith shall be commended and honoured. The strength of his faith appeared in the victory it won over his fears. And hereby he gave glory to God; for, as unbelief dishonours God by making him a liar (1 John 5:10), so faith honours God by setting to its seal that he is true (John 3:33). Abraham's faith gave God the glory of his wisdom, power, holiness, goodness, and especially of his faithfulness, resting upon the word that he had spoken... We never hear our Lord Jesus commending any thing so much as great faith (Matt. 8:10; 15:28), *therefore God gives honour to faith, great faith, because faith, great faith, gives honour to God.*

Romans 4

Hope

Lucius Florus relates it as a great instance of the bravery of the Roman citizens that in the time of the second Punic war, when Hannibal besieged Rome and was very near making himself master of it, a field on which part of his army lay, being offered to sale at that time, was immediately purchased, in a firm belief that the Roman

valour would raise the siege, (lib. 2, cap. 6). And have not we much more reason to venture our all upon the Word of God.

Jeremiah 32

Those that will deal with God must deal upon trust. It is acknowledged that one of the principal graces of a Christian is hope (1 Cor. 13:13), which necessarily implies a good thing to come, which is the object of that hope. *Faith respects the promise, hope the thing promised.* Faith is the evidence, hope the expectation, of things not seen. Faith is the mother of hope.

Romans 8

Those that rejoice in hope are likely to be patient in tribulation. It is a believing prospect of the joy set before us that bears up the spirit under all outward pressure.

Romans 12

The joy and peace of believers arise chiefly from their hopes. What is laid out upon them is but little, compared with what is laid up for them; therefore the more hope they have the more joy and peace they have.

Romans 15

A good hope of salvation, well founded and well built, will both purify the soul and keep it from being defiled by Satan, and it will comfort the soul and keep it from being troubled and tormented by Satan. He would tempt us to despair; but good hope keeps us trusting in God, and rejoicing in him.

Ephesians 6

Hospitality

The less they are in themselves, to whom we show kindness, the more there is of good will in it to Christ; the less it is for their sakes, the more it is for his, and he takes it accordingly. If Christ were personally among us, we think we should never do enough to welcome him; the poor, the poor in spirit, we have always with us, and they are his receivers. See (Matt. 25:35—40).

Matthew 18

Human Responsibility

Neither the patience of the saints under their sufferings, nor the counsel of God concerning their sufferings, will be any excuse for those that have any hand in their sufferings, or that persecute them.

Luke 22

Humility

Those are best prepared for the greatest mercies that see they are unworthy of the least.

Jacob doesn't say 'In this place I wrestled with God and prevailed' but, 'In this place I saw God face to face and my life was preserved'; not, 'It was my praise that I came off a conqueror' but 'It was God's mercy that I escaped with my life'. Note: It becomes those who God honours to take shame to themselves and to admire the condescensions of his grace to them.

Genesis 32

We must be content to have our excellences obscured and a veil drawn over them, not coveting to make a fair show in the flesh. Those that are truly desirous to be owned and accepted by God will likewise desire not to be taken notice of nor applauded by men.

Exodus 34

The ear of the learner is necessary to the tongue of the learned. (See Isa. 50:4).

Deuteronomy 1

When thy latter end is greatly increased, remember the smallness of thy beginnings.

Deuteronomy 6

True penitents, when they are under divine rebukes, call them not only just but good, not only submit to the punishment of their iniquity but accept of it, so Hezekiah did and by this it appeared that he was indeed humbled for the pride of his heart.

2 Kings 20

The more we do for God the more we are indebted to Him for the honour of being employed in his service and for grace enabling us in any measure to serve him. Does he, therefore, thank that servant? (Luke 17:9). No, but that servant has a great deal of reason to thank him. He thanks God that they were able to offer so willingly. It is a great instance of the power of God's grace in us to be able to do the work of God willingly.

'Who am I and what is my people?' David was the most

honourable person and Israel the most honourable people then in the world, yet thus does he speak of himself and think as unworthy the divine cognizance and favour. David now looks very great presiding in an august assembly appointing his successor and making a noble present to the honour of God and yet he is little and low in his own eyes.

1 Chronicles 29

As it is but little that he knows, and therefore he ought not to arraign the divine counsels, so it is but little that he can do, and therefore he ought not to oppose the proceedings of Providence.

Job 38

We must not imagine that we do anything for God by our own strength, or deserve anything from God by our own righteousness; but all the good we do is done by the power of his grace, and all the good we have is the gift of his mere mercy, and therefore he must have all the praise.

Psalm 115

Considering how safe, and quiet, and easy, those are that are of a humble spirit, what communion they have with God and comfort in themselves, we will say, 'With the lowly is wisdom.'

Proverbs 11

Humility, though it should expose us to contempt in the world, yet while it recommends us to the favour of God, qualifies us for his gracious visits, prepares us for his glory, secures us from many

temptations, and preserves the quiet and repose of our own souls, is much better than that high-spiritedness which, though it carry away the honour and wealth of the world, makes God a man's enemy and the devil his master.

Proverbs 16

Humility is the presage of honour and prepares men for it, and honour shall at length be the reward of humility, as he had said before (Ch. 15:33). That has need to be often said which men are so loth to believe.

Proverbs 18

He that knows his own heart knows so much more evil of himself than he does of any other that he cries out, 'Surely I cannot but think that I am more brutish than any man; surely no man has such a corrupt deceitful heart as I have. I have acted as one that has not the understanding of Adam, as one that is wretchedly degenerated from the knowledge and righteousness in which man was at first created; nay, I have not the common sense and reason of a man, else I should not have done as I have done.' Agur, when he was applied to by others as wiser than most, acknowledged himself more foolish than any. Whatever high opinion others may have of us, it becomes us to have low thoughts of ourselves.

Proverbs 30

We must be clothed with humility; for the proud in spirit are those that cannot bear to be trampled upon, but grow outrageous, and fret themselves, when they are hardly bestead. That will break a proud man's heart, which will not break a humble man's sleep. Mortify pride, therefore, and a lowly spirit will easily be reconciled to a low condition.

Ecclesiastes 7

The other evangelists tell us, that Matthew made a great feast, which the poor fishermen, when they were called, were not able to do. But when he comes to speak of this himself, he neither tells us that it was his own house, nor that it was a feast, but only that he sat at meat in the house; preserving the remembrance of Christ's favours to the publicans, rather than of the respect he had paid to Christ. Note, it well becomes us to speak sparingly of our own good deeds.

In the good we do, we must not seek our own praise, but only the glory of God. It must be more our care and endeavour to be useful, than to be known and observed to be so (Prov. 20:6; 25:27).

Matthew 9

Wise and good men, though they covet to do good, yet are far from coveting to have it talked of when it is done; because it is God's acceptance, not men's applause, that they aim at.

Matthew 12

You cannot speak so meanly and slightly of a humble believer, but he is ready to speak as meanly and slightly of himself. Some that seem to dispraise and disparage themselves, will yet take it as an affront if others do so too; but one that is humbled aright, will subscribe to the most abasing challenges, and not call them abusing ones. 'Truth, Lord; I cannot deny it; I am a dog, and have no right to the children's bread'.

David, thou hast done foolishly, very foolishly; 'Truth, Lord'. Asaph, thou hast been as a beast before God; 'Truth, Lord'. Agur, thou art more brutish than any man; 'Truth, Lord'. Paul, thou has been the chief of sinners, art less than the least of saints, not meet to be called an apostle; 'Truth, Lord.'

Matthew 15

The way to be great and chief is to be humble and serviceable. Those are to be best accounted of, and most respected, in the church, and will be so by all that understand things aright.

As he must become a fool that would be wise, so he must become a servant that would be chief. Paul was a great example of this, he 'laboured more abundantly than they all', made himself (as some would call it) a drudge to his work; and is not he chief? Do we not by consent call him the great apostle, though he called himself 'less than the least'?

Matthew 20

This enjoining of silence to the disciples, would likewise be of use to them, to prevent their boasting of the intimacy they were admitted to, that they might not be puffed up with the abundance of the revelations. It is a mortification to a man, to be tied up from telling of his advancements, and may help to hide pride from him.

Mark 9

Elisabeth was the wife of a priest, and in years, yet she grudges not that her kinswoman, who was many years younger than she, and every way her inferior, should have the honour of conceiving in her virginity, and being the mother of the Messiah, whereas the honour put upon her was much less; she rejoices in it, and is well pleased, as her son was afterwards, that she who cometh after her is preferred before her (John 1:27). Note, while we cannot but own that we are more favoured of God than we deserve, let us by no means envy that others are more highly favoured than we are.

Those that are filled with the Holy Ghost have low thoughts of their own merits, and high thoughts of God's favours. Her son the Baptist spoke to the same purport with this, when he said, 'Comest thou to me?' (Matt. 3:14).

Luke 1

He charged him to tell no man. This, it should seem, did not forbid him telling it to the honour of Christ, but he must not tell it to his own honour. Those whom Christ hath healed and cleansed must know that he hath done it in such a way as for ever excludes boasting.

Luke 5

The number of the apostles was twelve. Their names are here recorded; it is the third time that we have met with them, and in each of the three places the order of them differs, to teach both ministers and Christians not to be nice in precedency, not in giving it, much less in taking it, but to look upon it as a thing not worth taking notice of; let it be as it lights.

Luke 6

It is no new thing for a man's modesty to be turned against him, and improved to his prejudice; but it is better that men should take advantage of our low thoughts of ourselves, to trample upon us, than the devil take advantage of our high thoughts of ourselves, to tempt us to pride and draw us into his condemnation.

John 1

The more others magnify us, the more we must humble ourselves, and fortify ourselves against the temptation of flattery and applause, and the jealousy of our friends for our honour, by remembering our place, and what we are (1 Cor. 3:5).

John 3

It well becomes the disciples of Christ, when they are grown up to maturity in knowledge, frequently to reflect upon the follies and weaknesses of their first beginning, that free grace may have the glory of their proficiency, and they may have compassion on the ignorant.

John 12

Christ would teach Peter an implicit obedience: 'What I do thou knowest not now', and therefore art no competent judge of it, but must believe it is well done because I do it. Note, Consciousness to ourselves of the darkness we labour under, and our inability to judge of what God does, should make us sparing and modest in our censures of his proceedings; see Heb. 11:8.

John 13

It is no crime in a Christian, but much to his commendation, to take notice of the good that is in him, to the praise of divine grace. Spiritual pride is abominable: it is making use of the greatest favours of God to feed our own vanity, and make idols of ourselves. But to take notice of the favours of God to promote our gratitude to him, and to speak of them to his honour (be they of what sort they will), is but a proper expression of the duty and regard we owe him.

1 Corinthians 3

As much against the grain as it is with a proud man to acknowledge his infirmities, so much is it against the grain with a humble man to speak in his own praise. It is no pleasure to a good man to speak well of himself, yet in some cases it is lawful, namely, when it is for the advantage of others, or for our own necessary vindication; as thus it was here.

. . . He would not have them think that boasting of ourselves, or glorying in what we have, is a thing commanded by the Lord in general unto Christians, nor yet that this is always necessary in our own vindication; though it may be lawfully used, because not contrary to the Lord, when, strictly speaking, it is not after the Lord. It is the duty and practice of Christians, in obedience to the command and example of the Lord, rather to humble and abase themselves; yet prudence must direct in what circumstances it is needful to do that which we may do lawfully, even speak of what God has wrought for us, and in us, and by us too.

2 Corinthians 11

How much soever we are, or ought to be, esteemed by others, we ought always to think humbly of ourselves. See an example of this in this great apostle, who thought himself to be nothing, though in truth he was not behind the greatest apostles.

2 Corinthians 12

Those whom God advances to honourable employments he humbles and makes low in their own eyes; and, where God gives grace to be humble, there he gives all other grace. You may also observe in what a different manner the apostle speaks of himself and of his office. *While he magnifies his office, he debases himself.* Observe, a faithful minister of Christ may be very humble, and think very meanly of himself, even when he thinks and speaks very highly and honourably of his sacred function.

Ephesians 3

Paul had a great command of language; they called him Mercury, because he was the chief speaker (Acts 14:12), and yet he would have his friends ask of God the gift of utterance for him. He was a man of great courage, and often signalized himself for it; yet he would have them pray that God would give him boldness. He knew as well what to say as any man; yet he desires them to pray for him, that he may 'speak as he ought to speak'.

Ephesians 6

This is one of the things which 'accompany salvation' — to be able to rejoice that Christ is preached, though it be to the diminution of us and our reputation. This noble spirit appeared in John the Baptist, at the first public preaching of Christ.

Philippians 1

Humility is the great preserver of peace and order in all Christian churches and societies, consequently pride is the great disturber of them, and the cause of most dissensions and breaches in the church.

1 Peter 5

Husbands and Wives

She shall be subject, but it shall be to her own husband who loves her, not to a stranger, or an enemy: The sentence was not a curse to bring her to ruin, but a chastisement to bring her to repentance. It is well that enmity was not to be between the man and the woman, as there was between the serpent and the woman.

Genesis 3

Hymn Singing

Some have made it an objection against singing David's psalms that there are many who cannot say 'My heart is not haughty' etc. . . It is true there are, but we may sing it for the same purpose that we read it, to teach and admonish ourselves, and one another, what we ought to be, with repentance that we have come short of being so, and humble prayer to God for his grace to make us so.

Psalm 131

Hypocrisy

It is allowed that he has gained by his hypocrisy, has gained the praise and applause of men and the wealth of the world. Jehu gained a kingdom by his hypocrisy and the Pharisees many a widow's house. Upon this gain he builds his hope, such as it is. He hopes he is in good circumstances for another world, because he finds he is so for this, and he blesses himself in his own way. The wealth of this world, which he hoped in, he must leave behind him (Ps. 49: 17). The happiness of the other world, which he hoped for, he will certainly miss of.

Job 27

See the nature of hypocrisy: it lies in the heart, which is for the world and the flesh when the outside seems to be for God and religion.

Job 36

Note, a secret disaffection to God is often disguised with the specious colours of respect to him; and those who are resolved that they will not trust God yet pretend that they will not tempt him.

Isaiah 7

Great shows of piety and devotion may be found even among those who, though they keep up these forms of godliness, are strangers and enemies to the power of it. But what will such hypocritical services avail? Fasting without reforming and turning away from sin, will never turn away the judgments of God (Jonah 3:10). Notwithstanding this fast, God proceeded in his controversy with this people.

Jeremiah 36

They were not willing that those who saw them in God's house should see them in their own, lest they should see them contradict themselves and undo in private what they did in public.

Ezekiel 8

They did not pray for the favour or grace of God, that God would give them repentance, pardon their sins, and turn away his wrath, but only that he would not take away from them 'their corn and wine'. Note, carnal hearts, in their prayers to God, covet temporal mercies only, and dread and deprecate no other but temporal judgments, for they have no sense of any other.

Hosea 7

It is possible for a man to have his head full of scripture notions, and his mouth full of scripture expressions, while his heart is full of reigning enmity to God and all goodness. The knowledge which the devils have of the Scripture, increases both their mischievousness and their torment.

Matthew 4

The end specifies the action. It is of the last importance in religion, that we be right in our aims, and make eternal things, not temporal, our scope (2 Cor. 4:18). The hypocrite is like the waterman, that looks one way and rows another; the true Christian like the traveller, rather has his journey's end in his eye. The hypocrite soars like the kite, with his eye upon the prey below, which he is ready to come down to when he has a fair opportunity; the true Christian soars like the lark, higher and higher, forgetting the things that are beneath.

Matthew 6

There is no judging of men by their loose sayings; but by their fruits ye shall know them. Piety from the teeth outward is an easy thing. The most fair-spoken hypocrite cannot say better than to call Jesus the Son of God, and yet that the devil did.

Mark 5

Those who pretend subjection to Christ, but at the same time give themselves up to the service of the world and the flesh, do, in effect, the same that they did, who bowed the knee to him in mockery, and abused him with, 'Hail, king of the Jews', when they said, 'We have no king but Caesar'. Those that bow the knee to Christ, but do not bow the soul, that 'draw nigh to him with their mouths, and honour him with their lips, but their hearts are far from him', put the same affront upon him that these here did.

Mark 15

It is gross hypocrisy to condemn that in those who reprove us which yet we allow in those that flatter us.

It is not furnished with any true grace, but garnished with the pictures of all graces. Simon Magus was garnished with faith, Balaam with good desires, Herod with a respect for John, the Pharisees with many external performances. It is garnished, but it is like a 'potsherd covered with silver dross', it is all paint and varnish, not real, not lasting. The house is garnished, but the property is not altered; it was never surrendered to Christ, nor inhabited by the Spirit.

Luke 11

Christ's disciples were, for aught we know, the best men then in the world, yet they needed to be cautioned against hypocrisy.

Luke 12

He had no compassion towards them, no concern for them: what were the poor to him any further than he might serve his own ends by being overseer of the poor? Thus some warmly contend for the power of the church, as others for its purity, when perhaps it may be said, not that they care for the church; it is all one to them

whether its true interest sink or swim, but under the pretence of this they are advancing themselves. Simeon and Levi pretended zeal for circumcision, not that they cared for the seal of the covenant, any more than Jehu for the Lord of hosts, when he said, 'Come see my zeal'.

John 12

Those that boast of good works they never did, or promise good works they never do, or make the good works they do more or better than really they are, come under the guilt of Ananias's lie, which it concerns us all to dread the thought of.

Acts 5

Their words and speeches have a show of holiness and zeal for God. (It is an easy thing to be godly from the teeth outward).

Romans 16

In a vain religion there is much censuring, reviling, and detracting of others.

. . . When we hear people ready to speak of the faults of others, or to censure them as holding scandalous errors, or to lessen the wisdom and piety of those about them, that they themselves may seem the wiser and better, this is a sign that they have but a vain religion.

. . . Censuring is a pleasing sin, extremely compliant with nature, and therefore evinces a man's being in a natural state.

James 1

One would think to be once dead were enough; we none of

us, till grace renew us to a higher degree than ordinary, love to think of dying once, though this is appointed for us all. What then is the meaning of this being twice dead? They had been once dead in their natural, fallen, lapsed state; but they seemed to recover, and, as a man in a swoon, to be brought to life again, when they took upon them the profession of the Christian religion. But now they are dead again by the evident proofs they have given of their hypocrisy: Whatever they seemed, they had nothing truly vital in them.

Jude

Hypocrites

Balak pretended to honour the Lord with his sacrifices and to wait for the answer God would send him and yet when it didn't prove according to his mind he forgot God and flew into a great passion against Balaam as if it had been purely his doing. 'What hast thou done unto me'. 'How hast thou disappointed me'. Sometimes God makes the enemies of his Church a vexation one to another while he that sits in Heaven laughs at them and the efforts of their impotent malice.

Numbers 23

It is common for those that deny the power of godliness to boast of the form of it.

2 Chronicles 13

The hope of the hypocrite is woven out of his own bowels; it is the creature of his own fancy, and arises merely from a conceit of his own merit and sufficiency. There is a great deal of difference between the work of the bee and that of the spider. A diligent Christian, like the laborious bee, fetches in all his comfort from the heavenly dews of God's word; but the hypocrite, like the subtle spider, weaves out of a false hypothesis of his own concerning God, as if he were altogether such a one as himself.

Job 8

Those are hypocrites who, though they profess religion, neither take pleasure in it nor persevere in it, who reckon their religion a task and a drudgery, a weariness, and snuff at it, who make use of it only to serve a turn, and lay it aside when the turn is served, who will call upon God while it is in fashion, or while the pang of devotion lasts, but leave it off when they fall into other company, or when the hot fit is over.

Job 27

It is common for unhumbled hearts to be proud of their professions of humiliation, as the Pharisee (Luke 18:12), 'I fast twice in the week'. Observe what they expected from their performances. They thought God should take great notice of them, and own himself a debtor to them for their services. Note, it is a common thing for hypocrites, while they perform the external services of religion, to promise themselves that acceptance with God which he has promised only to the sincere; as if they must be accepted of course, or for a compliment.

Isaiah 58

They were weary of holy duties because their worldly business stood still the while; in this they were as in their element, but in God's sanctuary as a fish upon dry ground. Note, those are strangers to God, and enemies to themselves, that love market days better than Sabbath days, that would rather be selling corn than worshipping God.

Amos 8

Hypocrites tempt Jesus Christ; they try his knowledge, whether he can discover them through their disguises; they try his holiness and truth, whether he will allow of them in his church; but if they that of old tempted Christ, when he was but darkly revealed, were destroyed of serpents, of how much sorer punishment shall they be thought worthy who tempt him now in the midst of gospel light and love!

Matthew 22

Those are of all sinners most inexcusable that allow themselves in the sins they condemn in others, or in worse. This doth especially touch wicked ministers, who will be sure to have their portion appointed them with hypocrites (Ch. 24:51); for what greater hypocrisy can there be, than to press that upon others, to be believed and done, which they themselves disbelieve and disobey; pulling down in their practice what they build up in their preaching; when in the pulpit, preaching so well that it is a pity they should ever come out; but, when out of the pulpit, living so ill that it is a pity they should ever come in; like bells, that call others to church, but hang out of it themselves; or Mercurial posts, that point the way to others, but stand still themselves.

Matthew 23

When Christ would express the most severe punishment in the other world, he calls it the portion of hypocrites. If there be any place in hell hotter than other, as it is likely there is, it will be the allotment of those that have the form, but hate the power of godliness.

Matthew 24

All their care is to recommend themselves to their neighbours, whom they now converse with, not to approve themselves to Christ, whom they must hereafter appear before; as if any thing will serve, provided it will but serve for the present. Tell them of things not seen as yet, and you are like Lot to his sons-in-law, as one that mocked. They do not provide for hereafter, as the ant does, nor lay up for the time to come (1 Tim. 6:19).

Matthew 25

Idolatry

That creature which we place our happiness in, which we set our affections inordinately upon and which we can by no means find in our hearts to part with, of which we say 'what have we more', *that* we make an idol of. That is put in God's place and is a usurper which we are concerned about as if our life and comfort, our hope and happiness and our all were bound up in it.

Judges 18

They made a mongrel religion of it, worshipped the God of Israel for fear and their own idols for love . . . Our very ignorance concerning these idols teaches us the accomplishment of that word which God has spoken, that these false gods should all perish. (Jer. 10:11). They are all buried in oblivion while the name of the true God shall continue for ever.

2 Kings 17

Those that think one God too little will find two too many, and yet hundreds not sufficient.

Isaiah 2

God put a great honour upon man when, in respect of the powers and faculties of his soul, he made him after the image of God; but man does a great dishonour to God when he makes him, in respect of bodily parts and members, after the image of man.

Isaiah 44

The homage they should have paid to their Prince they paid to the statues that beautified the frontispiece of his palace; they worshipped the creatures instead of him that made them, the servants instead of him that commands them, and the gifts instead of him that gave them. With the queen of heaven they worshipped other gods, images of things not only in heaven above, but in earth beneath, and in the waters under the earth; for those that forsake the true God wander endlessly after false ones.

Jeremiah 7

Whatever creature we dote upon, pay homage to, and put a confidence in, we make an idol of that creature; and whatever we make an idol of we defile ourselves with.

Ezekiel 23

Whatever men make a god of they will mourn for the loss of; and an inordinate sorrow for the loss of any worldly good is a sign we made an idol of it.

Hosea 10

Ignorance

It is good for us to be made sensible of our own ignorance. Some have confessed their ignorance, and those that would not do this have betrayed it. But we must all infer from it what incompetent judges we are of the divine politics, when we understand so little even of the divine mechanics.

Job 37

Darkening the counsels of God's wisdom with our folly is a great affront and provocation to God. Concerning God's counsels we must own that we are without knowledge. They are a deep which we cannot fathom; we are quite out of our element, out of our aim, when we pretend to account for them. Yet we are too apt to talk of them as if we understood them, with a great deal of niceness and boldness; but alas! we do but darken them, instead of explaining them. We confound and perplex ourselves and one another when we dispute of the order of God's decrees, and the designs and reasons and methods, of his operations of providence and grace. A humble faith and sincere obedience shall see further and better into the secret of the Lord than all the philosophy of the schools, and the searches of science, so called.

Job 38

Men think themselves innocent because they are ignorant; so this ruler did. He said, 'All these have I kept from my youth up' (v. 21). He knows no more evil of himself than the Pharisee did (v. 11). He boasts that he began early in a course of virtue, that he had continued in it to this day, and that he had not in any instance transgressed. Had he been acquainted with the extent and spiritual nature of the divine law, and with the workings of his own heart, had he been but Christ's disciple a while, and learned of him, he would have said quite the contrary.

Luke 18

There was a veil upon his glory and upon their understandings; and how could they see through two veils? They wished his blood on them and their children; but, had they known what they did, they would have unwished it again.

Luke 23

Immutability

Thy throne is from generation to generation; the throne of glory, the throne of grace, and the throne of government, all are unchangeable, immovable; and this is matter of comfort to us when the crown has fallen from our head. When the thrones of princes, that should be our protectors, are brought to the dust, and buried in it, God's throne continues still; he still rules the world, and rules it for the good of the church. The Lord reigns, reigns for ever, even thy God, O Zion!

Lamentations 5

The ancient covenant, which seemed to be broken and forgotten, shall be renewed. By their idolatry, it should seem, they had cast God off; by their captivity, it should seem, God had cast them off. But when they were cured of their idolatry, and delivered out of their captivity, God and his Israel own one another again. God, by his good work in them, will make them his people; and then, by the tokens of his goodwill towards them, he will show that he is their God.

Ezekiel 11

The declarations of God's wrath against sinners are as inviolable as the assurances he has given of favour to his people; and the case of such is sad indeed, who have brought it to this issue, that either God must be false or they must be damned.

Ezekiel 24

Impatience

Job's friends, I doubt, had spirits too high to deal with a man in his low condition; and high spirits are impatient of contradiction, and think themselves affronted if all about them do not say as they say; they cannot bear a check, but they call it *the check of their reproach*, and then they are bound in honour to return it, if not to draw upon him that gave it . . . Men often mistake the dictates of their passion for the dictates of their reason, and therefore think they do well to be angry.

Job 20

Impenitence

He fell like him but didn't get up again like him. It is not so much sin as impenitence in sin that ruins men; not so much that they offend as that they do not humble themselves for their offences; not the disease but the neglect of the remedy.

2 Chronicles 33

God had sent them his prophets, to break up their fallow-ground; but they found them as hard and inflexible as the rock, rough and rugged, and they could do no good with them, nor work upon them, and therefore they shall not attempt it any more. They will not be reclaimed, and therefore shall not be reproved, but quite abandoned. Note, those who will not be cultivated as fields and vineyards shall be rejected as barren rocks and deserts (Heb. 6:7, 8).

Amos 6

Imprecatory Psalms

By this it appears that those passages in David's psalms which express his desire of and triumph in the ruin of his enemies, proceeded not from a spirit of revenge nor any irregular passion, but from a holy zeal for the glory of God and the public good for by what he did here when he heard of Saul's death, we may perceive that his natural temper was very tender and that he was kindly affected even to those that hated him.

2 Samuel 1

His prayer for their destruction comes not from a spirit of revenge, but from a spirit of prophecy, by which he foretold that all who rebel against God will certainly be destroyed by their own counsels. If it is a righteous thing with God to recompense tribulation to those that trouble his people, as we are told it is (2 Thess. 1:6), we pray that it may be done whenever we pray, Father thy will be done.

Psalm 5

This is not a prayer of malice, but a prayer of faith; for it has an eye to the word of God, and only desires the performance of that. There is truth in God's threatenings as well as in his promises, and sinners that repent not will find it so to their cost.

Psalm 54

Influence

Those who set bad examples, though they may repent themselves, yet cannot be sure that those who they have drawn into sin by their example, will repent. It is often otherwise.

2 Kings 21

Perhaps he found that his late affinity with the idolatrous house of Ahab and Kingdom of Israel had had a bad influence upon his own kingdom. Many, we may suppose, were emboldened to revolt to idolatry when they saw their reforming king so intimate with idolaters; and therefore he thought himself doubly obliged to do all he could to restore them. If we truly repent of our sin, we shall do our utmost to repair the damage we have any way done by it to religion or the souls of others. We are particularly concerned to recover those that have fallen into sin, or been hardened in it, by our example.

2 Chronicles 19

In this, the people were so forward and zealous that the priests and Levites blushed to see themselves outdone by the commonalty. To see them more ready to bring sacrifices than they were to offer them. This put them upon sanctifying themselves that the work might not stand still for the want of hands to carry it on. The notice we take of the zeal of others should make us ashamed of our own coldness and quicken us not only to do our duty but to do it well and to sanctify ourselves to it.

2 Chronicles 30

Good men's graces are sharpened by converse with those that are good, and bad men's lusts and passions are sharpened by converse with those that are bad, as iron is sharpened by its like, especially by the file. Men are filed, made smooth, and bright, and fit for business (who were rough and dull and inactive), by conversation. This is designed, 1. To recommend to us this expedient for sharpening ourselves, but with a caution to take heed whom we choose to converse with, because the influence upon us is so great, either for the better or the worse. 2. To direct us what we must have in our eye in conversation, namely to improve both others and ourselves, not to pass away time or banter one another, but to provoke one another to love and good works and so to make one another wiser and better.

Proverbs 27

Those that would convince others of and affect them with the word of God must make it appear, even in the most self-denying instances, that they do believe it themselves and are affected with it. If we would rouse others out of their security, and persuade them to sit loose to the world, we must ourselves be mortified to present things and show that we expect the dissolution of them.

Jeremiah 16

The people among whom they live shall be as the grass, which flourishes only by the blessing of God, and not by the art and care of man; they shall be beneficial to those about them by drawing down God's blessings on them, as Jacob on Laban's house, and by cooling and mitigating God's wrath, which otherwise would burn them up, as the dew preserves the grass from being scorched by the sun; so Dr. Pocock; they shall be mild and gentle in their behaviour, like their Master, who comes down 'like rain upon the new-mown grass' (Ps. 72:6).

Micah 5

Their not going in themselves was a hindrance to many; for, they having so great an interest in the people, multitudes rejected the gospel only because their leaders did.

Matthew 23

Here note, 1. The weakness and inconstancy of the best of men, when left to themselves, and how apt they are to falter in their duty to God, out of an undue regard to the pleasing of men. And 2. The great force of bad examples, especially the examples of great men and good men, such as are in reputation for wisdom and honour.

Galatians 2

Ingratitude

The more God gives us the more cheerfully we should serve him. Our abundance should be oil to the wheels of our obedience. God is a master that will be served with gladness and delights to hear us sing at our work. If, when we receive the gifts of God's bounty, we either do not serve him at all or serve him with reluctance, it is a righteous thing with him to make us know the hardships of want and servitude. Those deserve to have cause given them to complain who complain without a cause . . . Blush at thy own folly and ingratitude.

Deuteronomy 28

They had had joy and gladness in their fields and vineyards, singing and shouting at the treading of their grapes. Nothing is said of their praising God for their abundance, and giving him the glory of it. If they had made it the matter of their thanksgiving, they might still have had it the matter of their rejoicing; but they made it the food and fuel of their lusts.

Isaiah 16

The horrid ingratitude that there is in our sins against God and Jesus Christ is a great aggravation of them, and makes them appear exceedingly sinful. See how God argues to this purpose, *(Deut. 32:6; Jer. 2:5; Mic. 6:3).* We must not think it strange if we meet with those who not only hate us without cause, but are our adversaries for our love, (Ps. 35:12; 41:9).

John 10

Injustice

There Jeremiah remained many days, and, for aught that appears, nobody came near him or enquired after him. See what a world this is. The wicked princes, who are in rebellion against God, lie at ease, lie in state in their palaces, while godly Jeremiah, who is in the service of God, lies in pain, in a loathsome dungeon. It is well that there is a world to come.

Jeremiah 37

Inner Resources

He that does so shall be like a

tree planted by the waters, a choice tree, about which great care has been taken to set it in the best soil, so far from being like the heath in the wilderness; he shall be like a tree that spreads out its roots, and thereby is firmly fixed, spreads them out by the rivers, whence it draws abundance of sap, which denotes both the establishment and the comfort which those have who make God their hope; they are easy, they are pleasant, and enjoy a continual security and serenity of mind. A tree thus planted thus watered, shall not see when heat comes, shall not sustain any damage from the most scorching heats of summer; it is so well moistened from its roots that it shall be sufficiently guarded against drought.

Jeremiah 17

Interpreting Providences

Before he describes the temptation in its strength he lays down a great and unquestionable truth, which he resolves to adhere to, and which, if firmly believed, will be sufficient to break the force of temptation. This has been the way of God's people in grappling with this difficulty. Job, before he discourses of this matter, lays down the doctrine of God's omniscience (Job 24:1), Jeremiah the doctrine of His righteousness (Jer. 12:1), another prophet that of His holiness (Hab. 1:13), the psalmist that of his goodness and peculiar favour to his own people (Ps. 73:1), and that is it which Solomon here fastens

upon and resolves to abide by, that, though good and evil seem to be dispensed promiscuously, yet God has a particular care of and concern for his own people: The righteous and the wise, and their works, are in the hand of God, under his special protection and guidance; all their affairs are managed by him for their good.

Ecclesiastes 9

Jealousy

Eliab was now vexed that his younger brother should speak thus boldly against the Philistine which he himself durst not. He knew what honour David already had in the court and if he should now get honour in the camp (from which he thought he had found means effectually to seclude him) (v. 15), the glory of his elder brother would be eclipsed and stained and, therefore (such is the nature of jealousy) he would rather that Goliath should triumph over Israel than that David should be the man that should triumph over him. . . . God, by his grace keep us from such a spirit.

1 Samuel 17

As the elder brother, in the parable of the prodigal, repined at the reception of his younger brother, and complained of his father's generosity to him; so these labourers quarrelled with their master, and found fault, not because they had not enough, so much as because others were made equal with them.

There is a great proneness to

think that we have too little,
and others too much, of the
tokens of God's favour; and
that we do too much, and
others too little, in the work
of God. Very apt we all are to
undervalue the deserts of others,
and to overvalue our own.

If God be better in any respect
to others than to us, yet we
have no reason to complain
while he is so much better to
us than we deserve, in giving
us our penny, though we are
unprofitable servants.

The eye is often both the inlet
and the outlet of this sin. Saul
saw that David prospered, and
he eyed him (1 Sam. 18:9, 15).
It is an evil eye, which is displeased at the good of others,
and desires their hurt. What
can have more evil in it? It is
grief to ourselves, anger to
God, and ill-will to our neighbour; and it is a sin that has
neither pleasure, profit, nor
honour in it.

It is a dislike of his proceedings,
and a displeasure at what he
does, and is pleased with. It is
a direct violation of both the
two great commandments at
once; both that of love to God,
in whose will we should
acquiesce, and love to our
neighbour, in whose welfare we
should rejoice. Thus man's badness takes occasion from God's
goodness to be more exceedingly
sinful.

Matthew 20

Joy

Abraham laughed. It was a
laughter of delight, not of distrust. Even the promises of a
holy God, as well as his performances, are the joys of holy
souls; there is the joy of faith
as well as the joy of fruition.

Genesis 17

We must rejoice in God not
only because of what we have
received and are receiving from
him daily but because of what
he has promised and we expect
to receive yet further from
him. Because 'He shall bless
thee' therefore 'thou shalt
rejoice'. Those that make God
their Joy may rejoice in hope
for he is faithful that has
promised.

Deuteronomy 16

The joy of the Lord will arm
us against the assaults of our
spiritual enemies, and put our
mouths out of taste for those
pleasures with which the
tempter baits his hooks.

Nehemiah 8

'Thou hast hereby often put
gladness into my heart; not
only supported and refreshed
me, but filled me with joy
unspeakable; and therefore this
is what I will still pursue, what
I will seek after all the days of
my life'. When God puts grace
in the heart he puts gladness
in the heart; nor is any joy
comparable to that which
gracious souls have in the
communications of the divine
favour, no, not the joy of
harvest, of a plentiful harvest,
when the corn and wine
increase. This is gladness in the
heart, inward, solid, substantial
joy. The mirth of worldly
people is but a flash, a shadow;

149

even in laughter their heart is sorrowful (Prov. 14:13). 'Thou hast given gladness in my heart' so the word is. True joy is God's gift, not as the world giveth, (John 14:27). The saints have no reason to envy carnal worldlings their mirth and joy, but should pity them rather.

Psalm 4

They were required to be cheerful and pleasant, and to rejoice before God in all their approaches to him (Deut. 12:12). They had many feasts and good days, but only one day in all the year in which they were to afflict their souls.

Isaiah 43

'The garments of praise', such beautiful garments as were worn on thanksgiving days, instead of the 'spirit of heaviness', dimness or contraction — open joys for secret mournings. The 'spirit of heaviness' they keep to themselves (Zion's mourners weep in secret); but the joy they are recompensed with, they are clothed with as with a garment in the eye of others. Observe, where God gives the oil of joy, he gives the garment of praise.

Isaiah 61

The perishing of the harvest is the withering of the joy of the children of men. Those that place their happiness in the delights of sense, when they are deprived of them, or in any way disturbed in the enjoyment of them, lose all their joy; whereas the children of God, who look upon the pleasures of sense with holy indifference and contempt, and know what it is to make God their hearts'

delight, can rejoice in him as the 'God of their salvation' even when the 'fig tree does not blossom'; spiritual joy is so far from withering then, that it flourishes more than ever (Hab. 3:17, 18).

Joel 1

Joy in God is never out of season, nay, it is in a special manner seasonable when we meet with losses and crosses in the world, that it may then appear that our hearts are not set upon these things, nor our happiness bound up in them.

Habakkuk 3

The trouble of his soul was designed to ease the trouble of our souls; for, after this, he said to his disciples (ch. 14:1), 'Let not your hearts be troubled'; why should yours be troubled and mine too? Our Lord Jesus went on cheerfully in his work, in prospect of the joy set before him, and yet submitted to a trouble of soul. Holy mourning is consistent with spiritual joy, and the way to eternal joy.

John 12

They rejoiced, not only though they suffered shame (their troubles did not diminish their joy), but 'that they suffered shame'; *their troubles increased their joy, and added to it*. If we suffer ill for doing well, provided we suffer it well, and as we should, we ought to rejoice in that grace which enables us so to do.

Acts 5

Carnal joy puffs up the soul, but cannot fill it; therefore in laughter the heart is sad. True, heavenly, spiritual joy is filling to the soul; it has a satisfaction in it, answerable to the soul's vast and just desires. Thus does God satiate and replenish the weary soul. Nothing more than this joy, only more of it, even the perfection of it in glory, is the desire of the soul that hath it (Ps. 4:6, 7; 36:8; 63:5; 65:4).

Romans 15

It is the will of God that good Christians should be much in rejoicing; and those who are happy in good ministers have a great deal of reason to joy and rejoice with them. If the minister loves the people, and is willing to spend and be spent for their welfare, the people have reason to love the minister and to 'joy and rejoice with him'.

Philippians 2

It is our duty and privilege to rejoice in God, and to rejoice in him always; at all times, in all conditions; even when we suffer for him, or are afflicted by him. We must not think the worse of him or of his ways for the hardships we meet with in his service. *There is enough in God to furnish us with matter of joy in the worst circumstances on earth.*

Philippians 4

We must not sink into a sad and disconsolate frame of mind, which would make us faint under our trials; but we must endeavour to keep our spirits dilated and enlarged, the better to take in a true sense of our case, and with greater advantage to set ourselves to make the best

of it. Philosophy may instruct men to be calm under their troubles; but Christianity teaches them to be joyful, because such exercises proceed from love and not fury in God.

. . . There is the more reason for joy in afflictions if we consider the other graces that are promoted by them.

James 1

Every sound Christian has always something wherein he may greatly rejoice. Great rejoicing contains more than an inward placid serenity of mind or sensation of comfort; it will show itself in the countenance and conduct, but especially in praise and gratitude. The chief joy of a good Christian arises from things spiritual and heavenly, from his relation to God and to heaven. In these every sound Christian greatly rejoices; his joy arises from his treasure, which consists of matters of great value, and the title to them is sure.

1 Peter 1

The mystery of the Christian religion is directly calculated for the joy of mortals. It should be joy to us that the eternal Son should come to seek and save us, that he has made a full atonement for our sins, that he has conquered sin and death and hell, that he lives as our Intercessor and Advocate with the Father, and that he will come again to perfect and glorify his persevering believers. And therefore those live beneath the use and end of the Christian revelation who are not filled with spiritual joy. Believers should rejoice in their happy relation to God, as his sons and heirs, his beloved and adopted — in their happy relation to the Son of the Father, as being members of his beloved body, and co-heirs with himself — in the pardon of their sins, the sanctification of their natures, the adoption of their persons, and the prospect of grace and glory that will be revealed at the return of their Lord and head from heaven.

1 John 1

Judging Others

We cannot judge what men are by what they have been formerly nor what they will do by what they have done; age and experience may make men wiser and better. Those that had sold Joseph would not now abandon Benjamin.

Genesis 44

It is true, there may be overdoing in well-doing; but thence we must learn to be cautious ourselves, lest we run into extremes, but not to be censorious of others; because that which we may impute to the want of prudence, God may accept as an instance of abundant love. We must not say, those do too much in religion, that do more than we do, but rather aim to do as much as they.

Matthew 26

He is not to be understood of judging by persons in authority, within the verge of their office, nor of private judging concerning facts that are notorious; but of judging

persons' future state, or the secret springs and principles of their actions, or about facts doubtful in themselves. To judge in these cases, and give decisive sentence, is to assume the seat of God and challenge his prerogative. Note, how bold a sinner is the forward and severe censurer! How ill-timed and arrogant are his censures!

1 Corinthians 4

Judgment

But those as much deceive themselves who think to escape God's judgments as those who think to brave them. The feet of him that flees from them will as surely fail as the hands of him that fights against them.

2 Kings 25

God has weapons of all sorts; he has both *whet his sword and bent his bow* (Ps. 7; 12, 13); he can deal with his enemies *cominus vel eminus* — at hand or afar off. He has a sword for those that think to fight it out with him by their strength, and a bow for those that think to avoid him by their craft. See (Isa. 24; 17, 18; Jer. 48, 43, 44). He that is marked for ruin, though he may escape one judgment, will find another ready for him.

Job 20

Sometimes God makes an idolatrous nation, that serves him not at all, a scourge to a hypocritical nation, that serves him not in sincerity and truth.

Isaiah 10

Great laughters commonly end

in a sigh. Those that make the world their chief joy cannot rejoice evermore. When God sends his judgments into the earth he designs thereby to make those serious that were wholly addicted to their pleasures.

Isaiah 24

The hair that would not be trimmed and kept neat and clean by the admonitions of the prophets must be all shaved off by utter destruction. Those will be ruined that will not be reformed.

When God is dishonoured by the sins of men, he is said to be grieved (Ps. 95:10), so when he is honoured by their destruction he is said to be comforted. The struggle between mercy and judgment is over, and in this case judgment triumphs, triumphs indeed; for mercy that has been so long abused is now silent and gives up the cause, has not a word more to say on the behalf of such an ungrateful incorrigible people: 'My eye shall not spare, neither will I have any pity (v. 11). Divine compassion defers the punishment, or mitigates it; but here is judgment without mercy, wrath without any mixture or allay of pity.

Ezekiel 5

They had been under the rebukes of Providence for their sins, and yet they persisted in them (v. 27): 'I have stretched out my hand over thee', to threaten and frighten thee. So God did before he laid his hand upon them to ruin and destroy them; and that is his usual method, to try to bring men to repentance first by less judgments. He did so here. Before he brought such a famine upon them as broke the staff of bread he 'diminished their ordinary food', cut them short before he cut them off. When the overplus is abused, it is just with God to diminish that which is for necessity. Before he delivered them to the Chaldeans to be destroyed he delivered them to the 'daughters of the Philistines' to be ridiculed.

In the account which impenitent sinners shall be called to they will be told not only of the mercies for which they have been ungrateful, but of the afflictions under which they have been incorrigible (Amos 4:11).

Ezekiel 16

In the 'day of the revelation of the righteous judgment of God', which is now clouded and eclipsed, 'the righteousness of the righteous' shall appear before all the world to be 'upon him', to his everlasting comfort and honour, upon him as a robe, upon him as a crown; and the 'wickedness of the wicked' shall be 'upon him', to his everlasting confusion, upon him as a chain, upon him as a load, as a mountain of lead to sink him to the bottomless pit.

Ezekiel 18

It is a sad and sore judgment for any man to be let alone in sin, for God to say concerning a sinner, 'He is joined to his idols, the world and the flesh; he is incurably proud, covetous, or profane, an incurable drunkard or adulterer; let him alone; conscience, let him alone; minister, let him alone; providences, let him alone. Let nothing awaken him till the flames of hell do it.' The father corrects not the rebellious son any more when he determines to disinherit him. Those that are not disturbed in their sin will be destroyed for their sin.

Hosea 4

Oh that we could with an eye of faith see the flying roll of God's curse hanging over the guilty world as a thick cloud, not only keeping off the sunbeams of God's favour from them, but big with thunders, lightnings, and storms, ready to destroy them! How welcome then would the tidings of a Saviour be, who came to 'redeem us from the curse of the law' by being himself 'made a curse for us', and, like the prophet, 'eating this roll!' The vast length and breadth of this roll intimate what a multitude of curses sinners lie exposed to.

Zechariah 5

Though they were situated in a country like the garden of the Lord, yet, if in such a fruitful soil they abound in sin, God can soon turn a fruitful land into barrenness and a well-watered country into dust and ashes. Observe, No political union or confederacy can keep off judgments from a sinful people. Sodom and the neighbouring cities were no more secured by their regular government than the angels by the dignity of their nature or the old world by their vast number.

... Most heinous sins bring most grievous judgments. Those who were abominable in their vices were remarkable for their plagues. Those who are sinners exceedingly before the Lord must expect the most dreadful vengeance. The punishment of sinners in former ages is designed for the example of those who come after.

2 Peter 2

Observe, 1. The greatest calamities that can befall men will not bring them to repentance without the grace of God working with them. 2. Those that are not made better by the judgments of God are always the worse for them. 3. To be hardened in sin and enmity against God by his righteous judgments is a certain token of utter destruction.

Revelation 16

Judicial Blindness

If we shut our eyes against the light of divine truth, it is just with God to hide from our eyes the things that belong to our peace; and, if we use not our eyes as we should, it is just with him to let us be as if we had no eyes.

Isaiah 59

Justice

Though God has hardened Pharaoh's heart, yet Moses must repeat his applications to him. God suspends his grace and yet demands obedience to punish him for requiring bricks of the children of

Israel when he denied them straw.

Exodus 9

No life in it might be ransomed upon any terms; they must all be surely put to death (Lev. 27, 29); so he appoints from whom as creatures they had received their lives and to whom as sinners they had forfeited them and who may dispute his sentence? . . . God forbid we should entertain such a thought.

Joshua 6

Jeroboam did not deserve so good a post, but Israel deserved so bad a prince.

1 Kings 11

Ahaz walked in the ways of the kings of Israel and the king of Israel was the instrument God made use of for his punishment. It is just with God to make those our plagues whom we make our pattern or make ourselves partners with in sin. Vast numbers were slain and some of the first rank; the king's son for one. He had sacrificed some of his sons to Moloch, justly therefore is this sacrificed to the divine vengeance.

2 Chronicles 28

It is just with God to make men want that for necessity which they have abused to excess.

Isaiah 5

It is just with God to disappoint those expectations of mercy which his providence had given cause for when we disappoint those expectations of duty which our professions, pretensions, and fair promises, had given cause for. If we repent of the good we had purposed, God will repent of the good he had purposed. 'With the froward thou wilt show Thyself froward.'

Jeremiah 34

I will deal with them as they deserve. There needs no more than this to speak God righteous, that he does but render to men according to their deserts: and yet such are the deserts of sin that there needs no more than this to speak the sinner miserable.

Ezekiel 11

If God did this to the Son of his love, when he found sin but imputed to him, what shall he do to the generation of his wrath, when he finds sin reigning in them? If the father was pleased in doing these things to the green tree, why should he be loth to do it to the dry? Note, the consideration of the bitter sufferings of our Lord Jesus should engage us to stand in awe of the justice of God, and to tremble before him.

Luke 23

Mercy and truth are so met together, righteousness and peace have so kissed each other, that it is now become not only an act of grace and mercy, but an act of righteousness, in God, to pardon the sins of penitent believers, having accepted the satisfaction that Christ by dying made to his justice for them.

Romans 3

Justification

God is said to 'cast sin behind his back, to hide his face from it', which, and the like expressions, imply that the ground of our blessedness is not our innocency, or our not having sinned (a thing is, and is filthy, though covered; justification does not make the sin not to have been, or not to have been sin), but God's not laying it to our charge.

Romans 4

The apostle having at large asserted, opened, and proved, the great doctrine of justification by faith, for fear lest any should suck poison out of that sweet flower, and turn that grace of God into wantonness and licentiousness, he, with a like zeal, copiousness of expression, and cogency of argument, presses the absolute necessity of sanctification and a holy life, as the inseparable fruit and companion of justification; for, wherever Jesus Christ is made of God unto any soul righteousness, he is made of God unto that soul sanctification (1 Cor. 1:30). The water and the blood came streaming together out of the pierced side of the dying Jesus. And what God hath thus joined together let not us dare to put asunder.

Romans 6

Kindness

Though Abner was David's enemy and opposed his coming to the throne yet David would not oppose the preferment of his son but perhaps nominated him to this post of honour, which teaches us to render good for evil.

1 Chronicle 27

Knowing God

It is here promised, 'I will give them', not so much a head to know Me, but 'a heart to know Me', for the right knowledge of God consists not in notion and speculation, but in the convictions of the practical judgment directing and governing the will and affections. 'A good understanding have all those that do his commandments' (Ps. 111:10). Where God gives a sincere desire and inclination to know him he will give that knowledge. It is God himself that gives a heart to know him, else we should perish for ever in our ignorance.

Jeremiah 24

He prostrated himself in a humble sense of his own unworthiness of the honour now done him, and of the infinite distance which he now, more than ever, perceived to be between him and God; he fell upon his face in token of that holy awe and reverence of God with which his mind was possessed and filled. The more God is pleased to make known of himself to us, the more low we should be before him. He fell upon his face to adore the majesty of God, to implore his mercy and to deprecate the wrath he saw ready to break out against the children of his people.

Ezekiel 1

Knowledge

Our first parents, who knew so much did not know this, that they knew enough.

Genesis 3

Knowledge is the mother of devotion and of all obedience: blind sacrifices will never please a seeing God.

Psalm 100

The best way to improve in knowledge is to abide and abound in all the instances of serious godliness, for, 'If any man do his will, he shall know of the doctrine' of Christ, shall know more and more of it, (John 7:17). The love of the truth prepares for the light of it; 'the pure in heart shall see God' here.

Those that know much of the Word of God should still covet to know more; for there is more to be known. He does not say, 'Give me a further revelation,' but, 'Give me a further understanding'; what is revealed we should desire to understand, and what we know, to know better; and we must go to God for a heart to know.

Psalm 119

God is to be feared, to be reverenced, served, and worshipped; this is so the beginning of knowledge that those know nothing who do not know this. In order to the attaining of all useful knowledge this is most necessary, that we fear God; we are not qualified to profit by the instructions that are given us unless our minds be possessed with a holy reverence of God,

and every thought within us be brought into obedience to him.

Proverbs 1

The minds and manners of men are crooked and perverse. Solomon thought, with his wisdom and power together, thoroughly to reform his kingdom, and make that straight which he found crooked; but he was disappointed. All the philosophy and politics in the world will not restore the corrupt nature of man to its primitive rectitude; we find the insufficiency of them both in others and ourselves. Learning will not alter men's natural tempers, nor cure them of their sinful distempers; nor will it change the constitution of things in this world; a vale of tears it is and so it will be when all is done.

Ecclesiastes 1

Many a plain, honest, unlearned disciple of Christ, by meditation, experience, prayers, and especially obedience, attains to a more clear, sound, and useful knowledge of the word of God, than some great scholars with all their wit and learning. Thus David came to understand more than the ancients and all his teachers (Ps. 119:99, 100).

John 7

Large-Heartedness

He did not stay till they applied to him to beg for a night's lodging; but when he saw them (v. 17) enquired into their circumstances, and anticipated them with his kindness. A charitable disposition expects only opportunity,

not importunity, to do good.
Judges 19

The miseries of our country ought to be very much the grief of our souls. A gracious spirit will be a public spirit, a tender spirit, a mourning spirit. It becomes us to lament the miseries of our fellow-creatures, much more to lay to heart the calamities of our country, and especially of the church of God, to grieve for the affliction of Joseph. Jeremiah had prophesied the destruction of Jerusalem, and, though the truth of his prophecy was questioned, yet he did not rejoice in the proof of the truth of it by the accomplishment of it, preferring the welfare of his country before his own reputation. If Jerusalem had repented and been spared, he would have been far from fretting as Jonah did. Jeremiah had many enemies in Judah and Jerusalem, that hated, and reproached, and persecuted him; and in the judgments brought upon them God reckoned with them for it and pleaded his prophet's cause; yet he was far from rejoicing in it, so truly did he forgive his enemies and desire that God would forgive them.
Jeremiah 8

It is God's prerogative to judge of the principles men act upon; this is out of our line. Paul was so far from envying those who had liberty to preach the gospel while he was under confinement that he rejoiced in the preaching of it even by those who do it in pretence, and not in truth. How much more then should we rejoice in the preaching of the gospel by those who do it in truth, yea, though it should be with much weakness and some mistake!
Philippians 1

They were already possessed in some degree of these blessings, and he wishes them the continuation, the increase, and the perfection of them. Those who possess spiritual blessings in their own souls earnestly desire the communication of the same to others. The grace of God is a generous, not a selfish principle.
1 Peter 1

Law

The glass discovers the spots, but does not cause them. When the commandment came into the world sin revived, as the letting of a clearer light into a room discovers the dust and filth, which were there before, but were not seen.
Romans 5

As that which is straight discovers that which is crooked, as the looking-glass shows us our natural face with all its spots and deformities, so there is no way of coming to that knowledge of sin which is necessary to repentance, and consequently to peace and pardon, but by comparing our hearts and lives with the law.
Romans 7

The moral law was but for the searching of the wound, the ceremonial law for the shadowing forth of the remedy; but Christ is the end of both.
Romans 10

It is the grace of God that changes men's hearts; but the terrors of the law may be of use to tie their hands and restrain their tongues.

1 Timothy 1

Law and Grace

One of the first miracles Moses wrought was turning water into blood, but one of the first miracles our Lord Jesus wrought was turning water into wine; for the law was given by Moses and it was a dispensation of death and terror; but Grace and Truth which, like wine, make glad the heart came by Jesus Christ.

Exodus 7

By the touch of a leper ceremonial uncleanness was contracted. Everyone, therefore, was concerned to avoid it and the leper himself must give notice of the danger and this was all that the law could do in that it was weak through the flesh. It taught the leper to cry 'Unclean, Unclean' but the gospel has put another cry into lepers' mouths (Luke 17, 12—13), where we find ten lepers crying with a loud voice 'Jesus, Master, have mercy on us.' The law only shows us our disease; the gospel shows us our help in Christ.

Leveticus 13

Law and Order

What was the cause of this corruption? There was no king in Israel, no judge or sovereign prince to take (notice) of the setting up of these images (which doubtless the country about soon resorted to) and to give orders for the destroying of them, none to convince Micah of his error and to restrain and punish him, to take this disease in time by which the spreading of the infection might have been happily prevented. Every man did that which was right in his own eyes and then they soon did that which was evil in the sight of the Lord.

Judges 17

God is greatly offended with corruptions, not only in his own worship, but in the administration of justice between man and man, and the dishonesty of a people shall be the ground of his controversy with them as well as their idolatry and impiety; for God's laws are intended for man's benefit and the good of the community, as well as for God's honour, and the profanation of courts of justice shall be avenged as surely as the profanation of temples.

Hosea 10

The prophet complains that, Providence having delivered up the weaker to be a prey to the stronger, they were, in effect, made as 'the fishes of the sea' (v. 14). So they had been among themselves, preying upon one another as the greater fishes do upon the less (v. 3), and they were made so to the common enemy. They were 'as the creeping things', or swimming things (for the word is used for fish, Gen. 1:20), 'that have no ruler' over them, either to restrain them from devouring one another or to protect them from being devoured by their enemies.

Habakkuk 1

Leaving a Will

In the morning of youth lay out thyself to do good; give out of the little thou hast to begin the world with; and in the evening of old age yield not to the common temptation old people are in to be penurious; even then, withhold not thine hand, and think not to excuse thyself from charitable works by purposing to make a charitable will, but do good to the last.

Ecclesiastes 11

Legalism

The disciples could say little for themselves, especially because those who quarrelled with them seemed to have the strictness of the sabbath sanctification on their side; and it is safest to err on that hand: but Christ came to free his followers, not only from the corruptions of the Pharisees, but from their unscriptural impositions, and therefore has something to say for them, and justifies what they did, though it was a transgression of the canon.

Matthew 12

Lessons from Nature

God waters the earth with that with which he once drowned it, only dispensing it in another manner, to let us know how much we lie at his mercy, and how kind he is, in giving rain by drops that the benefit of it may be the further and the more equally diffused, as by an artificial water-pot.

Job 36

Liberality

'Give a portion to seven and also to eight', that is, be free and liberal in works of charity. Give much if thou hast much to give, not a pittance, but a portion, not a bit or two, but a mess, a meal; give a large dole, not a paltry one; give good measure (Luke 6:38), be generous in giving, as those were when, on festival days, they sent portions to those for whom nothing was prepared (Neh. 8:10), worthy portions. Give to many, to seven and to eight; if thou meet with seven objects of charity, give to them all, and then, if thou meet with an eighth, give to that, and if with eight more, give to them all too. Excuse not thyself with the good thou hast done from the good thou hast further to do.

Many make use of this as an argument against giving to the poor, because they know not what hard times may come when they may want themselves; whereas we should therefore the rather be charitable, that, when evil days come, we may have the comfort of having done good while we were able; we would then hope to find mercy both with God and man, and therefore should now show mercy. If by charity we trust God with what we have, we put it into good hands against bad times.

Ecclesiastes 11

Here was large money given for the advancing of that which they knew to be a lie, yet many grudge a little money for the advancement of that which they know to be the truth, though they have a promise of being reimbursed in the resurrection of the just. Let us never starve a good cause, when we see a bad one so liberally supported.

Matthew 28

When they were told of a famine at hand, they did not do as the Egyptians, hoard up corn for themselves; but, as became Christians, laid by for charity to relieve others, which is the best preparative for our own sufferings and want. It is promised to those that 'consider the poor that God will preserve them, and keep them alive, and they shall be blessed upon the earth' (Ps. 41:1, 2). And, 'those who show mercy, and give to the poor, shall not be ashamed in the evil time, but in the days of famine they shall be satisfied' (Ps. 37:19, 21). The best provision we can lay up against a dear time is to lay up an interest in these promises, by doing good, and communicating, (Luke 12:33). Many give it as a reason why they should be sparing, but the scripture gives it as a reason why we should be liberal, 'to seven, and also to eight', because 'we know not what evil shall be upon the earth'. (Ecclesiastes 11:2).

Acts 11

Liberty

The Pharisees complained of them to their Master for doing that which it was not lawful to do. Note, those are no friends to Christ and his disciples, who make that to be unlawful which God has not made to be so.

Matthew 12

By this it appears that the ministers of Christ may be of very different tempers and dispositions, very different ways of preaching and living, and yet all good and useful; diversity of gifts, but each given to profit withal. Therefore none must make themselves a standard to all others, nor judge hardly of those that do not do just as they do. John Baptist bore witness to Christ, and Christ applauded John Baptist, though they were the reverse of each other in their way of living.

Luke 7

But when it is insisted on as necessary, and his consenting to it, though only in a single instance, is likely to be improved as giving countenance to such an imposition, he has too great a concern for the purity and liberty of the gospel, to submit to it; he would not yield to those who were for the Mosaic rites and ceremonies, but would stand fast in the liberty wherewith Christ hath made us free, which conduct of his may give us occasion to observe that what under some circumstances may lawfully be complied with, yet, when that cannot be done without betraying the truth, or giving up the liberty of the gospel, it ought to be refused.

Galatians 2

Lies

Men could not arrive at such a pitch of impiety as to bear false witness (where to the guilt of a lie is added that of perjury and injury) if they had not advanced to it by allowing themselves to speak untruths in jest and banter, or under pretence of doing good.

Those that can swallow a false word debauch their consciences, so that a false oath will not choke them.

Proverbs 19

Listening to Sermons

This doctrine is fitly compared to rain and showers which come from above. To make the earth fruitful and accomplish that for which they are sent and depend not upon the wisdom or will of man (Micah 5:7). It is a mercy to have this rain come often upon us and our duty to drink it in (Heb. 6, 7).

Deuteronomy 32

We may expect that God will speak to us when we set ourselves to hearken to what He says. (Ps. 85:8, Hab. 2:1.) When we come to read the Word of God and to attend on the preaching of it, we should come thus disposed submitting ourselves to the commanding light and power of it. 'Speak, Lord, for thy servant heareth'.

1 Samuel 3

He begs that he would hearken to this discourse (v. 14), that he would pause awhile: Stand still and consider the wondrous works of God. What we hear is not likely to profit us unless we consider it, and we are not likely to consider things fully unless we stand still and compose ourselves to the consideration of them.

Job 37

Rebukes to hypocrites ought not to be terrors to the upright.

Psalm 50

God takes notice what returns our hearts make to the calls of his word, what we say and what we think when we have heard a sermon, what answer we give to the message sent us. When God calls us to 'return', we should answer as those did (Jer. 3:22), 'Behold we come'. But not as these here, 'Wherein shall we return?'

Malachi 3

How they come to be unprofitable hearers. The wicked one, that is, the devil, cometh and catcheth away that which was sown — such mindless, careless, trifling hearers are an easy prey to Satan; who, as he is the great murderer of souls, so he is the great thief of sermons, and will be sure to rob us of the word, if we take not care to keep it, as the birds pick up the seed that falls on the ground that is neither ploughed before nor harrowed after. If we break not up the fallow ground, by preparing our hearts for the word, and humbling them to it, and engaging our own attention; and if we cover not the seed afterwards, by meditation and prayer; if we give not a more earnest heed to the things which we have heard, we are as the highway ground. Note, the devil is a sworn enemy to our profiting by the Word of God; and none do more befriend his design than heedless hearers, who are thinking of something else, when they should be thinking of the things that belong to their peace.

The heart is, as the meal, soft and pliable; it is the tender heart that is likely to profit by the word: leaven among corn unground does not work, nor does the gospel in souls unhumbled and unbroken for sin; the law grinds the heart, and then the gospel leavens it.

. . . the meal must be kneaded, before it receive the leaven; our hearts, as they must be broken, so they must be moistened, and pains taken with them to prepare them for the word.

When the woman hides the leaven in the meal, it is with an intention that it should communicate its taste and relish to it; so we must treasure up the word in our souls, that we may be sanctified by it (John 17:17).

Matthew 13

It is good, in hearing the word, to keep the eye fixed upon the minister by whom God is speaking to us; for, as the eye affects the heart, so, usually, the heart follows the eye, and is wandering, or fixed, as that is.

Luke 4

How many are there in the midst of our assemblies, where the gospel is preached, that do not sit under the word, but sit by!

It is to them as a tale that is told them, not as a message that is sent them; they are willing that we should preach before them, not that we should preach to them.

Luke 5

They were ready to hear, not whatever he pleased to say, but what he was commanded of God to say. The truths of Christ were not communicated to the apostles to be published or stifled as they thought fit, but entrusted with them to be published to the world. We are ready to hear all, to come at the beginning of the service and stay to the end, and be attentive all the while, else how can we hear all? We are desirous to hear all that thou art commissioned to preach, though it be ever so displeasing to flesh and blood, and ever so contrary to our former notions or present secular interests. We are ready to hear all, and therefore let nothing be kept back that is profitable for us.

Acts 10

It is not enough to remember what we hear, and to be able to *repeat* it, and to *give testimony* to it, and *commend* it, and *write it,* and *preserve* what we have written; that which all this is in order to, and which crowns the rest, is that we be *doers* of the word.

James 1

Living in the Light of Eternity

Daniel sees his kingdom now at its last gasp, and therefore looks with contempt upon his gifts and rewards. And thus should we despise all the gifts and rewards that this world can give, did we see, as we may by faith, its final period hastening on. Let it give its perishing gifts to another; there are better gifts which we have our eyes and hearts upon; but let us do our duty in the world, do it all the real service we can, read God's writing to it in a profession of religion, and by an agreeable conversation make known the interpretation of it, and then trust God for his gifts, his rewards, in comparison with which all the world can give is mere trash and trifles.

Daniel 5

Living Sacrifice

That which pleased God was not the feeding of a beast, and making much of it, but killing it; so it is not the pampering of our flesh, but the mortifying of it, that God will accept. The sacrifice was bound, was bled, was burnt; so the penitent heart is bound by convictions, bleeds in contrition, and then burns in holy zeal against sin and for God. The sacrifice was offered upon the altar that sanctified the gift; so the broken heart is acceptable to God only through Jesus Christ; there is no true repentance without faith in him; and this is the sacrifice which he will not despise. Men despise that which is broken, but God will not. He despised the sacrifice of torn and broken beasts, but he will not despise that of a torn and broken heart.

Psalm 51

Loneliness

It is better to be serving God in solitude than serving sin with a multitude.

Psalm 84

Longsuffering

They began in their apostasy with omissions of good and so proceeded to commissions of evil. In like manner God will first suspend his favours and let them see what the issue of that will be, what a Friend they lose when they provoke God to depart and will try whether this will bring them to repentance.

Deuteronomy 32

We may here admire the grace of God in speaking to them and their obstinacy in turning a deaf ear to him, that either their badness did not quite turn away his goodness but still he waited to be gracious or that his goodness did not turn them from their badness but still they hated to be reformed.

2 Chronicles 33

How bad soever the world is, let us never think the worse of God nor of his government; but, from the abundance of wickedness that is among men, let us take occasion, instead of reflecting upon God's purity, as if he countenanced sin, to admire his patience, that he bears so much with those that so impudently provoke him, nay, and causes his sun to shine and his rain to fall upon them. If God's mercy were not in the heavens (that is, infinitely above the mercies of any creature), he would, long ere this, have drowned the world again. See (Isa. 55:8, 9; Hos. 11:9).

Psalm 36

The remembrance of former sins, notwithstanding which God did not cast off his people, is an encouragement to us to hope that though we are justly corrected for our sins, yet we shall not be utterly abandoned.

Psalm 106

As the supports of life, so the means of grace, are continued to us after they have been a thousand times forfeited.

Ezekiel 2

Parents and masters must not be angry at the forgetfulness of their children and servants, more than is necessary to make them take more heed another time; we are all apt to be forgetful of our duty. This should serve to excuse a fault, 'Peradventure it was an oversight'. See how easily Christ forgave his disciples' carelessness, though it was in such a material point as taking bread; and do likewise. But that which he chides them for is their little faith.

Matthew 16

See what is the language of an obstinate unbelief; it does, in effect, call the holy Jesus a blasphemer. It is hard to say which is more to be wondered at, that men who breathe in God's air should yet speak such things, or that men who have spoken such things should still be suffered to breathe God's air. The wickedness of man, and the patience of God, as it were, contend which shall be most wonderful.

John 10

Lord's Supper

To eat of the feast is to partake of the sacrifice, and so to be his guests to whom the sacrifice was offered, and this in token of friendship with him. Thus to partake of the Lord's table is to profess ourselves his guests and covenant people. This is the very purpose and intention of this symbolical eating and drinking; it is holding communion with God, and partaking of those privileges, and professing ourselves under those obligations, which result from the death and sacrifice of Christ; and this in conjunction with all true Christians, with whom we have communion also in this ordinance.

1 Corinthians 10

Our Saviour, having undertaken to make an offering of himself to God, and procure, by his death, the remission of sins, with all other gospel benefits, for true believers, did, at the institution, deliver his body and blood, *with all the benefits procured by his death,* to his disciples, and continues to do the same every time the ordinance is administered to true believers. This is here exhibited, or set forth, as the food of souls. And as food, though ever so wholesome or rich, will yield no nourishment without being eaten, here the communicants are to take and eat, or to receive Christ and feed upon him, his grace and benefits, and by faith convert them into nourishment to their souls. They are to take him as their Lord and life, yield themselves up to him, and live upon him. 'He is our life' (Col. 3:4).

1 Corinthians 11

Love

This expostulation is grounded upon a great truth that those only have our love, not that have our good words or our good wishes, but that have our hearts. That is love without dissimulation but it is falsehood and flattery of the highest degree to say we love those with whom our hearts are not. How can we say we love either our brother, whom we have seen, or God whom we have not seen, if our hearts be not with him.

Judges 16

It is required that we follow Christ, that we duly attend upon his ordinances, strictly conform to his pattern, and cheerfully submit to his disposals, and by upright and universal obedience observe his statutes, and keep his laws, and all this from a principle of love to him, and dependence on him, and with a holy contempt of everything else in comparison of him, and much more in competition with him. This is to follow Christ fully. To sell all, and give to the poor, will not serve, unless we come, and follow Christ. If I give all my goods to feed the poor, and have not love, it profits me nothing.

Matthew 19

If 'all that a man has he will give for his life', he that gives this for his friend gives all, and can give no more; this may sometimes be our duty (1 John 3:16).

John 15

In the enumeration of these commandments, the apostle puts the seventh before the sixth, and mentions this first, 'Thou shalt not commit adultery'; for though this commonly goes under the name of love (pity it is that so good a word should be so abused) yet it is really as great a violation of it as killing and stealing is, which shows that true brotherly love is love to the souls of our brethren in the first place. He that tempts others to sin, and defiles their minds and consciences, though he may pretend the most passionate love (Prov. 7:15, 18), does really hate them, just as the devil does, who wars against the soul.

Romans 13

A clear and deep head is of no signification, without a benevolent and charitable heart. It is not great knowledge that God sets a value upon, but true and hearty devotion and love.

Faith fixes on the divine revelation, and assents to that: hope fastens on future felicity, and waits for that: and in heaven faith will be swallowed up in vision, and hope in fruition. There is no room to believe and hope, when we see and enjoy. But love fastens on the divine perfections themselves.

In another world, there will

love be made perfect; there we shall perfectly love God, because he will appear amiable for ever, and our hearts will kindle at the sight, and glow with perpetual devotion. And there shall we perfectly love one another, when all the saints meet there, when none but saints are there, and saints made perfect. O blessed state! How much surpassing the best below! O amiable and excellent grace of charity! How much does it exceed the most valuable gift, when it outshines every grace, and is the everlasting consumation of them! When faith and hope are at an end, true charity will burn for ever with the brightest flame. Note, those border most upon the heavenly state and perfection whose hearts are fullest of this divine principle, and burn with the most fervent charity. It is the surest offspring of God.

1 Corinthians 13

Love of Ease

They had no great affection to their own land, and apprehended the difficulties in their way to it insuperable. This proceeded from a bad cause — a distrust of the power and promise of God, a love of ease and worldly wealth, and an indifference to the religion of their country and to the God of Israel himself; and it had a bad effect, for it was a tacit censure of those as foolish, rash, and given to change, that did return, and a weakening of their hands in the work of God. Such as these could not sing (Ps. 137) in their captivity, for they had

'forgotten thee O Jerusalem!' and were so far from preferring thee before their chief joy that they preferred any joy before thee. Here is therefore another proclamation issued out by the God of Israel, strictly charging and commanding all his freeborn subjects, wherever they were dispersed, speedily to return into their own land.

Zechariah 2

Love to God

We must love him 1. With a sincere love, not in word and tongue only saying we love him when our hearts are not with him, but inwardly and in truth . . . 2. With a strong love. The heart must be carried out toward him with great ardour and fervency of affection . . . 3. With a superlative love. We must love God above any creature whatsoever and love nothing besides him but what we love for him . . . 4. With an intelligent love . . . We must know him and, therefore, love him as those that see good cause to love him . . . 5. With an entire love. He is one, and therefore our hearts must be united in this love and the whole stream of our affections must run towards Him. Oh, that this love of God may be shed abroad in our hearts.

Deuteronomy 6

It greatly encouraged his confidence in God that he was conscious to himself of an entire affection to God and to his ordinances, and that he was in his element when in the way of his duty and in the way of increasing his acquaintance with him.

Psalm 27

True Christians have a sincere love to Jesus, because they believe in him. This love discovers itself in the highest esteem for him, affectionate desires after him, willingness to be dissolved to be with him, delightful thoughts, cheerful services and sufferings, etc.

1 Peter 1

Lowering of Standards

They looked no further than the burning of the sacrifice, and they pleaded that it was a pity to burn it if it was good for anything else. The people were so far convinced of their duty that they would bring sacrifices; they durst not wholly omit the duty, but they brought vain oblations, mocked God, and deceived themselves, by bringing the worst they had; and the priests, who should have taught them better, accepted the gifts brought to the altar and offered them up there, because, if they should refuse them, the people would bring none at all, and then they would lose their perquisites; and therefore, having more regard to their own profit than to God's honour, they accepted that which they knew he would not accept.

Malachi 1

Loyalty

If those that lived upon the crown thought themselves bound in gratitude thus to support the interest of it,

much more reason have we thus to argue ourselves into a pious concern for God's honour. We have our maintenance from the God of heaven and are salted with his salt, live upon his bounty and are the care of his providence and, therefore, it is not fit for us to see his dishonour without resenting it and doing what we can to prevent it.

Ezra 4

Lukewarmness

Lukewarmness or indifference in religion is the worst temper in the world. If religion is a real thing, it is the most excellent thing, and therefore we should be in good earnest in it; if it is not a real thing, it is the vilest imposture, and we should be earnest against it. If religion is worth anything, it is worth everything; an indifference here is inexcusable.

Christ expects that men should declare themselves in earnest either for him or against him.

He is sick of them, and cannot long bear them. They may call their lukewarmness 'charity, meekness, moderation', and a 'largeness of soul'; it is nauseous to Christ, and makes those so that allow themselves in it.

Revelation 3

Luxurious Living

The more men place their happiness in the gratification of sense the more pressing temporal afflictions are upon them. The drinkers of water needed not to care when the vine was laid waste; they could live as well without it as they had done; it was no trouble to the Nazarites. But the 'drinkers of wine' will 'weep and howl'. The more delights we make necessary to our satisfaction the more we expose ourselves to trouble and disappointment.

Joel 1

Man Helpless Before God's Judgments

Giants are but worms before God's Power.

Numbers 21

Balaam in his fury wished he had a sword to kill his ass with. See his impotency! Can he think by his curses to do mischief to Israel that has it not in his power to kill his own ass. This he cannot do . . . and what would he get by that but make himself so much the poorer (as many do) to gratify his passion and revenge.

Numbers 22

God is lord of hosts, has all creatures at his command, and, when he pleases, can humble and mortify a proud and rebellious people by the weakest and most contemptible creatures. Man is said to be a worm; and by this it appears that he is less than a worm, for, when God pleases, worms are too hard for him, plunder his country, eat up that for which he laboured, destroy the forage, and cut off the subsistence of a potent nation. The weaker the instrument is that God employs, the more is his power magnified.

Joel 1

Manifestations

It is observable that before Peter and John came to the sepulchre an angel had appeared there, rolled away the stone, frightened the guard, and comforted the women; as soon as they were gone from the sepulchre, Mary Magdalene here sees two angels in the sepulchre (v. 12), and yet Peter and John come to the sepulchre, and go into it, and see none. What shall we make of this? Where were the angels when Peter and John were at the sepulchre, who appeared there before and after? Angels appear and disappear at pleasure, according to the orders and instructions given them. They may be, and are really, where they are not visibly; nay, it should seem, may be visible to one and not to another, at the same time (Num. 22:23; 2 Kings 6:17). How they make themselves visible, then invisible, then visible again, it is presumption for us to enquire; but that they do so is plain from this story.

John 20

Marks of Grace

God's putting His law in our hearts and writing it in our inward parts furnish the surest evidence of our reconciliation to God and the best earnest of our happiness in Him. Moses is told to hew the tables; for the law prepares the heart by conviction and humiliation for the grace of God but it is only that grace that then writes the law in it.

Deuteronomy 10

The law of God written in the heart is a certain evidence of the love of God shed abroad there; we must reckon God's law one of the gifts of his grace.

Deuteronomy 33

Lamenting after God is as sure an evidence that we love him as rejoicing in God.

Psalm 42

Marriage

He that will not be counselled cannot be helped. It is especially prudent for young people to take advice in their marriages as Joash did who left it to his guardian to choose him his wives because Jezebel and Athaliah had been such plagues. This is a turn of life that often proves either the making or the marring of young people and therefore should be attended to with great care.

2 Chronicles 24

The relation between husband and wife is nearer than that between parents and children; now, if the filial relation may not easily be violated, much less may the marriage union be broken. May a child desert his parents, or may a parent abandon his children, for any cause, for every cause? No, by no means. Much less may a husband put away his wife, betwixt whom, though not by nature, yet by divine appointment, the relation is nearer, and the bond of union stronger, than between parents and children; for that is in a great measure superseded by marriage, when a man must leave his parents, to cleave to

his wife. See here the power of divine institution, that the result of it is a union stronger than that which results from the highest obligations of nature.

A man's children are pieces of himself, but his wife is himself. As the conjugal union is closer than that between parents and children, so it is in a manner equivalent to that between one member and another in the natural body. As this is a reason why husbands should love their wives, so it is a reason why they should not put away their wives; for no man ever yet hated his own flesh, or cut it off, but nourishes and cherishes it, and does all he can to preserve it. They two shall be one, therefore there must be but one wife, for God made but one Eve for one Adam (Mal. 2:15).

Matthew 19

It is very desirable, when there is a marriage, to have Jesus Christ present at it; to have his spiritual gracious presence, to have the marriage owned and blessed by him: the marriage is then honourable indeed; and they that marry in the Lord (1 Cor. 7:39) do not marry without him. They that would have Christ with them at their marriage must invite him by prayer; that is the messenger that must be sent to heaven for him; and he will come: 'Thou shalt call, and I will answer'. And he will turn the water into wine.

John 2

Material Prosperity

God gives and preserves outward blessings to wicked men to

show that these are not the best things but he has better in store for his own children.

Deuteronomy 2

Cedars, that used to be great rarities, were as common as sycamore trees. Such is the nature of worldly wealth, plenty of it makes it the less valuable; much more should the enjoyment of spiritual riches lessen our esteem of all earthly possessions.

1 Kings 10

'They were filled and their heart was exalted.' Their luxury and sensuality made them proud, insolent and secure. The best comment upon this is that of Moses (Deut. 32:13—15). But 'Jeshurun waxed fat and kicked'. When the body was stuffed up with plenty the soul was puffed up with pride. Then they began to think their religion a thing below them, and they could not persuade themselves to stoop to the services of it.

Worldly prosperity, when it feeds men's pride, makes them forgetful of God; for they remember Him only when they want Him. When Israel was filled, what more could the Almighty do for them?

Hosea 13

Means of Grace

Though the form and profession of godliness are kept up by many without the life and power of it, yet the life and power of it will not long be kept up without the form and profession. You take away grace

if you take away the means of grace.

Joshua 22

Let us not think it enough to pass through them, but let us lie down in them, abide in them; this is my rest for ever. It is by a constancy of the means of grace that the soul is fed.

Psalm 23

Those are mistaken who think that when they have robbed us of our Bibles, and our ministers, and our solemn assemblies, they have robbed us of our God; for, though God has tied us to them when they are to be had, he has not tied himself to them. We know where our God is, and where to find him, when we know not where his ark is, nor where to find that. Wherever we are, there is a way open heavenward.

Psalm 42

God's promises pertain to those, and those only, that dwell under the church's shadow, that attend on God's ordinances and adhere to his people, not those that flee to that shadow only for shelter in a hot gleam, but those that 'dwell under it' (Ps. 27:4).

Hosea 14

It is a righteous thing with God to withhold the blessings of grace from those that do not attend the means of grace, to deny the 'green pastures' to those that attend not the 'shepherd's tents'.

Zechariah 14

Meditation

David's prayers were not his

171

words only, but his meditations; as meditation is the best preparative for prayer, so prayer is the best issue of meditation. Meditation and prayer should go together. (19:14.) It is when we thus consider our prayers, and then only, that we may expect that God will consider them, and take that to his heart which comes from ours.

Psalm 5

They 'thought upon his name'; they seriously considered and frequently meditated upon the discoveries God has made of himself in his word and by his providences, and their 'meditation of him' was 'sweet' to them and influenced them. They 'thought on his name'; they consulted the honour of God and aimed at that as their ultimate end in all that they did. Note, those that know the name of God should often think of it and dwell upon it in their thoughts; it is a copious curious subject, and frequent thoughts of it will contribute very much to our communion with God and the stirring up of our devout affections to him.

Malachi 3

Meekness

It is observable that those creatures chosen for sacrifice were most mild and gentle, harmless and inoffensive to typify the innocence and meekness that were in Christ and to teach the innocence and meekness that should be in Christians.

Leviticus 1

See how quickly, how easily, how effectually the mutiny

among the soldiers was quelled by his patience and faith. When they spoke of stoning him, if he had spoken of hanging them or had ordered that the ringleaders of the faction should immediately have their heads struck off, though it would have been just, yet it might have been of pernicious consequence to his interest in this critical juncture and while he and his men were contending, the Amalekites would clearly have carried off their spoil but when he, as a deaf man, heard not, smothered his resentments and encouraged himself in the Lord his God, the tumult of the people was stilled by his gentleness and the power of God on their hearts; and being thus mildly treated they are now as ready to follow his foot as they were but a little before, to fly in his face.

1 Samuel 30

Meekness is wisdom. He rightly understands himself, and his duty and interest, the infirmities of human nature, and the constitution of human society, who is 'slow to anger', and knows how to excuse the faults of others as well as his own, how to adjourn his resentments, and moderate them, so as by no provocation to be put out of the possession of his own soul. A mild patient man is really to be accounted an intelligent man, one that learns of Christ, who is wisdom itself.

Proverbs 14

The meek are those who quietly submit themselves to God, to his word and to his rod, who follow his directions, and comply with his designs, and are gentle towards all men (Titus 3:2); who can bear provocation without being inflamed by it; are either silent or return a soft answer; and who can show their displeasure when there is occasion for it, without being transported into any indecencies; who can be cool when others are hot; and in their patience keep possession of their own souls, when they can scarcely keep possession of anything else. They are the meek, who are rarely and hardly provoked, but quickly and easily pacified; and who would rather forgive twenty injuries than revenge one, having the rule of their own spirits.

Matthew 5

Even that which is said without reason should be answered without passion; we should learn of our Master to reply with meekness even to that which is most impertinent and imperious, and, where it is easy to find much amiss, to seem not to see it, and wink at the affront.

Those who would be like Christ must put up with affronts, and pass by the indignities and injuries done them; must not regard them, much less resent them, and least of all revenge them. I, as a deaf man, heard not. When Christ was reviled, he reviled not again.

John 7

'Meekness', that excellent disposition of soul which makes men unwilling to provoke others, and not easily to be provoked or offended with their infirmities;

and it is opposed to angry resentments and peevishness.

Ephesians 4

Mercy

God quickly brought troubles upon them to awaken them and recover them to repentance before their hearts were hardened. It was but in the fourth year of Rehoboam that they began to corrupt themselves and in the fifth year the king of Egypt came up against them with a vast army.

2 Chronicles 12

He appeals to mercy, as one that knew he could not stand the test of strict justice. The best saints, even those that have been merciful to the poor, have not made God their debtor, but must throw themselves on his mercy. When we are under the rod we must thus recommend ourselves to the tender mercy of our God.

Psalm 41

The fountain of mercy is inexhaustibly full; the streams of mercy are inestimably rich.

Psalm 86

His mercy is everlasting; it is a fountain that can never be drawn dry. The saints, who are now the sanctified vessels of mercy, will be, to eternity, the glorified monuments of mercy.

Psalm 100

The repetition of it here twenty six times intimates, 1. That God's mercies to his people are thus repeated and drawn, as it were, with a continuando from the beginning to the end, with a progress and advance *ad infinitum*. 2. That in every particular favour we ought to take notice of the mercy of God, and to take notice of it as enduring still, the same now that it has been, and enduring for ever, the same always that it is.

3. That the everlasting continuance of the mercy of God is very much his honour and that which he glories in, and very much the saints' comfort and that which they glory in. It is that which therefore our hearts should be full of and greatly affected with, so that the most frequent mention of it, instead of cloying us, should raise us the more, because it will be the subject of our praise to all eternity. This most excellent sentence, that God's mercy endureth for ever, is magnified above all the truths concerning God, not only by the repetition of it here, but by the signal tokens of divine acceptance with which God owned the singing of it, both in Solomon's time (2 Chron. 5:13), when they sang these words, 'for his mercy endureth for ever', the house was filled with a cloud, and in Jehoshaphat's time (when they sung these words, God gave them victory, 2 Chron. 20:21, 22), which should make us love to sing, 'His mercies sure do still endure, eternally.'

Psalm 136

See how far off divine mercy will go, how far back it will look, to find out a reason for doing good to his people, when no present considerations appear but what make against them. Nay, it makes that a reason for relieving them which might have been used as a reason for abandoning them. He might have said, 'I have delivered them formerly, but they have again brought trouble upon themselves' (Prov. 19:19); therefore 'I will deliver them no more' (Judg. 10:13). But no, mercy rejoices against judgment, and turns the argument the other way: 'I have formerly delivered them and therefore will now.'

Isaiah 63

We that are sinful were forever undone if God were not merciful; but the goodness of his nature encourages us to hope that, if we by repentance undo what we have done against him, he will by a pardon unsay what he has said against us.

Jeremiah 3

So pleasing would it be to God to find any such that for their sake he would pardon the city; if there were but ten righteous men in Sodom, if but one of a thousand, of ten thousand, in Jerusalem, it should be spared. See how ready God is to forgive, how swift to show mercy.

Jeremiah 5

'They departed from Jerusalem'. See how ready God was to put a stop to his judgments, upon the first instance of reformation, so slow is he to anger and so swift to show mercy. As soon as ever they let their servants go free, God let them go free.

Jeremiah 34

God speaks as if he were conscious to himself of a strange striving of affections in compassion to Israel; as Lam. 1:20, 'My bowels are troubled; my heart is turned within me.' As it follows here, 'My repentings are kindled together'. His bowels yearned towards them, and his soul was grieved for their sin and misery (Judg. 10:16). Compare Jer. 31:20. 'Since I spoke against him my bowels are troubled for him.' When God was to give up his Son to be a sacrifice for sin, and a Saviour for sinners, he did not say, How shall I give him up? No, 'He spared not His own Son'; it 'pleased the Lord to bruise Him', and therefore God spared not him, that he might spare us.

Hosea 11

It becomes us, in many cases, to be gentle towards those that come under suspicion of having offended, to hope the best concerning them, and make the best of that which at first appears bad, in hopes that it may prove better. The rigour of the law is (sometimes) the height of injustice. That court of conscience which moderates the rigour of the law we call a court of equity. Those who are found faulty were perhaps overtaken in the fault, and are therefore to be restored with the spirit of meekness; and threatening, even when just, must be moderated.

Matthew 1

Love is his inclination to do us good considered simply as creatures; mercy respects us as apostate and as miserable creatures. Observe, God's eternal love or good-will towards his creatures is the fountain whence all his mercies vouchsafed to us proceed; and that love of God is great love, and that mercy of his is rich mercy, inexpressibly great and inexhaustibly rich.

Ephesians 2

Methods

Right notions of Christ's kingdom would keep us to right methods for advancing it.

John 6

Ministers

All the use they would make of the man of God was to be advised by him whether they should return home or if there were yet any hopes of finding the asses, which way they must go next. A poor business to employ a prophet about. Had they said 'Let us give up the asses for lost and now that we are so near the man of God, let us go and learn from him the good knowledge of God. Let us consult him how we may order our lives aright and enquire the law at his mouth since we may not have such another opportunity and then we shall not lose our journey' the proposal would have been such as became Israelites but to make prophecy, that glory of Israel, serve so mean a turn as this revealed too much of the manner of spirit they were of. Most people would rather be told their fortune than told their duty. If it were the business of the men of God to direct for the recovery of lost asses they would be consulted much more than they are now that it is their business to direct for the recovery of lost souls. So preposterous is the care of most men . . . Those that are prophets must first be seers; those who undertake to speak to others the things of God must have an insight into those things themselves.

1 Samuel 9

He could not see a lamb in distress but he would venture his life to rescue it. This temper made him fit to be a king to whom the lives of subjects should be dear and their blood precious (Ps. 72:14); and fit to be a type of Christ, the Good Shepherd who gathers the lambs in his arms and carries them in his bosom and who not only ventured but laid down his life for his sheep. Thus too was David fit to be an example to ministers with the utmost care and diligence to watch for souls that they be not a prey to the 'roaring lion'. *1 Samuel 17*

Nothing is more provoking to God than abuses given to his faithful ministers for what as done against them he takes it done against himself. Persecution was the sin that brought upon Jerusalem its final destruction by the Romans (Matt. 23; 34—37). Those that mock at God's faithful ministers and do all they can to render them despicable or odious, that vex and misuse them, to discourage them, and to keep others from hearkening to them, should be reminded that a wrong done to an ambassador is construed as done to the prince that sends him.

2 Chronicles 36

See what is the best learning of a minister, to know how to comfort troubled consciences, and to speak pertinently,

properly, and plainly, to the various cases of poor souls.

Isaiah 50

Ministers are watchmen on the church's walls (Isa. 62:6), watchmen that go about the city (Cant. 3:3). It is a toilsome office. Watchmen must keep awake, be they ever so sleepy, and keep abroad, be it ever so cold; they must stand all weathers upon the watch-tower, (Isa. 21:8; Gen. 31:40). It is a dangerous office. Sometimes they cannot keep their post, but are in peril of death from the enemy, who gain their point if they kill the sentinel; and yet they dare not quit their post upon pain of death from their general. Such a dilemma are the church's watchmen in; men will curse them if they be faithful, and God will curse them if they be false. But it is a needful office.

Ezekiel 3

Those that have public work to do for God and the souls of men have need to be much in private, to fit themselves for it. Ministers should spend much time in their chambers, in reading, meditation and prayer, that their 'profiting may appear'; and they ought to be provided with conveniences for this purpose.

Ezekiel 42

It was a great honour to him to be thus long employed in such good work, and a great mercy to the people to have a minister so long among them that so well knew their state, and naturally cared for it, one they had been long used to and who therefore was the more likely to be useful to them. And yet, for aught that appears, he did but little good among them; the longer they enjoyed him the less they regarded him; they despised his youth first, and afterwards his age.

Hosea 1

Amaziah, as a priest, aimed at nothing but the profits of his place, and he thought Amos, as a prophet, had the same views, and therefore advised him to prophesy where he might eat bread, where he might be sure to have as much as he chose; whereas Amos was to prophesy where God appointed him, and where there was most need of him, not where he would get most money.

Amos 7

Those whose business it is to call others to mourn for sin, and to mortify it, ought themselves to live a serious life, a life of self-denial, mortification, and contempt of the world. John the Baptist thus showed the deep sense he had of the badness of the time and place he lived in, which made the preaching of repentance needful; every day was a fast-day with him.

Matthew 3

Ministers should not leave empty spaces in their time, lest their lord should come in one of those empty spaces. As with a good God the end of one mercy is the beginning of another, so with a good man, a good minister, the end of one duty is the beginning of another. When Calvin was persuaded to remit his ministerial labours, he answered, with some resentment, 'What, would you have my master find me idle?'

A faithful minister of Jesus Christ is one that sincerely designs his master's honour, not his own; delivers the whole counsel of God, not his own fancies and conceits; follows Christ's institutions and adheres to them; regards the meanest, reproves the greatest, and doth not respect persons.

Matthew 24

Those that shall be put under your charge, must be as sheep under the charge of the shepherd, who is to tend them and feed them, and be a servant to them, not as horses under the command of the driver, that works them and beats them, and gets his pennyworths out of them.

Mark 10

Nothing is more likely to ensnare ministers, than bringing them to meddle with controversies about civil rights, and to settle land-marks between the prince and the subject, which it is fit should be done, while it is not at all fit that they should have the doing of it.

Mark 12

It was the hypocrisy of the Pharisees 'that they did not do as they taught' (Matt. 23:3), but pulled down with their lives what they built up with their preaching; for who will believe those who do not believe themselves? *Examples will govern more than rules.* The greatest obstructors of the success of the word are those whose bad lives contradict their good doctrine, who in the pulpit preach so well that it is a pity they should ever come out, and out of the pulpit live so ill that it is a pity they should ever come in.

Romans 2

It is a sign of true love to Jesus Christ to reckon that service and work for him truly honourable which the world looks upon with scorn, as mean and contemptible. The office of the ministry is an office to be magnified. Ministers are ambassadors for Christ, and stewards of the mysteries of God, and for their work's sake are to be esteemed highly in love.

Romans 11

He would derogate from none that had done service among them, nor would he be robbed of his own honour and respect. Note, faithful ministers may and ought to have a concern for their own reputation. Their usefulness depends much upon it.

1 Corinthians 3

The ministers of Christ should make it their hearty and continual endeavour to approve themselves trustworthy; and when they have the testimony of a good conscience, and the approbation of their Master, they must slight the opinions and censures of their fellow-servants: 'But with me', saith the apostle, 'it is a small thing that I should be judged of you, or of man's judgment' (v. 3). Indeed, reputation and esteem among men are a good step towards usefulness in the ministry; and Paul's whole argument upon this head shows he had a just concern for his own reputation. But he that would make

his chief endeavour to please men would hardly approve himself a faithful servant of Christ, (Gal. 1:10). He that would be faithful to Christ must despise the censures of men for his sake. He must look upon it as a very little thing (if his Lord approves him), what judgment men form of him. They may think very meanly or very hardly of him, while he is doing his duty; but it is not by their judgment that he must stand or fall. And happy is it for faithful ministers that they have a more just and candid judge than their fellow-servants; one who knows and pities their imperfections, though he has none of his own. It is better 'to fall into the hands of God than into the hands of men' (2 Sam. 24:14). The best of men are too apt to judge rashly, and harshly, and unjustly.

1 Corinthians 4

Ministers should not be of proud spirits, 'lording it over God's heritage', who are servants to the souls of men: yet, at the same time, they must avoid the meanness of spirit implied in becoming the servants of the humours or the lusts of men; if they should thus 'seek to please men, they would not be the servants of Christ' (Gal. 1:10).

2 Corinthians 4

From this we may note, 1. The very tender affection which faithful ministers bear towards those among whom they are employed; it is like that of the most affectionate parents to their little children. 2. That the chief thing they are longing and even travailing in birth for, on their account, is that Christ may be formed in them; not so much that they may gain their affections, much less that they may make a prey of them, but that they may be renewed in the spirit of their minds, wrought into the image of Christ, and more fully settled and confirmed in the Christian faith and life; and how unreasonably must those people act who suffer themselves to be prevailed upon to desert or dislike such ministers!

Galatians 4

The highest honour of the greatest apostle, and most eminent ministers, is to be the servants of Jesus Christ; not the masters of the churches, but the servants of Christ.

He mentions the church before the ministers, because the ministers are for the church, for their edification and benefit, not the churches for the ministers, for their dignity, dominion, and wealth.

Philippians 1

Observe, 1. A minister must expect afflictions in the faithful discharge of his duty. 2. He must endure them patiently, like a Christian hero. 3. These must not discourage him in his work, for he must do his work, and fulfil his ministry. 4. The best way to make full proof of our ministry is to fulfil it, to fill it up in all its parts with proper work.

2 Timothy 4

Ministers (Desire for)

'Lord, let the man of God come again unto us for we desire to be better acquainted with him'. Those that have heard from heaven cannot but wish to hear more thence, again and again to meet with the man of God. Observe — he does not go or send his servants abroad to find out this man of God but seeks him upon his knees, prays to God to send him and thus seeking, finds him. Would we have God's messengers, the ministers of his gospel, to bring a word proper for us and for our instruction, entreat the Lord to send them to us to teach us. (Romans 15:30−32.)

Judges 13

Miracles

The extracting of the blood of the grape every year from the moisture of the earth is no less a work of power, though, being according to the common law of nature, it is not such a work of wonder, as this.

Since no difficulties can be opposed to the arm of God's power, no improbabilities are to be objected against the word of his command.

John 2

Money

If men borrow large sums to trade with, to increase their stocks, or to purchase land, there is no reason why the lender should not share with the borrower in his profit; or if to spend upon their lusts, or repair what they have so spent, why should they not pay for their extravagances? But if the poor borrow to maintain their families, and we be able to help them, it is certain we ought either to lend freely what they have occasion for, or (if they be not likely to repay it) to give freely something towards it.

Nehemiah 5

To exact satisfaction for debts of injury, which tends neither to reparation nor to the public good, but purely for revenge, though the law may allow it, *in terrorem* — to strike terror, and for the hardness of men's hearts, yet savours not of a Christian spirit. To sue for money-debts, when the debtor cannot possibly pay them, and so let him perish in prison, argues a greater love of money, and a less love of our neighbour, than we ought to have (Neh. 5:7).

Matthew 18

Mortification

God prepared them for Canaan by humbling them for sin, teaching them to mortify their lusts, to follow God, and to comfort themselves in him. It is a work of time to make souls ready for Heaven and it must be done by a long train of exercises.

Deuteronomy 2

As in the destruction of the Canaanites by Joshua the sons of Anak were last subdued (Josh. 11:21), so here in the conquest of the Philistines, the giants of Gath were last brought down. In the conflicts between grace and corruption there are some sins which, like these giants, keep their ground a great while and are not mastered without much difficulty and a long struggle.

1 Chronicles 20

If there were no other way to restrain them (which, blessed be God, through his grace, there is), it were better for us to pluck out the eye, and cut off the hand, though the right eye and right hand, the more honourable and useful, than to indulge them in sin to the ruin of the soul. And if this must be submitted to, at the thought of which nature startles, much more must we resolve to keep under the body, and to bring it into subjection; to live a life of mortification and self-denial; to keep a constant watch over our own hearts, and to suppress the first rising of lust and corruption there; to avoid the occasions of sin, to resist the beginnings of it, and to decline the company of those who will be a snare to us, though ever so pleasing; to keep out of harm's way, and abridge ourselves in the use of lawful things, when we find them temptations to us; and to seek unto God for his grace, and depend upon that grace daily, and so to walk in the Spirit, so that we may not fulfil the lusts of the flesh; and this will be as effectual as cutting off a right hand or pulling out a right eye; and perhaps as much against the grain to flesh and blood; it is the destruction of the old man.

Matthew 5

Corrupt inclinations and

appetites must be checked and crossed; the beloved lust, that has been rolled under the tongue as a sweet morsel, must be abandoned with abhorrence. The outward occasions of sin must be avoided, though we thereby put as great a violence upon ourselves as it would be to cut off a hand, or pluck out an eye. When Abraham quitted his native country, for fear of being ensnared in the idolatry of it, and when Moses quitted Pharaoh's court, for fear of being entangled in the sinful pleasures of it, there was a right hand cut off. We must think nothing too dear to part with, for the keeping of a good conscience.

If the right hand of the old man be cut off, and its right eye plucked out, its chief policies blasted and powers broken, it is well; but there is still an eye and a hand remaining, with which it will struggle. They that are Christ's have nailed the flesh to the cross, but it is not yet dead.

Matthew 18

The pain of mortifying the flesh now is no more to be compared with the punishment for not mortifying it, than 'salting' with 'burning'.

Mark 9

Had they kept the books by them, there was danger lest, when the heat of the present conviction was over, they should have the curiosity to look into them, and so be in danger of liking them and loving them again, and therefore they burnt them. Note, those that truly repent of sin will keep themselves as far as possible from the occasions of it.

Acts 19

Motives

You are not aware what manner of spirit you are upon this occasion actuated by and how different from that of Elias. He did it in holy zeal, you in passion. He was concerned for God's glory, you for your own reputation only. God judges men's practices by their principles and his judgment is according to truth.

2 Kings 1

When they bring their gold and incense it shall not be to show the riches of their country, nor to gain applause to themselves for piety and devotion, but to 'show forth the praises of the Lord' (v. 6). Our greatest services and gifts to the church are not acceptable further than we have an eye to the glory of God in them. And this must be our business in our attendance on public ordinances, to 'give unto the Lord the glory due to his name'; for therefore, as these here, we are called out of darkness into light, that we should 'show forth the praises of him that called us.' (1 Pet. 2:9.)

Isaiah 60

There may be an open and lavish hand, where there is no liberal and charitable heart. The external act of giving alms may proceed from a very ill principle. Vainglorious ostentation, or a proud conceit of merit, may put a man to large expense this way who has no true love to God nor men. Our doing good to others will do none to us, if it be not well done, namely, from a principle of devotion and charity, love to God, and good-will to men. Note, If we leave charity out of religion, the most costly services will be of no avail to us. If we give away all we have, while we withhold the heart from God, it will not profit.

1 Corinthians 13

Mourning

Though mourning for the dead be a duty, yet it must always be kept under the government of religion and right reason, and we must not sorrow as those that have no hope, nor lament the loss of any creature, even the most valuable, and that which we could worst spare, as if we had lost our God, or as if all our happiness were gone with it; and, of this moderation in mourning, ministers, when it is their case, ought to be examples. We must at such a time study to improve the affliction, to accommodate ourselves to it, and to get our acquaintance with the other world increased, by the removal of our dear relations, and learn with holy Job to 'bless the name of the Lord' even when he takes as well as when he gives.

Ezekiel 24

Music

It is a pity that music which may be so serviceable to the good

temper of the mind, should ever be abused by any to the support of vanity and luxury and made an occasion of drawing the heart away from God and serious things. If this be to any the effect of it, it drives away the good spirit not the evil spirit.

1 Samuel 16

National Punishments

He has national judgments wherewith to take vengeance for national sins. Such nations as this was cannot long go unpunished. How shall I pardon thee for this? (v. 7). Not but that those who have been guilty of these sins have found mercy with God, as to their eternal state (Manasseh himself did, though so much accessory to the iniquity of these times); but nations, as such, being reward-able and punishable only in this life, it would not be for the glory of God to let a nation so very wicked as this pass without some manifest tokens of his displeasure.

Jeremiah 5

Nebuchadnezzar was very unjust and barbarous in invading the rights and liberties of his neigh-bours thus, and forcing them into subjection to him; yet God had just and holy ends in per-mitting him to do so, to punish these nations for their idolatry and gross immoralities. Those that would not serve the God that made them were justly made to serve their enemies that sought to ruin them.

Jeremiah 27

The decay of virtue in a nation brings on a decay of everything else; and when neighbours devour one another it is just with God to bring enemies upon them to devour them all.

Ezekiel 12

New Year

'On the first day of the first month' (upon New Year's Day) they were to offer a sacrifice for the 'cleansing of the sanctuary' (v. 18), that is, to make atonement for the iniquity of the holy things the year past, that they might bring none of the guilt of them into the services of the new year, and to implore grace for the preventing of that iniquity, and for the better performance of the service of the sanctuary the ensuing year.

Those that worship God together should often join in renewing their repentance for their manifold defects, and applying the blood of Christ for the pardon of them, and in renewing their covenants to be more careful for the future; and it is very seasonable to begin the year with this work, as Hezekiah did when it had been long neglected (2 Chron. 29:17).

Ezekiel 45

Obedience

Abraham did this though much might be objected against it. Though circumcision was painful, though to grown men it was shameful, though while they were sore and unfit for action their enemies might take advantage against them . . . Though Abraham was 99 years old and had been justified and accepted of God long since, though so strange a thing done religiously might be turned to his reproach by the Canaanite and the Perrizite that dwelt then in the land, yet God's command was sufficient to answer these and a thousand such objections; what God requires we must do not conferring with flesh and blood.

Genesis 17

We may be in the way of our duty and yet may meet with trouble and distress in that way. As prosperity will not prove us in the right, so cross events will not prove us in the wrong. We may be going where God calls us and yet may think our way hedged up with thorns. We may comfortably trust God with our safety while we carefully keep to our duty. If God be our guide he will be our guard.

Genesis 32

It ought to be the great care and endeavour of every one of us to follow the Lord fully. We must in a course of obedience to God's will and of service to his honour, follow him universally without dividing, uprightly without dissembling, cheerfully without disputing, and constantly without declining and this is following him fully.

Numbers 14

The end of their being taught was that they might do as they were taught . . . Good instructions from parents and ministers will but aggravate our condemnation if we do not live up to them.

Deuteronomy 6

Look which way we will, both our reviews and our prospects will furnish us with arguments for obedience.

Deuteronomy 8

The Lord thy God commands thee, therefore thou art bound in duty and gratitude to obey him and it is at thy peril if thou disobey. They are his laws, therefore thou shalt do them for to that end were they given thee. Do them and not dispute them; do them and not draw back from them; do them, not carelessly and hypocritically but with thy heart and soul, thy whole heart and thy whole soul.

Deuteronomy 26

That obedience pleases best which comes from a principle of delight in God's goodness.

Deuteronomy 28

If he had ordered this general circumcision just at this time of his own head he might justly have been censured as imprudent for how good soever the thing was in itself, in the eye of reason it was not seasonable at this time and might have been of dangerous consequence but when God commanded him to do it he must not consult with flesh and blood . . .

God would hereby show that the camp of Israel was not governed by the ordinary rules and measures of war but by immediate direction from God who, by thus exposing them in the most dangerous moments, magnified his own power in protecting them even then and this great instance of security in disabling themselves for action just when they were entering upon action, proclaimed such confidence in the divine care for their safety as would increase their enemies' fears much more when their scouts informed them not only of the thing itself that was done but of the meaning of it that it was a seal of the grant of this land to Israel.

Joshua 5

It intimates that he had more pleasure and satisfaction in reflecting upon his obedience to the commands of God in all this. war and valued himself more upon that than upon all the gains and triumphs with which he was enriched and advanced.

Joshua 11

God appointed these cattle to be sacrificed to him in the field and, therefore, will give them no thanks who bring them as a sacrifice to his altar, for he will be served in his own way and according to the rule he Himself has prescribed, nor will a good intention justify a bad action.

1 Samuel 15

He solemnly charges his people to continue and persevere in their duty to God having spoken to God for them, he here speaks from God to them and those only would fare the better for his prayers that were made better by his preaching. His admonition at parting is 'Let your heart be perfect with the Lord our God' (v. 61). 'Let your obedience be universal without dividing, upright without dissembling, constant without declining;' this is evangelical perfection.

1 Kings 8

The kingly and priestly offices were separated by the law of Moses not to be united again but in the person of the Messiah. If Uzziah did intend to honour God and gain acceptance with him in what he did, he was quite out in his aim for being a service purely of divine institution he could not expect that it should be accepted unless it were done in the way and by the hands that God had appointed.

2 Chronicles 26

The most obedient are accepted as the most intelligent; those understand themselves and their interest best that make God's law their rule and are in everything ruled by it. A great understanding those have that know God's commandments and can discourse learnedly of them, but a good understanding have those that do them and walk according to them.

Psalm 111

'Let it be as God wills', for, how cross soever it may be to our designs and interests, God's will is his wisdom. That counsel needs not to be altered, for there is nothing amiss in it, nothing that can be amended. If we could see it altogether at one view, we should see it so perfect that nothing can be put to it, for there is no deficiency in it, nor any thing taken from it, for there is nothing in it unnecessary, or that can be spared. As the Word of God, so the works of God are every one of them perfect in its kind, and it is presumption for us either to add to them or diminish from them (Deut. 4:2). It is therefore as much our interest, as our duty, to bring our wills to the will of God.

Ecclesiastes 3

Own God for your master; give up yourselves to him as his subjects and servants; attend to all the declarations of his mind and will, and make conscience of complying with them. 'Do my commandments', not only in some things, but 'according to all which I command you'; make conscience of moral duties especially and rest not in those that are merely ritual.

Jeremiah 11

God writes his law in the hearts of all believers, makes it ready and familiar to them, at hand when they have occasion to use it, as that which is written in the heart (Prov. 3:3). He makes them in care to observe it, for that which we are solicitous about is said to lie near our hearts. He works in them a disposition to obedience, a conformity of thought and affection to the rules of the divine law, as that of the copy to the original. This is here promised, and ought to be prayed for, that our duty may be done conscientiously and with delight.

Jeremiah 31

As soon as he understood that it was the mind of God he did it, and made no objections, was not disobedient to the heavenly vision; but, when he had done it, he desired better to understand why God had ordered him to do it, because the thing looked strange and unaccountable.

Note, 'though we are bound to follow God with an implicit obedience, yet we should endeavour that it may be more and more an intelligent obedience. We must never dispute God's statutes and judgments, but we may and must enquire, 'What mean these statutes and judgments? (Deut. 6:20.)

Jeremiah 32

If indeed he looked upon Jeremiah as a prophet, whose prayers might avail much both for him and his people, why did he not then believe him, and hearken to the words of the Lord which he spoke by him? He desired his good prayers, but would not take his good counsel, nor be ruled by him, though he spoke in God's name, and it appears by this that Zedekiah knew he did. Note, it is common for those to desire to be prayed for who yet will not be advised; but herein they put a cheat upon themselves, for how can we expect that God should hear others speaking to him for us if we will not hear them speaking to us from him and for him? Many who despise prayer when they are in prosperity will be glad of it when they are in adversity.

Jeremiah 37

They will do what God appoints them to do, whether it be good or whether it be evil: 'Though it may seem evil to us, yet we will believe that if God command it, it is certainly good, and we must not dispute it, but do it. Whatever God commands, whether it be easy or difficult, agreeable to our inclinations

or contrary to them, whether it be cheap or costly, fashionable or unfashionable, whether we get or lose by it in our worldly interests, if it be our duty, we will do it.

God has made that our duty which is really our privilege, and our obedience will be its own recompense.

Jeremiah 42

Here there was something peculiar, and Ezekiel, to make himself a sign to the people, must put a force upon himself and exercise an extraordinary piece of self-denial. Note, our dispositions must always submit to God's directions, and his command must be obeyed even in that which is most difficult and displeasing to us.

Ezekiel 24

God spoke to the fish, gave him orders to return him, as before he had given him orders to receive him. God speaks to other creatures, and it is done; they are all his ready obedient servants. But to man he speaks once, yea, twice, and he perceives it not, regards it not, but turns a deaf ear to what he says.

Jonah 2

As Zerubbabel's prudence and piety kept this from being any affront to him (as the setting up of a rival with him), so God's providence kept the kings of Persia from taking umbrage at it, as raising a rebellion against them. In doing what we are sure is God's pleasure, as this was, we may well venture men's displeasure.

Zechariah 6

Christ, as man, was obedient to the moral law, and, as Redeemer, to the mediatorial law; and in both he kept his Father's word, and his own word with the Father.

John 8

Though it is a great advantage to know our duty, yet we shall come short of happiness if we do not do our duty. *Knowing is in order to doing; that knowledge therefore is vain and fruitless which is not reduced to practice*; nay, it will aggravate the sin and ruin (Luke 12:47, 48; James 4:17). It is knowing and doing that will demonstrate us of Christ's kingdom, and wise builders. (see Ps. 103:17, 18.)

John 13

When they were showing their love to Christ by their grieving to think of his departure, and the sorrow which filled their hearts upon the foresight of that, he bids them, if they would show their love to him, do it, not by these weak and feminine passions, but by their conscientious care to perform their trust, and by a universal obedience to his commands; this is better than sacrifice, better than tears. 'Lovest thou me? Feed my lambs.'

He shows what an inseparable connection there is between love and obedience; love is the root, obedience is the fruit. Where a sincere love to Christ is in the heart, there will be obedience: 'If a man love me' indeed, that love will be such a commanding constraining principle in him, that, no question, he will 'keep my words'. Where there is true love to Christ there is a value for his favour, a veneration for his authority, and an entire surrender of the whole man to his direction and government. Where love is, duty follows of course, is easy and natural, and flows from a principle of gratitude.

John 14

Observe the description here given of the Christian profession: it is 'Obedience to the faith'. It does not consist in a notional knowledge or a naked assent, much less does it consist in perverse disputings, but in obedience.

The act of faith is the obedience of the understanding to God revealing, and the product of that is the obedience of the will to God commanding.

Romans 1

It is not enough to know well, and speak well, and profess well, and promise well, but we must do well: do that which is good, not only for the matter of it, but for the manner of it. We must do it well.

Romans 2

He once wrote his laws to them, now he will write his laws in them; that is, he will give them understanding to know and to believe his law; he will give them memories to retain them; he will give them hearts to love them and consciences to recognise them; he will give them courage to profess them and power to put them in practice; the whole habit and frame of their souls shall be a table and transcript of the law of God.

Hebrews 8

All that are chosen to eternal life as the end are chosen to obedience as the way. Unless a person be sanctified by the Spirit, and sprinkled with the blood of Jesus, there will be no true obedience in the life.

1 Peter 1

No sooner was the word of command given than it was immediately obeyed; no delay, no objection made. We find that some of the best of men, as Moses and Jeremiah, did not so readily come in and comply with the call of God to their work; but the angels of God excel not only in strength, but in a readiness to do the will of God. God says, 'Go your ways, and pour out the vials'; and immediately the work is begun. We are taught to pray that the will of God may be done on earth as it is done in heaven.

Revelation 16

Obstinacy

Note, those are obstinate indeed in their infidelity, who, when they can say nothing against a truth, will say nothing to it; and, when they cannot resist, yet will not yield.

Such a work of mercy should have engaged their love to him, and such a work of wonder their faith in him. But, instead of that, the Pharisees, who pretended to be oracles in the church, and the Herodians, who pretended to be the supporters of the state, though of opposite interests one to another, took counsel together against him, how they might destroy him.

Mark 3

If the patient be obstinate, and will not submit to the methods prescribed, but wilfully takes and does that which is prejudicial to him, the physician is not to be blamed if he give him up as in a desperate condition; and all the fatal symptoms that follow are not to be imputed to the physician, but to the disease itself and to the folly and wilfulness of the patient.

Romans 1

Old Age

Some old people bear up better than others under the decays of age, but, more or less, the days of old age are and will be evil days and of little pleasure. Great care therefore should be taken to pay respect and honour to old people, that they may have something to balance these grievances and nothing may be done to add to them. And all this, put together, makes up a good reason why we should remember our creator in the days of our youth, that he may remember us with favour when these evil days come, and his comforts may delight our souls when the delights of sense are in a manner worn off.

Ecclesiastes 12

Omissions

All that is charged upon them,

on which the sentence is grounded, is, omission; as, before, the servant was condemned, not for wasting his talent, but for burying it; so here he doth not say, 'I was hungry and thirsty, for you took my meat and drink from me; I was a stranger, for you banished me; naked, for you stripped me; in prison, for you laid me there': but, 'When I was in these distresses, you were so selfish, so taken up with your own ease and pleasure, made so much of your labour, and were so loth to part with your money, that you did not minister as you might have done to my relief and succour. You were like those epicures that were at ease in Zion, and were not grieved for the affliction of Joseph' (Amos 6:4—6). Note, omissions are the ruin of thousands.

Matthew 25

Opportunities

That peace gave him an opportunity to build it and, therefore, he resolved to set about it immediately. God has given me rest both at home and abroad and there is no adversary, no Satan (so the word is), no instrument of Satan to oppose it or to divert us from it. Satan does all he can to hinder temple work (1 Thess. 2, v. 18, Zech. 3:1), but when he is bound (Rev. 20:2), we should be busy. When there is no evil occurrent then let us be vigorous and zealous in that which is good and get it forward. When the churches have rest let them be edified (Acts 9:31). Days of peace and prosperity present us with a fair gale which we must

account for if we improve not.

1 Kings 5

Opposition

A jealous eye it seems they had upon them and no sooner did the Spirit of God stir up the friends of the temple to appear for it, than the evil spirit stirred up its enemies to appear against it. While the people built and ceiled their own houses, their enemies gave no molestation (Hag. 1:4), though the king's order was to put a stop to the building of the city (ch. 4:21) but when they fell to work again on the temple, then the alarm was taken and all heads were at work to hinder them (v. 3, 4).

Ezra 5

The objections which were made against Christ and his disciples gave occasion to some of the most profitable of his discourses; thus are the interests of truth often served, even by the opposition it meets with from gainsayers, and thus the wisdom of Christ brings good out of evil. This is the third instance of it in this chapter; his discourse of his power to forgive sin, and his readiness to receive sinners, was occasioned by the cavils of the scribes and Pharisees; so here, from a reflection upon the conduct of his family, arose a discourse concerning his tenderness for it.

Their quarrels with Christ for taking upon him to forgive sin (v. 3), for conversing with publicans and sinners (v. 11), for not fasting (v. 14), though spiteful enough, yet had some colour of piety, purity and devotion in them; but this (which they are left to, to punish them for those) breathes nothing but malice and falsehood, and hellish enmity in the highest degree.

Matthew 9

Oppression

Because he went beyond what he could afford, he defrauded his workmen of their wages, which is one of the sins that cries in the ears of the Lord of hosts (James 5:4). God takes notice of the wrong done by the greatest of men to their poor servants and labourers, and will repay those, in justice, that will not in justice pay those whom they employ, but use their neighbour's service without wages. Observe, the greatest of men must look upon the meanest as their neighbours, and be just to them accordingly, and love them as themselves.

Jeremiah 22

Those strong rods, we have reason to fear, had been instruments of oppression, assistant to the king in catching the prey and devouring men, and now they are destroyed with him. Tyranny is the inlet to anarchy; and, when the rod of government is turned into the serpent of oppression, it is just with God to say, 'There shall be no strong rod to be a sceptre to rule; but let men be as are the fishes of the sea, where the greater devour the less'.

Ezekiel 19

That which is but exactness with others is exaction upon the widows and the fatherless; nay, that not relieving and helping them as we ought is, in effect, oppressing them.

Zechariah 7

Optimism

As long as any of God's Israel remain (and a remnant God will have in the worst of times) there is hope be it ever so small a remnant for God can make him that remains though but one single person, triumph over the most proud and potent.

Judges 5

Original Sin

'Behold, I was shapen in iniquity'. He does not call upon God to behold it, but upon himself. 'Come, my soul, look unto the rock out of which I was hewn, and thou wilt find I was shapen in iniquity. Had I duly considered this before, I find I should not have made so bold with the temptation, nor have ventured among the sparks with such tinder in my heart; and so the sin might have been prevented.

Psalm 51

The case is, in short, this: though man is made to consist of body and soul, yet his spiritual part had then so much the dominion over his corporeal part that he was denominated a living soul (Gen. 2:7), but by indulging the appetite of the flesh, in eating forbidden fruit, he prostituted the just dominion of the soul to the tyranny of sensual lust, and became no longer a living soul, but flesh: 'Dust thou art'. The living soul became dead and inactive; thus in the day he sinned he surely died, and so he became earthly. In this degenerate state, he begat a son in his own likeness; he transmitted the human nature, which had been entirely deposited in his hands, thus corrupted and depraved; and in the same plight it is still propagated. Corruption and sin are woven into our nature; we are shapen in iniquity, which makes it necessary that the nature be changed.

John 3

We see the world under a deluge of sin and death, full of iniquities and full of calamities. Now, it is worth while to enquire what is the spring that feeds it, and you will find it to be the general corruption of nature; and at what gap it entered, and you will find it to have been Adam's first sin.

It is a great proof of original sin that little children, who were never guilty of any actual transgression, are yet liable to very terrible diseases, casualties, and deaths, which could by no means be reconciled with the justice and righteousness of God if they were not chargeable with guilt.

Romans 5

Paul had a very quick and piercing judgment, all the advantages and improvements of education, and yet never attained the right knowledge of indwelling sin till the Spirit by the law made it known to him. There is nothing about which

the natural man is more blind than about original corruption, concerning which the understanding is altogether in the dark till the Spirit by the law reveal it.

Romans 7

Outward Appearances Deceptive

Though we meet with prosperity and success in a way of sin, yet we must not therefore think the more favourably of it. They have a king, and if they conduct themselves well their king may be a very great blessing to them and yet Samuel will have them perceive and see that their wickedness was great in asking a king. We must never think well of that which God in his law frowns upon, though in his providence he may seem to smile upon it.

1 Samuel 12

He lays this down for a rule, that the love and hatred of God are not to be measured and judged of by men's outward condition. If prosperity were a certain sign of God's love, and affliction of his hatred, then it might justly be an offence to us to see the wicked and godly fare alike. But the matter is not so: No man knows either love or hatred by all that is before him in this world, by those things that are the objects of sense. These we may know by that which is within us; if we love God with all our heart, thereby we may know that he loves us, as we may know likewise that we are under his wrath if we be governed by that carnal mind which is enmity to Him. These will be known by that which shall be hereafter, by men's everlasting state; it is certain that men are happy or miserable according as they are under the love or hatred of God, but not according as they are under the smiles or frowns of the world; and therefore if God loves a righteous man (as certainly he does) he is happy, though the world frown upon him; and if he hates a wicked man (as certainly he does) he is miserable, though the world smile upon him.

Ecclesiastes 9

Parables

He preached by parables, because thereby the things of God were made more plain and easy to them who were willing to be taught, and at the same time more difficult and obscure to those who were willingly ignorant; and thus the gospel would be a 'savour of life' to some, and 'of death' to others. A parable, like the pillar of cloud and fire, turns a dark side towards Egyptians, which confounds them, but a light side towards Israelites, which comforts them, and so answers a double intention. The same light directs the eyes of some, but dazzles the eyes of others.

The disciples were well inclined to the knowledge of gospel mysteries, and would search into the parables, and by them would be led into a more intimate acquaintance with those mysteries; but the carnal hearers that rested in bare hearing, and would

not be at the pains to look further, nor to ask the meaning of the parables, would be never the wiser, and so would justly suffer for their remissness. A parable is a shell that keeps good fruit for the diligent, but keeps it from the slothful.

Matthew 13

Parents

(God adds to the command that we respect our parents) and 'keep my Sabbaths''. If God provides by his law for the preserving of the honour of parents, parents must use their authority over their children for the preserving of the honour of God particularly the honour of his Sabbaths the custody of which is very much committed to parents by the fourth commandment 'thou and thy son and thy daughter'. The ruin of young people has often been observed to begin in the contempt of their parents and the profaning of the Sabbath.

Leviticus 19

It is a comfort to parents when they come to die if, though they smart themselves for their own sin, yet they are not conscious to themselves of any of those iniquities which God visits upon the children.

Numbers 27

Little did Elimelech think, when he went to sojourn in Moab, that ever his sons would thus join in affinity with Moabites. But those that bring young people into bad acquaintance, and take them out of the way of public ordinances, though they may think them well-principled and armed against temptation, know not what they do, nor what will be the end thereof.

Ruth 1

Let parents take heed of sin, especially the sin of cruelty and oppression, for their poor children's sake who may be smarting for it by the just hand of God when they themselves are in their graves. Guilt and a curse are a bad entail upon a family. It should seem Saul's posterity trod in his steps for it is called a 'bloody house'. It was the spirit of the family and, therefore, they are justly reckoned with for his sin as well as for their own.

2 Samuel 21

He knew David was not one of those that envy their children's greatness and that, therefore, he would not be disquieted at this prayer nor take it as an affront but would heartily say 'Amen' to it. The wisest and best man in the world desires his children may be wiser and better than he for he, himself, desires to be wiser and better than he is and wisdom and goodness are true greatness.

1 Kings 1

His reign was short and inconsiderable. He reigned but three months and then was removed and carried captive to Babylon as his father, it is likely, would have been if he had lived but so much longer. What an unhappy young prince was this that was thrust into a falling house, a sinking throne. What an unnatural father had he, who begat him to suffer for him and by his own sin and folly had left himself nothing to bequeath to his son but his own miseries. Yet this young prince reigned long enough to show that he justly smarted for his father's sins for he trod in their steps.

2 Kings 24

Those that love their seed must leave their sins lest they perish not alone in their iniquity but bring ruin on their families with themselves.

1 Chronicles 10

He takes it for granted that parents will, with all the wisdom they have, instruct their children, and, with all the authority they have, give law to them for their good. They are reasonable creatures, and therefore we must not give them law without instruction; we must draw them with the cords of a man, and when we tell them what they must do we must tell them why. But they are corrupt and wilful, and therefore with the instruction there is need of a law. Abraham will not only catechize, but command, his household.

Proverbs 1

David having thus recommended wisdom to his son, no marvel that when God bade him ask what he would he prayed, Lord, 'give me a wise and an understanding heart'. We should make it appear by our prayers how well we are taught.

He was tender, and only beloved, in the sight of his mother. Surely there was such a manifest reason for making such a distinction when both the parents made it. Now we see *how they showed their love;* they catechised him, kept him to his book, and held him to a strict discipline. Though he was a prince, and heir-apparent to the crown, yet they did not let him live at large; nay, therefore they tutored him thus. And perhaps David was the more strict with Solomon in his education because he had seen the ill effects of an undue indulgence in Adonijah, whom he had not crossed in anything (1 Kings 1:6), as also in Absalom.

Proverbs 4

Chasten thy son while there is hope, for, perhaps, if he be let alone awhile, he will be past hope, and a much greater chastening will not do that which now a less would effect. It is easiest plucking up weeds as soon as they spring up, and the bullock that is designed for the yoke should be betimes accustomed to it.

It is better that he should cry under thy rod than under the sword of the magistrate, or, which is more fearful, that of divine vengeance.

Proverbs 19

If a reproof will serve without the rod, it is well, but the rod must never be used without a rational and grave reproof; and then, though it may be a present uneasiness both to the father and to the child, yet it will give wisdom.

Proverbs 29

The child of a very godly father,

notwithstanding all the instructions given him, the good education he has had and the needful rebukes that have been given him, and the restraints he has been laid under, after all the pains taken with him and prayers put up for him, may yet prove notoriously wicked and vile, the grief of his father, the shame of his family, and the curse and plague of his generation. He is here supposed to allow himself in all those enormities which his good father dreaded and carefully avoided, and to shake off all those good duties which his father made conscience of and took satisfaction in; he undoes all that his father did, and goes counter to his example in everything.

Ezekiel 18

If parents be careless, and do not give their children good instructions as they ought, the children ought to make up the want by studying the Word of God so much the more carefully and diligently themselves when they grow up; and the bad examples of parents must be made use of by their children for admonition, and not for imitation.

Ezekiel 20

Let not the greatest be excused, but 'assemble the elders', the judges and magistrates. Let not the meanest be passed by, but 'gather the children, and those that suck the breasts'. It is good to bring little children, as soon as they are capable of understanding any thing, to religious assemblies, that they may be trained up betimes in the way wherein they should go; but these were brought even when they were at the breast and were kept fasting, that by their cries for the breast the hearts of the parents might be moved to repent of sin, which God might justly so visit upon their children that the 'tongue of the sucking child' might 'cleave to the roof of his mouth' (Lam. 4:4), and that on them God might have compassion, as he had on the infants of Nineveh (Jonah 4:11).

Joel 2

Some observe what a mixture there was of good and bad in the succession of these kings; as for instance wicked Roboam begat wicked Abia; wicked Abia begat good Asa; good Asa begat good Josaphat; good Josaphat begat wicked Joram (v. 7, 8). Grace does not run in the blood, neither does reigning sin. God's grace is his own, and he gives or withholds it as he pleases.

Matthew 1

A master of a family cannot give faith to those under his charge, nor force them to believe, but he may be instrumental to remove external prejudices, which obstruct the operation of the evidence, and then the work is more than half done. Abraham was famous for this (Gen. 18:19), and Joshua, (ch. 24:15). This was a nobleman, and probably he had a great household; but, when he comes into Christ's school, he brings them all along with him.

John 4

It is good to train up children in a respect to good people and good ministers. This was particularly remarkable at Tyre, which we have not met with anywhere else, that they brought their wives and children to attend Paul, to do him the more honour and to receive benefit by his instructions and prayers; and as angry notice was taken of the children of the idolaters of Bethel, that mocked a prophet, so, no doubt, gracious notice was taken of the children of the disciples at Tyre, that honoured an apostle, as Christ accepted the hosannas of the little children.

Acts 21

Thus, when duty fails on one side, it commonly fails on the other. Disobedient children are justly punished with unnatural parents; and, on the contrary, unnatural parents with disobedient children.

Romans 1

Though God has given you power, you must not abuse that power, remembering that your children are, in a particular manner, pieces of yourselves, and therefore ought to be governed with great tenderness and love. Be not impatient with them; use no unreasonable severities and lay no rigid injunctions upon them. When you caution them, when you counsel them, when you reprove them, do it in such a manner as not to 'provoke them to wrath'. In all such cases deal prudently and wisely with them, endeavouring to convince their judgments and to work upon their reason.

Ephesians 6

Partiality

It is a fundamental error in the administration of justice, and that which cannot but lead men to abundance of transgression, to consider the parties concerned more than the merits of the cause, so as to favour one because he is a gentleman, a scholar, my countryman, my old acquaintance, has formerly done me a kindness, or may do me one, or is of my party and persuasion, and to bear hard on the other party because he is a stranger, a poor man, has done me an ill turn, is or has been my rival, or is not of my mind, or has voted against me. Judgment is perverted when any consideration of this kind is admitted into the scale, anything but pure right.

Proverbs 28

Patience

We are taught hereby how necessary it is that we wait on our God continually. Saul lost his kingdom for want of two or three hours' patience.

1 Samuel 13

Stoical apathy and Christian patience are very different: by the one men become in some measure, insensible of their afflictions; but by the other they become triumphant in and over them. Let us take care, in times of trial, that patience and not passion, be set at work in us.

When we bear all that God appoints, and as long as he appoints, and with a humble obedient eye to him, and when we not only bear troubles, but rejoice in them, then patience hath its perfect work.

James 1

Peace

In heaven there is perfect peace; for there is perfect holiness, and there is God, who is love.

Job 25

If God give inward peace to a man only, the quietness and everlasting assurance which are the effect of righteousness, neither the accusations of Satan, nor the afflictions of this present time, no, nor the arrests of death itself, can give trouble. What can make those uneasy whose souls dwell at ease in God?

Job 34

Such a river of peace as the springs of the world's comforts cannot send forth and the dams of the world's troubles cannot stop nor drive back nor its sands rack up, such a river of peace as will carry us to the ocean of boundless and endless bliss.

Isaiah 66

Solid peace cannot be enjoyed where there is no true grace; first grace, then peace. Peace without grace is mere stupidity; but grace may be true where there is for a time no actual peace; as Heman was distracted with terror, and Christ was once in an agony.

1 Peter 1

Peacemakers

We should deny ourselves both in our rights and in our conveniences rather than quarrel. A wise and a good man will rather retire into obscurity like Isaac into a valley, than sit high to be the butt of envy and ill-will.

Genesis 26

When quarrels happen we should be willing to be friends again upon any terms; peace and love are such valuable jewels that we can scarcely buy them too dearly. Better sit down losers than go on in strife.

Genesis 31

We should be ambitious and industrious how to be calm and quiet in our minds, in patience to possess our own souls, and to be quiet towards others; or of a meek and mild, a gentle and peaceable disposition, not given to strife, contention, or division. Satan is very busy to disquiet us; and we have that in our own hearts that disposes us to be disquiet; therefore let us *study* to be quiet.

1 Thessalonians 4

Persecution

So precious shall their blood be unto him that not a drop of it shall be shed, by the deceit or violence of Satan or his instruments without being reckoned for. Christ is a king, who, though he calls his subjects sometimes to resist unto blood for him, yet is not prodigal of their blood, nor will ever have it parted with but upon a valuable consideration to his glory and theirs, and the filling up of the measure of their enemies' iniquity.

Psalm 72

Those who can agree in nothing else can agree to persecute a good man. Herod and Pilate will unite in this, and in this they resemble Satan, who is not divided against himself, all the devils agreeing in Beelzebub.

Psalm 140

Those that are for keeping up and advancing the kingdom of sin in the world look upon Jerusalem, even the church of God, as the great obstacle to their designs, and they must have it out of the way; but they will find it heavier than they think it is.

Zechariah 12

Surely hell itself must be let loose, and devils, those desperate and despairing spirits, that have no part or lot in the great salvation, must become incarnate, ere such spiteful enemies could be found to a doctrine, the substance of which was 'good will toward men' and the 'reconciling of the world to God'; no, would you think it? All this mischief arises to the preachers of the gospel, from those to whom they came to preach salvation. Thus the 'blood-thirsty hate the upright, but the just seek his soul.' (Prov. 29:10). And therefore heaven is so much opposed on earth, because earth is so much under the power of hell (Eph. 2:2).

Matthew 10

The way of sin, especially the

sin of persecution, is down-hill; and when once a respect to Christ's ministers is cast off and broken through in one instance, that is at length done, which the man would sooner have thought himself a dog than to have been guilty of, (2 Kings 8:13).

Matthew 14

Whatever is pretended, the real cause of the world's enmity to the gospel is the testimony it bears against sin and sinners. Christ's witnesses by their doctrine and conversation torment those that dwell on the earth, and therefore are treated so barbarously (Rev. 11:10). But it is better to incur the world's hatred, by testifying against its wickedness, than gain its goodwill by going down the stream with it.

John 7

Lazarus is singled out to be the object of their special hatred, because God has distinguished him by the tokens of his peculiar love, as if they had made a league offensive and defensive with death and hell, and resolved to be severe upon all deserters. One would think that they should rather have consulted how they might have joined in friendship with Lazarus and his family, and by their mediation have reconciled themselves to this Jesus whom they had persecuted; but the god of this world had 'blinded their minds'.

John 12

Whom Christ blesseth the world curseth. The favourites and heirs of heaven have never been the darlings of this world, since the

old enmity was put between the seed of the woman and of the serpent. Why did Cain hate Abel, but 'because his works were righteous'? Esau hated Jacob because of the blessing; Joseph's brethren hated him because his father loved him; Saul hated David because 'the Lord was with him'; Ahab hated Micaiah because of his prophecies; such are the causeless causes of the world's hatred.

John 15

In threatening times, our care should not be so much that troubles may be prevented as that we may be enabled to go on with cheerfulness and resolution in our work and duty, whatever troubles we may meet with. Their prayer is not, 'Lord, behold their threatenings', and frighten them, and stop their mouths, and fill their faces with shame; but, 'Behold their threatenings', and animate us, open our mouths and fill our hearts with courage. They do not pray, 'Lord, give us a fair opportunity to retire from our work, now that it is become dangerous', but, 'Lord, give us grace to go on in our work, and not to be afraid of the face of man.'

Acts 4

Though persecution may not drive us off from our work, yet it may send us, as a hint of Providence, to work elsewhere.

Acts 8

Saul's sufferings for Christ shall redound so much to the honour of Christ and the service of the church, shall be so balanced with spiritual comforts and recompensed with eternal glories, that it is no discouragement to him to be told how great things he must suffer for Christ's name's sake.

Acts 9

The proceedings of persecutors have often been illegal even by the law of nations, and often inhuman, against the law of nature, but always sinful, and against God's law.

Acts 16

Those afflictions which may be truly persecution as far as men are concerned in them are fatherly rebukes and chastisements as far as God is concerned in them. Persecution for religion is sometimes a correction and rebuke for the sins of professors of religion. Men persecute them because they are religious; God chastises them because they are not more so: men persecute them because they will not give up their profession; God chastises them because they have not lived up to their profession.

Hebrews 12

To suffer for righteousness sake is the honour and happiness of a Christian; to suffer for the cause of truth, a good conscience, or any part of a Christian's duty, is a great honour; the delight of it is greater than the torment, the honour more than the disgrace, and the gain much greater than the loss.

1 Peter 3

All the great persecutions that ever were in the world were raised, spirited up, and conducted, by the devil; he is the grand persecutor, as well as 'the deceiver and accuser, of the

brethren'; men are his willing spiteful instruments, but he is the chief adversary that wars against Christ and his people (Gen. 3:15; Rev. 12:12). The design of Satan in raising persecutions against the faithful servants of God is to bring them to apostasy, by reason of their sufferings, and so to destroy their souls.

1 Peter 5

Perseverance

To those that are sincere in their religion God will give grace to persevere in it. Those that follow God faithfully will be divinely strengthened to continue following him. And observe, following God is a work that is its own wages. It is the matter of a promise as well as a precept.

1 Samuel 12

Perspective

What little reason have we to value the wealth of this world when so great a churl as Nabal abounds and so great a saint as David suffers want.

1 Samuel 25

Never let the Church's friends be disheartened by the power and pride of the Church's enemies. We need not fear great men against us while we have the great God for us. What will a finger more on each hand do or a toe more on each foot, in contest with Omnipotence?

1 Chronicles 20

All is well that ends well,

everlastingly well; but nothing well that ends ill, everlastingly ill. The righteous man's afflictions end in peace, and therefore he is happy; the wicked man's enjoyments end in destruction, and therefore he is miserable.

Psalm 73

Perversity of Human Nature

So perversely did they misconstrue providence, though God, by His prophets, had so often explained it to them, and the thing itself spoke the direct contrary. Since we forsook our idolatries we have wanted all things, and have been consumed by the sword, the true reason of which was because they still retained their idols in their hearts and an affection to their old sins; but they would have it thought that it was because they had forsaken the acts of sin. Thus the afflictions which should have been for their welfare, to separate between them and their sins, being misinterpreted, did but confirm them in their sins. Thus, in the first ages of Christianity, when God chastised the nations by any public calamities for opposing the Christians and persecuting them, they put a contrary sense upon the calamities, as if they were sent to punish them for conniving at the Christians and tolerating them, and cried, *'Christianos ad leones'* — 'Throw the Christians to the lions'.

Jeremiah 44

Christ conversed familiarly with all sorts of people, not affecting any peculiar strictness or austerity; he was affable and easy of access, not shy of any company, was often at feasts, both with Pharisees and publicans, to try if this would win upon those who were not wrought upon by John's reservedness: those who were not awed by John's frowns, would be allured by Christ's smiles; from whom Paul learned to become all things to all men (1 Cor. 9:22). Now our Lord Jesus, by his freedom, did not at all condemn John, any more than John did condemn him, though their deportment was so very different. Note, though we are never so clear in the goodness of our own practice, yet we must not judge of others by it. There may be a great diversity of operations, where it is the same God that worketh all in all (1 Cor. 12:6), and this various manifestation of the Spirit is given to every man to profit withal (v. 7). Observe especially, that God's ministers are variously gifted: the ability and genius of some lie one way, of others, another way: some are Boanerges — sons of thunder; others, Barnabases — sons of consolation; yet all these worketh that one and the selfsame Spirit (1 Cor. 12:11), and therefore we ought not to condemn either, but to praise both, and praise God for both, who thus tries various ways of dealing with persons of various tempers, that sinners may be either made pliable or left inexcusable, so that, whatever the issue is, God will be glorified.

Matthew 11

They now tempted Christ as

Israel did (1 Cor. 10:9). And observe their perverseness; then, when they had signs from heaven, they tempted Christ, saying, 'Can he furnish a table in the wilderness?' Now that he had furnished a table in the wilderness, they tempted him, saying, 'Can he give us a sign from heaven?'

Matthew 16

Philosophy

Upon the whole, therefore, he concluded that great scholars do but make themselves great mourners; for in much wisdom is much grief (v. 18). There must be a great deal of pains taken to get it, and a great deal of care not to forget it; the more we know the more we see there is to be known, and consequently we perceive with greater clearness that our work is without end, and the more we see of our former mistakes and blunders, which occasions much grief. The more we see of men's different sentiments and opinions (and it is that which a great deal of our learning is conversant about) the more at a loss we are, it may be, which is in the right. Those that increase knowledge have so much the more quick and sensible perception of the calamities of this world, and for one discovery they make that is pleasing, perhaps, they make ten that are displeasing, and so they increase sorrow. Let us not therefore be driven off from the pursuit of any useful knowledge, but put on patience to break through the sorrow of it; but let us despair of finding true happiness in this knowledge, and expect it only in the knowledge of God.

Ecclesiastes 1

Pity

Even those that suffer justly, and for their sins, are yet to be pitied and not trampled upon. If the father corrects one child, he expects the rest should tremble at it, not triumph in it.

Ezekiel 35

Pleasures

See the vanity of all the pleasures of sense; they soon surfeit, but never satisfy; the longer they are enjoyed, the less pleasant they grow.

John 2

Possessions

Observe a proportion in thy expenses; reduce not thy food in order to gratify thy pride, nor thy clothing in order to gratify thy voluptuousness. Be neat, wear clean linen, and be not slovenly. Or, let thy garments be white in token of joy and cheerfulness, which were expressed by white raiment (Rev. 3:4); and as a further token of joy, let thy head lack no ointment that is fit for it. Our Saviour admitted this piece of pleasure at a feast (Matt. 26:7), and David observes it among the gifts of God's bounty to him. 'Thou anointest my head with oil' (Ps. 23:5). Not that we must place our happiness in any of the delights of sense, or set our hearts upon them, but what God has given us we must make as comfortable a use of as we can afford, under the limitations of sobriety and wisdom, and not forgetting the poor.

Ecclesiastes 9

Some lavish gold out of the bag to make an idol of it in the house, while others hoard up gold in the bag to make an idol of it in the heart.

Isaiah 46

Creature comforts are as sparks, short-lived and soon gone; yet the children of this world, while they last, warm themselves by them, and walk with pride and pleasure in the light of them.

Isaiah 50

They did not call it their own, because they had, in affection, forsaken all for Christ, and were continually expecting to be stripped of all for their adherence to him. They did not say that aught was their own. for we can call nothing our own but sin. What we have in the world is more God's than our own; we have it from him, must use it for him, and are accountable for it to him.

Acts 4

Poverty

It is no strange thing for saints in this world to want necessaries for the support of their natural life. In those primitive times prevailing persecutions must needs reduce many of the suffering saints to great extremities;

and, still the poor, even the poor saints, we have always with us. Surely the things of this world are not the best things; if they were, the saints, who are the favourites of heaven, would not be put off with so little of them.

Romans 12

Praising God

This is here called a service and the persons employed in it workmen, not but that it is the greatest liberty and pleasure to be employed in praising God: what is heaven but that? But it intimates that it is our duty to make a business of it and stir up all that is within us to it and that in our present state of corruption and infirmity it will not be done as it should be done without labour and struggle. We must take pains with our hearts to bring them and keep them to this work and to engage all that is within us.

1 Chronicles 25

Wherefore David blessed the Lord, not only alone in his closet, but before all the congregation. This I expected when we read 'that David rejoiced with great joy' (v. 9), for such a devout man as he, would no doubt make that the matter of his thanksgiving which was so much the matter of his rejoicing. He that looked round with comfort would certainly look up with praise . . . The nearer we come to the world of everlasting praise, the more we should speak the language and do the work of that world . . . All that we can in our most exalted praises, attribute to him he has an unquestionable title to . . . All the glory we can give him with our hearts, lips and lives comes infinitely short of what is his due.

We must give God all the glory of all the good that is at any time done by ourselves or others. Our own good works must not be the matter of our pride nor the good works of others the matter of our flattery but both the matter of our praise for certainly it is the greatest honour and pleasure in the world faithfully to serve God.

1 Chronicles 29

(The glory of God appeared) when they were in their praises celebrating the everlasting mercy and goodness of God. As there is no one saying oftener repeated in Scripture than this, 'His mercy endureth for ever' (26 times in one Psalm, Psalm 136 and quite often elsewhere), so there is none more signally owned from heaven for it was not the expression of some rapturous flights that the priests were singing when the glory of God appeared, but this plain song 'He is good and his mercy endureth for ever.' This should endear those words to us. God's goodness is his glory and he is pleased when we give him the glory of it.

2 Chronicles 5

Even sorrow for sin must not put us out of tune for praising God. By faith we must rejoice in Christ Jesus as our righteousness.

2 Chronicles 29

The work of angels is to praise God. The more we abound in holy, humble, thankful, joyful praise, the more we do the will of God as they do it; and, whereas we are so barren and defective in praising God, it is a comfort to think that they are doing it in a better manner.

Job 38

In singing this we must triumph in the name of Christ as above every name, must give him honour ourselves, rejoice in the honours others do him, and in the assurance we have that there shall be a people praising him on earth when we are praising him in heaven.

Psalm 22

We must praise God, and we must sacrifice praise, direct it to God, as every sacrifice was directed; put it into the hands of the priest, our Lord Jesus, who is also the altar; see that it be made by fire, that it be kindled with the flame of holy and devout affection; we must be fervent in spirit, praising the Lord. This he is pleased in infinite condescension, to interpret as glorifying him.

Psalm 50

It cast a damp particularly upon his praises; when he had lost the joys of his salvation his harp was hung upon the willow-trees; therefore he prays, 'Lord, open my lips', put my heart in tune for praise again. To those that are tongue-tied by reason of guilt, the assurance of the forgiveness of their sins says effectually, *Ephphatha* — Be opened.

Psalm 51

Faithful prayers may quickly be turned into joyful praises, if it be not our own fault. 'Let the hearts of those rejoice that seek the Lord' (105:3), and let them praise him for working those desires in them, and giving them assurance that he will satisfy them. David was now in a wilderness, and yet had his heart much enlarged in blessing God. Even in affliction we need not want matter for praise, if we have but a heart to it.

Those that have their hearts refreshed with the tokens of God's favour ought to have them enlarged in his praises.

Psalm 63

We ought to praise God as good in himself, but we do it most feelingly when we observe how good he has been to us.

Psalm 86

Review what he has made known of himself in his word and in his works, and you will see, and say, that God is great and greatly to be feared; for his name is holy, his infinite purity and rectitude appear in all that whereby he has made himself known, and because it is holy, therefore it is reverend. . The angels have an eye to God's holiness when they cover their faces before him, and nothing is more man's honour than his sanctification. It is in his holy places that God appears most terrible (Ps. 68:35; Lev. 10:3).

Psalm 111

It is an easy thing to praise God in word and tongue; but those only are well learned in this mystery who have learned to praise him with uprightness of heart, that is, are inward with him in praising him, and sincerely aim at his glory in the course of their conversation as well as in the exercises of devotion. God accepts only the praises of the upright.

Psalm 119

It is a heaven upon earth to be praising God; and the pleasure of that should quite put our mouths out of taste for the pleasures of sin.

The psalmist had suggested to us the goodness of God, as the proper matter of our cheerful praises; here he suggests to us the greatness of God as the proper matter of our awful praises; and on this he is most copious, because this we are less forward to consider.

Psalm 135

We are never so earnestly called upon to pray and repent as to give thanks; for it is the will of God that we should abound most in the most pleasant exercises of religion, in that which is the work of heaven.

In all our adorations we must have an eye to God's excellency as transcendent, and to his power and dominion as incontestably and uncontrollably supreme.

We must give thanks to God, not only for that mercy which is now handed out to us here on earth, but for that which shall endure for ever in the glories and joys of heaven.

Psalm 136

The five foregoing psalms were all of a piece, all full of prayers; this, and the five that follow it to the end of the book, are all of a piece too, all full of praises; and though only this is entitled David's psalm, yet we have no reason to think but that they were all his as well as all the foregoing prayers. And it is observable that after five psalms of prayer follow six psalms of praise; for those that are much in prayer shall not want matter for praise, and those that have sped in prayer must abound in praise. Our thanksgivings for mercy, when we have received it, should even exceed our supplications for it when we were in pursuit of it. David, in the last of his begging psalms, had promised to praise God (144:9), and here he performs his promise.

Psalm 145

Holy joy or delight are required as the principle of it, and that is pleasant to us as men; giving glory to God is the design and business of it, and that is pleasant to us as saints that are devoted to his honour. Praising God is work that is its own wages; it is heaven upon earth; it is what we should be in as in our element.

Psalm 147

There he is praised continually in a far better manner than we can praise him. And it is a comfort to us, when we find we do it so poorly, that it is so well done there.

. . . Not that our praises can bear any proportion to God's greatness, for it is infinite, but, since he is greater than we can

express or conceive, we must raise our conceptions and expressions to the highest degree we can attain to.

. . . Praise God with a strong faith, praise him with holy love and delight; praise him with an entire confidence in Christ; praise him with a believing triumph over the powers of darkness; praise him with an earnest desire towards him and a full satisfaction in him; praise him by a universal respect to all his commands; praise him by a cheerful submission to all his disposals; praise him by rejoicing in his love and solacing yourselves in his great goodness; praise him by promoting the interests of the kingdom of his grace; praise him by a lively hope and expectation of the kingdom of his glory.

Let us often take a pleasure in thinking what glorified saints are doing in heaven, what those are doing whom we have been acquainted with on earth, but who have gone before us thither; and let it not only make us long to be among them, but quicken us to do this part of the will of God on earth as those do it that are in heaven. And let us spend as much of our time as may be in this good work because in it we hope to spend a joyful eternity.

Psalm 150

The voice of thanksgiving is the same with the voice of those that make merry; for whatever is the matter of our joy should be the matter of our praise. Is any merry? Let him sing psalms. What makes us cheerful should make us thankful. 'Serve the Lord with gladness'.

Jeremiah 30

Prayer

God often grants the desires of sinners in wrath while he denies the desires of his own people in love.

Numbers 11

The privilege to draw near to the God of Israel is not a small thing in itself and, therefore, must not appear small to us. To those who neglect opportunities of drawing near to God, who are careless and formal in it, to whom it is a task and not a pleasure, we may properly put this question 'Seemeth it a small thing to you that God has made you a people near unto him?'

Numbers 16

God has wicked men in a chain . . . it was in anger that God said to Balaam 'Go with them' and we have reason to think that Balaam himself so understood it, for we do not find him pleading this allowance when God reproved him for going. As God sometimes denies the prayers of his people in love so sometimes he grants the desires of the wicked in wrath.

Numbers 22

'If iniquity be in thy hand (that is, if there be any sin which thou dost yet live in the practice of) *put it far away*, forsake it with detestation and a holy indignation, steadfastly resolving not to return to it, nor to have any thing more to do with it. (Ezek. 18:31; Hos. 14:9; Isa. 30:22). If any of the gains of iniquity, any goods gotten by fraud or oppression, be in thy hand, make restitution thereof' (as Zaccheus, Luke 19:8, 'and shake thy hands from holding them,') (Isa. 33:15). The guilt of sin is not removed if the gain of sin be not restored.

Job 11

Prayer has prevailed to change God's way and his providence, but never was his will or purpose changed; for *known unto God are all* his works.

Job 23

It will be a great comfort to us if trouble, when it comes, find the wheels of prayer a-going, for then we may come with the more boldness to the throne of grace. Tradesmen are willing to oblige those that have been long their customers.

Psalm 17

'The Lord grant thee according to thine own heart'. This they might in faith pray for, because they knew David was a man after God's own heart, and would design nothing but what was pleasing to him. Those who make it their business to glorify God may expect that God will, in one way or other, gratify them, and those who walk in his counsel may promise themselves that he will fulfil theirs. 'Thou shalt devise a thing and it shall be established unto thee.' (1 John 3:22).

Psalm 20

We are to look upon our daily worship, alone, and with our families, to be both the most needful of our daily occupations and the most delightful of our daily comforts.

Psalm 65

In all the parts of prayer the soul must ascend upon the wings of faith and holy desire, and be lifted up to God, to meet the communications of his grace, and in an expectation raised very high of great things from him.

When God hears our prayers it is fitly said that he bows down his ear to them, for it is admirable condescension in God that he is pleased to take notice of such mean creatures as we are and such defective prayers as ours are . . . Not that God needs to have his affections stirred up by anything that we can say; but thus we must express our desire of his favour.

It is thus our duty to pray always, without ceasing, and to continue instant in prayer; and then we may hope to have our prayers heard which we make in the time of trouble, if we have made conscience of the duty at other times, at all times. It is comfortable if an affliction finds the wheels of prayer a-going, and that they are not then to be set a-going.

Psalm 86

It should be our care that God would graciously hear us; for, if our prayers be not pleasing to God, they will be to no purpose to ourselves.

Psalm 102

Are we in pursuit of any mercy, and wrestling with God for it? We must take our encouragement, in prayer, from God only, and have an eye to his glory more than to our own benefit in it. 'Lord, do so and so for us, not that we may have the credit and comfort of it, but that thy mercy and truth may have the glory of it.' This must be our highest and ultimate end in our prayers, and therefore it is made the first petition in the Lord's prayer, as that which guides all the rest, 'Hallowed be thy name.'

Psalm 115

See how the desire and prayer of a good man exactly agree with the will and command of a good God.

The best are sensible of their aptness to wander; and the more we have found of the pleasure there is in keeping God's commandments the more afraid we shall be of wandering from them and the more earnest we shall be in prayer to God for his grace to prevent our wanderings.

Psalm 119

God is in heaven, where he reigns in glory over us and all the children of men, where he is attended with an innumerable company of holy angels and is far exalted above all our blessing and praise. We are on earth, the footstool of his throne; we are mean and vile, unlike God, and utterly unworthy to receive any favour from him or to have any communion with him. Therefore we must be grave, humble and serious, and be reverent in speaking to him, as we are when we speak to a great man that is much our superior; and, in token of this, let our words be few, that they may be well chosen (Job 9:14). This does not condemn all long prayers; were they not good, the Pharisees would not have used them for a pretence; Christ prayed all night; and we are directed to 'continue in prayer'. But it condemns careless heartless, praying, vain repetitions (Matt. 6:7), repeating *Pater-nosters* by tale. Let us speak to God, and of him, in his own words, words which the Scripture teaches; and let our words, words of our own invention, be few, lest, not speaking by rule, we speak amiss.

Ecclesiastes 5

When we meet with the greatest difficulties, then is a time to stir up not ourselves only, but others also, to take hold on God. Prayer is the midwife of mercy, that helps to bring it forth.

The prayer that reaches heaven must be lifted up by a strong faith, earnest desires, and a direct intention to the glory of God, all which should be quickened when we come to the last stake.

Isaiah 37

It is an ill omen to a people when God restrains the spirits of his ministers and people from praying for them, and gives them to see their case so desperate that they have no heart to speak a good word for them. Those that will not regard good ministers' preaching cannot expect any benefit by their praying. If you will not hear us when we speak from God to you, God will not hear us when we speak to Him for you.

Jeremiah 7

God's having heard our voice when we cried to him, even out of the low dungeon, is an encouragement for us to hope that he will not at any time hide his ear. Observe how he calls prayer his breathing; for in prayer we breathe towards God, we breathe after him. Though we be but weak in prayer, cannot cry aloud, but only breathe in groanings that cannot be uttered, yet we shall not be neglected if we be sincere. Prayer is the breath of the new man, sucking in the air of mercy in petitions and returning it in praises; it is both the evidence and the maintenance of spiritual life.

Lamentations 3

Though we may not quarrel with God, yet we may plead with him; and, though we may not conclude that he has cast off, yet we may (with the prophet, Jer. 12:1) humbly reason with him concerning his judgments, especially the continuance of the desolations of his sanctuary.

Lamentations 5

Though Daniel was a great man, he did not think it below him to be thrice a day upon his knees before his maker and to be his own chaplain; though he was an old man, he did not think himself past it; nor, though it had been his practice from his youth up, was he weary of this well doing. Though he was a man of business, vast business, for the service of the public, he did not think that would excuse him from the daily exercises of devotion. How inexcusable then are those who have but little to do in the world, and yet will not do thus much for God and their souls! Daniel was a man famous for prayer, and for success in it (Ezek. 14:14), and he came to be so by thus making a conscience of prayer and making a business of it daily; and in thus doing God blessed him wonderfully.

Daniel 6

We must take good words with us, by taking good thoughts and good affections with us. Those who master a subject are seldom at a loss for language. Note, when we come to God we should consider what we have to say to him; for, if we come without an errand, we are likely to go without an answer. (Ezra 9:10) 'What shall we say?' We must take with us words from the Scripture, take them from the Spirit of grace and supplication, who teaches us to cry, *Abba*, Father, and makes intercession in us.

Hosea 14

The complaints of the brute-creatures here are for want of water ('The rivers are dried up', through the excessive heat), and for want of grass, for 'the fire has devoured the pastures of the wilderness'. And what better are those than beasts who never cry to God but for corn and wine, and complain of nothing but the want of the delights of sense? Yet their crying to God in those cases shames the stupidity of those who cry not to God in any case.

Joel 1

You may as soon find a living man without breath as a living saint without prayer.

Zechariah 12

Secret prayer is to be performed in retirement, that we may be unobserved, and so may avoid ostentation; undisturbed, and so may avoid distraction; unheard, and so may use the greater freedom; yet if the circumstances be such that we cannot possibly avoid being taken notice of, we must not therefore neglect the duty, lest the omission be a greater scandal than the observation of it.

Matthew 6

It was well they had him so near them. They awoke him with their prayers; 'Lord, save us, we perish'. Note, they who would learn to pray must go to sea. Imminent and sensible dangers will drive people to him who alone can help in time of need. Their prayer has life in it, 'Lord, save us, we perish'.

Matthew 8

In following Christ with our prayers, we must expect to meet with hindrances and manifold discouragements from within and from without, something or other that bids us hold our peace. Such rebukes are permitted, that faith and fervency, patience and perseverance, may be tried.

Christ knew well enough; but he would know it from them, whether they begged only for an alms, as from a common person, or for a cure, as from the Messiah. Note, it is the will of God that we should in everything make our requests known to him by prayer and supplication; not to inform or move him, but to qualify ourselves for the mercy. The waterman in the boat, who with his hook takes hold of the shore, does not thereby pull the shore to the boat, but the boat to the shore. So in prayer we do not draw the mercy to ourselves, but ourselves to the mercy.

Matthew 20

Where there are many sins to be confessed, and many wants to pray for the supply of, and many mercies to give thanks for, there is occasion for long prayers. But the Pharisees' long prayers were made up of vain repetitions, and (which was the end of them) they were for a pretence.

Matthew 23

And thus the cure is the sooner wrought, the nobleman's mistake rectified, and his faith confirmed; so that the thing was better done in Christ's way. When he denies what we ask, he gives what is much more to our advantage; we ask for ease, he gives patience.

John 4

The promise is as express as we can desire. We are taught here how to seek; we must 'ask the Father in Christ's name'; we must have an eye to God as a Father, and come as children

to him; and to Christ as mediator, and come as clients. Asking of the Father includes a sense of spiritual wants and a desire of spiritual blessings, with a conviction that they are to be had from God only. It includes also humility of address to him, with a believing confidence in him, as a Father able and ready to help us. Asking in Christ's name includes an acknowledgment of our own unworthiness to receive any favour from God, a complacency in the method God has taken of keeping up a correspondence with us by his Son, and an entire dependence upon Christ as 'the Lord our Righteousness'.

See what a generous benefactor our Lord Jesus is, above all benefactors; he gives liberally, and is so far from upbraiding us with the frequency and largeness of his gifts that he rather upbraids us with the seldomness and straitness of our requests.

Would we have our joy full, as full as it is capable of being in this world, we must be 'much in prayer'. When we are told to 'rejoice evermore', it follows immediately, 'Pray without ceasing'. See how high we are to aim in prayer — not only at peace, but joy, a 'fulness of joy'.

John 16

All repetitions in prayer are not to be counted 'vain repetitions'; Christ 'prayed, saying the same words' (Matt. 26:44), and yet 'prayed more earnestly'. What his Father had promised him, and he was assured of, yet he must pray for; promises are not designed to supersede prayers, but to be the guide of our desires and the ground of our hopes.

John 17

Before they were first sent forth Christ spent time in prayer for them, and now they spent time in prayer for themselves. They were waiting for the descent of the Spirit upon them, and therefore abounded thus in prayer. The Spirit descended upon our Saviour when he was praying, (Luke 3:21). Those are in the best frame to receive spiritual blessings that are in a praying frame. Christ had promised now shortly to send the Holy Ghost; now this promise was not to supersede prayer, but to quicken and encourage it. God will be enquired of for promised mercies, and the nearer the performance seems to be the more earnest we should be in prayer for it.

Acts 1

Christ was so pleased to find Paul praying that he must have others to take notice of it: 'Rejoice with me, for I have found the sheep which I had lost'. It denotes also the strangeness of it: Behold, and wonder, that he who but the other day breathed nothing but threatenings and slaughter, now breathes nothing but prayer. But was it such a strange thing for Saul to pray? Was he not a Pharisee? and have we not reason to think he did, as the rest of them did, make long prayers in the synagogues and the corners of the streets? Yes; but now he began

to pray after another manner than he had done; *then* he said his prayers, *now* he prayed them. Regenerating grace evermore sets people on praying; you may as soon find a living man without breath as a living Christian without prayer; if breathless, lifeless; and so, if prayerless, graceless.

Acts 9

From morning to night we should think to be too long to be without meat; yet who thinks it is too long to be without prayer?

Acts 10

Hereby Christians are distinguished from the profane and atheistical, that they dare not live without prayer; and hereby they are distinguished from Jews and Pagans, that they call on the name of Christ.

1 Corinthians 1

Though God accepts the prayer of faith, yet he does not always answer it in the letter; *as he sometimes grants in wrath, so he sometimes denies in love.*

2 Corinthians 12

The perfecting, establishing, strengthening, and settling, of good people in grace, and their perseverance therein, is so difficult a work, that only the God of all grace can accomplish it; and therefore he is earnestly to be sought unto by continual prayer, and dependence upon his promises.

1 Peter 5

To this end we must remember that our Lord obliges us, 1. To forgive those who offend us

(Matt. 6:14) and 2. To reconcile ourselves to those whom we have offended (Matt. 5:23, 24). As goodwill to men was proclaimed from heaven, so goodwill to men, and particularly to the brethren, must be carried in the hearts of those who go to God and heaven.

1 John 3

Prayer (Acceptable)

Samuel's sacrifice without his prayer would have been an empty shadow. His prayer without the sacrifice would not have been so prevalent but both together teach us what great things we may expect from God in answer to those prayers which are made with faith in Christ's sacrifice.

1 Samuel 7

Prayers that have much life and affection in them are in a special manner pleasing to God.

2 Kings 20

God gave him strength in his soul, and that is a real and valuable answer to the prayer of faith in the day of affliction. If God give us strength in our souls to bear the burdens, resist the temptations, and do the duties of an afflicted state, if he strengthen us to keep hold of himself by faith, to maintain the peace of our own minds and to wait with patience for the issue, we must own that he has answered us, and we are bound to be thankful.

Psalm 138

Prayer (Delays)

Instead of blaming Christ, or charging him with unkindness, she seems rather to suspect herself, and lay the fault upon herself. She fears lest, in her first address, she had not been humble and reverent enough, and therefore now 'she came, and worshipped him', and paid him more respect than she had done; or she fears that she had not been earnest enough, and therefore now she cries, 'Lord, help me.' Note, When the answers of prayer are deferred, God is thereby teaching us to pray more, and pray better.

Matthew 15

But God will now, in giving this mercy, look a great way back to the prayers that he had made long since for and with his wife, as Isaac for and with his (Gen. 25:21). Note, prayers of faith are filed in heaven, and are not forgotten, though the thing prayed for is not presently given in. Prayers made when we were young and coming into the world may be answered when we are old and going out of the world.

Luke 1

Prayer (Earnestness in)

The psalm concludes with the same petition that had been put up twice before, and yet it is no vain repetition (v. 19): 'Turn us again'. The title given to God rises (v. 3) 'O God!', (v. 7) 'O God! of hosts!', (v. 19) 'O Lord Jehovah, God of hosts! When we come to God for his grace, his goodwill towards us and his good work in us, we should pray earnestly, continue instant in prayer, and pray more earnestly.

Psalm 80

He prayed with his heart, and prayer is acceptable no further than the heart goes along with it. Lip-labour, if that be all, is lost labour. He was importunate with God in prayer; he cried, as one in earnest, with fervour of affection and a holy vehemence and vigour of desire. He cried with his whole heart; all the powers of his soul were not only engaged and employed, but exerted to the utmost, in his prayers. Then we are likely to speed when we thus strive and wrestle in prayer.

Psalm 119

David loved prayer, and he begs of God that his prayers might be heard and answered (v. 1, 2). David cried unto God. His crying denotes fervency in prayer; he prayed as one in earnest. His crying to God denotes faith and fixedness in prayer.

Those that cry in prayer may hope to be heard in prayer, not for their loudness, but for their liveliness.

Those that know how to value God's gracious presence will be importunate for it and humbly impatient of delays. He that believes does not make haste, but he that prays may be earnest with God to make haste.

Prayer is of a sweet-smelling savour to God, as incense, which yet has no savour without fire;

nor has prayer without the fire of holy love and fervour.

Psalm 141

What we utter before God must come from the heart, and therefore we must not be rash with the mouth, never let our tongue outrun our thoughts in our devotions; the words of our mouth must always be the product of the meditation of our hearts. Thoughts are words to God, and words are but wind if they be not copied from the thoughts. Lip-labour, though ever so well laboured, if that be all, is but lost labour in religion (Matt. 15:8, 9).

Ecclesiastes 5

The 'it may be' of the prospect of the haven of blessings should quicken us with double diligence to ply the oar of prayer.

The prayer that reaches heaven must be lifted up by a strong faith, earnest desires, and a direct intention to the glory of God, all which should be quickened when we come to the last stake.

Isaiah 37

To pray is to take hold of God, by faith to take hold of the promises and the declarations God has made of his goodwill to us *and to plead them with him* — to take hold of him as of one who is about to depart from us, earnestly begging of him not to leave us, or of one that has departed, soliciting his return — to take hold of him as he that wrestles takes hold of him he wrestles with; for the seed of Jacob wrestle with him and so prevail. But when we take hold of God it is as the boatman with his hook takes hold on the shore, as if he would pull the shore to him, but really it is to pull himself to the shore; so we pray, not to bring God to our mind, but to bring ourselves to his. Those that would take hold of God in prayer so as to prevail with him must *stir up themselves to do it*; all that is within us must be employed in the duty *(and all little enough)*, our *thoughts fixed*, and our *affections flaming*. In order hereunto all that is within us must be engaged and summoned into the service.

Isaiah 64

He had prayed (Ch. 32:16), but he must pray again. Note, those that expect to receive comforts from God must continue instant in prayer.

Promises are given, not to supersede, but to quicken and encourage prayer. See (Ezek. 36:37).

Jeremiah 33

They cried out as men in earnest; men in want are earnest, of course. Cold desires do but beg denials. Those that would prevail in prayer, must stir up themselves to take hold on God in the duty. When they were discountenanced in it, they cried the more. The stream of fervency, if it be stopped, will rise and swell the higher.

The sincere and serious beggars at Christ's door commonly meet with the worst rebukes from those that follow him but in pretence and hypocrisy. But they would not be beaten off so; when they were in pursuit of such a mercy, it was no time to compliment, or to practise a timid delicacy; no, 'they cried the more'.

Matthew 20

The prayers and supplications that Christ offered up were joined with strong cries and tears, herein setting us an example not only to pray, but to be fervent and importunate in prayer. How many dry prayers, how few wet ones, do we offer up to God!

Hebrews 5

Prayer (Encouragement to)

Hear what this haughty king says (What is thy petition, and what is thy request? It shall be granted thee), and say shall not God hear and answer the prayers of his own elect, that cry day and night to him? Esther came to a proud imperious man; *we* come to the God of love and grace. She was not called; *we* are: the Spirit says *'Come'* and the bride says, *'Come'*. She had a law against her; *we* have a promise, many a promise in favour of us: *Ask, and it shall be given you.* She had no friend to introduce her, or intercede for her, while on the contrary, he that was then the king's favourite was her enemy; but *we* have an advocate with the Father, in whom he is well pleased. Let us therefore come boldly to the throne of grace.

Esther 5

It is thus expressed because

others despise their praying, they themselves fear God will despise it, and he was thought to despise it while their affliction was prolonged and their prayers lay unanswered. When we consider our own meanness and vileness, our darkness and deadness, and the manifold defects in our prayers, we have cause to suspect that our prayers will be received with disdain in heaven; but we are here assured of the contrary, for we have an advocate with the Father.

Psalm 102

Thou feedest the young ravens that cry, with food proper for them; and wilt thou not feed me with spiritual food, the bread of life, which my soul needs and craves, and cannot subsist without? 'The earth is full of thy mercy'; and is not heaven too? Wilt thou not then give me spiritual blessings in heavenly places? A gracious heart will fetch an argument from any thing to enforce a petition for divine teaching. Surely he that will not let his birds be unfed will not let his children be untaught.

Psalm 119

When God is about to give his people the expected good he pours out a spirit of prayer, and it is a good sign that he is coming towards them in mercy. Then, when you see the expected end approaching, then you shall call upon me. Note, promises are given, not to supersede, but to quicken and encourage prayer: and when deliverance is coming we must by prayer go forth to meet it. When Daniel understood that the 70 years were near expiring, then he set his face with more fervency than ever to seek the Lord (Dan. 9:2, 3).

. . . and this we must do with our heart (that is, in sincerity and uprightness), and with our whole heart (that is, with vigour and fervency, putting forth all that is within us in prayer).

Jeremiah 29

When God intends great mercy for his people, the first thing he does is to set them a praying; thus he seeks to destroy their enemies by stirring them up to seek to him that he would do it for them; because, though he has proposed it and promised it, and it is for his own glory to do it, yet he will 'for this be enquired of by the house of Israel (Ezek. 36: 37). 'Ask, and it shall be given'. This honour will he have to himself, and this honour will he put upon prayer and upon praying people. And it is a happy presage to the distressed church of deliverance approaching, and is, as it were, the dawning of its day, when his people are stirred up to cry mightily to him for it.

Zechariah 12

Prayer (Matters for)

It is a sin against God not to pray for the Israel of God, especially for those of them that are under our charge and good men are afraid of the guilt of omissions.

1 Samuel 12

God gives us leave to be earnest

with him in prayer for particular blessings from a confidence in his power and general mercy though we have no particular promise to build upon. We cannot be sure, yet let us pray for who can tell but God will be gracious to us in this or that particular. When our relations and friends have fallen sick, the prayer of faith has prevailed much while there is life there is hope and while there is hope there is room for prayer.

2 Samuel 12

If any good have got possession of our hearts or the hearts of our friends, it is good, by prayer, to commit the custody of it to the grace of God. 'Lord, keep it there, keep it for ever there.'

1 Chronicles 29

He knew they were a praying people and had heard that God was nigh to them in all that which they called upon him for. He was sensible; he needed their prayers and might receive benefit by them and was kind to them in order that he might have an interest in their prayers. It is the duty of God's people to pray for those that are in authority over them, not only for the good and gentle but also for the froward but they are particularly bound in gratitude to pray for their protectors and benefactors and it is the wisdom of princes to desire their prayers and to engage them. Let not the greatest princes despise the prayers of the meanest saints. It is desirable to have them for us and dreadful to have them against us.

Ezra 6

Though we are to pray for our enemies as such, yet we are to pray against God's enemies as such, against their enmity to him and all their attempts upon his kingdom.

Psalm 68

Prayer (Pleading God's Attributes)

Our experiences of God's power and favour should be improved for the support of our expectations. 'Thou hast, therefore, not only thou canst but we trust thou wilt' is good arguing.

Exodus 15

He pleads with God for speedy relief: 'Lord, thou art good, thou art faithful, thou art righteous; these attributes of thine will be made known in my deliverance, but, if it be not hastened, it will come too late; for I shall be dead and past relief, dead and not capable of receiving any comfort, very shortly.'

Psalm 88

The best saints count this their best plea for any blessing, 'Let me have it according to thy mercy'; for we deserve no favour from God, nor can we claim any as a debt, but we are most likely to be easy when we cast ourselves upon God's mercy and refer ourselves to it. Particularly, when we come to him for instruction, we must beg it, as a mercy, and reckon that in being taught we are well dealt with.

Psalm 119

Prayer (Pleading God's Word)

The best we can say to God in prayer is what he has said to us. God's promises, as they are the surest guide of our desires in prayer and furnish us with the best petitions, so they are the firmest ground of our hopes and furnish us with the best pleas. 'Lord, thou hast said this and wilt thou not be as good as thy Word. The Word upon which thou hast caused me to hope?' (Ps. 119:49).

Genesis 32

'Lord, thou hast put me into this place, therefore I can, in faith, ask of thee grace to enable me to do the duty of it.' What service we have reason to believe God calls us to, we have reason to hope he will qualify us for . . . Note first, God's promises are our best pleas in prayer. 'Remember thy word unto thy servant'.

2 Chronicles 1

He could not in faith have asked God to show such a peculiar favour to this house above any other if he himself had not said it should be his rest for ever. The prayer that will speed must be warranted by the Word. We may with humble confidence pray to God to be well pleased with us in Jesus Christ because he has declared himself well pleased in him 'Jesus, my beloved Son' . . . Even Christ's intercessions do not supersede but encourage our supplications.

2 Chronicles 6

Many passages in this acknowledgement of sins and mercies are taken from (Ezek. 20: 5—26), as will appear by comparing those verses with these; for the word of God is of use to direct us in prayer, and by what he says to us we may learn what to say to him.

Nehemiah 9

The former part is taken out of Psalm 57:7, the latter out of Psalm 60:5, and both with very little variation, to teach us that we may in prayer use the same words that we have formerly used, provided it be with new affections. It intimates likewise that it is not only allowable, but sometimes convenient, to gather some verses out of one psalm and some out of another, and to put them together, to be sung to the glory of God.

Psalm 108

Those that are governed by the precepts of the word and are resolved to keep them (v. 57) may plead the promises of the word and take the comfort of them.

Psalm 119

This, and that other word, 'Into thy hands I commit my spirit', he fetched from David's psalms (though he could have expressed himself in his own words), to teach us of what use the Word of God is to us, to direct us in prayer, and to recommend to us the use of scripture-expressions in prayer, which will help our infirmities.

Matthew 27

217

Prayer (Public)

We find that when this psalm (or at least the closing verses of it) was sung, all the people said, 'Amen', and praised the Lord by saying 'Hallelujah'. By these two comprehensive words it is very proper, in religious assemblies, to testify their joining with their ministers in the prayers and praises which, as their mouth, they offer up to God, according to his will, saying 'Amen' to the prayers and 'Hallelujah' to the praises.

Psalm 106

Prayer (Unacceptable)

Hezekiah prayed for his own life and David for the life of his child after both had been expressly threatened; the former prevailed though the latter did not . . . What God does not think fit to grant we should not think fit to ask. God takes such a pleasure in the prayer of the upright that it is no pleasure to him, no, not in any particular instance, to give a denial to it.

Deuteronomy 3

Those who expect God to hear their prayers must be willing to hear reason, to hear a faithful reproof and to hear the complaints and appeals of wronged innocency. If we turn away our ear from hearing the law, our prayer will be an abomination.

Judges 9

If true repentance come upon him, God will hear his cry and accept him (Isa. 1:18); but, if he continue impenitent and unchanged, let him not think to find favour with God.

Those who in prosperity slighted God, either prayed not at all or were cold and careless in prayer, when trouble comes will make their application to him and cry as men in earnest. But, will God hear him then? In the troubles of this life, God has told us that he will not hear the prayers of those who regard iniquity in their hearts (Ps. 66: 19) and set up their idols there (Ezek. 14:4), nor of those who turn away their ear from hearing the law (Prov. 28:9). Get you to the gods whom you have served (Judg. 10:14).

Job 27

When we only pore upon the afflictions we are under, and neglect the consolations of God which are treasured up for us, it is just with God to reject our prayers.

Job 35

Those are in a sad case indeed that are cut off from the benefit of prayer. 'I will not hear them when they cry', and therefore do not thou pray for them. Note, those that have so far thrown themselves out of God's favour that he will not hear their prayers cannot expect benefit by the prayers of others for them.

Jeremiah 11

They had forfeited all benefit by the prophet's prayers for them because they had not regarded his preaching to them. This is the meaning of that repeated prohibition given to the prophet (v. 11): 'Pray not thou for this people for their good', as before (ch. 7:16; 11:14). This did not forbid him thus to express his good-will to them (Moses continued to intercede for Israel after God had said 'Let me alone' (Exod. 32:10), but it forbade them to expect any good effect from it as long as they 'turned away their ear from hearing the law'.

Jeremiah 14

Preachers

We often find the prophets admonished, whose business it was to admonish others, as (Isa. 8:11). Ministers have lessons to learn as well as lessons to teach, and must themselves hear God's voice and preach to themselves.

Jeremiah 12

He had always been a lively affectionate preacher, and since he began to speak in God's name he always spoke as a man in earnest; he cried aloud and did not spare, spared neither himself nor those to whom he preached; and this was enough for those to laugh at who hated to be serious. It is common for those that are unaffected with, and disaffected to, the things of God themselves, to ridicule those that are much affected with them. Lively preachers are the scorn of careless unbelieving hearers.

Jeremiah 20

As God appointed Jeremiah to confirm his predictions of the approaching destruction of Jerusalem by his own practice in living unmarried, so he now appointed him to confirm his predictions of the future restoration of Jerusalem by his own practice in purchasing this field.

Note, it concerns ministers to make it to appear in their whole conversation that they do themselves believe that which they preach to others; and that they may do so, and impress it the more deeply upon their hearers, they must many a time deny themselves, as Jeremiah did in both these instances.

Jeremiah 32

'Whosoever shall receive one such child', a preacher of the gospel that is of such a disposition as this, he placeth his respect aright, and receiveth me; and whosoever receiveth me, in such a minister, receiveth him that sent me; and what greater honour can any man attain to in this world than to be received by men as a messenger of God and Christ, and to have God and Christ own themselves received and welcomed in him.

Luke 9

Preaching

Here the matter was settled by consent of both parties that God should henceforward speak to us by men like ourselves, by Moses and the Prophets, by the Apostles and the Evangelists and if we believe not these neither should we be persuaded, though God should speak to us as he did to Israel at Mount Sinai or send expresses from heaven or hell.

Deuteronomy 5

He as inoffensively as possible, reminded them of what was written in the Law. Let them but look into their Bibles and there they would find 1. The precept they broke; you transgressed the commandments of the Lord. You know you do so . . . 2. The penalty they incurred. You know if the Word of God be true, you cannot prosper in this evil way. Never expect to do ill and fare well. Nay, you find already that because you have forsaken the Lord, he has forsaken you as he told you he would. (Deut. 29:25; 31:16, 17). This is the work of ministers, by the Word of God as a lamp and a light to expose the sin of men and expound the providences of God.

2 Chronicles 24

Men would gladly have their prophets thus under their girdles as we say, to speak just when and what they would have them speak and not otherwise.

2 Chronicles 25

He did not deliver his head and observations at random, as they came to mind, but methodised them, and set them in order that they might appear in more strength and lustre. He put what he had to say in such a dress as he thought would be most pleasing: He sought to find out acceptable words, words of delight; he took care that good matter might not be spoiled by a bad style, and by the ungratefulness and incongruity of the expression. Ministers should study, not for big words, nor for fine words, but acceptable words, such as are likely to please men for their good, to edification (1 Cor. 10:33). Those that would win souls must contrive how to win upon them with words fitly spoken.

He does not say 'Do you hear it' but, 'Let us hear it'; for preachers must themselves be hearers of that word which they preach to others, must hear it as from God; those are teachers by the halves who teach others and not themselves (Rom. 2:21).

Ecclesiastes 12

He shall cry, in the preaching of his word, cry like a travailing woman; for the ministers of Christ preached as men in earnest, and that travailed in birth again till they saw Christ formed in the souls of the people (Gal. 4:19). He shall cry, yea, roar, in the gospel woes, which are more terrible than the roaring of a lion, and which must be preached along with gospel blessings to awaken a sleeping world.

Isaiah 42

He must not, as other watchmen, look round to spy danger and gain intelligence, but he must look up to God, and further he need not look: Hear the word at my mouth (v. 17). Note, those that are to preach must first hear; for how can those teach others who have not first learned themselves?

As a watchman must have eyes in his head, so he must have a tongue in his head; if he be dumb, it is as bad as if he were blind (Isa. 56:10).

Ezekiel 3

The power of imagination, if it be rightly used, and kept under the direction and correction of reason and faith, may be of good use to kindle and excite pious and devout affections, as it was here to Ezekiel and his attendants. 'Methinks I see so and so, myself dying, time expiring, the world on fire, the dead rising, the great tribunal set', and the like, may have an exceedingly good influence upon us; for fancy is like fire, a good servant, but a bad master.

Ezekiel 4

The birth of Christ was notified to the Jewish shepherds by an angel, to the Gentile philosophers by a star: to both God spoke in their own language, and in the way they were best acquainted with.

Matthew 2

He speaks as one that came not to preach *before* them, but to preach *to* them. Though his education was private, he was not bashful when he appeared in public, nor did he fear the face of man,, for he was full of the Holy Ghost and of power.

Matthew 3

Intelligent hearers; they hear the word and understand it; they understand not only the sense and meaning of the word, but their own concern in it: they understand it as a man of business understands his business. God in his word deals with men as men, in a rational way, and gains possession of the will and affections by opening the understanding: whereas Satan, who is a thief and a robber, comes not in by that door, but climbeth up another way.

Matthew 13

Here is a woe to them whom all men speak well of, that is, who make it their great and only care to gain the praise and applause of men, who value themselves upon that more than upon the favour of God and his acceptance (v. 26): 'Woe unto you'; that is, it would be a bad sign that you were not faithful to your trust, and to the souls of men, if you preached so as that nobody would be disgusted; for your business is to tell people of their faults, and, if you do that as you ought, you will get that ill will which never speaks well.

We should desire to have the approbation of those that are wise and good, and not be indifferent to what people say of us; but, as we should despise the reproaches, so we should also despise the praises, of the fools in Israel.

Luke 6

Ministers must preach as those that are in earnest, and are themselves affected with those things with which they desire to affect others. Those words are not likely to thaw the hearers' hearts that freeze between the speaker's lips.

The mistakes of preachers often give rise to the prejudices of hearers.

John 1

The corrupt and wicked heart of man often makes that an occasion of offence which is indeed matter of the greatest comfort. Christ foresaw that they would thus take offence

221

at what he said, and yet he said it. That which is the undoubted word and truth of Christ must be faithfully delivered, whoever may be offended at it. Men's humours must be captivated to God's word, and not God's word accommodated to men's humours.

John 6

The advantage of having faithful remembrancers near us, who, though they cannot tell us more than we know already, yet may remind us of that which we know, but have forgotten. The crowing of the cock to others was an accidental thing, and had no significance; but to Peter it was the voice of God, and had a blessed tendency to awaken his conscience, by putting him in mind of the word of Christ.

John 18

Preaching the gospel is the best work, and the most proper and needful that a minister can be employed in, and that which he must give himself wholly to (1 Tim. 4:15), which that he may do, he must not entangle himself in the affairs of this life (2 Tim. 2:4), no, not in the outward business of the house of God. (Neh. 11:16).

Acts 6

The instruction, edification, and comfort of the church, is that for which God instituted the ministry. And surely ministers should, as much as possible, fit their ministrations to these purposes.

1 Corinthians 14

An old sermon may be preached with new affections; what we say often we may say again, if we say it affectionately, and are ourselves under the power of it.

Philippians 3

It is 'powerful'. When God sets it home by His Spirit, it convinces powerfully, converts powerfully, and comforts powerfully. It is so powerful as to pull down strong holds (2 Cor. 10:4, 5), to raise the dead, to make the deaf to hear, the blind to see, the dumb to speak, and the lame to walk. It is powerful to batter down Satan's kingdom, and to set up the kingdom of Christ upon the ruins thereof.

Hebrews 4

The business of a faithful minister is to apply general truths to the particular condition and state of his hearers. The apostle quotes a passage (v. 6) out of the prophet, and applies it severally to good and bad. This requires wisdom, courage, and fidelity; but it is very profitable to the hearers.

1 Peter 2

Prejudice

Who call drunkenness good fellowship, and covetousness good husbandry, and, when they persecute the people of God, think they do him good service — and, on the other hand, who call seriousness ill-nature, and sober singularity ill-breeding, who say all manner of evil falsely concerning the ways of godliness, and do what they can to form in men's minds prejudices against them, and this in defiance of evidence as plain and convincing as that of sense, by which we distinguish, beyond contradiction, between light and darkness, and between that which to the taste is sweet and that which is bitter.

Isaiah 5

Josephus speaks of some in his time who did it; we read of Jewish exorcists (Acts 19:13), and of some that in Christ's name cast out devils, though they did not follow him (Mark 9:38), or were not faithful to him (ch. 7:22). These the Pharisees condemned not, but imputed what they did to the Spirit of God, and valued themselves and their nation upon it. It was therefore merely from spite and envy to Christ, that they would own that others cast out devils by the Spirit of God, but suggest that he did it by compact with Beelzebub. Note, it is the way of malicious people, especially the malicious persecutors of Christ and Christianity, to condemn the same thing in those they hate, which they approve of and applaud in those they have a kindness for.

Matthew 12

Let him say what he would in his own justification, they are resolved, right or wrong, to find him guilty of sabbath breaking. When malice and envy sit upon the bench, reason and justice may even be silent at the bar, for whatever they can say will undoubtedly be overruled.

John 5

He was not to be blamed for changing his thoughts, when God had changed the thing. In things of this nature we must act according to our present light; yet must not be so wedded to our opinion concerning them as to be prejudiced against further discoveries, when the matter may either be otherwise or appear otherwise; and God may reveal even this unto us (Phil. 3:15).

Acts 11

It is very hard for men suddenly to get clear of their prejudices: those that had been Pharisees, even after they became Christians, retained some of the old leaven. All did not so, witness Paul, but some did; and they had such a jealousy for the ceremonial law, and such a dislike of the Gentiles, that they could not admit the Gentiles into communion with them, unless they would be circumcised, and thereby engage themselves to keep the law of Moses.

Acts 15

Presence of God

They were content with the altars without the Ark. So easily can formal professors rest satisfied in a round of external performances without any tokens of God's presence or acceptance.

1 Samuel 7

He calls God his strength (v. 19). When we cannot rejoice in God as our song, yet let us stay ourselves upon him as our strength, and take the comfort of spiritual supports when we cannot come at spiritual delights.

Psalm 22

223

Christ doth not leave the soul, when extraordinary joys and comforts leave it. Though more sensible and ravishing communications may be withdrawn, Christ's disciples have, and shall have, his ordinary presence with them always, even to the end of the world, and that is it we must depend upon. Let us thank God for daily bread, and not expect a continual feast on this side of heaven.

Mark 9

They welcomed Christ into the ship; they willingly received him. Note, Christ's absenting himself for a time is but so much the more to endear himself, at his return, to his disciples, who value his presence above any thing; see (Cant. 3:4).

John 6

Presumption

If even a righteous man engage in an unrighteous cause, let him not expect to prosper. God is no respecter of persons. (Prov. 3:30; 25:8).

2 Chronicles 35

Pride

Let none be puffed up with conceit of visions and revelations when even an ass saw an angel.

Numbers 22

That will break a proud man's heart that will not break a humble man's sleep.

2 Samuel 17

What is more commonly and (as we think) more innocently done than to show strangers the riches and rarities of a country, to show our friends our houses and their furniture, our gardens, stables and libraries. But if we do this in the pride of our hearts as Hezekiah did to gain applause from men and not giving praise to God, it turns into sin to us as it did to him . . . Isaiah, who had often been his comforter, is now his reprover — the blessed Spirit is both (John 16, 7, 8). Ministers must be both as there is occasion . . . It is just with God to take that from us which we make the matter of our pride and in which we put our confidence.

2 Kings 20

He invaded the dignity of the priesthood which he had no right to and for that he was deprived even of his royal dignity which he had a right to. Those that covet forbidden honours forfeit the allowed ones. Adam by catching at the tree of knowledge of which he might not eat, debarred himself from the tree of life of which he might have eaten. Let all that read it say, the Lord is righteous.

2 Chronicles 26

God left him to himself to be proud of his wealth to keep him from being proud of his holiness. It is good for us to know ourselves and our weakness and sinfulness, that we might not be conceited or self-confident but may always think meanly of ourselves and live in a dependence upon divine grace. We know not the corruption of our own hearts nor what we shall do if God leave us to ourselves. Lord, lead us not into temptation . . . When Hezekiah had destroyed other idolatries he began to idolise himself. Oh what need have great men and good men and useful men to study their own infirmities and follies and their obligations to free grace that they may never think highly of themselves and to beg earnestly of God that he will hide pride from them and always keep them humble.

2 Chronicles 32

. . . His high spirit resented what Job had said as if it had been the greatest affront imaginable. Proud men are apt to think themselves slighted more than they really are.

Job 18

God is often angry at that in us which we are ourselves proud of and sees much amiss in that which we think was done well.

Job 42

Pride is a sin which men have reason to be themselves ashamed of; it is a shame to a man who springs out of the earth, who lives upon alms, depends upon God, and has forfeited all he has, to be proud.

Proverbs 11

Pride makes men impatient of contradiction in either their opinions or their desires, impatient of competition and rivalship, impatient of contempt, or anything that looks like a slight, and impatient of concession, and receding, from a conceit of certain right and truth on their side; and hence arise quarrels among relations and neighbours, quarrels in states and kingdoms, in churches and Christian societies. Men will be revenged, will not forgive, because they are proud.

Proverbs 13

Over-praising a man makes him the object of envy; every man puts in for a share of reputation, and therefore reckons himself injured if another monopolize it or have more given him than his share. And the greatest danger of all is that it is a temptation to pride; men are apt to think of themselves above what is meet when others speak of them above what is meet. See how careful blessed Paul was not to be over-valued (2 Cor. 12:6).

Proverbs 27

It is just with God to take that from us which we make the matter of our pride, and on which we build a carnal confidence. When David was proud of the numbers of his people God took a course to make them fewer; and when Hezekiah boasts of his treasures, and looks upon them with too great a complacency, he is told that he acts like the foolish traveller who shows his money and gold to one that proves a thief and is thereby tempted to rob him.

Isaiah 39

He that knows what is in man knew that Jehoiakim did this in the pride of his heart, which makes that to be sinful, exceedingly sinful, which is in itself lawful. Those therefore that are enlarging their houses, and making them more sumptuous, have need to look well to the frame of their own spirits in the doing of it, and carefully to watch against all the workings of vain-glory.

Many have unhumbled hearts under humbling providences, and look most haughty when God is bringing them down. This is striving with our maker.

Jeremiah 22

It is just with God that our enemies should make that their prey which we have made our pride. The King of Tyre's palace, his treasury, his city, his navy, his army, these he glories in as his brightness, these, he thinks, make him illustrious and glorious as a god on earth. But all these the victorious enemy shall defile, shall deface, shall deform.

Ezekiel 28

The people were, generally, extremely proud of their privileges, confident of justification by their own righteousness, insensible of sin; and, though now under the most humbling providences, being lately made a province of the Roman Empire, yet they were unhumbled; they were much in the same temper as they were in Malachi's time, insolent and haughty, and ready to contradict the Word of God.

Matthew 3

Advancement in the world makes a man a fair mark for Satan to shoot his fiery darts at. God casts down, that he may raise up; the devil raises up, that he may cast down;

therefore they who would take heed of falling, must take heed of climbing.

Matthew 4

It is sad that men who have, in some measure, mastered their pleasure, which is sensual wickedness, should be ruined by their pride, which is spiritual wickedness, and no less dangerous. Here also, they have their reward, that praise and applause of men which they court and covet so much; they have it, and it is their all.

This direction about laying up our treasure, may very fitly be applied to the foregoing caution, of not doing what we do in religion to be seen of men. Our treasure is our alms, prayers, and fastings, and the reward of them; if we have done these only to gain the applause of men, we have laid up this treasure on earth, have lodged it in the hands of men, and must never expect to hear any further of it. Now it is folly to do this, for the praise of men we covet so much is liable to corruption: it will soon be rusted, and moth-eaten and tarnished; a little folly, like a dead fly, will spoil it all (Eccl. 10:1). Slander and calumny are thieves that break through and steal it away, and so we lose all the treasure of our performances; we have run in vain, and laboured in vain, because we misplaced our intentions in doing of them. Hypocritical services lay up nothing in heaven (Isa. 58:3); the gain of them is gone, when the soul is called for (Job. 27:8). But if we have prayed and fasted and

given alms in truth and uprightness, with an eye to God and to
his acceptance, and have
approved ourselves to him therein, we have laid up that treasure
in heaven.

Matthew 6

They envied him, as Saul did his
father David, because of what
the women sang of him (1 Sam.
18:7, 8). Note, those who bind
up their happiness in the praise
and applause of men, expose
themselves to a perpetual uneasiness upon every favourable word
that they hear said of any other.
The shadow of honour followed
Christ, who fled from it, and
fled from the Pharisees, who
were eager in the pursuit of it.

Matthew 12

They strive who it should be,
each having some pretence or
other to it. Peter was always
the chief speaker, and already
had the keys given him; he
expects to be lord-chancellor, or
lord-chamberlain of the household, and so to be the greatest.
Judas had the bag, and therefore he expects to be lord-
treasurer, which, though now
he come last, he hopes, will
then denominate him the greatest. Simon and Jude are nearly
related to Christ, and they
hope to take place of all the
great officers of state, as princes
of the blood. John is the beloved
disciple, the favourite of the
Prince, and therefore hopes to
be the greatest. Andrew was
first called, and why should not
he be first preferred? Note, we
are very apt to amuse and
humour ourselves with foolish
fancies of things that will never
be.

He that had nothing to pay
with (v. 25) fancied he could
pay all. See how close pride
sticks, even to awakened
sinners; they are convinced,
but not humbled.

Matthew 18

It is a gracious ambition to
covet to be really more holy
than others, but it is a proud
ambition to covet to appear
so. It is good to excel in real
piety, but not to exceed in
outward shows; for overdoing
is justly suspected of design
(Prov. 27:14). It is the guise
of hypocrisy to make more
ado than needs in external
services.

For him that is taught in the
word to give respect to him
that teaches is commendable
enough in him that gives it; but
for him that teaches to love it,
and demand it, and affect it, to
be puffed up with it, and to be
displeased if it be omitted, is
sinful and abominable; and,
instead of teaching, he has
need to learn the first lesson
in the school of Christ, which
is humility.

If God gives them repentance,
they will be abased in their
own eyes, and will abhor themselves for it; if they repent not,
sooner or later they will be
abased before the world.
Nebuchadnezzar, in the height
of his pride, was turned to be
a fellow-commoner with the
beasts; Herod, to be a feast
for the worms: and Babylon,
that sat as a queen, to be the
scorn of the nations. God
made the proud and aspiring
priests contemptible and base

(Mal. 2:9), and the lying prophet to be the tail (Isa. 9:15). But if proud men have not marks of humiliation set upon them in this world, there is a day coming when they shall rise to everlasting shame and contempt (Dan. 12:2); so plentifully will he reward the proud doer! (Ps. 31:23).

Matthew 23

O what need have good men to take heed of pride, a corruption that arises out of the ashes of other corruptions!

Luke 15

Considering how great these Pharisees were, and what abundance of respect was paid them, one would think they needed not grudge Christ so inconsiderable a piece of honour as was now done him; but proud men would monopolize honour, and have none share with them, like Haman.

John 12

It is but too common for persons of very moderate knowledge and understanding to have a great measure of self-conceit.

1 Corinthians 3

Those who receive all should be proud of nothing (Ps. 115:1). Beggars and dependents may glory in their supports; but to glory in themselves is to be proud at once of meanness, impotence, and want. Note, due attention to our obligations to divine grace would cure us of arrogance and self-conceit.

1 Corinthians 4

Self-conceit is but self-deceit: as it is inconsistent with that charity we owe to others (for 'charity vaunteth not itself, is not puffed up') (1 Cor. 13:4), so it is a cheat upon ourselves; and there is not a more dangerous cheat in the world than self-deceit.

Galatians 6

The proud resists God; in his understanding he resists the truths of God; in his will he resists the laws of God; in his passions he resists the providences of God; and therefore no wonder that God sets himself against the proud.

James 4

There is a mutual opposition between God and the proud, so the word signifies; they war against him, and he scorns them; 'he resisteth the proud', because they are like the devil, enemies to himself and to his kingdom among men (Prov. 3:34).

1 Peter 5

Priorities

The nearer the world comes to its period the less value we should put on it. Because the time is short and the fashion of the world passes away let those that buy be as though they possessed not. One would put little value on an old house that is ready to drop down.

Leviticus 25

Now that the people were numbered, orders given for the dividing of the land and a General of the forces nominated and commissioned, one would have expected that the next chapter should begin the history of the campaign or at least should give us an account of the ordinances of war. No, it contains the ordinances of worship and provides that now as they were on the point of entering Canaan they should be sure to take their religion along with them.

Numbers 28 (Intro.)

Lastly, he built for pleasure in Lebanon, for his hunting perhaps, or other diversions there. Let piety begin and profit proceed, and leave pleasure to the last.

1 Kings 9

When David is advanced to wealth and power, see what his cares and projects are. Not 'what shall I do for my children to get portions for them,' 'What shall I do to fill my coffers and enlarge my dominions?' but 'What shall I do for God to serve and honour him?' Those that are contriving where to bestow their fruits and their goods would do well to enquire what condition the ark is in and whether some may not be well bestowed upon it.

1 Chronicles 17

Canaan was a rich country and yet must send to Ophir for gold. The Israelites were a wise and understanding people and yet must be beholden to the king of Tyre for men that had knowledge of the seas and yet Canaan was God's peculiar land and the Israelites God's peculiar people. This teaches us that grace and not gold is the best riches and acquaintance with God and his law, not with

arts and sciences, the best knowledge.

2 Chronicles 8

Hezekiah immediately threw the church doors open and brought in the priests and Levites; he found Judah low and naked yet did not make it his first business to revive the civil interests of his kingdom but to restore religion to its good posture again. Those that begin with God begin at the right end of their work and it will prosper accordingly.

2 Chronicles 29

That which he chose for his study was the law of the Lord. The Chaldeans among whom he was born and bred were famed for literature especially the study of the stars to which, being a studious man, we may suppose that Ezra was tempted to apply himself but he got over the temptation; the law of his God was more to him.

Ezra 7

A godly man has thoughts of the world, but they are his outward thoughts; his inward thought is reserved for God and heavenly things: but a worldly man has only some floating foreign thoughts of the things of God, while his fixed thought, his inward thought is about the world; that lies nearest his heart, and is upon the throne there.

Psalm 49

Heavenly wisdom is better than worldly wealth, and to be preferred before it. Grace is more valuable than gold. Grace is the gift of God's peculiar favour; gold only of common providence. Grace is for ourselves, gold for others. Grace is for the soul and eternity; gold only for the body and time. Grace will stand us in stead in a dying hour, when gold will do us no good.

Proverbs 16

The array of Solomon was very splendid and magnificent: he that had the peculiar treasure of kings and provinces, and so studiously affected pomp and gallantry, doubtless had the richest clothing, and the best made up, that could be got; especially when he appeared in his glory on high days. And yet, let him dress himself as fine as he could, he comes far short of the beauty of the lilies, and a bed of tulips outshines him. Let us, therefore, be ambitious of the wisdom of Solomon, in which he was outdone by none (wisdom to do our duty in our places), rather than the glory of Solomon, in which he was outdone by the lilies. Knowledge and grace are the perfection of man, not beauty, much less fine clothes.

Matthew 6

'True it is', said Bishop Hooper, the night before he suffered martyrdom, 'that life is sweet, and death is bitter, but eternal death is more bitter, and eternal life is more sweet.' As the happiness of heaven with Christ is enough to countervail the loss of life itself for Christ, so the gain of all the world in sin is not sufficient to countervail the ruin of the soul by sin.

Mark 8

Judas asked, 'Why was it not given to the poor?' To which it is easy to answer, Because it was better bestowed upon the Lord Jesus.

We need wisdom, when two duties come in competition, to know which to give the preference to, which must be determined by the circumstances. Opportunities are to be improved, and those opportunities first and most vigorously which are likely to be of the shortest continuance, and which we see most speedily hastening away. That good duty which may be done at any time ought to give way to that which cannot be done but just now.

John 12

The Romans were whole, and needed not the physician as other poor places that were sick and dying. While men and women were every day dropping into eternity, and their precious souls perishing for lack of vision, it was no time for Paul to trifle. There was now a gale of opportunity, the fields were white unto the harvest; such a season slipped might never be retrieved; the necessities of poor souls were pressing, and called aloud, and therefore Paul must be busy. It concerns us all to do that first which is most needful.

Romans 15

Private Devotion

Our accustomed devotions morning and evening alone and with our families must not be omitted upon any pretence whatsoever; no, not when extraordinary services are to be performed. Whatever is added these must not be diminished.

Leviticus 9

If our devotions are ignorant and cold and trifling and full of distractions we offer the blind, the lame and the sick for sacrifices.

Leviticus 22

It is hereby intimated that we must not seek occasions to abate our zeal in God's service nor be glad of an excuse to omit a good duty but rather rejoice in an opportunity of accumulating and doing more than ordinary in religion. If we perform family worship we must not think that this will excuse us from our secret devotions; nor that on the days we go to Church we need not worship God alone and with our families; but we should always abound in the work of the Lord. . . No extraordinary services should jostle out our stated devotions.

Numbers 29

Privileges

As the ignorance of the un-circumcised shall not excuse their wickedness, so neither shall the privileges of the circumcised excuse theirs, but they shall be punished together. Note, the Judge of all the earth is impartial, and none shall fare the better at his bar for any external advantages.

Jeremiah 9

When we are ready to surfeit on the children's bread, we should remember how many there are, that would be glad of the crumbs. Our broken meat in spiritual privileges, would be a feast to many a soul; (Acts 13:42).

Matthew 15

Procrastination

If these five kings had humbled themselves in time and had begged peace instead of waging war, they might have saved their lives but now the decree had gone forth and they found no place for repentance or the reversal of the judgment. It was too late to expect it though perhaps they sought it carefully with tears.

Joshua 10

Perhaps when Amon sinned as his father did in the beginning of his days he promised himself that he should repent as his father did in the latter end of his days but his case shows what a madness it is to presume upon that. If he hoped to repent when he was old he was wretchedly disappointed for he was cut off when he was young.

2 Chronicles 33

It will be no thanks to us to leave the pleasures of sin when they have left us, nor to return to God when need forces us. It is the greatest absurdity and ingratitude imaginable to give the cream and flower of our days to the devil, and reserve the bran, and refuse, and dregs of them, for God; this is offering the torn and the lame, and the sick for sacrifice; and besides, old age being thus clogged with infirmities, it is the greatest folly imaginable to put off that needful work till then, which requires the best of our strength, when our faculties are in their prime, and especially to make the work more difficult by a longer continuance in sin, and, laying up treasures of guilt in the conscience, to add to the burdens of age and make them heavier.

Ecclesiastes 12

Where Satan cannot persuade men to look upon the judgment to come as a thing doubtful and uncertain, yet he gains his point by persuading them to look upon it as a thing at a distance, so that it loses its force: if it be sure, yet it is not near; whereas, in truth, 'the Judge stands before the door.'

Ezekiel 11

When ministers attend such as have been mindless of God and their souls all their days, but are under death-bed convictions; and, because true repentance is never too late, direct them to repent, and turn to God, and close with Christ; yet, because late repentance is seldom true, they do but as these wise virgins did by the foolish, even make the best of bad. They can but tell them what is to be done, if it be not too late; but whether the door may not be shut before it is done, is an unspeakable hazard. It is good advice now, if it be taken in time, 'Go to them that sell, and buy for yourselves'. Note, those that would have grace, must have recourse to, and attend upon, the means of grace; see Isa. 55:1.

With regard to those that put off their great work to the last, it is a thousand to one, that they have not time to do it then. Getting grace is a work of time, and cannot be done in a hurry. While the poor awakened soul addresses itself, upon a sick bed, to repentance and prayer, in awful confusion, it scarcely knows which end to begin at, or what to do first; and presently death comes, judgment comes, and the work is undone, and the poor sinner undone for ever. This comes of having oil to buy when we should burn it, and grace to get when we should use it.

Matthew 25

Promises

God's promises are to be the guide and measure of our desires and expectations.

Genesis 28

This promise that he would drive them out from before the children of Israel plainly supposes it as the condition of the promise that the children of Israel must themselves attempt their extirpation, must go up against them, else they could not be said to be driven out before them. If afterwards Israel, through sloth or coward- ice or affection to these idola- ters, sit still and left them alone, they must blame themselves and not God if they be not driven out . . . We must resist our spiritual enemies and then God will tread them under our feet.

Joshua 13

Gideon expected more from 300 men supported by a particular

promise than from so many thousands supported only by their own valour.

Judges 8

He prays for the performance of God's promise. I desire no more and I expect no less so full is the promise and so firm. Thus we must turn God's promises into prayers and then they shall be turned into performances for with God saying and doing are not two things as they often are with men. God will do as he has said.

2 Samuel 7

The promises of God are not only the best foundation of prayer, telling us what to pray for and encouraging our faith and hope in prayer, but they are a present answer to prayer. Let the prayer be made according to the promise, and then the promise may be read as a return to the prayer; and we are to believe the prayer is heard because the promise will be performed.

We value the promise by the character of him that makes it. We may therefore depend upon God's promises; for good and upright is the Lord, and therefore he will be as good as his word. He is so kind that he cannot deceive us, so true that he cannot break his promise. Faithful is he who hath promised who also will do it. He was good in making the promise, and therefore will be upright in performing it.

Psalm 25

God's word of promise, being a firm foundation of hope, is a full fountain of joy to all believers.

Psalm 60

Make sure grace and glory, and other things shall be added. This is a comprehensive promise, and is such an assurance of the present comfort of the saints that whatever they desire and think they need, they may be sure that either Infinite Wisdom sees it is not good for them or Infinite Goodness will give it to them in due time. Let it be our care to walk uprightly, and then let us trust God to give us everything that is good for us.

Psalm 84

Though our expectations are in some particular instances disappointed, yet God's promises are not disannulled; they are established in the very heavens (that is, in his eternal counsels); they are above the changes of this lower region and out of the reach of the opposition of hell and earth. The stability of the material heavens is an emblem of the truth of God's Word; the heavens may be clouded by vapours arising out of the earth, but they cannot be touched, they cannot be changed.

Psalm 89

When the ten tribes were lost in Assyria, and the two almost lost in Babylon, the strength of that nation was weakened, and, in all appearance, its day shortened; for they said 'Our hope is lost, we are cut off for our parts' (Ezek. 37:11). And then what becomes of the promise that Shiloh should arise out of Judah, the star out of Jacob, and the Messiah out of the family of David? If these fail, the promise fails.

Psalm 102

What he has promised, he will perform, for it is the word both of his truth and of his power. An active faith can rejoice in what God has said, though it be not yet done; for with him, saying and doing are not two things, whatever they are with us.

Psalm 108

He pleads the promise of God, guides his desires by it, and grounds his hopes upon it.

Psalm 119

We doubt not of the birth of the child that is conceived, though we know not how it is formed; nor need we doubt of the performance of the promise, though we perceive not how things work towards it. And we may well trust God to provide for us that which is convenient without our anxious disquieting cares, and therein to recompense us for our charity, since it was without any knowledge or forecast of ours that our bodies were curiously wrought in secret and our souls found the way into them.

Ecclesiastes 11

God was ready to fulfil the promise, but then they must fulfil the condition; if not, the promise is void, and it is just with God to turn them out of possession. Being brought in upon their good behaviour, they had no wrong done them if they were turned out upon their ill behaviour. Obedience was the rent reserved by the lease, with a power to re-enter for non-payment.

Jeremiah 11

Though the return of the church's prosperity do not come in our time, we must not therefore despair of it, for it will come in God's time. Though those who said, 'The vessels of the Lord's house shall *shortly*' be brought again, prophesied a lie (v. 16), yet he that said, 'They shall *at length* be brought again', prophesied the truth. We are apt to set our clock before God's dial, and then to quarrel because they do not agree; but the Lord is a God of judgment, and it is fit that we should wait for him.

Jeremiah 27

'As I have brought all this great evil upon them', pursuant to the threatenings, and for the glory of divine justice, 'So I will bring upon them all this good', pursuant to the promise, and for the glory of divine mercy. He that is faithful to his threatenings will much more be so to his promises; and he will comfort his people 'according to the time he has afflicted them.'

Jeremiah 32

If God will do his part according to the promise, we must do ours according to the precept. Note, the promise of God's grace to enable us for our duty should engage and quicken our constant care and endeavour to do our duty. God's promises must drive us to his precepts as our rule, and then his precepts must send us back to his promises for

strength, for without his grace we can do nothing.
Ezekiel 36

God's promises are intended, not to supersede, but to excite and encourage, our prayers; and, when we see the day of the performance of them approaching, we should the more earnestly plead them with God and put them in suit.
Daniel 9

God often answers prayer with good words, when he does not immediately appear in great works; and those good words are real answers to prayer. Men's good words will not feed the body (James 2:16), but God's good words will feed the faith, for saying and doing with him are not two things, though they are with us.
Zechariah 1

Christ's promises make his precepts easy, and his yoke not only tolerable, but pleasant, and sweet, and very comfortable; yet this promise was as much a trial of this young man's faith as the precept was of his charity, and contempt of the world.
Matthew 19

Faith is the soul, prayer is the body; both together make a complete man for any service. Faith, if it be right, will excite prayer; and prayer is not right, if it do not spring from faith. This is the condition of our receiving — we must ask in prayer, believing. The requests of prayer shall not be denied; the expectations of faith shall not be frustrated. We have many promises to this purport

from the mouth of our Lord Jesus, and all to encourage faith, the principal grace, and prayer, the principal duty, of a Christian.

'All things', in general; 'whatsoever', bring it to particulars; though generals include particulars, yet such is the folly of our unbelief, that, though we think we assent to promises in the general, yet we fly off when it comes to particulars.
Matthew 21

It was a great mercy that God's words should be fulfilled in their season, notwithstanding his sinful distrust. The unbelief of man shall not make the promises of God of no effect, they shall be fulfilled in their season, and he shall not be for ever dumb, but only till the day that these things shall be performed, and then thy lips shall be opened, that thy mouth may show forth God's praise. Thus, though God chastens the iniquity of his people with the rod, yet his loving kindness he will not take away.
Luke 1

An earnest secures the promise, and is part of the payment. The illumination of the Spirit is an earnest of everlasting light; the quickening of the Spirit is an earnest of everlasting life; and the comforts of the Spirit are an earnest of everlasting joy. Note, the veracity of God, the mediation of Christ, and the operation of the Spirit, are all engaged that the promises shall be sure to all the seed.
2 Corinthians 1

Prophecy

But now they see both plainly enough when the sentence is executed; now he that runs may read, and publish the exact agreement that appears between the present providences and the former predictions which then were slighted, between the present punishments and the former sins which then were persisted in. Now they cannot but say, 'The Lord is righteous' (Dan. 9:11—13).

Zechariah 1

Christ's preaching was mostly practical; but, in this chapter, we have a prophetical discourse, a prediction of things to come; such however as had a practical tendency, and was intended, not to gratify the curiosity of his disciples, but to guide their consciences and conversations, and it is therefore concluded with practical application. The church has always had particular prophecies, besides general promises, both for direction and for encouragement to believers; but it is observable, Christ preached this prophetical sermon in the close of his ministry, as the Apocalypse is the last book of the New Testament, and the prophetical books of the Old Testament are placed last, to intimate to us, that we must be well grounded in plain truths and duties, and those must first be well digested, before we dive into those things that are dark and difficult; many run themselves into confusion by beginning their Bible at the wrong end.

Matthew 24

We commonly give it as a reason why the prophecies of scripture are expressed darkly and figuratively, because, if they did plainly describe the event, the accomplishment would thereby either be defeated or necessitated by a fatality inconsistent with human liberty; and yet this plain and express prophecy of Peter's denying Christ did neither, nor did in the least make Christ accessory to Peter's sin.

John 13

It is possible that men may be fulfilling scripture prophecies, even when they are breaking scripture precepts, particularly in the persecution of the church, as in the persecution of Christ. And this justifies the reason which is sometimes given for the obscurity of scripture prophecies, that, if they were too plain and obvious, the accomplishment of them would thereby be prevented.

Acts 13

Prophets

The prophets were sent in the first place to teach them the knowledge of God, to remind them of their duty, and direct them in it. If they succeeded not in that, their next work was to reprove them for their sins and to set them in view before them, that they might repent and reform and return to their duty. If in this they prevailed not, but sinners went on frowardly, their next work was to foretell the judgments of God that the terror of them might awaken those to repentance who would not be made sensible of the obligations of his love or else that the execution of them in their season might be a demonstration of the divine mission of the prophets that foretold them.

2 Kings 21

Prosperity of the Wicked

Before Job will enquire into the reasons of the prosperity of wicked men he asserts God's omniscience, as one prophet, in a similar case, asserts his righteousness (Jer. 12:1) another his holiness (Hab. 1:13), another his goodness to his own people (Ps. 73:1). General truths must be held fast, though we may find it difficult to reconcile them to particular events.

Job 24

'When the wicked spring as the grass' in spring (so numerous, so thickly sown, so green, and growing so fast) 'and all the workers of iniquity do flourish' in pomp, and power, and all the instances of outward prosperity, are easy and many, and succeed in their enterprises, one would think that all this was in order to their being happy, that it was a certain evidence of God's favour and an earnest of something as good or better in reserve; but it is quite otherwise; it is 'that they shall be destroyed for ever'. The very 'prosperity of fools shall slay them.' (Prov. 1:32). The sheep that are designed for the slaughter are put into the fattest pasture.

Psalm 92

Prosperity is the unhappy occasion of much iniquity; it makes people conceited of themselves, indulgent of the flesh, forgetful of God, in love with the world, and deaf to the reproofs of the Word. See (30:6). It is good for us, when we are afflicted, to remember how and wherein we went astray before we were afflicted, that we may answer the end of the affliction.

Psalm 119

Protection

This was done and recorded in order to encourage God's people in all ages to trust in him in the greatest straits. What cannot he do who did this? What will he not do for those who fear and love him who did this for those murmuring, unbelieving Israelites?

Exodus 14

Those places only are walled up to heaven that are compassed with God's favour as with a shield.

Deuteronomy 1

When God pleads his people's cause, he can deal with giants as with grasshoppers.

Deuteronomy 3

Those that are in the way of God and their duty may expect that Providence will protect them but this will not excuse them from taking all prudent methods for their own safety. God will keep us but then we must not wilfully expose ourselves. Providence must be trusted but not tempted. Calvin thinks that their charge to

Rahab to keep this matter secret and not to utter it was intended for her safety lest she, boasting of her security from the sword of Israel should, before they came to protect her, fall into the hands of the King of Jericho and be put to death for treason. Thus do they prudently advise her for her safety as she advised them for theirs.

Joshua 2

The wisdom of God is never at a loss for ways and means to preserve his people. As this Saul was diverted, so another Saul was converted just then when he was breathing out threatenings and slaughter against the saints of the Lord.

1 Samuel 23

Saul for the present desisted from the persecution. . . He went home . . . vexed that when at last he had found David he could not at that time find in his heart to destroy him as he had designed. God has many ways to tie the hands of persecutors, when he does not turn their hearts.

1 Samuel 24

Never let the Church's friends be disheartened by the power and pride of the Church's enemies. We need not fear great men against us while we have the great God for us. What will a finger more on each hand do or a toe more on each foot, in contest with Omnipotence?

1 Chronicles 20

Those whose hearts are upright with him may be sure of his protection and have all the reason in the world to depend upon it. He is able to protect them in the way of their duty (for wisdom and might are his) and he actually intends their protection. A practical disbelief of this is at the bottom of all our departures from God and double dealing with him. Asa could not trust God and, therefore, made court to Benhadad.

2 Chronicles 16

He was out of the way of his duty, had been out upon an expedition which he could not well account for to God and his conscience and yet he returned in peace for God is not extreme to mark what we do amiss nor does he withdraw his protection every time we forfeit it.

2 Chronicles 19

If we think to secure ourselves by prayer only, without watchfulness, we are slothful and tempt God; if by watchfulness, without prayer, we are proud and slight God; and, either way, we forfeit his protection.

Nehemiah 4

God's peculiar people are taken under his special protection, they and all that belong to them; divine grace makes a hedge about their spiritual life, and divine providence about their natural life, so they are safe and easy.

Job 1

God easily can, and (as far as is for his glory) certainly will, blast and defeat all the designs of his and his people's enemies. How were the plots of Ahithophel, Sanballat, and Haman baffled! How were the confederacies of Syria and Ephraim against Judah, of Gebal, and Ammon, and Amalek, against God's Israel, the kings of the earth and the princes against the Lord and against his anointed, broken! The hands that have been stretched out against God and his church have not performed their enterprise, nor have the weapons formed against Sion prospered.

Job 5

There is no flying from God's hand but by flying to it. It is very comfortable, when we are in fear of the power of man, to see it dependent upon and in subjection to the power of God. (See Isa. 10: 6, 7, 15).

Psalm 17

God protects believers, 1. With the greatest tenderness and affection which is intimated in that, 'He shall cover thee with his feathers, under his wings', which alludes to the hen gathering her chickens under her wings . . . 2. With the greatest power and efficacy. Wings and feathers, though spread with the greatest tenderness, are yet weak, and easily broken through, and therefore it is added, 'His truth shall be thy shield and buckler', a strong defence. God is as willing to guard his people as the hen is to guard the chickens, and as able as a man of war in armour.

Psalm 91

He that devotes himself to God's guidance and government, with an entire dependence upon God's wisdom, power and goodness, has a better security to make him easy than if all the kings and potentates of the earth should undertake to protect him.

Psalm 118

Those that love God and are beloved of him, have their minds easy and live very comfortably without this ado. Solomon was called Jedidiah-Beloved of the Lord (2 Sam. 12:25); to him the kingdom was promised, and then it was in vain for Absalom to rise up early, to wheedle the people, and for Adonijah to make such a stir, and to say, 'I will be king'. Solomon sits still, and being, 'beloved of the Lord', to him he gives sleep and the kingdom too.

Psalm 127

'Lord, thou has kept me in the day of battle with the Philistines, suffer me not to fall by the treacherous intrigues of false-hearted Israelites.' God is as able to preserve his people from secret fraud as from open force; and the experience we have had of his power and care, in dangers of one kind, may encourage us to trust in him and depend upon him in dangers of another nature; for nothing can shorten the Lord's right hand.

Psalm 140

The wicked have fallen into the distresses which they thought themselves far from, nay, which they had been instrumental to bring the righteous into, so that they seem to come in their stead, as a ransom for the just. Mordecai is saved from the gallows, Daniel from the lion's den, and Peter from the prison; and their persecutors come in their stead. The Israelites are delivered out of the Red Sea and the Egyptians drowned in it. So precious are the saints in God's eye that he gives men for them (Isa. 43:3, 4).

Proverbs 11

He will keep it constantly, night and day, and not without need, for the enemies are restless in their designs and attempts against it, and, both night and day, seek an opportunity to do it a mischief. God will keep it in the night of affliction and persecution, and in the day of peace and prosperity, the temptations of which are no less dangerous.

Isaiah 27

'Come not near any man upon whom is the mark'; do not so much as threaten or frighten any of them; it is promised them that there shall no evil come nigh them, and therefore you must keep at a distance from them. The king of Babylon gave particular orders that Jeremiah should be protected. Baruch and Ebed-melech were secured, and, it is likely, others of Jeremiah's friends, for his sake. God had promised that it should go well with his remnant and they should be well treated (Jer. 15:11); and we have reason to think that none of the mourning praying remnant fell by the sword of the Chaldeans, but that God found out some way or other to secure them all, as, in the last destruction of Jerusalem by the Romans, the Christians were all secured in a city called Pella,

and none of them perished with the unbelieving Jews.

Ezekiel 9

The angel's presence made even the lions' den his strong-hold, his palace, his paradise; he had never had a better night in his life. See the power of God over the fiercest creatures, and believe his power to restrain the roaring lion that 'goes about continually seeking to devour' from hurting those that are his. See the care God takes of his faithful worshippers, especially when he calls them out to suffer for him. If he keeps their souls from sin, comforts their souls with his peace, and receives their souls to himself, he does in effect 'stop the lions' mouths', that they cannot hurt them. See how ready the angels are to minister for the good of God's people, for they own themselves their 'fellow servants'.

Daniel 6

God calls those to serve the interests of his church whom he either finds, or makes fit, for it. If there be horns (which denote the force and fury of beasts) against the church, there are carpenters (which denote the wisdom and forecast of men) for the church, by which they find ways to master the strongest beasts, for 'every kind of beast is tamed, and has been tamed, of mankind' (James 3:7).

Zechariah 1

Some think it alludes to shepherds that made fires about their flocks, or travellers that made fires about their tents in desert places, to frighten wild beasts from them. God will not only 'make a hedge' about them as he did about Job (ch. 1:10), not only make walls and bulwarks about them (Isa. 26:1) (those may be battered down), not only be as the mountains round about them (Ps. 125:2), (mountains may be got over), but he will be a wall of fire round them, which cannot be broken through, nor scaled, nor undermined, nor the foundations of it sapped, nor can it be attempted, or approached, without danger to the assailants. God will not only make a wall of fire about her, but he will himself be such a wall; for 'our God is a consuming fire' to his and his church's enemies. He is a wall of fire, not on one side only, but round about on every side.

Zechariah 2

It is true, there is such a promise of the ministration of angels, for the protection of the saints. The devil knows it by experience; for he finds his attempts against them fruitless, and he frets and rages at it, as he did at the hedge about Job, which he speaks of so sensibly (Job 1:10).

Matthew 4

Christ had his hour set, which was to put a period to his day and work on earth; so have all his people and all his ministers, and, till that hour comes, the attempts of their enemies against them are ineffectual, and their day shall be lengthened as long as their Master has any work for them to do; nor can all the powers of hell and earth prevail against them, until they have finished their testimony.

John 7

The safety and preservation of the saints are owing, not only to the divine grace in proportioning the strength to the trial, but to the divine providence in proportioning the trial to the strength.

John 18

Providence

God sometimes removes useful men when we think they can ill be spared but this ought to satisfy us that they are never removed till they have done the work which was appointed them.

Numbers 31

The case was indeed very lamentable that so good a man, a prophet so faithful and so bold in God's cause, should for one offence die as a criminal, while an old lying prophet lives as at ease and an idolatrous prince in pomp and power. Thy way, O God, is in the sea and thy path in great waters. We cannot judge of men by their sufferings nor of sins by their present punishments.

1 Kings 13

Jacob had foretold that the seed of Ephraim should become a multitude of nations and yet that plant is thus nipped in the bud. God's providences often seem to contradict his promises but when they do so they really magnify the promise and make the performance of it notwithstanding so much the more illustrious.

1 Chronicles 7

If God give quietness who then

can make trouble (Job 34:29). Those have rest indeed to whom God gives rest; peace indeed to whom Christ gives peace; not as the world giveth (John 14:27). Now Asa takes notice of the rest they had as the gift of God . . . God must be acknowledged with thankfulness in the rest we are blessed with of body and mind, family and country and as the reward of the reformation begun because we have sought the Lord our God he has given us rest. N.B. As the frowns and rebukes of Providence should be observed for a check to us in an evil way, so the smiles of Providence should be taken notice of for our encouragement in that which is good.

2 Chronicles 14

God governs the world in infinite wisdom and the creatures and all their actions are continually under his eye. The eye of Providence is quicksighted. It runs, it is intent, it runs to and fro, it reaches far through the whole earth no corner of which is from under it, not the most dark or distant and his eye directs his hand and the arm of his power for he shows himself strong. Does Satan walk to and fro in the earth? Providence runs to and fro, is never out of the way, never to seek, never at a loss.

2 Chronicles 16

God has all men's hearts in his hand and turns them as he pleases, contrary to their own first intentions, to serve his purposes. Many are moved unaccountably both to themselves and others but an invisible power moves them. Wicked

Ahab, disguising himself, arming himself, thereby as he thought securing himself and yet slain. No art, no arms can save those whom God has appointed to ruin. What can hurt those whom God will protect and what can shelter those whom God will destroy? Jehoshaphat is safe in his robes. Ahab killed in his armour for the race is not to the swift nor the battle to the strong.

2 Chronicles 18

What is intended for the prejudice of the church has often by the over-ruling providence of God, been made serviceable to it (Phil. 1:12). The enemies of the Jews in appealing to Darius hoped to get an order to suppress them but instead of that they got an order to supply them, thus out of the eater comes forth meat.

Ezra 6

Observe: 1. How kind the king was to him. He granted him all his requests, whatever he desired to put him in a capacity to serve his country. 2. How kind his people were to him. When he went many more went with him, because they desired not to stay in Babylon when he had gone thence and because they would venture to dwell in Jerusalem when he had gone thither. 3. How kind his God was to him. He obtained this favour from his king and country by the good hand of the Lord that was upon him. (v. 6, 9).
Note: Every creature is that to us which God makes it to be . . . As we must see the events that shall occur in the hand of God, so we must see

the hand of God in the events that do occur and acknowledge him with thankfulness when we have reason to call it his good hand.

Ezra 7

He gained his point, *not* according to his merit, his interest in the king, or his good management, but according to the good hand of his God upon him. Gracious souls take notice of God's hand, his good hand, in all events which turn in favour of them. This is the Lord's doing, and therefore doubly acceptable.

Nehemiah 2

We cannot now expect such miracles to be wrought for us as were for Israel when they were brought out of Egypt, but we may expect that in such ways as God here took to defeat Haman's plot he will still protect his people.

Esther (Intro.)

Her case was at present very discouraging. Providence so ordered it that, just at this juncture, she was under a cloud, and the king's affections cooled towards her, for she had been kept from his presence thirty days, that her faith and courage might be the more tried, and that God's goodness in the favour she now found with the king notwithstanding might shine the brighter.

Esther 4

Whatever happens to us, it is God that performs it (Ps. 57:2), and an admirable performance the whole will appear to be when the mystery of God shall be finished. He performs all that, and that only, which was appointed, and in the appointed time and method. This may silence us, for what is appointed cannot be altered. But to consider that, when God was appointing us to eternal life and glory as our end, he was appointing to this condition, this affliction, whatever it is, in our way, this may do more than silence us, it may satisfy us that it is all for the best; though what he does we know not now, yet we shall know hereafter.

Job 23

What is lighter than the wind? Yet God hath ways of poising it. He knows how to make the weight for the winds, which he brings out of his treasuries (Ps. 135:7), keeping a very particular account of what he draws out, as men do of what they pay out of their treasuries, not at random, as men bring out their trash. Nothing sensible is to us more unaccountable than the wind. We hear the sound of it, yet cannot tell whence it comes, nor whither it goes; but God gives it out by weight, wisely ordering both from what point it shall blow and with what strength. The waters of the sea, and the rain-waters, he both weighs and measures, allotting the proportion of every tide and every shower. A great and constant communication there is between clouds and seas, the waters above the firmament and those under it. Vapours go up, rains come down, air is condensed into water, water rarefied into air; but the great God keeps an exact account of all the stock with which this trade is carried on for the public benefit and sees that none of it be lost.

Now if, in these things, Providence be so exact, much more in dispensing frowns and favours, rewards and punishments, to the children of men, according to the rules of equity.

Job 28

God's great and gracious design, in all the dispensations of his providence towards the children of men, is to save them from being for ever miserable and to bring them to be for ever happy (v. 29, 30). All these things God is working with the children of men. He deals with them by conscience, by providences, by ministers, by mercies, by afflictions. He makes them sick and makes them well again. All these are his operations.

All providences are to be looked upon as God's workings with man, his strivings with him. He uses a variety of methods to do men good; if one affliction do not do the work, he will try another; if neither do, he will try a mercy; and he will send a messenger to interpret both. He often works such things as these twice, thrice; so it is in the original referring to (v. 14). He speaks once, yea twice; if that prevail not, he works twice, yea thrice; he changes his method (we have piped, we have mourned), returns again to the same method, repeats the same applications. Why does he take all this pains with man? It is to bring back his soul from the pit (v. 30). If God did not

take more care of us than we do of ourselves, we should be miserable; we would destroy ourselves, but he would have us saved, and devises means, by his grace, to undo that by which we were undoing ourselves.

Job 33

God does nothing mean. This is a good reason why we should acquiesce in all the operations of his providence concerning us in particular. His visible works, those of nature, and which concern the world in general, are such as we admire and commend, and in which we observe the Creator's wisdom, power, and goodness; shall we then find fault with his dispensations concerning us, and the counsels of his will concerning our affairs?

Job 36

This is a remarkable instance of the extent of the divine providence to things that seem minute, as this of the exact number of a man's cattle, as also of the harmony of providence, and the reference of one event to another; for 'known unto God are all his works, from the beginning to the end'. Job's other possessions, no doubt, were increased in proportion to his cattle, lands, money, servants, etc. So that, if before, he was the greatest of all the men of the east, what was he now?

Job 42

God's providences concerning his people are commonly mixed — mercy and judgment; God has set the one over against the other, and appointed them April-days, showers and sunshine.

It was so with David and his family; when there was mercy in the return of the ark there was judgment in the death of Uzza.

Psalm 101

He looks round, and takes notice of the works of God in the visible creation, and the providential government of the world: 'I meditate on all thy works.' Many see them, but do not see the footsteps of God's wisdom, power, and goodness in them, and do not receive the benefit they might by them because they do not meditate upon them; they do not dwell on that copious curious subject, but soon quit it, as if they had exhausted it, when they have scarcely touched upon it.

Psalm 143

We *must* believe that he is able to do what he will, wise to do what is best, and good, according to his promise, to do what is best for us, if we love him and serve him. . . In all our conduct we *must* be diffident of our own judgment, and confident of God's wisdom, power and goodness, and therefore must follow Providence and not force it. That often proves best which was least our own doing. . . We *must* not only in our judgment believe that there is an over-ruling hand of God ordering and disposing of us and all our affairs, but we must solemnly own it, and address ourselves to him accordingly. . . In all our ways that prove direct, and fair, and pleasant, in which we gain our point to our satisfaction, we

must acknowledge God with thankfulness. In all our ways that prove cross and uncomfortable, and that are hedged up with thorns, we must acknowledge God with submission.

Proverbs 3

God can change men's minds, can, by a powerful insensible operation upon their spirits, turn them from that which they seemed most intent upon, and incline them to that which they seemed most averse to, as the husbandman, by canals and gutters, turns the water through his grounds as he pleases, which does not alter the nature of the water, nor put any force upon it, any more than God's providence does upon the native freedom of man's will, but directs the course of it to serve his own purpose.

Proverbs 21

He makes some poor, to exercise their patience, and contentment, and dependence upon God, and others rich, to exercise their thankfulness and beneficence.

Proverbs 22

While the picture is in drawing, and the house in building, we see not the beauty of either; but when the artist has put his last hand to them, and given them their finishing strokes, then all appears very good. We see but the middle of God's works, not from the beginning of them (then we should see how admirably the plan was laid in the divine counsels), nor to the end of them, which crowns the action (then we should see

245

the product to be glorious); but we must wait till the veil be rent, and not arraign God's proceedings nor pretend to pass a judgment on them.

Ecclesiastes 3

The little difference there is between the conditions of the righteous and the wicked in this world: there is one event to both. Is David rich? So is Nabal. Is Joseph favoured by his prince? So is Haman. Is Ahab killed in a battle? So is Josiah. Are the bad figs carried to Babylon? So are the good (Jer. 24:1). There is a vast difference between the original, the design, and the nature, of the same event to the one and to the other; the effects and issues of it are likewise vastly different; the same providence to the one is a savour of life unto life, to the other, of death unto death, though, to outward appearance, it is the same.

Ecclesiastes 9

This short chapter helps us to put a very comfortable construction upon a great many long ones, by showing us that the same providence which to some is a 'savour of death unto death' may by the grace and blessing of God be made to others a 'savour of life unto life'; and that, 'though God's people share with others in the same calamity, yet it is not the same to them that it is to others, but is designed for their good and shall issue in their good; to them it is a correcting rod in the hand of a tender Father, while to others it is an avenging sword in the hand of a righteous Judge.

Jeremiah 24

Those do better for themselves who patiently submit to the rebukes of Providence than those who contend with them.

Jeremiah 38

Both the powers of nature and the wills of men are all made to serve the intention, which they infallibly and irresistibly effect, though perhaps they mean not so, neither doth their heart think so (Isa. 10:7; Micah 4:11, 12). Thus, though the will of God's precepts be not done on earth as it is done in heaven, yet the will of his purpose and counsel is, and shall be. The wheel is said to have four faces, looking four several ways (v. 15), denoting that the providence of God exerts itself in all parts of the world, east, west, north, and south, and extends itself to the remotest corners of it.

Ezekiel 1

But though the sword cut off the righteous and the wicked (for it devours one as well as another) (2 Sam. 11:25), yet far be it from us to think that the righteous are as the wicked (Gen. 18:25). No, God's graces and comforts make a great difference when his providence seems to make none. The good figs are sent into Babylon for their good (Jer. 24:5, 6). It is only in outward appearance that there is one event to the righteous and to the wicked (Eccles. 9:2).

Ezekiel 21

Providence seemed to favour

his design, and give him an opportunity to escape. We may be out of the way of duty and yet may meet with a favourable gale. The ready way is not always the right way.

Jonah 1

Some think that Christ here alludes to the two sparrows that were used in cleansing the leper (Lev. 14:4—6); the two birds in the margin are called sparrows; of these, one was killed, and so fell to the ground, the other was let go. Now it seemed a casual thing which of the two was killed; the persons employed took which they pleased, but God's providence designed, and determined which. Now this God, who has such an eye to the sparrows, because they are his creatures, much more will have an eye to you, who are his children.

Matthew 10

God has a sovereignty over all his creatures and an exclusive right in them, and may make them serviceable to his glory in such a way as he thinks fit, in doing or suffering; and if God be glorified, either by us or in us, we were not made in vain.

John 9

'As many as had possession of lands or houses sold them' (v. 34). Dr. Lightfoot computes that this was the year of jubilee in the Jewish nation, the fiftieth year (the twenty-eighth since they settled in Canaan fourteen hundred years ago), so that, what was sold that year being not to return till the next jubilee, lands then took a good

price, and so the sale of those lands would raise the more money.

Acts 4

A strange chemistry of Providence this, to extract so great a good as the enlargement of the gospel out of so great an evil as the confinement of the apostle.

Philippians 1

Prudence

A just man may perish in his righteousness, but let him not, by his own imprudence and rash zeal, pull trouble upon his own head, and then reflect upon Providence as dealing hardly with him. 'Be not righteous overmuch' (v. 16). In the acts of righteousness govern thyself by the rules of prudence, and be not transported, no, not by a zeal for God, into any intemperate heats or passions, or any practices unbecoming thy character or dangerous to thy interests.' Note, there may be over-doing in well-doing. Self denial and mortification of the flesh are good; but if we prejudice our health by them, and unfit ourselves for the service of God, we are righteous overmuch. To reprove those that offend is good, but to cast that pearl before swine, who will turn again and rend us, is to be righteous overmuch.

Why shouldest thou destroy thyself, as fools often do by meddling with strife that belongs not to them? Why shouldst thou provoke authority, and run thyself into the briers, by needless contradictions, and by going out of thy sphere to correct what is amiss? Be wise as serpents, beware of men.

Ecclesiastes 7

It is the will of Christ that his people and ministers, being so much exposed to troubles in this world, as they usually are, should not needlessly expose themselves, but use all fair and lawful means for their own preservation. Christ gave us an example of this wisdom (ch. 21:24, 25; 22:17–19; John 8:6, 7); besides the many escapes he made out of the hands of his enemies, till his hour was come. See an instance of Paul's wisdom (Acts 23:6, 7). In the cause of Christ we must sit loose to life and all its comforts, but must not be prodigal of them. It is the wisdom of the serpent to secure his head, that that may not be broken, 'to stop his ear to the voice of the charmer' (Ps. 58:4, 5), and to take shelter in the clefts of the rocks; and herein we may be wise as serpents. We must be wise, not to pull trouble upon our own heads; wise to keep silence in an evil time, and not to give offence, if we can help it.

Matthew 10

Therefore Christ drops that argument, and considers, that if he should refuse this payment, it would increase people's prejudice against him and his doctrine, and alienate their affections from him, and therefore he resolve to pay it. Note, Christian prudence and humility teach us, in many cases, to recede from our right, rather than give offence by insisting upon it. We must never decline our duty for fear of giving offence (Christ's preaching and miracles offended them, yet he went on with them (Matt. 15: 12, 13), better offend men than God); but we must sometimes deny ourselves in that which is our secular interest, rather than give offence; as Paul (1 Cor. 8: 13; Rom. 14:13).

Matthew 17

In times of imminent peril and danger, it is not only lawful, but our duty, to seek our own preservation by all good and honest means; and if God opens a door of escape, we ought to make our escape, otherwise we do not trust God but tempt him.

While we only go out of the way of danger, not out of the way of duty, we may trust God to provide a dwelling for his outcasts (Isa. 16:4, 5). In times of public calamity, when it is manifest that we cannot be serviceable at home and may be safe abroad, Providence calls us to make our escape. He that flees, may fight again.

Matthew 24

The prudence of the serpent would have directed them to be silent, and, though they could not with a good conscience promise that they would not preach the gospel any more, yet they needed not tell the rulers that they would. But the boldness of the lion directed them thus to set both the authority and the malignity of their persecutors at defiance.

Acts 4

The ceremonial law, though it was by no means to be imposed upon the Gentile converts (as the false teachers would have it, and thereby endeavoured to subvert the gospel), yet it was not become unlawful as yet to those that had been bred up in the observance of it, but were far from expecting justification by it. It was dead, but not buried; dead, but not yet deadly.

Acts 21

Public Worship

God has a love for the dwellings of Jacob, has a gracious regard to religious families and accepts their family worship. Yet, he loves the gates of Zion better, not only better than any, but better than all, of the dwellings of Jacob. God was worshipped in the dwellings of Jacob, and family worship is family duty, which must by no means be neglected; yet, when they come in competition, public worship (other things being equal) is to be preferred before private.

Psalm 87

Thy faithfulness and the truth of thy promise, that rock on which the church is built, shall be praised in the congregation of the saints, who owe their all to that faithfulness, and whose constant comfort it is that there is a promise, and that he is faithful that promised. It is expected from God's saints on earth that they praise him; who should, if they do not? Let every saint praise him, but especially the congregation of saints; when they come together, let them join in praising God. The more

the better; it is the more like heaven.

In religious assemblies God has promised the presence of his grace, but we must also, in them, have an eye to his glorious presence, that the familiarity we are admitted to may not breed the least contempt; for he is terrible in his holy places, and therefore greatly to be feared. A holy awe of God must fall upon us, and fill us, in all our approaches to God.

Psalm 89

Pulpit Exchanges

Ezekiel is now among the captives in Babylon; but, as Jeremiah at Jerusalem wrote for the use of the captives though they had Ezekiel upon the spot with them (ch. 29), so Ezekiel wrote for the use of Jerusalem, though Jeremiah himself was resident there; and yet they were far from looking upon it as an affront to one another, or an interference with one another's business; for ministers have need of one another's help both by preaching and writing. Jeremiah wrote to the captives for their consolation, which was the thing they needed; Ezekiel here is directed to write to the inhabitants of Jerusalem for their conviction and humiliation, which was the thing they needed.

Ezekiel 16

Reactions

To render good for good is human, evil for evil is brutish,

good for evil is Christian, but evil for good is devilish; it is so very absurd and wicked a thing that we cannot think but God will avenge it.

Jeremiah 18

Rebellion Against God

This description of the war-horse will help to explain that character which is given of presumptuous sinners (Jer. 8:6). Every one turneth to his course, as the horse rusheth into the battle. When a man's heart is fully set in him to do evil, and he is carried on in a wicked way by the violence of inordinate appetites and passions, there is no making him afraid of the wrath of God and the fatal consequences of sin. Let his own conscience set before him the curse of the law, the death that is the wages of sin, and all the terrors of the Almighty in battle-array; he mocks at this fear, and is not affrighted, neither turns he back from the flaming sword of the cherubim. Let ministers lift up their voice like a trumpet, to proclaim the wrath of God against him, he believes not that it is the sound of the trumpet, nor that God and his heralds are in earnest with him; but what will be in the end hereof it is easy to foresee.

Job 39

Rebukes

One of them which Bath-Sheba bore to him he called Nathan, probably in honour of Nathan the prophet who reproved him

for his sin in that matter and was instrumental to bring him to repentance. It seems he loved him the better for it as long as he lived. It is wisdom to esteem those our best friends that deal faithfully with us.

1 Chronicles 3

If God's professing people degenerate from what themselves and their fathers were, they must expect to be told of it; and it is well if a just reproach will help to bring us to a true repentance.

Psalm 79

Many that would be very well pleased to hear the information of the wise, and much more to have their commendations and consolations yet do not care for hearing their rebukes, that is, care not for being told of their faults, though ever so wisely; but therein they are no friends to themselves, for reproofs of instruction are the way cf life (Prov. 6:23), and, though they be not so pleasant as the song of fools, they are more wholesome. To hear, not only with patience, but with pleasure, the rebuke of the wise, is a sign and means of wisdom.

Ecclesiastes 7

Peter was not so sharply reproved for disowning and denying his master in his sufferings as he was for dissuading him from them; though that was the defect, this the excess of kindness.

Matthew 16

Recording God's Visits

It may be of use to keep an account when and where God has been pleased to manifest himself to our souls in a peculiar manner, that the return of the day, and our return to the place of the altar (Gen. 13:4), may revive the pleasing grateful remembrance of God's favour to us. 'Remember, O my soul! and never forget what communications of divine love thou didst receive at such a time, at such a place; tell others what God did for thee'.

Ezekiel 1

Reformation

As justice and charity will never atone for atheism and profaneness, so prayers and sacrifices will never atone for fraud and oppression; for righteousness towards men is as much a branch of pure religion as religion towards God is a branch of universal righteousness.

If we make ourselves clean by repentance and reformation (v. 16), God will make us white by a full remission.

Isaiah 1

Corruptions that are crept into any ordinance of God must be purged out by having recourse to the primitive institution. If the copy be vicious, it must be examined and corrected by the original. Thus, when St. Paul would redress the grievances in the church of Corinth about the Lord's Supper, he appealed to the appointment (1 Cor. 11:23), so and so 'I received from the Lord'. Truth was from the beginning; we must therefore enquire for the good old way (Jer. 6:16), and must reform, not by later patterns, but by ancient rules.

Matthew 19

The house is swept, but it is not washed; and Christ hath said, 'If I wash thee not, thou hast no part with me'; the house must be washed, or it is none of his. Sweeping takes off only the loose dirt, while the sin that besets the sinner, the beloved sin, is untouched. It is swept from the filth that lies open to the eye of the world, but it is not searched and ransacked for secret filthiness (Matt. 23:25). It is swept, but the 'leprosy is in the wall', and will be till something more be done.

Luke 11

Refuge of Lies

The prophets gave them fair warning, but they turned it off with a jest: 'They do but talk so, because it is their trade; they are words of course, and words are but wind. It is not the word of the Lord that is in them; it is only the language of their melancholy fancy or their ill will to their country, because they are not preferred.' Note, impenitent sinners are not willing to own anything to be the word of God that makes against them, that tends either to part them from, or disquiet them in, their sins.

Jeremiah 5

Jerusalem shall shortly be as miserable as ever Shiloh was: 'Therefore will I do unto this house as I did to Shiloh', ruin it, and lay it waste (v. 14). Those that tread in the steps of the wickedness of those that went before them must expect to fall by the like judgments, for all these things happened to them for ensamples. The temple at Jerusalem, though ever so strongly built, if wickedness was found in it, would be as unable to keep its ground and as easily conquered as even the tabernacle in Shiloh was, when God's day of vengeance had come. 'This house' (says God) 'is called by my name, and therefore you may think that I should protect it; it is the house in which you trust, and you think that it will protect you; this land is the place, this city the place, which I gave to you and your fathers, and therefore you are secure of the continuance of it, and think that nothing can turn you out of it; but the men of Shiloh thus flattered themselves and did but deceive themselves.

Jeremiah 7

Remembrancers

This is the office of the best ministers, even the apostles themselves; they are 'The Lord's remembrancers' (Isa. 62:6); they are especially bound to make mention of the promises, and put God in mind of his engagements to do good to his people; and they are the people's remembrancers, making mention of God's precepts, and putting them in mind of the doctrines and duties of Christianity, that they may remember God's commandments, to do them.

2 Peter 1

Repentance

Those who truly believe the divine revelation concerning the ruin of sinners and the grant of the heavenly land to God's Israel will give diligence to flee from the wrath to come and to lay hold on eternal life by joining themselves to God and to his people.

Joshua 2

True repentance strikes at the darling sin and will with a peculiar zeal and resolution put away that sin which most easily besets us.

1 Samuel 7

Ahab's care was not to lose all the beasts, many being already lost, but he took no care about his soul not to lose that. He took a deal of pains to seek grass but none to seek the favour of God, fencing against the effect but not enquiring how to remove the cause.

1 Kings 18

Those do not truly nor acceptably repent or reform who only part with the sins that they lose by but continue their affection to the sins that they get by.

2 Kings 3

True conversion is not only from wasteful sins but from gainful sins. Not only from those sins that are destructive to the secular interest but from those that support and befriend it, in forsaking which is the great trial whether we can deny ourselves and trust God.

2 Kings 10

Those whose hearts condemn them will go anywhere in a day of distress rather than to God.

2 Kings 16

The armed men, though being armed they might by force have maintained their title to what they got by the sword, acquiesced and left their captives and the spoil to the disposal of the princes and herein they showed more truly heroic bravery than they did by taking them. It is a great honour for any man to yield to the authority of reason and religion against his interest.

2 Chronicles 28

Atonement must be made for the sins of the last reign. They thought it not enough to lament and forsake those sins but they brought a sin offering. Even our repentance and reformation will not obtain pardon but in and through Christ who was made sin (that is a sin-offering) for us. No peace but through his blood; no, not for penitence.

2 Chronicles 29

See how ready God is to accept and welcome returning sinners and how swift to show mercy. Let not great sinners despair when Manasseh himself, upon his repentance, found favour with God. In him God showed forth a pattern of long-suffering

as (1 Tim. 1:16; Isa. 1:18) . . . Those that truly repent of their sins will not only return to God themselves but will do all they can to recover those that have, by their example, been seduced and drawn away from God, else they do not thoroughly, as they ought, undo what they have done amiss nor make the plaster as wide as the wound.

2 Chronicles 33

Holy shame is as necessary an ingredient in true and ingenuous repentance as holy sorrow . . . Penitent sinners never see so much reason to blush and be ashamed as when they come to *lift up their faces before God.* A natural sense of our own honour which we have injured will make us ashamed, when we have done a wrong thing, to look men in the face; but a gracious concern for God's honour will make us much more ashamed to look him in the face. The publican, when he went to the temple to pray, hung down his head more than ever, as one ashamed (Luke 18:13).

. . . There is not a surer nor sadder presage of ruin to any people than revolting to sin, to the same sins again, after great judgments and great deliverances. Those that will be wrought upon neither by the one nor by the other are fit to be rejected, as reprobate silver, for the *founder melteth in vain.*

Ezra 9

What is said with a stiff neck must be unsaid again with a broken heart, or we are undone.

Psalm 75

When we cast our sins behind our back, and take no care to repent of them, God sets them before his face, and is ready to reckon for them; but when we set them before our face in true repentance, as David did when his sin was ever before him, God casts them behind his back.

Isaiah 38

What it is to repent. There are two things involved in repentance: 1. It is to turn from sin; it is to forsake it. It is to leave it, and to leave it with loathing and abhorrence, never to return to it again. The wicked must forsake his way, his evil way, as we would forsake a false way that will never bring us to the happiness we aim at, and a dangerous way, that leads to destruction. Let him not take one step more in that way. Nay, there must be not only a change of way, but a change of mind; the unrighteous must forsake his thoughts. Repentance, if it be true, strikes at the root, and washes the heart from wickedness. We must alter our judgments concerning persons and things, dislodge the corrupt imaginations and quit the vain pretences under which an un-sanctified heart shelters itself. Note, it is not enough to break off from evil practices, but we must enter a caveat against evil thoughts. Yet this is not all. 2. To repent is to return to the Lord; to return to him as our God, our sovereign Lord, against whom we have rebelled, and to whom we are concerned to reconcile ourselves; it is to return to the Lord as the fountain of life and living waters,

which we had forsaken for broken cisterns.

Isaiah 55

True repentance begins in a serious and impartial enquiry into ourselves, what we have done, arising from a conviction that we have done amiss.

Jeremiah 8

They shall come with weeping and with supplications, weeping for sin, supplication for pardon; for the goodness of God shall lead them to repentance; and they shall weep with more bitterness and more tenderness for sin, when they are delivered out of their captivity, than ever they did when they were groaning under it. Weeping and praying do well together; tears put life into prayers, and express the liveliness of them, and prayers help to wipe away tears.

The way God takes of converting souls to himself is by opening the eyes of their understandings, and all good follows thereupon: After that I was instructed I yielded, I smote upon my thigh. When sinners come to a right knowledge they will come to a right way. Ephraim was chastised, and that did not produce the desired effect, it went no further: I was chastised, and that was all. But, when the instructions of God's Spirit accompanied the corrections of his providence, then the work was done, then he smote upon his thigh, was so humbled for sin as to have no more to do with it.

Jeremiah 31

He is to turn from his wickedness and from his wicked way. It is not enough for a man to turn from his wicked way by an outward reformation, which may be the effect of his sins leaving him rather than of his leaving his sins, but he must turn from his wickedness, from the love of it and the inclination to it, by an inward regeneration; if he do not so much as turn from his wicked way, there is little hope that he will turn from his wickedness.

Ezekiel 3

True penitents see sin to be an abominable thing, that abominable thing which the Lord hates and which makes sinners, and even their services, odious to him (Jer. 44:4; Isa. 1:11). It defiles the sinner's own conscience, and makes him, unless he be past feeling, an abomination to himself. Those gratifications which the hearts of sinners were set upon as delectable things, the hearts of penitents are turned against as detestable things.

Ezekiel 6

When men begin to complain more of their sins than of their afflictions then there begins to be some hope of them; and this is that which God requires of us, when we are under his correcting hand, that we own ourselves in a fault and justly corrected.

Hosea 5

Were the child which the mother is in travail of capable of understanding its own case, we should reckon it an unwise child that would choose to stay long in the birth; for the 'captive exile hasteth to be loosed, lest he die in the pit' (Isa. 51:14). Note, those may justly be reckoned their own destroyers who defer and put off their own repentance, by which alone they might help themselves. Those are in danger of miscarrying in conversion who delay it, and will not put forth themselves to speed the work and bring it to an issue.

Hosea 13

The manner of the expectation is very humble and modest: 'Who knows if he will?' Some think it is expressed thus doubtfully to check the presumption and security of the people, and to quicken them to a holy carefulness and liveliness in their repentance, as (Josh. 24:19). Or, rather, it is expressed doubtfully because it is the removal of a temporal judgment that they here promise themselves, of which we cannot be so confident as we can that, in general, God is gracious and merciful. There is no question at all to be made but that if we truly repent of our sins God will forgive them, and be reconciled to us; but whether he will remove this or the other affliction which we are under may well be questioned, and yet the probability of it should encourage us to repent. Promises of temporal good things are often made with a peradventure. 'It may be you shall be hid' (Zeph. 2:3). David's sin is pardoned, and yet the child shall die, and, when David prayed for its life, he said, as here, 'Who can tell whether God will be gracious to me' in this matter likewise (2 Sam. 12:22).

The Ninevites repented and reformed upon such a consideration as this (Jonah 3:9).

We must 'turn to the Lord our God', not only because he has been just and righteous in punishing us for our sins, the fear of which should drive us to him, but because he is gracious and merciful, in receiving us upon our repentance, the hope of which should draw us to him.

When the sinner's mind is changed, God's way towards him is changed; the sentence is reversed, and the curse of the law is taken off. Note, that is genuine, ingenuous, and evangelical repentance which arises from a firm belief of the mercy of God, which we have sinned against, and yet are not in despair. 'Repent, for the kingdom of heaven is at hand.' The goodness of God, if it be rightly understood, instead of emboldening us to go on in sin, will be the most powerful inducement to repentance (Ps. 130:4). The act of indemnity brings those to God whom the act of attainder frightened from him.

Joel 2

It becomes penitents to be humble and low in their own eyes, to be thankful for the least mercy, patient under the greatest affliction, to be watchful against all appearances of sin, and approaches towards it, to abound in every duty, and to be charitable in judging others.

It is vain presumption to think that our having good relations will save us, though we be not good ourselves. What though we be descended from pious ancestors; have been blessed with a religious education; have our lot cast in families where the fear of God is uppermost; and have good friends to advise us and pray for us; what will all this avail us, if we do not repent, and live a life of repentance?

Consider your ways, change your minds; you have thought amiss; think again, and think aright. Note, true penitents have other thoughts of God and Christ, and sin and holiness, and this world and the other, than they have had, and stand otherwise affected toward them. The change of the mind produces a change of the way. Those who are truly sorry for what they have done amiss, will be careful to do so no more.

Matthew 3

All those, and those only, are invited to rest in Christ, that are sensible of sin as a burden, and groan under it; that are not only convinced of the evil of sin, of their own sin, but are contrite in soul for it; that are really sick of their sins, weary of the service of the world and of the flesh; that see their state sad and dangerous by reason of sin, and are in pain and fear about it, as Ephraim (Jer. 31: 18—20), the prodigal (Luke 15: 17), the publican (Luke 18:13), Peter's hearers (Acts 2:37), Paul (Acts 9:4, 6, 9), the jailor (Acts 16:29, 30). This is a necessary preparative for pardon and peace. The Comforter must first convince (John 16:8); I have torn and then will heal.

Matthew 11

Though he was convinced that John was a prophet, and one owned of God, yet he does not express the least remorse or sorrow for his sin in putting him to death. The devils believe and tremble, but they never believe and repent. Note, there may be the terror of strong convictions, where there is not the truth of a saving conversion.

Matthew 14

They did not like a religion which insisted so much on humility, self-denial, contempt of the world, and spiritual worship. Repentance was the door of admission into this kingdom, and nothing could be more disagreeable to the Pharisees, who justified and admired themselves, than to repent, that is, to accuse and abase and abhor themselves; therefore they went not in themselves.

Matthew 23

As it commends the good father's kindness that he showed it before the prodigal expressed his repentance, so it commends the prodigal's repentance that he expressed it after his father had shown him so much kindness.

Even those that have received the pardon of their sins, and the comfortable sense of their pardon, must have in their hearts a sincere contrition for it, and with their mouths must make a penitent confession of it, even of those sins which they have reason to hope are pardoned. David penned the fifty-first psalm after Nathan had said, 'The Lord has taken away thy sin, thou shalt not die'. Nay, the comfortable sense of the pardon of sin should increase our sorrow for it; and that is ingenuous evangelical sorrow which is increased by such a consideration. See (Ezek. 16: 63), 'Thou shalt be ashamed and confounded, when I am pacified towards thee.'

Luke 15

The true penitent casts away from him his transgressions, 'Away with them, away with them' (Isa. 2:20; 30:22), 'crucify them, crucify them'; it is not fit that they should live in my soul (Hos. 14:8).

John 19

Peter, though he had denied his Master, had not deserted his Master's friends; by this appears the sincerity of his repentance, that he associated with the disciple whom Jesus loved. And the disciples' keeping up their intimacy with him as formerly, notwithstanding his fall, teaches us to restore those with a spirit of meekness that have been faulty. If God has received them upon their repentance, why should not we?

John 20

Repetition

Such humble thoughts had Paul of himself, though he excelled in knowledge, that he would not pretend to tell them that which they did not know before, but only to remind them of that in which they had formerly been by others instructed. So Peter

(2 Peter 1:12; 3:1). People commonly excuse themselves from hearing the word with this, that the minister can tell them nothing but what they knew before. If it be so, yet have they not need to know it better, and to be put in mind of it?

Romans 15

Those who have had ever so good teaching are apt to forget, and need to have their memories refreshed. The same truth, taught over again, if it give no new light, may make new and quicker impression.

1 Corinthians 4

Reprobates

It was in vain to think of reforming them, for various methods had been tried with them, and all to no purpose (v. 29, 30). He compares them to ore that was supposed to have some good metal in it, and was therefore put into the furnace by the refiner, who used all his art, and took abundance of pains about it, but it proved all dross, nothing of any value could be extracted out of it. God by his prophets and by his providences had used the most proper means to refine this people and to purify them from their wickedness; but it was all in vain. By the continual preaching of the word, and a series of afflictions, they had been kept in a constant fire, but all to no purpose. The bellows have been still kept so near the fire to blow it, that they are burnt with the heat of it, or they are quite worn out

with long use and thrown into the fire as good for nothing. The prophets have preached their throats sore with crying aloud against the sins of Israel, and yet they are not convinced and humbled. The lead, which was then used in refining silver, as quicksilver is now, is consumed of the fire, and has not done its work. The founder melts in vain; his labour is lost, for the wicked are not plucked away, no care is taken to separate between the precious and the vile, to purge out the old leaven, to cast out of communion those who, being corrupt themselves, are in danger of infecting others.

Jeremiah 6

Reproof

We are commanded to rebuke our neighbour in love ... friendly reproof is a duty we owe to one another and we ought to give it and take it in love. 'Let the righteous smite me and it shall be a kindness (Ps. 141:5). Faithful and useful are those wounds of a friend (Prov. 27:5, 6). It is here strictly commanded 'Thou shalt in any wise do it and not omit it under any pretence.' Consider the guilt we incur by not reproving. It is construed here into a hating of our brother. We are ready to argue that such a one is a friend I love, therefore, I will not make him uneasy by telling him of his faults; but we should rather say, therefore I will do him the kindness to tell him of them. Love covers sin from others but not from the sinner himself . . . must we help the ass of an enemy that has fallen under his burden and shall we not help the soul of a friend?

Leviticus 19

Those that complain that their ministers are too harsh with them should remember that while they keep to the Word of God they are but messengers and must say as they are bidden and be willing, as Saul himself here was, that they should 'Say on'. Samuel delivers his message faithfully.

1 Samuel 15

Many things not in themselves sinful, turn into sin to us by our delighting in them. Joab was aware of David's vanity herein but he, himself, was not. It would be good for us to have a friend that would faithfully admonish us when we say or do anything proud or vainglorious for we often do so and are not ourselves aware of it.

2 Samuel 24

Most people would rather be told their fortune than their faults or their duty . . . Some have, by sickness, been reminded of their forgotten ministers and praying friends. He sent to Ahijah because he had told him he should be king. 'He was once the messenger of good tidings, surely he will be so again.' Those that by sin disqualify themselves for comfort and yet expect their ministers, because they are good men, should speak peace and comfort to them, greatly wrong both themselves and their ministers.

1 Kings 14

Is this Asa, is this he whose heart was perfect with the Lord his God all his days? Well, let him that thinks he stands take heed lest he fall. A wise man and yet in a rage, an Israelite and yet in a rage with a prophet. A good man and yet impatient of reproof and that cannot bear to be told of his faults. Lord, what is man when God leaves him to himself. Those that idolise their own conduct cannot bear contradiction . . . God's prophets meet with many that cannot bear reproof but take it much amiss, yet they must do their duty.

2 Chronicles 16

He hearkened to and preferred those that humoured him before the good prophet that gave him fair warning of his danger. Those do best for themselves that give their friends leave, and particularly their ministers, to deal plainly and faithfully with them and take their reproofs not only patiently but kindly. That counsel is not always best for us that is most pleasing to us.

2 Chronicles 18

Sinners ought to consider that how little notice soever they take of them, an account is kept of the words of the seers that speak to them from God to admonish them of their sins, warn them of their danger and call them to their duty, which will be produced against them in the great day.

2 Chronicles 33

Wise men are not so perfectly wise but there is that in them which needs a reproof; and we must not connive at any man's

faults because we have a veneration for his wisdom, nor must a
wise man think that his wisdom
exempts him from reproof when
he says or does anything
foolishly; but the more wisdom
a man has the more desirous he
should be to have his weaknesses shown him, because a
little folly is a great blemish
to him that is in reputation for
wisdom and honour.

Proverbs 9

If the scorner will not be
recovered from his sin, the
disease being inveterate, yet
the simple will beware of venturing upon the sin which
exposes men thus. If it cure
not the infected, it may prevent the spreading of the
infection. The reproof of wise
men will be a means of good
to themselves. They need not
be smitten, a word to the wise
is enough.

Proverbs 19

If it be well given, by a wise
reprover, and well taken, by an
obedient ear, it is an earring of
gold and an ornament of fine
gold, very graceful and well
becoming both the reprover and
the reproved; both will have
their praise, the reprover for
giving it so prudently and the
reproved for taking it so
patiently and making a good
use of it. Others will commend them both, and they will
have satisfaction in each other;
he who gave the reproof is
pleased that it had the desired
effect, and he to whom it was
given has reason to be thankful
for it as a kindness. That is well
given, we say, that is well taken;
yet it does not always prove

that that is well taken which
is well given. It were to be
wished that a wise reprover
should always meet with an
obedient ear, but often it is
not so.

Proverbs 25

The same strings, though generally unpleasing ones, are harped
upon in this chapter that were
in those before. People care not
to be told either of their sin or
of their danger by sin; and yet
it is necessary, and for their
good, that they should be told
of both, nor can they better
hear of either than from the
Word of God and from their
faithful ministers, while the sin
may be repented of and the
danger prevented.

Hosea 13

They take it as an affront to
be 'told of their faults', and
called upon to amend them;
they are ready to say, 'What ado
do these prophets make about
returning and repenting; why
are we disgraced and disturbed
thus, our own consciences and
our neighbours stirred up against
us?' It is ill with those who
thus count reproofs reproaches,
and 'kick against the pricks.'

Malachi 3

The consideration of what is
amiss in ourselves, though it
ought not to keep us from
administering friendly reproof,
ought to keep us from magis-
terial censuring, and to make
us very candid and charitable
in judging others. 'Therefore
restore with the spirit of meekness, considering thyself' (Gal.
6:1); what thou hast been, what
thou art, and what thou wouldst

be, if God should leave thee to thyself.

Matthew 7

Faithful reproofs, if they do not profit, usually provoke; if they do not do good, they are resented as affronts, and they that will not bow to the reproof, will fly in the face of the reprover and hate him, as Ahab hated Micaiah (1 Kings 22:8). See (Prov. 9:8; 15:10, 12). *Veritas odium parit* — Truth produces hatred.

Matthew 14

Where the fault is plain and great, the person proper for us to deal with, and we have an opportunity for it, and there is no apparent danger of doing more hurt than good, we must with meekness and faithfulness tell people of what is amiss in them. Christian reproof is an ordinance of Christ for the bringing of sinners to repentance, and must be managed as an ordinance. 'Let the reproof be private, between thee and him alone; that it may appear you seek not his reproach, but his repentance.' Note, it is a good rule, which should ordinarily be observed among Christians, not to speak of our brethren's faults to others, till we have first spoken of them to themselves.

Matthew 18

When those who hear the reproofs of the Word, perceive that it speaks of them, if it do not do them a great deal of good, it will certainly do them a great deal of hurt. If they be not pricked to the heart with conviction and contrition, as

they were (Acts 2:37), they will be cut to the heart with rage and indignation, as they were (Acts 5:33).

Matthew 21

Carnal people can easily honour the memories of faithful ministers that are dead and gone, because they do not reprove them, nor disturb them, in their sins.

They can pay respect to the writings of the dead prophets, which tell them what they should be; but not the reproofs of the living prophets, which tell them what they are.

Matthew 23

These people complimented Christ with Rabbi, and showed him great respect, yet he told them thus faithfully of their hypocrisy; his ministers must hence learn not to flatter those that flatter them, nor to be bribed by fair words to cry peace to all that cry 'rabbi' to them, but to give faithful reproofs where there is cause for them.

John 6

Frequently those that need reproof most, and deserve it best, though they have wit enough to discern a 'tacit' one, have not grace enough to bear a 'just' one.

John 9

People's being unwilling to hear of their faults is no good reason why they should not be faithfully told of them. It is a common excuse made for not reproving sin that the times will not bear it. But those whose office it is to reprove must not be awed by this; the times must bear it, and shall bear it. 'Cry aloud and spare not'; cry aloud and fear not.

Acts 5

In reproving for sin, we should have a tender regard to the reputation, as well as the reformation, of the sinner. We should aim to distinguish between them and their sins, and take care not to discover any spite against them ourselves, nor expose them to contempt and reproach in the world. Reproofs that expose commonly do but exasperate, when those that kindly and affectionately warn are likely to reform. When the affections of a father mingle with the admonitions of a minister, it is to be hoped that they may at once melt and mend; but to lash like an enemy or executioner will provoke and render obstinate.

1 Corinthians 4

Hereby he teaches us that in reproving others we should take care to convince them that our reproofs do not proceed from any private pique or resentment, but from a sincere regard to the honour of God and religion and their truest welfare; for they are then likely to be most successful when they appear to be most disinterested.

Galatians 4

This may give us occasion to observe that, in reproving sin and error, we should always distinguish between the leaders and the led, such as set themselves to draw others thereinto and such as are drawn aside by them. Thus the apostle softens and alleviates the fault of these Christians, even while he is reproving them, that he might the better persuade them to return to, and stand fast in, the liberty wherewith Christ had made them free.

Galatians 5

The sharpest reproofs must aim at the good of the reproved; they must not be of malice, nor hatred, nor ill will, but of love; not to gratify pride, passion, nor any evil affection in the reprover, but to reclaim and reform the erroneous and the guilty.

Titus 1

And we may here observe with what esteem and affection he speaks of him who had formerly publicly withstood and sharply reproved Peter. If a righteous man smite one who is truly religious, it shall be received as a kindness; and let him reprove, it shall be as an excellent oil, which shall soften and sweeten the good man that is reproved when he does amiss.

2 Peter 3

Resolution

Those who keep their eye upon heaven as their end will keep their feet in the paths of religion as their way, whatever difficulties and discouragements they meet with in it. He will not only hold on his way notwithstanding, but will grow *stronger and stronger*. By the sight of other good men's trials, and the experience of his own, he will be made more vigorous and lively in his duty, more warm and affectionate, more resolute and undaunted; the worse others are the better he will be; that which dismays others emboldens him. The blustering wind makes the traveller gather his cloak the closer about him and gird it the faster. Those that are truly wise and good will be continually growing wiser and better. Proficiency in religion is a good sign of sincerity in it.

Job 17

Responsibility

Those that are entrusted with the charge of the Sanctuary will have a great deal to answer for. Who would covet the care of souls who considers the account that must be given of that care.

Numbers 18

It is taken for granted that the tribe of Judah would be both a praying tribe and an active tribe. 'Lord,' says Moses, 'hear his prayers and give success to all his undertakings; let his hands be sufficient for him both in husbandry and in war.' The voice of prayer should always be attended with the hand of endeavour and then we may expect prosperity.

Deuteronomy 33

The assurance God had given them of success in this day's action, instead of making them remiss and presumptuous, set all heads and hands on work for the effecting of what God had promised.

Judges 20

Those that do not restrain the sins of others when it is in the power of their hand to do it, make themselves partakers of the guilt and will be charged as accessories. Those in authority will have a great deal to answer for if they make not the sword they bear a terror to evil workers.

1 Samuel 3

God had decreed the end but Ahab must use the means.

1 Kings 20

The call that is given to this people (v. 18): 'Hear, you deaf, and attend to the joyful sound, and look you blind, that you may see the joyful light.' There is no absurdity in this command, nor is it unbecoming the wisdom and goodness of God to call us to do that good which yet of ourselves we are not sufficient for; for those have natural powers which they may employ so as to do better than they do, and may have supernatural grace if it be not their own fault, who yet labour under a moral impotency to that which is good. This call to the deaf to hear and the blind to see is like the command given to the man that had the withered hand to stretch it forth; though he could not do this, because it was withered, yet, if he had not attempted to do it, he would not have been healed, and his being healed thereupon was owing, not to his act, but to the divine power.

Isaiah 42

If it contract so heinous a guilt as it does to be accessory to the murder of a dying body, what is it to be accessory to the ruin of an immortal soul?

Ezekiel 3

Those who perish are as inexcusable as this man would have been, if he had not attempted to stretch forth his hand, and so had not been healed. But those who are saved have no more to boast of than this man had of contributing to his own cure, by stretching forth his hand, but are as much indebted to the power and grace of Christ as he was.

Matthew 12

A candle gives light but a little way, and but a little while, and is easily blown out, and continually burning down and wasting. Many who are lighted as candles, put themselves under a bed, or under a bushel; they do not manifest grace themselves, nor minister grace to others; they have estates, and do no good with them; they have their limbs and senses, wit and learning perhaps, but nobody is the better for them; they have spiritual gifts, but do not use them; like a taper in an urn, they burn to themselves.

We are not born for ourselves.

Mark 4

Restlessness

People are never long easy and satisfied: there is no end, no rest, of all the people; they are continually fond of changes, and know not what they would have. This is no new thing, but it has been the way of all that have been before them; there have been instances of this in every age: even Samuel and David could not always please. As it has been, so it is likely to be still: those that come after will be of the same spirit, and shall not long rejoice in him whom at first they seemed extremely fond of. Today, hosanna — tomorrow, crucify.

Ecclesiastes 4

Restraints Upon Sin

Crosses and obstacles in an evil course are great blessings, and are so to be accounted. They are God's hedges, to keep us from transgressing, to restrain us from wandering out of the green pastures, to 'withdraw man from his purpose' (Job 33:17), to make the way of sin difficult, that we may not go on in it, and to keep us from it whether we will or not. We have reason to bless God both for restraining grace and for restraining providences.

Hosea 2

Wicked men are restrained from the most wicked practices, merely by their secular interest, and not by any regard to God. A concern for their ease, credit, wealth, and safety, being their reigning principle, as it keeps them from many duties, so it keeps them from many sins, which otherwise they would not be restrained from; and this is one means by which sinners are kept from being overmuch wicked (Eccl. 7:17). The danger of sin that appears to sense, or to fancy only, influences men more than that which appears to faith. Herod feared that the putting of John to death might raise a mutiny among the people, which it did not; but he never feared it might raise a mutiny in his own conscience, which it did (v. 2). Men fear being hanged for that which they do not fear being damned for.

Matthew 14

Restoring Backsliders

Yet there is a mixture of mercy in this sentence. God deals not in severity, as he might have done, with those who had dealt treacherously with him, but mitigates the sentence (vs. 11, 14). They are deprived but in part, *'ab officio'* — of their office, and, it should seem, not at all *'a beneficio'* — of their emoluments. They shall help to 'slay the sacrifice', which the Levites were permitted to do, and which in this temple was done, not at the altar, but 'at the tables' (ch. 40:39). They shall be porters 'at the gates of the house', and they shall be 'keepers of the charge of the house, for all the service thereof.' Note, those who may not be fit to be employed in one kind of service may yet be fit to be employed in another; and even those who have offended may yet be made use of, and not quite thrown aside, much less thrown away.

Ezekiel 44

Resurrection

The resurrection of Christ, considered as an act of power, is common to all the three persons, but as an act of judgment it is peculiar to the Father, who as a Judge released Christ, raised him from the grave, and gave him glory, proclaimed him to all the world to be his Son by his resurrection from the dead, advanced him to heaven, crowned him with glory and honour, invested him with all power in heaven and earth, and glorified him with that glory which he had with God before the world was.

1 Peter 1

Revelation

The Gospel of Christ is not a doubtful opinion, like an hypothesis or new notion in philosophy, which every one is at liberty to believe or not; but it is a revelation of the mind of God, which is of eternal truth in itself, and of infinite concern to us.

John 3

This was very much the character of the pretenders to philosophy and the Grecian learning and wisdom in that day. Such a man receives not the things of the Spirit of God. Revelation is not with him a principle of science; he looks upon it as delirium and dotage, the extravagant thought of some deluded dreamer. It is no way to wisdom among the famous masters of the world; and for that reason he can have no knowledge of things revealed, because they are only spiritually discerned, or made known by the revelation of the Spirit.

1 Corinthians 2

Revenge

Nay, if persons wronged in seeking the defence of the law, and magistrates in granting it, act from any particular personal pique or quarrel, and not from a concern that public peace and order be maintained and right done, even such proceedings, though seemingly regular, will fall under this prohibited self-revenging.

Romans 12

To 'render evil for evil, or railing for railing', is a sinful unchristian practice; the magistrate may punish 'evil-doers', and private men may seek a legal remedy when they are wronged; but private revenge by duelling, scolding, or secret mischief, is forbidden (Prov. 20:22; Luke 6:27; Rom. 12:17; 1 Thess. 5:15). To rail is to revile another in bitter, fierce, and reproachful terms; but for ministers to rebuke sharply, and to preach earnestly against the sins of the times, is not railing; all the prophets and apostles practised it (Isa. 56:10; Zeph. 3:3; Acts 20:29).

1 Peter 3

Reverence

Outward expressions of inward reverence and a religious awe of God well become us and are required of us whenever we approach to him in solemn ordinances.

Joshua 5

Eglon pays respect to a message from God. Though a king, though a heathen king, though rich and powerful, though now tyrannising over the people of God, though a fat, unwieldly man that could not easily rise nor stand long, though in private and what he did was not under observation, yet, when he expected to receive orders from heaven, he rose out of his seat, whether it was low and easy or whether it was high and stately, he quitted it and stood up when God was about to speak to him, thereby owning God as superior. This shames the irreverence of many who are called Christians and yet, when a message from God is delivered to them, study to show by all the marks of carelessness how little they regard it.

Judges 3

Let no man think that his service done for God will justify him in any instance of disrespect or irreverence towards the things of God . . . It is an offence to God if we think meanly of his ordinances because of the meanness of the manner of their administration.

1 Samuel 6

The courts of Solomon and Ahasuerus were magnificent; but, compared with the glorious majesty of God's kingdom, they were but as glow-worms to the sun. The consideration of this should strike an awe upon us in all our approaches to God.

Psalm 145

An excellent direction to maintain high thoughts of God in our minds at all times: Be thou in the fear of the Lord every day and all the day long. We must be in the fear of the Lord as in our employment, exercising ourselves in holy adorings of God, in subjection to his precepts, submission to his providences, and a constant care to please him; we must be in it as in our element, taking a pleasure in contemplating God's glory and complying with his will. We must be devoted to his fear (Ps. 119:38); and governed by it as our commanding principle in all we say and do. All the days of our life we must constantly keep up an awe of God in our spirits, must pay a deference to his authority, and have a dread of his wrath. We must be always so in his fear as never to be out of it.

Proverbs 23

Though angels' faces, doubtless, are much fairer than those of the children of men (Acts 6:15), yet, in the presence of God, they cover them, because they cannot bear the dazzling lustre of the divine glory, and because, being conscious of an infinite distance from the divine perfection, they are ashamed to show their faces before the holy God, who charges even his angels with folly if they should offer to vie with him (Job 4:18). If angels be thus reverent in their attendance on God, with what godly fear should we approach his throne!

Isaiah 6

We sanctify the Lord God in our hearts when we with sincerity and fervency adore him, when our thoughts of him are aweful and reverend, when we rely upon his power, trust to his faithfulness, submit to his wisdom, imitate his holiness, and give him the glory due to his most illustrious perfections. We sanctify God before others when our deportment is such as invites and encourages others to glorify and honour him; both are required (Lev. 10:3).

An aweful sense of the divine perfections is the best antidote against the fear of sufferings; did we fear God more, we should certainly fear men less.

1 Peter 3

A holy awe and reverential fear of God are necessary in order to our worshipping and glorifying him, and a belief of the inconceivable distance between him and us is very proper to beget and maintain that religious fear of the Lord which is the beginning of wisdom.

If men have no knowledge or belief of the eternal God, they will be very apt to think him such a one as themselves.

2 Peter 3

Revival

And he that made dry land in the waters can produce waters in the driest land.

Isaiah 43

At 'evening-time', when our hopes are quite spent with waiting all day to no purpose, nay, when we fear it will be quite dark, when things are at the worst and the case of the church is most deplorable. As to the church's enemies 'the sun goes down at noon', so to the church it rises at night; unto the upright springs 'light out of darkness' (Ps. 112:4); deliverance comes when the tale of bricks is doubled, and when God's people have done looking for it, and so it comes with a pleasing surprise.

Zechariah 14

Rewards

He mentions it to God in prayer, not as if he thought he had hereby merited any favour from God, as a debt, but to show that he looked not for any recompense of his generosity from men, but depended upon God only to make up to him what he had lost and laid out for his honour; and he reckoned the favour of God reward enough. 'If God do but think upon me for good, I have enough.' His thoughts to us-ward are our happiness (Ps. 40:5). He refers it to God to recompense him in such a manner as he pleased. 'If men forget me, let my God think on me, and I desire no more.'

Nehemiah 5

Dominion is not founded in grace. Those that have not any colourable title to eternal happiness may yet have a justifiable title to their temporal good things. Nebuchadnezzar is a very bad man, and yet God calls him his servant, because he employed him as an instrument of his providence for the chastising of the nations, and particularly his own people; and for his service therein he thus liberally repaid him. Those whom God makes use of shall not lose by him; much more will he be found the bountiful rewarder of all those that designedly and sincerely serve him.

Jeremiah 27

As Judah had his lot next the sanctuary on one side, so Benjamin had, of all the tribes, his lot nearest to it on the other side, which honour was reserved for those who adhered to the house of David and the temple at Jerusalem when the other ten tribes went astray from both. It is enough if treachery and apostasy, upon repentance, be pardoned, but constancy and fidelity shall be rewarded and preferred.

Ezekiel 48

What shall we have? Christ looked at the joy set before him, and Moses at the recompense of reward. For this end it is set before us, that by a patient continuance in well-doing we may seek for it. Christ encourages us to ask what we shall gain by leaving all to follow him; that we may see he doth not call us to our prejudice, but unspeakably to our advantage. As it is the language of an obediential faith to ask, 'What shall we do?' with an eye to the precepts; so it is of a hoping, trusting faith, to ask, 'What shall we have?', with an eye to the promises. But observe, the disciples had long since left all to engage themselves in the service of Christ, and yet never till now asked, 'What shall we have?'

Matthew 19

In heaven, every vessel will be full, brimful, though every vessel is not alike large and capacious. In the distribution of future joys, as it was in the gathering of the manna, he that shall gather much, will have nothing over, and he that shall gather little, will have no lack (Exod. 16:18). Those whom Christ fed miraculously, though of different sizes, men, women, and children, did all eat, and were filled.

Matthew 20

Sacraments

The ministry of the Word and sacraments is designed for no other end than to lead people to Christ, and to make him more and more manifest.

John 1

The nature of sacraments in general: they are signs and seals — signs to represent and instruct, seals to ratify and confirm.

Romans 4

Sacrifice

Surely it was in a way of righteous judgment, because they had changed the glory of God into the similitude of a beast, that God gave them up to such vile affections that changed them into worse than beasts. God says of this that it was what he commanded them not, neither came it into his heart, which is not meant of his not commanding them thus to worship Moloch (this he had expressly forbidden them), but he had never commanded that his worshippers should be at such an expense, nor put such a force upon their natural affection, in honouring him; it never came into his heart to have children offered to him, yet they had forsaken his service for the service of such gods as, by commanding this, showed themselves to be indeed enemies to mankind.

Jeremiah 7

See the deficiency of the legal sacrifices for sin; they were therefore often repeated, not only every year, but every feast, every day of the feast, because they could not make the comers thereunto perfect (Heb. 10:1, 3). See the necessity of our frequently repeating the same religious exercises. Though the sacrifice of atonement is offered once for all, yet the sacrifices of acknowledgment, that of a broken heart, that of a thankful heart, those spiritual sacrifices which are acceptable to God through Christ Jesus, must be every day offered.

Ezekiel 45

Salvation

He hath saved us from the dominion of sin, which is darkness (1 John 1:6), from the dominion of Satan, who is the 'prince of darkness' (Eph. 6: 12), and from the damnation of hell, which is 'utter darkness' (Matt. 25:30). They are 'called out of darkness' (1 Peter 2:9).

Colossians 1

Samaritans

The Samaritans were the adversaries of Judah (Ezra 4:1), were upon all occasions mischievous to them. The Jews were extremely malicious against the Samaritans, 'looked upon them as having no part in the resurrection, excommunicated and cursed them by the sacred name of God, by the glorious writing of the tables, and by the curse of the upper and lower house of judgment, with this law. That no Israelite eat of anything that is a Samaritan's, for it is as if he should eat swine's flesh'. So Dr. Lightfoot, out of 'Rabbi Tanchum'.

She had little reason to boast of their fathers; for, when Antiochus persecuted the Jews, the Samaritans, for fear of sharing with them in their sufferings, not only renounced all relation to the Jews, but surrendered their temple to Antiochus, with a request that it might be dedicated to Jupiter Olympius, and called by his name.

John 4

Sanctification

We must not only not quench the Spirit but we must stir up the gift that is in us. Though we be not always sacrificing yet we must keep the fire of holy love always burning and thus we must pray always.

Leviticus 6

New dispositions and inclinations, new sympathies and antipathies; the understanding enlightened, the conscience softened, the thoughts rectified; the will bowed to the will of God, and the affections made spiritual and heavenly: so that the man is not what he was — old things are passed away, all things are become new; he acts from new principles, by new rules, with new designs.

Romans 12

The persons and things which are acceptable to God should be approved of us. Should not we be pleased with that which God is pleased with? What is it to be sanctified, but to be of God's mind?

Romans 14

Satan

His own children he tempts first, and draws them to sin, and afterwards torments, when thereby he has brought them to ruin; but this child of God he tormented with affliction, and then tempted to make a bad use of his affliction.

Job 2

See why he called Peter, Satan, when he suggested this to him; because, whatever stood in the way of our salvation, he looked upon as coming from the devil, who is a sworn enemy to it. The same Satan that afterward entered into Judas, maliciously to destroy him in his undertaking, here prompted Peter plausibly to divert him from it. Thus he changes himself into an angel of light.

Matthew 16

The devil does all he can to keep us from believing, to make us not believe the word when we read and hear it; or, if we heed it for the present, to make us forget it again, and let it slip (Heb. 2:1); or, if we remember it, to create prejudices in our minds against it, or divert our minds from it to something else; and all is lest we should believe and be saved, lest we should believe and rejoice, while he believes and trembles.

Luke 8

By two particular instances, they resembled the devil — murder and lying. The devil is an enemy to life, because God is the God of life and life is the happiness of man; and an enemy to truth, because God is the God of truth and truth is the bond of human society.

John 8

They are under the influence and power of the devil, who is here called 'the god of this world', and elsewhere 'the prince of this world', because of the great interest he has in this world, the homage that is paid to him by multitudes in this world, and the great sway that, by divine permission, he bears in the world, and in the hearts of his subjects, or rather slaves. And as he is the prince of darkness, and ruler of the darkness of this world, so he darkens the understandings of men, and increases their prejudices, and supports his interest by keeping them in the dark, blinding their minds with ignorance, and error, and prejudices, that they should not 'behold the light of the glorious gospel of Christ, who is the image of God'.

2 Corinthians 4

Satan's Devices

The great thing Satan aims at is to make people forget God, and all that whereby he has made himself known; and he has many subtle methods to bring them to this. Sometimes he does it by setting up false gods (bring men in love with Baal, and they soon forget the name of God), sometimes by misrepresenting the true God, as if he were altogether such a one as ourselves. Pretences to new revelation may prove as dangerous to religion as the denying of all revelation; and false prophets in God's name may perhaps do more mischief to the power of godliness than false prophets in Baal's name, as being less guarded against.

Jeremiah 23

See, and be amazed to see, how this world is imposed upon: 1. Satan's sworn enemies are represented as his friends, the Apostles, who pulled down the devil's kingdom, were called devils. Thus men laid to their charge, not only things which they knew not, but things which they abhorred, and were directly contrary to, and the reverse of. 2. Satan's sworn servants would be thought to be his enemies, and they never more effectually do his work, than when they pretend to be fighting against him. Many times they who themselves are nearest akin to the devil, are most apt to father others upon him; and those that paint him on others' clothes have him reigning in their own hearts. It is well there is a day coming, when (as it follows here), (v. 26), that which

is hid will be brought to light.
Matthew 10

Note, first, we must take heed lest anything that occurs in our way to holy ordinances unfit us for, or divert us from, our due attendance on them. Let us proceed in the way of our duty, notwithstanding the artifices of Satan, who endeavours, by the perverse disputings of men of corrupt minds, and many other ways, to ruffle and discompose us. Secondly, we must not, for the sake of private feuds and personal piques, draw back from public worship. Though the Pharisees had thus maliciously cavilled at Christ, yet he went into their synagogue. Satan gains this point, if, by sowing discord among brethren, he prevail to drive them, or any of them, from the synagogue, and the communion of the faithful.
Matthew 12

It is the subtlety of Satan, to send temptations to us by the unsuspected hands of our best and dearest friends. Thus he assaulted Adam by Eve, Job by his wife, and here Christ by his beloved Peter. It concerns us therefore not to be ignorant of his devices, but to stand against his wiles and depths, by standing always upon our guard against sin, whoever moves us to it. Even the kindnesses of our friends are often abused by Satan, and made use of as temptations to us.
Matthew 16

Satisfaction

Thanks to our Maker, we have plenty and variety enough allowed us. To prevent our being uneasy at the restraints of religion, it is often good to take a view of the liberties and comforts of it.
Genesis 3

Note, gracious persons, though they still covet more of God, never covet more than God; but, being satisfied of his lovingkindness, they are abundantly satisfied with it, and envy not any their carnal mirth and sensual pleasures and delights, but account themselves truly happy in what they have, and doubt not but to be completely happy in what they hope for.
Psalm 16

Those that hunger and thirst after righteousness in Christ shall have all they can desire to satisfy them and make them easy, and shall not labour, as they have done, for that which satisfies not. Those that are much in praying shall be much in thanksgiving: those shall praise the Lord that seek him.
Psalm 22

Those that labour for the world, labour for the wind, for that which has more sound than substance, which is uncertain, and always shifting its point, unsatisfying and often hurtful, which we cannot hold fast, and which, if we take up with it as our portion, will no more feed us than the wind (Hos. 12:1). Men will see that they have laboured for the wind when at death they find the profit of their labour is all gone, gone like the wind, they know not whither.

Ecclesiastes 5

Christ disappointed the expectations of those who looked for a Messiah according to their fancies, as the carnal Jews, but outdid theirs who looked for such a Messiah as was promised.

Isaiah 52

It is comfortable dwelling in a habitation of justice and a mountain of holiness. 'And the husbandmen and shepherds shall eat of the fruit of their labours; for I have satiated the weary and sorrowful soul.' That is, those that came weary from their journey, and have been long sorrowful in their captivity, shall now enjoy great plenty. This is applicable to the spiritual blessings God has in store for all true penitents, for all that are just and holy; they shall be abundantly satisfied with divine graces and comforts. In the love and favour of God the weary soul shall find rest and the sorrowful soul joy.

Jeremiah 31

Those that in sincerity join themselves to the true God find enough in him for their satisfaction; and, though they still desire more of God, yet they never desire more than God. But those that forsake this living fountain for broken cisterns will find themselves soon surfeited, but never satisfied; they have soon enough of the gods they have, and are still enquiring after more.

Ezekiel 16

'I will drink no more of the fruit of the vine', as it is a bodily refreshment. I have done with it. No one, having tasted spiritual delights, straightway desires sensitive ones, for he saith, 'The spiritual is better' (Luke 5:39); but everyone that hath tasted spiritual delights, straightway desires eternal ones, for he saith those are better still; and therefore 'let me drink no more of the fruit of the vine', it is dead and flat to those that have been made to drink of the river of God's pleasures; but, Lord, hasten the day, when I shall drink it new and fresh in the kingdom of God, where it shall be for ever new, and in perfection.

Mark 14

Saturday Night

They were to leave off all their worldly labour and compose themselves to the work of the day approaching, some time before sunset on the ninth day . . . The eves of solemn days ought to be employed in solemn preparation. When work for God and our souls is to be done we should not (limit) ourselves in time for the doing of it for how can we spend our time better?

Leviticus 23

The market place they sit in is to some a place of idleness (ch. 20:3); to others a place of worldly business (James 4:13); to all a place of noise or diversion; so that if you ask the reason why people get so little good by the means of grace, you will find it is because they are

273

slothful and trifling, and do not love to take pains; or because their heads, and hands, and hearts are full of the world, the cares of which choke the Word, and choke their souls at last (Ezek. 33:31; Amos 8:5); and they study to divert their own thoughts from everything that is serious.

Matthew 11

The day before the sabbath should be a day of preparation for the sabbath, not of our houses and tables, but of our hearts, which, as much as possible, should be freed from the cares and business of the world, and fixed, and put in frame for the service and enjoyment of God. Such work is to be done, and such advantages are to be gained on the sabbath day, that it is requisite we should get ready for it a day before; nay, the whole week should be divided between the improvement of the foregoing sabbath and the preparation for the following sabbath.

Mark 15

'Six days before the passover'. Devout men set time apart before, to prepare themselves for that solemnity, and thus it became our Lord Jesus to 'fulfil all righteousness'. Thus he has set us an example of solemn self-sequestration, before the solemnities of the gospel passover; let us hear the voice crying, 'Prepare ye the way of the Lord'.

John 12

They would not drive it too late on the day of preparation for the sabbath. What is to be done

the evening before the sabbath should be so contrived that it may neither intrench upon sabbath time, nor indispose us for sabbath work.

John 19

Schism

Our Master had himself foretold that divisions and offences would come, but had entailed a woe on those by whom they come (Matt. 18:7), and against such we are here cautioned. Those who burden the church with dividing and offending impositions, who uphold and enforce those impositions, who introduce and propagate dividing and offending notions, which are erroneous or justly suspected, who out of pride, ambition, affectation of novelty, or the like, causelessly separate from their brethren, and by perverse disputes, censures, and evil surmisings, alienate the affections of Christians one from another — these cause divisions and offences, contrary to, or different from (for that also is implied), the 'doctrine which we have learned'.

Romans 16

There may be schism where there is no separation of communion. Persons may come together in the same church, and sit down at the same table of the Lord, and yet be schismatics. Uncharitableness, alienation of affection, especially if it grows up to discord, and feuds, and contentions, constitute schism. Christians may separate from each other's communion, and yet be charitable one towards another; they may continue in the same communion, and yet be uncharitable. This latter is schism, rather than the former.

1 Corinthians 11

Scorn

Though he was a man of honour, a man of great prudence, and had done eminent services to his country, yet because he was a devout, conscientious man, 'the proud had him greatly in derision'; they ridiculed him, bantered him, and did all they could to expose him to contempt; they laughed at him for his praying, and called it 'cant', for his seriousness, and called it 'mopishness', for his strictness, and called it 'needless preciseness'. They were the proud that sat in the scorner's seat and valued themselves on so doing.

Psalm 119

Secession

When the church ceases to be the pillar and ground of truth, we may and ought to forsake her; for our regard to truth should be greater than our regard to the church; we are no longer obliged to continue in the church than she continues to be the pillar and ground of truth.

1 Timothy 3

Seeing Ourselves as we are

He owns himself an offender, and has nothing to say in his own justification (v. 4): 'Behold I am vile, not only mean and contemptible, but vile and abominable, in my own eyes.' He is now sensible that he has sinned, and therefore calls himself vile. Sin debases us, and penitents abase themselves, reproach themselves, are ashamed, yea, even confounded. 'I have acted undutifully to my Father, ungratefully to my benefactor, unwisely for myself; and therefore I am vile.' Job now vilifies himself as much as ever he had justified and magnified himself. Repentance changes men's opinion of themselves. Job had been too bold in demanding a conference with God, and thought he could make his part good with him: but now he is convinced of his error, and owns himself utterly unable to stand before God or to produce anything worth his notice, the veriest dunghill-worm that ever crawled upon God's ground. While his friends talked with him, he answered them, for he thought himself as good as they; but when God talked with him, he had nothing to say, for, in comparison with him, he sees himself nothing, less than nothing, worse than nothing, vanity and vileness itself; and therefore, 'What shall I answer thee?'

Job 40

Seeking God

Did any ever seek the Lord and not find him? Yes, Saul did. The Lord answered him not; took no notice of either his petitions or of his enquiries. . . He could not expect an answer of peace for 1. he enquired in such a manner that it was as if he had not enquired at all. Therefore, it is said (1 Chr. 10: 14) he enquired not of the Lord for he did it faintly and coldly and with a secret design, if God did not answer him, to consult the devil. He did not enquire of the Lord in faith but with a double, unstable mind. 2. He enquired of the Lord when it was too late, when the days of his probation were over and he was finally rejected. Seek the Lord while he may be found for there is a time when he will not be found. 3. He had forfeited the benefit of all the methods of enquiry. Could he that hated and persecuted Samuel and David who were both prophets expect to be answered by prophets? Could he that had slain the high priest expect to be answered by Urim or could he that had sinned away the Spirit of grace expect to be answered by dreams? No, be not deceived God is not mocked.

1 Samuel 28

Self-Control

Man's government of himself by the freedom of his will has in it more of God's image than his government of the creatures.

Genesis 1

Joshua gives the reproof very mildly. He does not load them with any ill names, does not give them any harsh provoking language . . . he only asks them 'Why have you beguiled us?' In the greatest provocations it is our wisdom and duty to keep our temper and to bridle our passion. A just cause needs not anger to defend it and a bad one is made never the better by it.

Joshua 9

He longed for the water of the well of Bethlehem but when he had it he wouldn't drink it because he would not so far humour himself and gratify a foolish fancy. He that has such a rule as this over his own spirit is better than the mighty. It is an honour to a man to have the command of himself but he that will command himself must sometimes cross himself.

1 Chronicles 11

It is bad to think amiss, but it is much worse to speak amiss, for that is an allowance of the evil thought, and gives it an imprimatur — a sanction; it is publishing the seditious libel; and therefore, if thou hast thought evil, lay thy hand upon thy mouth and let it go no further (Prov. 30:32) and that will be an evidence for thee that that which thou thoughtest thou allowest not.

Job 40

A prudent man covers shame. He covers the passion that is in his own breast; when his spirit is stirred, and his heart hot within him, he keeps his mouth as with a bridle, and suppresses his resentments, by smothering and stifling them. Anger is shame, and, though a wise man be not perfectly free from it, yet he is ashamed of it, rebukes it, and suffers not the evil spirit to speak.

It is a kindness to ourselves, and contributes to the repose of our own minds, to extenuate and excuse the injuries and affronts that we receive, instead of aggravating them and making the worst of them, as we are apt to do.

Proverbs 12

'The glory of a man is to pass over a transgression'; it is the duty of a reasonable, and therefore certainly of a Christian man, whose reason is improved and advanced by religion; such may not, and will not, presently fall foul on one who has offended him, but, like God, will be 'slow to anger, and ready to forgive'. Contention and strife arise from men's lusts, and exorbitant unruly passions, which must be curbed and moderated, not indulged; and Christians need to be reminded of these things, that they do not by a wrathful contentious spirit and behaviour displease and dishonour God and discredit religion, promoting feuds in the places where they live. 'He that is slow to anger is better than the mighty,' and he 'that ruleth his spirit than he that taketh a city.'

Titus 3

Our blessed Redeemer was perfectly holy, and so free from sin that no temptation, no provocation whatsoever, could extort from him so much as the least sinful or indecent word. Provocations to sin can never justify the commission of it. The rudeness, cruelty, and injustice of enemies, will not justify Christians in reviling and revenge; the reasons for sin can never be so great, but we have always stronger reasons to avoid it.

1 Peter 2

Self-Deception

We are apt to think that we trust in God, and are entitled to the blessings here promised to those who do so. But this is a thing about which our own hearts deceive us as much as anything. We think that we trust in God when really we do not, as appears by this, that our hopes and fears rise or fall according as second causes smile or frown.

Jeremiah 17

As if God could not see it, though he is all eye, or did not heed it, though his name is Jealous, or had forgotten it, though he is an eternal mind that can never be unmindful, or would not reckon for it, though he is the 'Judge of heaven and earth'. This is the sinner's atheism; as good say that there is no God as say that he is either ignorant or forgetful, that there is 'none that judges in the earth' as that he remembers not the things he is to give judgment upon.

Hosea 7

Even counterfeit graces will serve a man to make a show of when he comes to die, as well as they have done all his life long; the hypocrite's hopes blaze when they are just expiring.

Matthew 25

They thought themselves well-furnished in their souls; they

had learning, and they took it for religion; they had gifts, and they took them for grace; they had wit, and they took it for true wisdom; they had ordinances, and they took up with them instead of the God of ordinances. How careful should we be not to put the cheat upon our own souls!

Revelation 3

Self-Denial

Many are kept from doing their duty by the fear of trouble, the love of ease and an inordinate affection to their worldly business and advantage.

Judges 5

Making excuses (Luke 14:18) is interpreted making light of Christ (Matt. 22:5), and so it is. Those put a great contempt upon Christ that cannot find in their hearts to bear a cold blast for him, or get out of a warm bed.

Song of Solomon 5

Wine is indeed given to 'make glad the heart of man' and we are allowed the sober and moderate use of it; but we are so apt to abuse it and get hurt by it, and a good man, who has his heart made continually glad with the 'light of God's countenance', has so little need of it for that purpose (Ps. 4: 6, 7), that it is a commendable piece of self-denial either not to use it at all or very sparingly and medicinally, as Timothy used it (1 Tim. 5:23).

Jeremiah 35

Temperance, self-denial, and

mortification to the world, do very much befriend the exercises of piety, and help to transmit the observance of them to posterity. The more dead we are to the delights of sense, the better we are disposed for the service of God; but nothing is more fatal to the entail of religion in a family than pride and luxury.

Jeremiah 35

God's servants must learn to endure hardness, and to deny themselves the use of lawful delights, when they may thereby serve the glory of God, evidence the sincerity of their faith, and express their sympathy with their brethren in affliction. The body must be kept under and brought into subjection. Nature is content with a little, grace with less, but lust with nothing. It is good to stint ourselves of choice, that we may the better bear it if ever we should come to be stinted by necessity.

Ezekiel 4

This fitly follows upon denying ourselves; for he that will not deny himself the pleasures of sin, and the advantages of this world for Christ, when it comes to the push, will never have the heart to take up his cross. 'He that cannot take up the resolution to live a saint, has a demonstration within himself, that he is never likely to die a martyr'; so Archbishop Tillotson.

Matthew 16

It is very good for us to straiten and deny ourselves, that we may be able to give the more to the poor; to deny ourselves not only superfluities, but even conveniences, for the sake of charity. We should in many cases pinch ourselves, that we may supply the necessities of others; this is loving our neighbours as ourselves.

Mark 12

The expectation we have of being without bodily appetites in a future life is a very good argument against being under their power in the present life.

1 Corinthians 6

That man has very little of the spirit of the Redeemer who had rather his brother should perish than himself be abridged, in any respect, of his liberty. He who hath the Spirit of Christ in him will love those whom Christ loved, so as to die for them, and will study to promote their spiritual and eternal welfare, and shun everything that would unnecessarily grieve them, and much more everything that would be likely to occasion their stumbling, or falling into sin.

1 Corinthians 8

Those who would aright pursue the interests of their souls must beat down their bodies, and keep them under. They must combat hard with fleshly lusts, till they have subdued them; and not indulge a wanton appetite, and long for heathenish sacrifices, nor eat them, to please their flesh, at the hazard of their brethren's souls. The body must be made to serve the mind, not suffered to lord over it.

1 Corinthians 9

Self-Discipline

His care and industry. He rose up early in the morning that he might lose no time and to show how intent his mind was upon his business. Those that would maintain their spiritual conflicts must not love their ease.

Joshua 8

Self-Examination

The word signifies a fixed abiding thought. Some make it an allusion to those who work embroidery, who are very exact and careful to cover the least flaw, or to those who cast up their accounts, who reckon with themselves, 'What do I owe? What am I worth?' 'I thought not on my wealth (as the covetous man) (49:11) but on my ways, not on what I have but what I do'; for what we do will follow us into another world when what we have must be left behind. Many are critical enough in their remarks upon other people's ways who never think of their own.

Psalm 119

I thought I could have counted them one by one, and have found out the account. He desired to find them out as a penitent, that he might the more particularly acknowledge them; and, generally, the more particular we are in the confession of sin the more comfort we have in the sense of the pardon; he desired it also as a preacher, that he might the more particularly give warning to others. Note, a sound

279

conviction of one sin will put us upon enquiring into the whole confederacy; and the more we see amiss in ourselves the more diligently we should enquire further into our own faults, that what we see not may be discovered to us (Job 34:32).

Ecclesiastes 7

Let us search and try our ways, search what they have been, and then try whether they have been right and good or no; search as for a malefactor in disguise, that flees and hides himself, and then try whether guilty or not guilty. Let conscience be employed both to search and to try, and let it have leave to deal faithfully, to accomplish a diligent search and to make an impartial trial. Let us try our ways, that by them we may try ourselves, for we are to judge of our state not by our faint wishes, but by our steps, not by one particular step, but by our ways, the ends we aim at, the rules we go by, and the agreeableness of the temper of our minds and the tenor of our lives to those ends and those rules. When we are in affliction it is seasonable to consider our ways (Hag. 1:5), that what is amiss may be repented of and amended for the future, and so we may answer the intention of the affliction. We are apt, in times of public calamity, to reflect upon other people's ways, and lay blame upon them; whereas our business is to search and try our own ways. We have work enough to do at home.

Lamentations 3

Christianity is something more than humanity. It is a serious question, and which we should frequently put to ourselves, 'What do we more than others?' 'What excelling thing do we do?' We know more than others; we talk more of the things of God than others; we profess, and have promised, more than others; God has done more for us, and therefore justly expects more from us than from others; the glory of God is more concerned in us than in others; but what do we more than others? Wherein do we live above the rate of the children of this world?

Matthew 5

They ask the reason why they could not cast out the devil at this time (v. 19); 'they came to Jesus apart'. Note, Ministers, who are to deal for Christ in public, have need to keep up a private communion with him, that they may in secret, where no eye sees, bewail their weakness and straitness, their follies and infirmities, in their public performances, and enquire into the cause of them. We should make use of the liberty of access we have to Jesus apart, where we may be free and particular with him. Such questions as the disciples put to Christ, we should put to ourselves, in communing with our own hearts upon our beds; why were we so dull and careless at such a time? Why came we so much short in such a duty? That which is amiss may, when found out, be amended.

Matthew 17

They were apt to suspect themselves; 'Lord, is it I?' Though they were not conscious to themselves of any inclination that way (no such thought had ever entered into their mind), yet they feared the worst, and asked him who knows us better than we know ourselves, 'Lord, is it I?'. Note, it well becomes the disciples of Christ always to be jealous over themselves with a godly jealousy, especially in trying times. We know not how strongly we may be tempted, nor how far God may leave us to ourselves, and therefore have reason, not to be high-minded, but fear. It is observable that our Lord Jesus, just before he instituted the Lord's Supper, put his disciples upon this trial and suspicion of themselves, to teach us to examine and judge ourselves, and so to eat of that bread, and drink of that cup.

Matthew 26

To be exact and severe on ourselves and our own conduct is the most proper way in the world not to fall under the just severity of our heavenly Father. We must not judge others, lest we be judged (Matt. 7:1); but we must judge ourselves, to prevent our being judged and condemned by God. We may be critical as to ourselves, but should be very candid in judging others.

1 Corinthians 11

It requires a great deal of diligence and labour to make sure our calling and election; there must be a very close examination of ourselves, a very narrow search and strict enquiry, whether we are thoroughly converted, our minds enlightened, our wills renewed, and our whole souls changed as to the bent and inclination thereof; and to come to a fixed certainty in this requires the utmost diligence, and cannot be attained and kept without divine assistance, as we may learn from (Ps. 139:23; Rom. 8:16).

2 Peter 1

Self-Indulgence

Fulness of bread, as it was one of Jerusalem's mercies, so it had become one of her sins (Ezek. 16:49). The plenty was abused to luxury and excess, which were therefore thus justly punished with famine. It is a righteous thing with God to deprive us of those enjoyments which we have made the food and fuel of our lusts.

Ezekiel 4

Self-Pity

We are apt to call reproofs reproaches, and to think ourselves mocked when we are but advised and admonished: this peevishness is our folly, and a great wrong to ourselves and to our friends.

Job 12

What was the cause of their mourning; not their sin, but their punishment. They did not lament their fall into idolatry, and luxury, and persecution, but their fall into ruin — the loss of their traffic and of their wealth and power. The spirit of antichrist is a worldly spirit, and their sorrow is a mere worldly sorrow, they did not lament for the anger of God, that had now fallen upon them, but for the loss of their outward comforts.

Revelation 18

Self-Sufficiency

Those who trust to their own sufficiency, and are so confident of it that they neither exert themselves to the utmost nor seek unto God for his grace, are the youths and the young men, who are strong, but are apt to think themselves stronger than they are. And they shall faint and be weary, yea, they shall utterly fail in their services, in their conflicts, and under their burdens; they shall soon be made to see the folly of trusting to themselves. But those that wait upon the Lord, who make conscience of their duty to him and by faith rely upon him and commit themselves to his guidance, shall find that God will not fail them.

Isaiah 40

As before they knew not what they asked, so now they know not what they answered. 'We are able'; they would have done well to put in, 'Lord, by thy strength and in thy grace, we are able, otherwise we are not.' But the same that was Peter's temptation, to be confident of his own sufficiency, and presume upon his own strength, was here the temptation of James and John; and it is a sin we are all prone to. They knew not what Christ's cup was, nor what his baptism, and therefore they were thus bold in promising for themselves. But those are commonly most confident, that are least

acquainted with the cross.

Matthew 20

Separation

Let all take warning by his fall carefully to preserve their purity and to watch against all fleshly lusts for all our glory has gone and our defence departed from us when the covenant of our separation to God as spiritual Nazarites is profaned.

Judges 16

Those that know not how to quit a place at court when they cannot keep it without sinning against God and wronging their consciences, do not rightly value the divine favour.

2 Kings 5

(See) the great danger of bad company even to good men. Those that have most wisdom, grace and resolution cannot be sure that they can converse familiarly with wicked people and not get hurt by them. Jehoshaphat here in complaisance to Ahab sits in his robes patiently hearing the false prophets speaking lies in the name of the Lord, can scarcely find in his heart to give him a too mild and gentle reproof for hating a prophet of the Lord and dares not rebuke that false prophet who basely abused the faithful seer nor oppose Ahab who committed him to prison. Those who venture among the seats of the scornful cannot come off without a great deal of the guilt attaching to at least the omission of their duty unless they have such measures of wisdom and courage as few can pretend to.

2 Chronicles 18

Those that durst not eat the meat yet made bold with the broth, because they would come as near as might be to that which was forbidden, to show how they coveted the forbidden fruit. Perhaps this is here put figuratively for all forbidden pleasure and profits which are obtained by sin, that abominable thing which the Lord hates; they loved to be dallying with it, to be tasting of its broth. But those who thus take a pride in venturing upon the borders of sin, and the brink of it, are in danger of falling into the depths of it.

Isaiah 65

Why the dimensions of it were made thus large. It was to 'make a separation', by putting a very large distance 'between the sanctuary and the profane place'; and therefore there was a wall surrounding it, to keep off those that were unclean and to separate between 'the precious and the vile'. Note, a difference is to be put between common and sacred things, between God's name and other names, between his day and other days, his Book and other books, his institutions and other observances; and a distance is to be put between our worldly and religious actions, so as still to go about the worship of God with a solemn pause.

Ezekiel 42

God says, 'thou shalt call me Ishi, and call me no more Baali';

both signify 'my husband', and both had been made use of concerning God (Isa. 54:5). 'Thy Maker is thy husband', thy 'Baal' (so the word is), thy owner, patron, and protector. It is probable that many good people had, accordingly, made use of the word Baali in worshipping the God of Israel; when their wicked neighbours bowed the knee to Baal they gloried in this, that God was their Baal. 'But', says God, 'you shall call me so no more, because I will have the very names of Baalim taken away.' Note, that which is very innocent in itself should, when it has been abused to idolatry, be abolished, and the very use of it taken away, that nothing may be done to keep idols in remembrance, much less to keep them in reputation. When calling God 'Ishi' will do as well, and signify as much, as 'Baali', let that word be chosen rather, lest, by calling him Baali, others should be put in mind of their 'quondam' Baals.

Hosea 2

Those that would be kept from sin, and not fall into the devil's hands, must studiously avoid the occasions of sin and not come upon the devil's ground.

Hosea 4

He that is not with me is against me. In the little differences that may arise between the disciples of Christ among themselves, we are taught to lessen the matters in variance, and to seek peace, by accounting those who are not against us, to be with us (Luke 9:50); but in the great quarrel between Christ and the devil, no peace is to be sought, nor any such favourable construction to be made of any indifference in the matter; he that is not hearty for Christ, will be reckoned with as really against him: he that is cold in the cause, is looked upon as an enemy. When the dispute is between God and Baal, there is no halting between two (1 Kings 18: 21), there is no trimming between Christ and Belial.

Matthew 12

Bad company is to many an occasion of sin; and those who needlessly thrust themselves into it, go upon the devil's ground, venture into his crowds, and may expect either to be tempted and ensnared, as Peter was, or to be ridiculed and abused, as his Master was; they scarcely can come out of such company, without guilt or grief, or both.

Matthew 26

Those that receive Christ's good will and good word must expect the world's ill will and ill word. Gospel ministers have been in a particular manner hated by the world, because they call men out of the world, and separate them from it, and teach them not to conform to it, and so condemn the world. 'Father, keep them', for it is for thy sake that they are exposed; they are sufferers for thee. Thus the psalmist pleads, 'For thy sake I have borne reproach' (Ps. 69:7).

John 17

He desired to be thought 'one of them', that he might not be suspected to be a disciple of Christ. Is this Peter? What a contradiction is this to the prayer of every good man, 'Gather not my soul with sinners'! 'Saul among the prophets' is not so absurd as David among the Philistines. Those that deprecate the lot of the scornful hereafter should dread the 'seat of the scornful' now. It is ill warming ourselves with those with whom we are in danger of burning ourselves (Ps. 141:4).

John 18

Christ was separated from this world, as those that are buried have nothing more to do with this world, nor this world with them; and therefore our complete separation from sin is represented by our being 'buried with Christ'. And a good Christian will be willing to be buried alive with Christ.

Acts 13

Service

We must first see to it that our peace be made with God and then we may expect that our services for his glory will be accepted.

Leviticus 5

They owe their service to those to whom they owe their lives.

Joshua 9

His lying prostrate was a posture of greater reverence, but his standing up would be a posture of greater readiness and fitness for business. Our adorings of God must not hinder, but rather quicken and excite, our actings for God. He fell on his face in a holy fear and awe of God, but he was quickly raised up again; for those that humble themselves shall be exalted. God delights not in the dejections of his servants, but the same that brings them low will raise them up.

Ezekiel 2

Paul's strait was not between living in this world and living in heaven; between these two there is no comparison: but his strait was between serving Christ in this world and enjoying him in another. Still it was Christ that his heart was upon: though, to advance the interest of Christ and his church, he chose rather to tarry here, where he met with oppositions and difficulties, and to deny himself for awhile the satisfaction of his reward.

Philippians 1

Could Paul think it worth while to shed his blood for the service of the church, and shall we think it much to take a little pains? Is not that worth our labour which he thought worth his life?

Philippians 2

Shining Christians

Let them shine so bright, appear so glorious in the eye of the world, cast such benign influences, be as much out of the reach of their enemies who curse the rising sun because it scorches them; let them rejoice as a strong man to run a race (Ps. 19:5), let them as burning and shining lights in their places dispel the mists of darkness and shine with more and more

lustre and power unto the perfect day.

Judges 5

Sickness

Diseases are God's servants; they go where he sends them and do what he bids them. It is, therefore, good for the health of our bodies to mortify the sin of our souls.

Deuteronomy 7

So it directs us, not only to apply ourselves to Christ, who has power over bodily diseases, for the cure of them, but it also teaches us in what manner to apply ourselves to him; with an assurance of his power, believing that he is as able to cure diseases now, as he was when on earth, but with a submission to his will; Lord, if thou wilt, thou canst. As to temporal mercies, we cannot be so sure of God's will to bestow them, as we may of his power, for his power in them is unlimited, but his promise of them is limited by a regard to his glory and our good. When we cannot be sure of his will, we may be sure of his wisdom and mercy, to which we may cheerfully refer ourselves.

Matthew 8

Sin

Eve lays all the blame upon the serpent. Sin is a brat which nobody is willing to own, a sign that it is a scandalous thing.

Genesis 3

Satan drives his vassals from

presumption to despair. We cannot think too ill of sin provided we do not think it unpardonable.

Genesis 4

Omissions are sins and must come into judgment but what had been omitted at one time might be done at another and so to obey was better than sacrifice but a commission was past recall.

From all these laws concerning the sin offerings we may learn to hate sin and to watch against it. That is certainly a very bad thing to make atonement for which so many innocent and useful creatures must be slain and mangled thus.

Leviticus 4

To show the loathsomeness of the sin for which it was offered it must not be made grateful either to the taste by oil or to the smell by frankincense. The unsavouriness of the offering was to intimate that the sinner must never relish his sin again as he had done.

Leviticus 5

Though the pollution contracted was only ceremonial, yet the neglect of the purification prescribed would turn into moral guilt. 'He that shall be unclean and shall not purify himself, that soul shall be cut off'. It is a dangerous thing to despise divine institutions though they may seem minute. A slight wound, if neglected, may prove fatal. A sin we call little, if not repented of, will be our ruin. When great sinners that repent shall find mercy. Our uncleanness separates us from God but it is our being unclean and not purifying purselves that will separate us for ever from him. It is not the wound that is fatal so much as the contempt of the remedy.

Why did the law make a dead corpse such a defiling thing? Because death is the wages of sin, entered into the world by it and reigns by the power of it. Death to mankind is another thing from what it is to other creatures; it is a curse, it is the execution of the law and, therefore, the defilement of death signifies the defilement of sin . . . when the dead body was buried . . . then he began to reckon his days. Then and then only we may with comfort apply Christ's merit to our souls, when we have forsaken sin and cease all fellowship with the unfruitful works of death and darkness.

Numbers 19

God often makes men's sin their punishment.

Deuteronomy 28

By this he shows that there is no sin little because no little God to sin against.

1 Samuel 13

Those that ease their cares by sinful pleasures, increase their wealth by sinful pursuits, escape their troubles by sinful projects, and evade sufferings for righteousness' sake by sinful compliances against their consciences, make a choice they will repent of; for there is more evil in the least sin than in the greatest affliction.

Job 36

When, after one sin, David's heart smote him, and, after another, Nathan was sent to tell him, 'Thou art the man', God restored his soul. Though God may suffer his people to fall into sin, he will not suffer them to lie still in it.

Psalm 23

Nothing will disquiet the heart of a good man so much as the sense of God's anger, which shows what a fearful thing it is to fall into his hands. The way to keep the heart quiet is to keep ourselves in the love of God and to do nothing to offend him.

Psalm 38

It is his truth that by wilful sin we deny, his conduct that we despise, his command that we disobey, his promise that we distrust, his name that we dishonour, and it is with him that we deal deceitfully and disingenuously.

This should greatly humble us for all our sins, that they have been committed under the eye of God which argues either a disbelief of his omniscience or a contempt of his justice.

Psalm 51

The sins of God's professing people do not only anger him, but grieve him, especially their distrust of him. . . If our sins have grieved God, surely they should grieve us, and nothing in sin should grieve us so much as that.

Psalm 95

Those that make light of sin make light of Christ. Those are fools that make light of sin, for they make light of that which God complains of (Amos 2:13), which lay heavily upon Christ, and which they themselves will have other thoughts of shortly.

Proverbs 14

We sin even in our doing good; there is something defective, nay, something offensive, in our best performances. That which, for the substance of it, is good, and pleasing to God, is not so well done as it should be, and omissions in duty are sins, as well as omissions of duty.

Ecclesiastes 7

The angels had celebrated the purity and holiness of God; and therefore the prophet, when he reflects upon sin, calls it uncleanness; for the sinfulness of sin is its contrariety to the holy nature of God, and upon that account especially it should appear both hateful and frightful to us.

Isaiah 6

The confusion and emptiness that shall overspread the face of the whole country shall be like that of the whole earth when it was 'Tohu' and 'Bohu' (the very words here used) — without form and void (Gen. 1:2). Sin will soon turn a paradise into a chaos, and sully the beauty of the whole creation.

Isaiah 34

See here sin in its colours, sin exceedingly sinful, withdrawing the creature from his allegiance to his Creator; and see sin in its consequences, sin exceedingly hurtful, separating us from God, and so separating us not only from all good, but to all evil (Deut. 29:21) which is the very quintessence of the curse.

Isaiah 59

Sin is the great mischief-maker between God and a people; it forfeits the benefits of his promises and spoils the success of their prayers. It defeats his kind intentions concerning them (Hos. 7:1) and baffles their pleasing expectations from him. It ruins their comforts, prolongs their grievances, brings them into straits, and retards their deliverances (Isa. 59:1, 2).

Jeremiah 18

It becomes us to speak of sin with the utmost dread and detestation as an abominable thing; it is certainly so, for it is that which God hates, and we are sure that his judgment is according to truth. Call it grievous, call it odious, that we may by all means possible put ourselves and others out of love with it. It becomes us to give warning of the danger of sin, and the fatal consequences of it, with all seriousness and earnestness: 'O, do not do it. If you love God, do not, for it is provoking to him; if you love your own souls, do not, for it is destructive to them.' Let conscience do this for us in an hour of temptation, when we are ready to yield. O take heed! Do not this abominable thing which the Lord hates; for, if God hates it, thou shouldst hate it.

Jeremiah 44

What should they do with the places when the services had become an abomination? He has now abhorred his sanctuary (v. 7); it has been defiled with sin, that only thing which he hates, and for the sake of that he abhors even his sanctuary, which he had delighted in and called his rest for ever (Ps. 132:14).

Lamentations 2

Those that will not be kept from sin by fear and shame shall by fear and shame be punished for it; such is the confusion that sin will end in.

Ezekiel 7

If God can work such deliverance as no other can, he may demand such obedience as no other may. He gives him the glory of his goodness, that he was ready to do it (v. 28): 'He has sent his angel and delivered his servants'. Bel could not save his worshippers from being burnt at the mouth of the furnace, but the God of Israel saved his from being burnt when they were cast into the midst of the furnace because they refused to 'worship any other god'. By this Nebuchadnezzar was plainly given to understand that all the great success which he had had, and should yet have, against the people of Israel, which he gloried in, as if he had therein overpowered the God of Israel, was owing purely to 'their sin': if the body of that nation had faithfully adhered to their own God and the worship of him only, as these three men did, they would all have been delivered out of his hand as these three men were.

Daniel 3

He does not say, 'So shall the king of Assyria do to you;' but, 'So shall Bethel do to you.' Note, whatever mischief is done to us it is sin that does it. Are the fortresses spoiled? Are the women and children murdered? Is the king cut off? It is sin that does all this. It is sin that ruins soul, body, estate, all. So shall Bethel do unto you. It is thy own wickedness that corrects thee and thy backslidings that reprove thee.

Hosea 10

When we are confessing our sins it is good to take notice of the mercies of God as the aggravations of our sins, that we may be the more humbled and ashamed, and call ourselves by the scandalous name of ungrateful.

Nehemiah 9

Guilt and corruption are our two great discouragements when we stand before God. By the guilt of the sins committed by us we have become obnoxious to the justice of God; by the power of the sin that dwells in us we have become odious to the holiness of God.

Zechariah 3

For this sin John reproved him; not by tacit and oblique allusions, but in plain terms, 'It is not lawful for thee to have her'. He charges it upon him as a sin; not, it is not honourable, or, it is not safe, but, it is not lawful; the sinfulness of sin, as it is the transgression of the law, is the worst thing in it. This was Herod's own iniquity, his beloved sin, and therefore John Baptist tells

him of this particularly.

Matthew 14

When he began to reckon, one of the first defaulters appeared to owe ten thousand talents. There is no evading the enquiries of divine justice; your sin will be sure to find you out. The debt was ten thousand talents, a vast sum, amounting by computation to one million eight hundred and seventy five thousand pounds sterling; a king's ransom or a kingdom's subsidy, more likely than a servant's debt; see what our sins are.

Matthew 18

Sin is a brat that nobody is willing to own; and many deceive themselves with this, that they shall bear no blame if they can but find any to lay the blame upon; but it is not so easy a thing to transfer the guilt of sin as many think it is. The condition of him that is infected with the plague is not the less dangerous, either for his catching the infection from others, or his communicating the infection to others; we may be tempted to sin, but cannot be forced. The priests threw it upon Judas; 'See thou to it'; and now Pilate throws it upon them; 'See ye to it'; 'for with what measure ye mete, it shall be measured to you.'

Matthew 27

He was 'made sin for us', and therefore was thus sorrowful; he fully knew the malignity of the sins he was to suffer for; and having the highest degrees of love to God, who was offended by them, and of love to man, who was damaged and endangered by them, now that those were set in order before him, no marvel that his soul was 'exceeding sorrowful'. Now he was made to serve with our sins, and was thus wearied with our iniquities.

Mark 14

We were by sin become odious to God's holiness, which cried, 'Away with them, away with them', for God is 'of purer eyes than to behold iniquity.' We were also become obnoxious to God's justice, which cried against us, 'Crucify them, crucify them', let the sentence of the law be executed. Had not Christ interposed, and been rejected of men, we had been for ever rejected of God.

Dead bodies and graves are noisome and offensive; hence sin is compared to a 'body of death' and an 'open sepulchre'; but Christ's sacrifice, being to God as a sweet-smelling savour, hath taken away our pollution.

John 19

Every wilful sin is a quarrel with God, it is 'striving with our Maker' (Isa. 45:9), the most desperate contention. The Spirit of God strives with sinners (Gen. 6:3), and impenitent sinners strive against the Spirit, rebel against the light (Job 24: 13), hold fast deceit, strive to retain that sin which the Spirit strives to part them from.

Romans 2

Some of the strongest and best arguments against all sorts of sin

are taken from the sufferings of Christ. All sympathy and tenderness for Christ as a sufferer are lost if you do not put away sin. He died to destroy it; and, though he could cheerfully submit to the worst sufferings, yet he could never submit to the least sin.

1 Peter 4

All that was made for man's use is subject to vanity by man's sin; and if the sin of man has brought the visible heavens, and the elements and earth, under a curse, from which they cannot be freed without being dissolved, what an abominable evil is sin, and how much to be hated by us!

2 Peter 3

Sin is filthiness; it renders men odious and vile in the sight of the most holy God, and makes them (sooner or later, as penitent or as punished to extremity and without resource) vile in their own eyes, and in a while they become vile in the eyes of all about them.

Jude

Sin (Consequences of)

Many must be involved in the guilt. Joab, the general to whom the blood of his soldiers, especially the worthies, ought to be precious, must do it; he and all that retire from Uriah when they ought in conscience to support and second him, become guilty of his death. Uriah cannot thus die alone; the party he commands is in danger of being cut off with him; and it proved so; some of the people, even the servants of David (so they are called, to aggravate David's sin in being so prodigal of their lives), fell with him (v. 17). Nay, this wilful misconduct by which Uriah must be betrayed might be of fatal consequence to the whole army, and might oblige them to raise the siege. It will be the triumph and joy of the Ammonites, the sworn enemies of God and Israel; it will gratify them exceedingly. David prayed for himself, that he might not fall into the hands of men, nor flee from his enemies (ch. 24:13, 14), yet he sells his servant Uriah to the Ammonites and not for any iniquity in his hand.

2 Samuel 11

Ahaz walked in the ways of the kings of Israel and the king of Israel was the instrument God made use of for his punishment. It is just with God to make those our plagues whom we make our pattern or make ourselves partners with in sin. Vast numbers were slain and some of the first rank; the king's son for one. He had sacrificed some of his sons to Moloch, justly, therefore, is this sacrificed to the divine vengeance.

2 Chronicles 28

Sincerity

Those that sincerely set themselves against sin will set themselves against all sin.

2 Chronicles 31

God and man will look upon those as meaning well, and approve of them, who make conscience of their duty, though they have their mistakes. What is honestly intended shall be well taken.

Psalm 111

The poorest beggar, that asked a miracle for the relief of his necessity, was never denied; but this proud prince, that asked a miracle merely for the gratifying of his curiosity, is denied.

Luke 23

Singing

Sing praise, sing with the voice of a psalm. Express your joy, thus proclaim it, thus excite it yet more, and thus propagate it among others. Let these be assisted with sacred music, not only with the soft and gentle melody of the harp, but since it is a victorious King whose glory is to be celebrated, who goes forth conquering and to conquer, let him be proclaimed with the martial sound of the trumpet and cornet.

Psalm 98

When God in his providence exercises us with a mixture of mercy and judgment it is our duty to sing, and sing unto him both of the one and of the other; we must be suitably affected with both, and make suitable acknowledgments to God for both. The Chaldee-paraphrase of this is observable: 'If Thou bestowest mercy upon me', or 'If Thou bring any judgment upon me, before Thee, O Lord, will I sing my hymns for all.' Whatever our outward condition is, whether joyful or sorrowful, still we must give glory to God, and sing praises to him; neither the laughter of a prosperous condition nor the tears of an afflicted condition must put us out of tune for sacred songs.

Psalm 101

Sloth

It did not bode well at all that God's Israel began to think much of their labour and contrived how to spare their pains . . . it has likewise often proved of bad consequence to make light of an enemy . . . it will awaken our care and diligence in our Christian warfare to consider that we wrestle with principalities and powers.

Joshua 7

Those that have no heart to their work pretend that their way is hedged up with thorns, and they cannot do their work at all (as if God were a hard Master, reaping where he had not sown), at least that their way is strewed with thorns, that they cannot do their work without a great deal of hardship and danger; and therefore they go about it with as much reluctance as if they were to go barefoot through a thorny hedge.

Proverbs 15

The observation is too true in the affairs of religion; he that is trifling and careless in praying and hearing is brother to him that does not pray or hear at all; and omissions of duty and in duty are as fatal to the soul as commissions of sin.

Proverbs 18

Those who have least to do for God, frequently do least of what they have to do. Some make it an excuse for their laziness, that they have not the opportunities of serving God that others have; and because they have not wherewithal to do what they say they would, they will not do what we are sure they can, and so sit down and do nothing; it is really an aggravation of their sloth, that when they have but one talent to take care about, they neglect that one.

He that is slothful in his work, and neglects the good that God has commanded, is brother to him that is a great waster, by doing the evil that God has forbidden (Prov. 18:9). He that is careless in God's work, is near akin to him that is busy in the devil's work. To do no good is to incur very serious blame. Omissions are sins, and must come into judgment.

Matthew 25

Whatever may be the pretences of slothful professors, in excuse of their slothfulness, the true reason of it is a reigning indifference to the interests of Christ and his kingdom, and their coldness therein. They care not whether religion gets ground or loses ground, so they can but live at ease.

Luke 19

Social Justice

A just man will not take advantage of his neighbour's necessity to make a prey of him, nor indulge himself in ease and idleness to live upon the sweat and toil of others, and therefore will not take increase from those who cannot make increase of what he lends them, nor be rigorous in exacting what was agreed for from those who by the act of God are disabled to pay it; but he is willing to share in loss as well as profit.

Ezekiel 18

Soul

The gourd which Jonah had pity on 'perished in a night'; it withered, and there was an end of it. But the precious souls in Nineveh that God had pity on are not so short-lived; they are immortal, and therefore to be carefully and tenderly considered. One soul is of more value than the whole world, and the gain of the world will not countervail the loss of it; surely then one soul is of more value than many gourds, of more value than many sparrows; so God accounts, and so should we, and therefore have a greater concern for the children of men than for any of the inferior creatures, and for our own and others' precious souls than for any of the riches and enjoyments of this world.

Jonah 4

Every man has a soul of his own. The soul is the spiritual and immortal part of man, which thinks and reasons, has a power of reflection and prospect, which actuates the body now, and will shortly act in a separation from the body. Our souls are our own not in respect of dominion and property (for we are not our own, 'All souls are Mine', saith God), but in respect of nearness and concern; our souls are our own, for they are ourselves.

One soul is worth more than all the world; our own souls are of greater value to us than all the wealth, honour, and pleasures of this present time, if we had them. Here is the whole world set in the scale against one soul, and *'Tekel'* written upon it; it is weighed in the balance, and found too light to weigh it down. This is Christ's judgment upon the matter, and he is a competent Judge; he had reason to know the price of souls, for he redeemed them; nor would he underrate the world, for he made it.

Matthew 16

Source of Spiritual Courage

We found before, when the Spirit of the Lord came upon Saul (11:6) none could be more daring nor forward to answer the challenge of Nahash the Ammonite but now that the Spirit of the Lord had departed from him, even the big looks and big words of the single Philistine make him change colour. . . As the best, so the bravest men are no more than what God makes them.

1 Samuel 17

What God works in his people by his grace contributes more to their preservation and defence than what he works for them by his providence. 'The God of Israel gives strength and power to his people', that they may do their part, and

293

then he will not be wanting to do his. It is the glory of God to strengthen the weak, that most need his help, that see and own their need of it, and will be the most thankful for it.

See what divine grace does; it makes children not only men, but champions, makes weak saints to be not only good soldiers, but great soldiers, like David. And see how God often does his own work as easily and effectually, and more to his own glory, by weak and obscure instruments than by the most illustrious.

Zechariah 12

Sowing and Reaping

They prepare destruction for themselves by preparing themselves for destruction, loading themselves with guilt and submitting themselves to their corruptions.

Psalm 7

He foretells that God will reward them, not only according to their deeds, but according to the wickedness of their endeavours; for sinners shall be reckoned with, not only for the mischief they have done, but for the mischief they would have done, which they designed, and did what they could to effect. And, if God go by this rule in dealing with the wicked, surely he will do so in dealing with the righteous, and will reward them, not only for the good they have done, but for the good they have endeavoured to do, though they could not accomplish it.

Psalm 28

Spirit of the Age

The Romans, living in the imperial city, which reigned over the kings of the earth (Rev. 17: 18), and was at that time in the meridian of its splendour, were perhaps ready to take occasion thence to think the better of themselves. Even the holy seed were tainted with this leaven. Roman Christians would be ready to look scornfully upon other Christians.

Romans 12

Spiritual Blindness

They had been followed with one judgment after another, but they had not profited by those means of grace as might be expected; they were still unreformed, and how could they expect that 'they should possess the land'? 'Shall you possess the land?' What! such wicked people as you are? 'How shall I put thee among the children and give thee a pleasant land?' (Jer. 3:19). Surely you never reflect upon yourselves, else you would rather wonder that you are in the land of the living than expect to possess this land. For do you not know how bad you are?

Ezekiel 33

Sinners that were wedded to their lusts loved their ignorance and mistakes, which supported them in their sins, rather than the truths of Christ, which would have parted them from their sins. Man's apostasy began in an affectation of forbidden knowledge, but is kept up by an affectation of forbidden ignorance. Wretched man is in love with his sickness, in love with his slavery, and will not be made free, will not be made whole.

The labour of ministers is all lost labour, unless the grace of God make it effectual. Men do not understand that which is made most plain, nor believe that which is made most evident, unless it be given them from heaven to understand and believe it.

John 3

They said nothing to him concerning his miracles, by which he had done so much good, and proved his doctrine beyond contradiction, because of these they were sure they could take no hold. Thus the adversaries of Christ, while they are industriously quarrelling with his truth, wilfully shut their eyes against the evidences of it, and take no notice of them.

John 18

They knew not who he was, nor what errand he came into the world upon; for, 'if they had known, they would not have crucified the Lord of Glory'. Christ owned this in extenuation of their crime: 'They know not what they do'; and so did Peter: 'I wot that through ignorance you did this' (ch. 3:17). It was also because they knew not the voice of the prophets though they heard them read every sabbath day.

Acts 13

'And makest thy boast of God'. See how the best things may be perverted and abused. A believing, humble, thankful glorying in God, is the root and summary of all religion (Ps. 34:2; Isa. 45:25; 1 Cor. 1:31). But a proud vainglorious boasting in God, and in the outward profession of his name, is the root and summary of all hypocrisy. Spiritual pride is of all kinds of pride the most dangerous.

Romans 2

See here too what a different notion the word gives of a sensual and fleshly life from what the world generally has of it. Carnal people think they enjoy their pleasures; the word calls it servitude and vassalage: they are very drudges and bond slaves under them.

Titus 3

Spiritual Desertion

Many have lost the favourable presence of God and are not aware of it. They have provoked God to withdraw from them but are not sensible of their loss nor ever complain of it. Their souls languish and grow weak. Their gifts wither. Everything goes cross with them and yet they impute not this to the right cause. They are not aware that God has departed from them nor are they in any care to reconcile themselves to him or to recover his favour. When God has departed we cannot do as at other times.

Judges 16

'Why hast thou forsaken me?' is the language of a heart

295

binding up its happiness in God's favour. When we are lamenting God's withdrawings, yet still we must call hin our God, and continue to call upon him as ours. When we want the faith of assurance we must live by a faith of adherence. 'However it be, yet God is good, and he is mine; though he slay me, yet will I trust in him'; though he do not answer me immediately, I will continue praying and waiting; though he be silent, I will not be silent.

Psalm 22

Nothing grieves a child of God so much as God's hiding his face from him, nor is there anything he so much dreads as God's casting off his soul. If the sun be clouded, that darkens the earth; but if the sun should abandon the earth, and quite cast it off, what a dungeon would it be!

Psalm 88

Her gates are gone in an instant, so that one would think they were sunk into the ground with their own weight, and he has destroyed and broken her bars, those bars of Jerusalem's gates which formerly he had strengthened (Ps. 147:13). Gates and bars will stand us in no stead when God has withdrawn his protection.

The ark was God's footstool, under the mercy-seat, between the cherubim; this was of all others the most sacred symbol of God's presence (it is called his footstool (1 Chron. 28:2; Ps. 99:5; Ps. 132:7); there the *Shechinah* rested, and with an

eye to this Israel was often protected and saved; but now he remembered not his footstool. The ark itself was suffered, as it should seem, to fall into the hands of the Chaldeans. God, being angry, threw that away; for it shall be no longer his footstool; the earth shall be so, as it had been before the ark was (Isa. 66:1). Of what little value are the tokens of his presence when his presence is gone! Nor was this the first time that God gave his ark into captivity (Ps. 78:61). God and his kingdom can stand without that footstool.

Lamentations 2

That Christ's being forsaken of his Father was the most grievous of his sufferings, and that which he complained most of. Here he laid the most doleful accents; he did not say, 'Why am I scourged? And why spit upon? And why nailed to the cross?' Nor did he say to his disciples, when they turned their back upon him 'Why have ye forsaken me?' But when his Father stood at a distance, he cried out thus; for this was it that put wormwood and gall into the affliction and misery. This brought the waters into the soul (Ps. 69:1–3).

Matthew 27

A sight of angels and their smiles will not suffice without a sight of Christ and God's smiles in him. Nay, the sight of angels is but an opportunity of pursuing here enquiries after Christ. All creatures, the most excellent, the most dear, should be used as means, and but as means, to bring us into acquaintance with God in Christ. The angels asked her, 'Why weepest thou?' I have cause enough to weep, says she, for 'they have taken away my Lord', and, like Micah, 'What have I more?' Do you ask why I weep? 'My beloved has withdrawn himself, and is gone.' Note, none know, but those who have experienced it, the sorrow of a deserted soul, that has had comfortable evidences of the love of God in Christ, and hopes of heaven, but has now lost them, and walks in darkness; such a 'wounded spirit who can bear?'.

John 20

Spiritual Fluctuation

And see here how the passions that run into an extreme one way commonly run into an extreme the other way. Jonah, who was in transports of joy when the gourd flourished, is in pangs of grief when the gourd has withered. Inordinate affection lays a foundation for inordinate affliction; what we are over-fond of when we have it we are apt to over-grieve for when we lose it, and we may see our folly in both.

Jonah 4

Spiritual Gifts

Among God's Israel there is to be found a great variety of dispositions contrary to each other yet all contributing to the beauty and strength of the body. Judah like a lion, Issachar like an ass, Dan like a serpent, Naphtali like a hind.

Let not those of different temperaments and gifts censure one another nor envy one another any more than those of different statures and complexions.

Genesis 49

Let none be puffed up with conceit by visions and revelations when even an ass saw an angel.

Numbers 22

It should seem these two tribes were differently armed both offensively and defensively. The men of Judah guarded themselves with targets, the men of Benjamin with shields, the former of which were much larger than the latter (1 Kings 10:16, 17). The men of Judah fought with spears when they closed in with the enemy. The men of Benjamin drew bows to reach the enemy at a distance. Both did good service and neither could say to the other 'I have no need of thee.' Different gifts and employments are for the common good.

2 Chronicles 14

There may be a faith of miracles, where there is no justifying faith; none of that faith which works by love and obedience. Gifts of tongues and healing would recommend men to the world, but it is real holiness or sanctification that is accepted of God. Grace and love are a more excellent way than removing mountains, or speaking with the tongues of men and of angels (1 Cor. 13:1, 2). Grace will bring a man to heaven without working miracles, but working miracles will never bring a man to heaven without grace.

Matthew 7

Spiritual gifts are bestowed, that men may with them profit the church and promote Christianity. They are not given for show, but for service; not for pomp and ostentation, but for edification; not to magnify those that have them, but to edify others.

1 Corinthians 12

Spiritual Understanding

It is matter of wonder that God should give Satan such a permission as this, should *deliver the soul of his turtle-dove* into the hand of the adversary, such a lamb to such a lion; but he did it for his own glory, the honour of Job, the explanation of Providence, and the encouragement of his afflicted people in all ages, to make a case which, being adjudged, might be a useful precedent. He suffered Job to be tried, as he suffered Peter to be sifted, but he took care that *his faith should not fail* (Luke 22:32) and then the trial of it was found unto praise, and honour, and glory (1 Peter 1:7).

Job 1

'They understood not thy wonders in Egypt'. They saw them, but they did not rightly apprehend the *meaning* and *design* of them. Blessed are those who have not seen, and yet have understood. They *thought* the plagues of Egypt were intended for their deliverance, *whereas* they were intended *also* for their instruction and conviction, not only to force them out of their Egyptian slavery, but to *cure* them of their inclination to Egyptian idolatry, by evidencing the sovereign power and dominion of the God of Israel, above all gods, and his particular concern for them. We lose the benefit of providences for want of understanding them.

Psalm 106

To eat the flesh of Christ! this is a hard saying, but to believe that Christ died for me, to derive from that doctrine strength and comfort in my approaches to God, my oppositions to sin and preparations for a future state, this is the spirit and life of that saying, and, construing it thus, it is an excellent saying. The reason why men dislike Christ's sayings is because they mistake them. The literal sense of a parable does us no good, we are never the wiser for it, but the spiritual meaning is instructive.

John 6

Strong Drink

Those that would be kept from any sin must keep themselves from all the occasions and beginnings of it, and be afraid of coming within the reach of its allurements, lest they be overcome by them.

If this be the end of the sin, with good reason were we directed to stop at the beginning of it: Look not upon the wine when it is red.

Proverbs 23

Stubbornness

The Lord God called to baldness and girding with sackcloth, but behold painting and dressing, walking contrary to God (Isa. 22:12, 13). There is not a surer presage of ruin than an unhumbled heart under humbling providences.

2 Kings 9

Carnal hearts, in time of trouble, see their sickness and see their wound, but do not see the sin that is the cause of it, nor will be brought to acknowledge that, no, nor to acknowledge the hand of God, his 'mighty hand', much less his righteous hand, in their trouble; and therefore, instead of going the next way to the Creator, who could relieve them, they take a great deal of pains to go about to creatures, who can do them no service. Those who repent not that they have offended God by their sins are loth to be beholden to him in their afflictions, but would rather seek relief anywhere than with him.

Hosea 5

Submissiveness

Let him do to me as seemeth good to him; I have nothing to object. All is well that God does. Observe with what satisfaction and holy complacency he speaks of the divine disposal — not only he can do what he will subscribing to his power (Job 9:12), or he has a right to do what he will, subscribing to his sovereignty (Job 33:13), or he will do what he will, subscribing to his unchangeableness (Job 23:13, 15), but let him do what he will, subscribing to his wisdom and goodness.

Note: It is our interest as well as duty, cheerfully to acquiesce in the will of God whatever befalls us. That we may not complain of what is, let us see God's hand in all events and that we may not be afraid of what shall be, let us see all events in God's hand.

2 Samuel 15

Zophar here speaks very good things concerning God and his greatness and glory, concerning man and his vanity and folly: these two compared together, and duly considered, will have a powerful influence upon our submission to all the dispensations of the divine Providence.

See here what God is, and let him be adored.

He is an incomprehensible being, infinite and immense, whose nature and perfections our finite understandings cannot possibly form any adequate conception of, and whose counsels and actings we cannot therefore, without the greatest presumption, pass a judgment upon. We that are so little acquainted with the divine nature are incompetent judges of the divine providence; and, when we censure the dispensations of it, we talk of things that we do not understand. We cannot find out God; how dare we then find fault with him . . . we may apprehend him, but we cannot comprehend him, we may know that he is, but cannot know what he is.

Job 11

He is under no obligation to show us a reason for what he does, neither to tell us what he designs to do (in what method, at what time, by what instruments) nor to tell us why he deals thus with us. He is not bound either to justify his own proceedings or to satisfy our demands and enquiries; his judgments will certainly justify themselves. If we do not satisfy ourselves in them, it is our own fault. It is therefore daring impiety for us to arraign God at our bar, or challenge him to show cause for what he doeth, to say unto him, 'What doest thou?'

Job 33

We must follow Providence, and not force it, subscribe to Infinite Wisdom and not prescribe.

Psalm 37

Let the obsequiousness even of the unstable waters teach us obedience to the word and will of God; for shall man alone of all the creatures be obstinate? Let their retiring to and resting in the place assigned them teach us to acquiesce in the disposals of that wise providence which appoints us the bounds of our habitation.

Psalm 104

This yields abundant satisfaction to those who have bound up all their comforts in God's counsels, that his counsel shall undoubtedly stand; and, if we are brought to this, that *whatever pleases God pleases us*, nothing can contribute more to make us easy than to be assured of this, that God will do all his pleasure (Ps. 135:6).

Isaiah 46

Is it their wisdom to submit to the heavy iron yoke of a cruel tyrant, that they may secure the lives of their bodies? And is it not much more our wisdom to submit to the sweet and easy yoke of our rightful Lord and Master Jesus Christ, that we may secure the lives of our souls? Bring down your spirits to repentance and faith, and that is the way to bring up your spirits to heaven and glory, and with much more cogency and compassion may we expostulate with perishing souls than Jeremiah here expostulates with a perishing people.

Jeremiah 27

Because we feel most from our own burden, and cannot be persuaded to reconcile ourselves to it, we are ready to cry out, Surely never was sorrow like unto our sorrow; whereas, if our troubles were to be thrown into a common stock with those of others, and then an equal dividend made, share and share alike, rather than stand to that we should each of us say, 'Pray, give me my own again.'

Lamentations 1

When afflicting providences deprive us of our relations, possessions, and enjoyments, we must bear it patiently, must not be angry at God, must not be angry for the gourd. It is comparatively but a small loss, the loss of a shadow; that is the most we can make of it. It was a gourd, a withering thing; we could expect no other than that it should wither. Our being angry for the withering of it will not recover it; we ourselves shall shortly wither like it. If one gourd be withered, another gourd may spring up in the room of it; but that which should especially silence our discontent is that though our gourd be gone our God is not gone, and there is enough in him to make up all our losses. Let us therefore own that we do ill, that we do very ill, to be angry for the gourd; and let us under such events quiet ourselves 'as a child that is weaned from his mother'.

Jonah 4

We are apt, in such cases, to add to our own trouble, by fancying what 'might have been'. 'If such a method had been taken, such a physician employed, my friend had not died,' which is more than we know: but what good does this do? When God's will is done, our business is to submit to him.

John 11

Suffering

Christ's sufferings are continued in the suffering of the saints for his name. The devil tempts them, casts them into prison, persecutes and slays them, and so bruises the heel of Christ, who is afflicted in their afflictions. But while the heel is bruised on earth, it is well that the head is safe in heaven.

Genesis 3

God brings his people into danger and distress that he may have the honour of bringing about their deliverance, and suffers the enemies of his church to prevail awhile, though they profane his name by their sin, that he may have the honour of prevailing at last and sanctifying his own name in their ruin.

Ezekiel 38

The cross is here put for all sufferings, as men or Christians; providential afflictions, persecutions for righteousness' sake, every trouble that befalls us, either for doing well or for not doing ill. The troubles of Christians are fitly called crosses, in allusion to the death of the cross, which Christ was obedient to; and it should reconcile us to troubles, and take off the terror of them, that they are what we bear in common with Christ, and such as he hath borne before us.

Matthew 16

Even in this, consolation doth more abound. It is but a cup, not an ocean; it is but a draught, bitter perhaps, but we shall see the bottom of it; it is a cup in the hand of a Father (John 18: 11); and it is full of mixture (Ps. 75:8). It is but a baptism; if dipped, that is the worst of it, not drowned; perplexed, but not in despair. Baptism is an ordinance by which we join ourselves to the Lord in covenant and communion; and so is suffering for Christ (Ezek. 20: 37; Isa. 48:10). Baptism is 'an outward and visible sign of an inward and spiritual grace'; and so is suffering for Christ, for unto us it is given (Phil. 1:29).

Matthew 20

Whether it make for us or against us, we must abide by

this rule, that we cannot judge of men's sins by their sufferings in this world; for many are thrown into the furnace as gold to be purified, not as dross and chaff to be consumed.

Luke 13

We are not called to suffer, while we may avoid it without sin; and therefore, though we may not, for our own preservation, change our religion, yet we may change our place. Christ secured himself, not by a miracle, but in a way common to men, for the direction and encouragement of his suffering people. *John 4*

Reference is here had to the divine counsels concerning his sufferings, by virtue of which it behoved him thus to submit and suffer. Note, this should reconcile us to the darkest hours of our lives, that we were all along designed for them; *see (1 Thess. 3:3).*

John 12

We are apt to justify our complaints of injuries done us with this, that they are causeless, whereas the more they are so the more they are like the sufferings of Christ, and may be the more easily borne.

John 15

Sunday Observance

Those that covenant to keep all God's commandments must particularly covenant to keep sabbaths well; for the profanation of them is an inlet to other instances of profaneness. The sabbath is a market day for our souls, but not for our bodies.

Nehemiah 10

They must rest from their worldly employment on the sabbath day, must do no servile work. They must bear no burden into the city nor out of it, into their houses nor out of them; husbandmen's burdens of corn must not be carried in, nor manure carried out; nor must tradesmen's burdens of wares or merchandises be imported or exported. There must not a loaded horse, or cart, or wagon, be seen on the sabbath day either in the streets or in the roads, the porters must not ply on that day, nor must the servants be suffered to fetch in provisions or fuel. It is a day of rest, and must not be made a day of labour, unless in case of necessity.

Where God is jealous we must be cautious. 'Take heed to yourselves', for it is at your peril if you rob God of that part of your time which he has reserved for himself. 'Take heed to your souls' (so the word is); in order to the right sanctifying of sabbaths, we must look well to the frame of our spirits and have a watchful eye upon all the motions of the inward man. Let not the soul be burdened with the cares of this world on sabbath days, but let that be employed, even all that is within us, in the work of the day.

Jeremiah 17

Now that which our Lord Jesus here lays down is, that the

works of necessity and mercy are lawful on the sabbath day, which the Jews in many instances were taught to make a scruple of. Christ's industrious explanation of the fourth commandment, intimates its perpetual obligation to the religious observation of one day in seven as a holy sabbath. He would not expound a law that was immediately to expire, but doubtless intended hereby to settle a point which would be of use to his church in all ages; and so it is to teach us, that our Christian sabbath, though under the direction of the fourth commandment, is not under the injunctions of the Jewish elders.

The priests in the temple did a great deal of servile work on the sabbath day; killing, flaying, burning the sacrificed beasts, which in a common case would have been profaning the sabbath; and yet it was never reckoned any transgression of the fourth commandment, because the temple service required and justified it. This intimates, that those labours are lawful on the sabbath day which are necessary, not only to the support of life, but to the service of the day; as tolling a bell to call the congregation together, travelling to church, and the like. Sabbath rest is to promote, not to hinder, sabbath worship.

Matthew 12

The sabbath is a sacred and divine institution; but we must receive and embrace it as a privilege and a benefit, not as a task and a drudgery. First, God never designed it to be an imposition upon us, and therefore we must not make it so to ourselves. Man was not made for the sabbath, for he was made a day before the sabbath was instituted. Man was made for God, and for his honour and service, and he must rather die than deny him; but he was not made for the sabbath, so as to be tied up by the law of it, from that which is necessary to the support of his life.

What care we ought to take not to make those exercises of religion burdens to ourselves or others, which God ordained to be blessings; neither adding to the command by unreasonable strictness, nor indulging those corruptions which are adverse to the command, for thereby we make those devout exercises a penance to ourselves, which otherwise would be a pleasure.

Mark 2

Though she was under this infirmity, by which she was much deformed, and made to look mean, and not only so, but, as is supposed, motion was very painful to her, yet she went to the synagogue on the sabbath day. Note, even bodily infirmities, unless they be very grievous indeed, should not keep us from public worship on sabbath days; for God can help us, beyond our expectation.

Luke 13

Sympathy

This is a request like that of Job (ch. 19:21), 'Have pity upon me, have pity upon me, O you my friends.' It helps to make a burden sit lighter if our friends sympathize with us, and mingle their tears with ours, for this is an evidence that, though we are in affliction, we are not in contempt, which is commonly as much dreaded in an affliction as anything.

Lamentations 1

Tact

Every thing that is true and good is not suitable and seasonable. To one that was humbled, and broken, and grieved in spirit, as Job was, he ought to have preached of the grace and mercy of God, rather than of his greatness and majesty, to have laid before him the consolations rather than the terrors of the Almighty. Christ knows how to speak what is proper for the weary (Isa. 50:4) and his ministers should learn rightly to divide the word of truth, and not make those sad whom God would not have made sad.

Job 26

Talkative

But these Corinthians excelled most churches in spiritual gifts, and particularly in utterance; and yet this was not in them, as in too many, both the effect and evidence of ignorance; for with their utterance there appeared knowledge, abundance of knowledge. They had a treasury of things new and old, and in their utterance they brought out of this treasury. They abounded also in all diligence. Those who have great

knowledge and ready utterance are not always the most diligent Christians. *Great talkers are not always the best doers; but these Corinthians were diligent to do, as well as know and talk, well.*

2 Corinthians 8

Taxes

What we have, we have as stewards; others have an interest in it, and must have their dues.

Render to all their dues; and that readily and cheerfully, not tarrying till you are by law compelled to it.

Romans 13

Teachers

Observe the method: he first learned and then taught. Sought the law of the Lord and so laid up a good treasure and then instructed others and laid out what he had laid up. He also first did and then taught — practised the commandments himself and then directed others in the practice of them, thus his example confirmed his doctrine.

Ezra 7

Teaching Methods

He did not name John, but gives them such a description of him as would put them in mind of what he had said to them formerly concerning him; 'This is Elias'. This is a profitable way of teaching; it engages the learners' own thoughts, and makes them, if not their own teachers, yet their own remembrancers; and thus knowledge becomes easy to him that understands. When we diligently use the means of knowledge, how strangely are mists scattered and mistakes rectified!

Matthew 17

Many are taught with the briars and thorns of affliction that would not learn otherwise. God gives wisdom by the rod and reproof, chastens and teaches and by correction opens the ear to discipline. Our blessed Saviour, though he was a Son, yet learned obedience by the things which he suffered. Let every pricking briar and grieving thorn, especially when it becomes a thorn in the flesh, be thus interpreted, thus improved. By this God designs to teach me. What good lesson shall I learn?

Judges 8

Temperament

Ezra and Nehemiah were both of them very wise, good, useful men, yet, in cases not unlike, there was a great deal of difference between their management: when Ezra was told of the sin of the rulers in marrying strange wives he rent his clothes and wept, and prayed, and was hardly persuaded to attempt a reformation, fearing it to be impracticable, for he was a man of a mild tender spirit; when Nehemiah was told of as bad a thing he kindled immediately, reproached the delinquents, incensed the people against them, and never rested till, by all the rough methods

he could use, he forced them to reform; for he was a man of a hot and eager spirit. Note: 1. Very holy men may differ much from each other in their natural temper and in other things that result from it. 2. God's work may be done, well done, and successfully and yet different methods taken in the doing of it, which is a good reason why we should neither arraign the management of others nor make our own a standard. There are diversities of operation, but the same Spirit.

Nehemiah 5

Comparing this story with that in (Luke 10:38) etc., we may observe the different tempers of these two sisters, and *the temptations and advantages of each*. Martha's natural temper was active and busy; she loved to be here and there, and at the end of every thing; and this had been a snare to her when by it she was not only careful and cumbered about many things, but hindered from the exercises of devotion: but now in a day of affliction this active temper did her a kindness, kept the grief from her heart, and made her forward to meet Christ, and so she received comfort from him the sooner. On the other hand, Mary's natural temper was contemplative and reserved. This had been formerly an advantage to her, when it placed her at Christ's feet, to hear his word, and enabled her there to attend upon him without those distractions with which Martha was cumbered; but now in the day of affliction that same temper proved a snare to her, made her less able to grapple with her grief, and disposed her to melancholy: 'But Mary sat still in the house'. See here how much it will be our wisdom carefully to watch against the temptations, and improve the advantages, of our natural temper.

John 11

Peter ought not to be censured for casting himself into the sea, but commended for his zeal and the strength of his affection; and so must those be who, in love to Christ, quit the world, with Mary, to 'sit at his feet'. But others serve Christ more in the affairs of the world. They continue in that ship, drag the net, and bring the fish to shore, as the other disciples here; and such ought not to be censured as worldly, for they, in their place, are as truly serving Christ as the other, even in serving tables. If all the disciples had done as Peter did, what had become of their fish and their nets? And yet if Peter had done as they did we had wanted this instance of holy zeal. *Christ was well pleased with both, and so must we be.*

. . . all that are faithful are not alike forward.

John 21

Temporary Expedients

While a house is in the building, a great deal of dirt and rubbish are suffered to lie by it which must be taken away when the house is built.

Deuteronomy 12

Temptation

Had Eve kept close to the side out of which she was lately taken, she would have been less exposed. There are many temptations to which solitude gives great advantage; but the communion of saints contributes much to their strength and safety.

Satan tempted Eve, that by her he might tempt Adam; so he tempted Job by his wife, and Christ by Peter. It is his policy to send temptations by un-suspected hands, and theirs that have most interest in us and influence upon us.

Genesis 3

When we enter into a parley with temptations, we are in great danger of being overcome by them . . . those are a fair mark for Satan's temptation that speak diminishingly of divine prohibitions as if they amounted to no more than the denial of a permission and as if to go against God's law were only to go without his leave.

It is very probable that he sent double money in the hands of his messengers but beside that, now he tempted him with honours, laid a bait not only for his covetousness but for his pride and ambition. How earnestly should we beg of God daily to mortify in us these two limbs of the old man. Those that know how to look with a holy contempt upon worldly wealth and preferment will find it not so hard a matter as most men

do to keep a good conscience.
Numbers 22

We are more endangered by the charms of a smiling world than by the terrors of a frowning world.
Numbers 25

We must expect trouble and affliction from that, whatever it is, which we sinfully indulge; that which we are willing should tempt us we shall find will vex us.
Numbers 33

These are two of the blackest and most horrid of all Satan's temptations, and yet such as good men have sometimes been violently assaulted with. Nothing is more contrary to natural conscience than blaspheming God, nor to natural sense than self-murder; therefore the suggestion of either of these may well be suspected to come immediately from Satan.
Job 2

What we must not meddle with we must not lust after; and what we must not lust after we must not look at; not the forbidden wealth (Prov. 23:5), not the forbidden wine (Prov. 23:31), not the forbidden woman (Matt. 5:28).
Job 31

If we carefully avoid all the paths of sin, it will be very comfortable in the reflection, when we are in trouble. If we keep ourselves, that the wicked one touch us not with his temptations (1 John 5:18), we may hope he will not be able to touch us with his terrors.
Psalm 17

Those that would be kept from harm must keep out of harm's way. Such tinder there is in the corrupt nature that it is madness, upon any pretence whatsoever, to come near the sparks. If we thrust ourselves into temptation, we mocked God when we prayed, 'Lead us not into temptation.'
Proverbs 5

'You have broken one of the rules of your order, in coming to live at Jerusalem; why may you not break this too, and when you are in the city do as they do?' But they peremptorily refused.
Jeremiah 35

Those that would avoid sin must not parley with temptation. When that which we are allured or affrighted to is manifestly evil, the motion is rather to be rejected with indignation and abhorrence than reasoned with; stand not to pause about it, but say, as Christ has taught us, 'Get thee behind me Satan'.
Daniel 3

That which Satan aimed at, in all his temptations, was, to bring him to sin against God, and so to render him for ever incapable of being a sacrifice for the sin of others. Now, whatever the colours were, that which he aimed at was, to bring him, 1. To despair of his Father's goodness. 2. To presume upon his Father's power. 3. To alienate his Father's honour, by giving it to Satan. In the two former, that which he tempted him *to*, seemed innocent, and therein appeared the subtlety of the tempter; in the last, that which he tempted him *with*, seemed desirable. The two former are artful temptations, which there was need of great wisdom to discern; the last was a strong temptation, which there was need of great resolution to resist; yet he was baffled in them all.

The great thing Satan aims at, in tempting good people, is to overthrow their relation to God as a Father, and so to cut off their dependence on him, their duty to him, and their communion with him.

Finding Christ so confident of his Father's care of him, in point of nourishment, he endeavours to draw him to presume upon that care in point of safety. We are in danger of missing our way, both on the right hand, and on the left, and therefore must take heed, lest, when we avoid one extreme, we be brought by the artifices of Satan, to run into another; lest, by overcoming our prodigality, we fall into covetousness. Nor are any extremes more dangerous than those of despair and presumption, especially in the affairs of our souls. Some who have obtained a persuasion that Christ is able and willing to save them *from* their sins, are then tempted to presume that he will save them *in* their sins. Thus when people begin to be zealous in religion. Satan hurries them into bigotry and intemperate heats.

Matthew 4

Those who have their spiritual senses exercised, will be aware of the voice of Satan, even in a friend, a disciple, a minister, that dissuades them from their duty. We must not regard who speaks, so much as what is spoken; we should learn to know the devil's voice when he speaks in a saint as well as when he speaks in a serpent. Whoever takes us off from that which is good, and would have us afraid of doing too much for God, speaks Satan's language.

Matthew 16

They that think it dangerous to be in company with Christ's disciples, because thence they may be drawn in to suffer for him, will find it much more dangerous to be in company with his enemies, because there they may be drawn in to sin against him.

Mark 14

As by retiring into the wilderness he showed himself perfectly indifferent to the world, so by his fasting he showed himself perfectly indifferent to the body; and Satan cannot easily take hold of those who are thus loosened from, and dead to, the world and the flesh. The more we keep under the body, and bring it into subjection, the less advantage Satan has against us.

Luke 4

But there are some sins in their own nature so exceedingly sinful, and to which there is so little temptation from the world and the flesh, that it is plain Satan lays the egg of them in a heart disposed to be the nest to hatch them in.

From yesterday's pardon, we should fetch an argument against this day's temptation.

John 13

Temptation (Victory Over)

In the midst of all these grievances he did not speak a word amiss; and we have no reason to think but that he also preserved a good temper of mind, so that, though there might be some stirrings and risings of corruption in his heart, yet grace got the upper hand and he took care that the root of bitterness might not spring up to trouble him (Heb. 12:15). The *abundance of his heart* was for God, produced good things, and suppressed the evil that was there, which was outvoted by the better side. If he did think any evil, yet he *laid his hand upon his mouth* (Prov. 30:32), stifled the evil thought and let it go no further, by which it appeared, not only that he had true grace, but that it was strong and victorious: in short that he had not forfeited the character of a perfect and upright man; for so *he* appears to be who, in the midst of such temptations, offends not in word (James 3:2; Ps. 17:3).

Job 2

Testimony

We may be for ever singing God's mercies, and yet the subject will not be drawn dry. We must sing of God's mercies as long as we live, train up others to sing of them when we are gone, and hope to be singing them in heaven world without end; and this is singing of the mercies of the Lord for ever. With my mouth, and with my pen (for by that also do we speak), will I make known thy faithfulness to all generations, assuring posterity, from my own observation and experience, that God is true to every word that he has spoken, that they may learn to put their trust in God (78:6).

Psalm 89

We ought to show to others God's dealings with us, both the rebukes we have been under and the favours we have received; and though the account hereof may reflect disgrace upon ourselves, as this did upon Nebuchadnezzar, yet we must not conceal it, as long as it may redound to the glory of God. Many will be forward to tell what God has done for their souls, because that turns to their own praise, who care not for telling what God has done against them, and how they deserved it; whereas we ought to give glory to God, not only by praising him for his mercies, but by confessing our sins, accepting the punishment of our iniquity, and in both taking shame to ourselves, as this mighty monarch here does.

Daniel 4

Testing

Many commandments God gave them which there would have been no occasion for if they had not been led through the wilderness, as those relating to the manna (Exod. 16:28) and

God thereby tried them as our first parents were tried by the trees of the garden, whether they would keep God's commandments or not . . . God often brings his people low that he might have the honour of helping them.

Deuteronomy 8

God's time to appear for the deliverance of his people is when things are at the worst with them. God tries his people's faith and stirs up prayer by letting things go to the worst and then magnifies his own power and fills the faces of his enemies with shame and the hearts of his people with so much the greater joy by rescuing them out of extremity.

Deuteronomy 32

Thankfulness

Later mercies should bring to remembrance former mercies and revive our thankfulness for them.

Joshua 4

Observe what great things she says of God. She takes little notice of the particular mercy she was, now rejoicing in, does not commend Samuel for the prettiest child, the most toward and sensible for his age that she ever saw, as fond parents are too apt to do. No, she overlooks the gift and praises the giver whereas most forget the giver and fasten only on the gift. Every stream should lead us to the fountain.

1 Samuel 2

The more we do for God the more we are indebted to him for the honour of being employed in his service and for grace enabling us in any measure to serve him. Does he, therefore, thank that servant (Luke 17:9)? No, but that servant has a great deal of reason to thank him. He thanks God that they were able to offer so willingly. It is a great instance of the power of God's grace in us to be able to do the work of God willingly.

1 Chronicles 29

What a pity is it that this earth, which is so full of God's goodness, should be empty of his praises, and that of the multitudes that live upon his bounty there are so few that live to his glory!

Psalm 33

Whatever are the premises, God's glory must always be the conclusion. God has heard me and therefore blessed be God.

Psalm 66

The psalmist has a very sad complaint to make of the deplorable condition of the family of David at this time, and yet he begins the psalm with songs of praise; for we must, in everything, in every state, give thanks; thus we must glorify the Lord in the fire. We think, when we are in trouble, that we get ease by complaining; but we do more— we get joy, by praising. Let our complaints therefore be turned into thanksgivings.

Psalm 89

'Forget not all his benefits'. If

we do not give thanks for them, we do forget them; and that is unjust as well as unkind, since in all God's favours there is so much that is memorable. O my soul, to thy shame be it spoken, thou hast forgotten many of his benefits; but surely thou wilt not forget them all, for thou shouldst not have forgotten any.

Psalm 103

Was Daniel thus thankful to God for making known that to him which was the saving of the lives of him and his fellows? Much more reason have we to be thankful to him for making known to us the great salvation of the soul, to us and not to the world, to us and not to the wise and prudent.

Daniel 2

Thanksgiving is a proper answer to dark and disquieting thoughts, and may be an effectual means to silence them. Songs of praise are sovereign cordials to drooping souls, and will help to cure melancholy. When we have no other answer ready to the suggestions of grief and fear, we may have recourse to this, 'I thank thee, O Father'; let us bless God that it is not worse with us than it is.

Matthew 11

Miracles, which are the matter of our wonder, must be the matter of our praise; and mercies, which are the matter of our rejoicing, must be the matter of our thanksgiving. Those that were healed, glorified God; if he heal our diseases, all that is within us must bless his holy name; and if we have been graciously preserved from blindness, and lameness, and dumbness, we have as much reason to bless God as if we had been cured of them; nay, and the standers-by glorified God. Note, God must be acknowledged with praise and thankfulness in the mercies of others as in our own.

Matthew 15

Thoughtfulness for Others

Special notice is taken of his great tenderness in providing old soft rags for Jeremiah to put under his arm-holes, to keep the cords wherewith he was to be drawn up from hurting him, his arm-holes being probably galled by the cords wherewith he was let down. Nor did he throw the rags down to him, lest they should be lost in the mire, but carefully let them down (v. 11, 12). Note, those that are in distress should not only be relieved, but relieved with compassion and marks of respect, all which shall be placed to account and abound to a good account in the day of recompense.

Jeremiah 38

Thoughts

Even in good thoughts there is a fickleness and inconstancy which may well be called vanity. It concerns us to keep a strict guard upon our thoughts, because God takes particular notice of them. Thoughts are words to God, and vain thoughts are provocations.

Psalm 94

Carnal pleasure, worldly profit

and honour, the things of sense and time, are the things of the flesh, which unregenerate people mind. The favour of God, the welfare of the soul, the concerns of eternity, are the things of the Spirit, which those that are after the Spirit do mind. *The man is as the mind is.*

Romans 8

Thunder

The emperor Caligula would hide himself under his bed when it thundered. Horace, the poet, owns that he was reclaimed from atheism by the terror of thunder and lightning, which he describes somewhat like this of David.

Psalm 29

Time

See how industrious our Lord Jesus was to redeem time, to husband every minute of it, and to fill up the vacancies of it. When the disciples were gone into the town, his discourse with the woman was edifying, and suited to her case; when she was gone into the town, his discourse with them was no less edifying, and suited to their case; it were well if we could thus gather up the fragments of time, that none of it may be lost.

John 4

Tithing

Let their readiness to part with their rings to make an idol shame us out of our niggardli-ness in the service of the true God. Shall we grudge the expenses of our religion or starve so good a cause?

Exodus 32

Though they paid great taxes to the kings of Persia, and had much hardship put upon them. they would not make that an excuse for not paying their tithes, but would render to God the things that were his, as well as to Caesar the things that were his.

Nehemiah 10

They can be thus prodigal of their goods when it is for the saving of their lives, and yet how sparing of them in works of piety and charity, and in suffering for Christ, though they are told by eternal Truth itself that those shall be recompensed more than a thousand fold 'in the resurrection of the just'.

Acts 27

Tolerance

We are to believe that many have the root of the matter in them who are not in every thing of our mind — who have their follies, and weaknesses, and mistakes — and to conclude that it is at our peril if we persecute any such. Woe to him that offends one of these little ones! God will resent and revenge it. Job and his friends differed in some notions concerning the methods of providence, but they agreed in the root of the matter, the belief of another world, and therefore should not persecute one another for these differences.

Job 19

Piety is disgraced in all the shows of it, if there be not charity. That tongue confutes itself which one while pretends to adore the perfections of God, and to refer all things to him, and another while will condemn even good men if they do not just come up to the same words or expressions used by it.

James 3

Tongue

It is very observable that no mention is here made of Solomon's departure from God in his latter days, not the least hint given of it, because the Holy Ghost would teach us not to take delight in repeating the faults and follies of others. If those that have been in reputation for wisdom and honour misbehave, though it may be of use to take notice of their misconduct for warning to ourselves and others, once speaking of it is enough. Why should that unpleasing string be again struck upon? Why can we not do as the sacred historian does, speak largely of that in others which is praiseworthy without saying anything of their blemishes though they have been gross and obvious. This is but doing as we would be done by.

2 Chronicles 9

What is good in men we should take all occasions to speak of and often repeat it. What is evil we should make mention of but sparingly and no more than is needful.

2 Chronicles 24

When they came to see and sit with him he thought he might speak his mind freely to them, and that the more bitter his complaints to them were the more they would endeavour to comfort him. This made him take a greater liberty than otherwise he would have done. David, though he smothered his resentments when the wicked were before him, would proably have given vent to them if none had been by but friends (Ps. 39:1). But this freedom of speech, which their professions of concern for him made him use, had exposed him to their censures.

Job 6

Those are not the wisest of the company, but the weakest rather, who covet to have all the talk.

Job 8 (Intro.)

The tongue is death or life, poison or medicine, as it is used. There are words that are cutting and killing, that are like the piercings of a sword. Opprobrious words grieve the spirits of those to whom they are spoken, and cut them to the heart. Slanders, like a sword, wound the reputation of those of whom they are uttered, and perhaps incurably. Whisperings and evil surmises, like a sword, divide and cut asunder the bonds of love and friendship, and separate those that have been dearest to each other.

There are words that are curing and healing: the tongue of the wise is health, closing up those wounds which the backbiting tongue had given, making all whole again, restoring peace, and accommodating matters in variance and persuading to reconciliation. Wisdom will find out proper remedies against the mischiefs that are made by detraction and evil-speaking.

Proverbs 12

Nothing stirs up anger and sows discord, like grievous words, calling foul names, as *Raca*, and thou fool, upbraiding men with their infirmities and infelicities, their extraction or education, or anything that lessens them and makes them mean; scornful, spiteful reflections, by which men affect to show their wit and malice, stir up the anger of others, which does but increase and inflame their own anger. Rather than lose a jest some will lose a friend and make an enemy.

Proverbs 15

The way to preserve peace among relations and neighbours is to make the best of everything, not to tell others what has been said or done against them when it is not at all necessary to their safety, nor to take notice of what has been said or done against ourselves, but to excuse both, and put the best construction upon them. It was an oversight, therefore overlook it. It was done through forgetfulness, therefore forget it. It perhaps made nothing of you, do you make nothing of it.

Proverbs 17

The testimony of our consciences will be for us, or against us, according as we have or have not governed our tongues well. According as the fruit of the mouth is good or bad, unto iniquity or unto righteousness, so the character of the man is, and consequently the testimony of his conscience concerning him.

A man may do a great deal of good, or a great deal of hurt, both to others and to himself, according to the use he makes of his tongue. Many a one has been his own death by a foul tongue, or the death of others by a false tongue; and, on the contrary, many a one has saved his own life, or procured the comfort of it, by a prudent gentle tongue, and saved the lives of others by a seasonable testimony or intercession for them, and, if by our words we must be justified or condemned, death and life are no doubt, in the power of the tongue.

Proverbs 18

By a constant watchfulness over our words we shall prevent abundance of mischiefs which an ungoverned tongue runs men into. Keep thy heart, and that will keep thy tongue from sin; keep thy tongue, and that will keep thy heart from trouble.

Proverbs 21

We must keep the evil thought we have conceived in our minds from breaking out in any evil speeches. Do not give the evil thought an *'imprimatur'* — a license; allow it not to be published; but lay thy hand upon thy mouth; use a holy violence with thyself, if need be, and enjoin thyself silence; as Christ suffered not the evil spirits to speak. It is bad to think ill, but it is much worse to speak it, for that implies a consent to the evil thought and a willingness to infect others with it.

Proverbs 30

'Raca' is a scornful word, and comes from pride, 'Thou empty fellow'; it is the language of that which Solomon calls 'proud wrath' (Prov. 21:24), which tramples upon our brother. . . 'Thou fool' is a spiteful word, and comes from hatred; looking upon him, not only as mean and not to be honoured, but as vile and not to be loved; 'thou wicked man, thou reprobate'. The former speaks a man without sense, this (in Scripture language) speaks a man without grace; the more the reproach touches his spiritual condition, the worse it is; the former is a haughty taunting of our brother, this is a malicious censuring and condemning of him, as abandoned of God. Now this is a breach of the sixth commandment; malicious slanders and censures are poison under the tongue, that kills secretly and slowly; bitter words are as arrows that wound suddenly (Ps. 64:3), or as a sword in the bones. The good name of our neighbour, which is better than life, is thereby stabbed and murdered; and it is an evidence of such an ill-will to our neighbour as would strike at his life, if it were in our power.

Matthew 5

See what malignity there is in tongue-sins, when the only unpardonable sin is so.

Matthew 12

It is not the disciples that defile themselves with what they eat, but the Pharisees that defile themselves with what they speak spitefully and censoriously of them. Note, those who charge guilt upon others for transgressing the commandments of men, many times bring greater guilt upon themselves, by transgressing the law of God against rash judging. Those most defile themselves, who are most forward to censure the defilements of others.

Matthew 15

We have reason to suspect the truth of that which is backed with rash oaths and imprecations. None but the devil's sayings need the devil's proofs. He that will not be restrained by the third commandment from mocking his God, will not be kept by the ninth from deceiving his brother.

Matthew 26

'My tongue was glad'. In the psalm it is, 'My glory rejoiceth'; which intimates that our tongue is our glory, the faculty of speaking is an honour to us, and never more so than when it is employed in praising God.

Acts 2

Total Depravity

'There is none that doeth good, no not one', till the free and mighty grace of God has wrought a change. Whatever good is in any of the children of men, or is done by them, it is not of themselves, it is God's work in them. When God had made the world he looked upon his own work and all was very good (Gen. 1:31); but some time after, he looked upon man's work, and behold, all was very bad (Gen. 6:5), every operation of the thought of man's heart was evil, only evil, and that continually. They have gone aside from the right way of their duty, the way that leads to happiness, and have turned into the paths of the destroyer. In singing this, let us lament the corruption of our own nature, and see what need we have of the grace of God; and, since that which is born of the flesh is flesh, let us not marvel that we are told we must be born again.

Psalm 14

So stupid are we that nothing less than the mighty hand of divine grace, known experimentally, can make us know rightly the name of God as it is revealed to us.

Jeremiah 16

It is observable that, to prove the general corruption of nature, he quotes some scriptures which speak of the particular corruptions of particular persons, as of Doeg (Ps. 140:3), of the Jews (Isa. 59:7, 8), which shows that the same sins that are committed by one are in the nature of all.

Romans 3

Touchline Christians

Whatever cost he was at in rearing the structure, if he had neglected the worship that was to be performed there, it would all have been to no purpose. Assisting the devotion of others will not atone for our own neglects.

2 Chronicles 8

Tradition

Learn, the uncertainty of human tradition, and the folly of building our faith upon it. Here was a tradition, a saying that 'went abroad among the brethren'. It was early; it was common; it was public; and yet it was false. How little then are those unwritten traditions to be relied upon which the council of Trent hath decreed to be received with a 'veneration and pious affection equal to that which is owing to the holy Scripture.' Here was a traditional exposition of Scripture. No new saying of Christ's advanced, but only a construction put by the brethren upon what he did really say, and yet it was a misconstruction.

John 21

Tranquility of Spirit

The injuries men do us should drive us to God, for to him we may commit our cause. Nay, he sings to the Lord; his spirit was not ruffled by it, nor cast down, but so composed and cheerful that he was still in tune for sacred songs and it did not occasion one jarring string in his harp. Thus let the injuries we receive from men, instead of provoking our passions, kindle and excite our devotions.

Psalm 7

All our outward concerns must be committed to the providence of God, and to the sovereign, wise, and gracious disposal of that providence. Roll thy works upon the Lord (so the word is); roll the burden of thy care from thyself upon God. Lay the matter before him by prayer. Make known thy works unto the Lord (so some read it), not only the works of thy hand, but the workings of thy heart; and then leave it with him, by faith and dependence upon him, submission and resignation to him. The will of the Lord be done. We may then be easy when we resolve that whatever pleases God shall please us.

Proverbs 16

Trials

We may well imagine how unfit that people would have been for Canaan had they not first gone through the discipline of the wilderness.

Deuteronomy 32

Many are taught with the briars and thorns of affliction that would not learn otherwise. God gives wisdom by the rod and reproof, chastens and teaches and by correction opens the ear to discipline. Our blessed Saviour, though he was a Son, yet learned obedience by the things which he suffered. Let every pricking briar and grieving thorn, especially when it becomes a thorn in the flesh, be thus interpreted, thus improved. By this God designs to teach me. What good lesson shall I learn?

Judges 8

As the promise tried her faith so this precept tried her obedience for God requires both from

those on whom he will bestow his favours.

Judges 13

Outward losses drive good people to their prayers but bad people to their curses.

Judges 17

Saul had driven him from his country, the Philistines had driven him from their camp, the Amalekites had plundered his city, his wives were taken prisoners and now, to complete his woe, his own familiar friends in whom he trusted, whom he had sheltered and who did eat of his bread, instead of sympathising with him and offering him any relief, lifted up the heel against him and threatened to stone him. Great faith must expect such severe exercises but it is observable that David was reduced to this extremity just before his accession to the throne.

1 Samuel 30

Good men, even when God frowns upon them, think well of him.

1 Chronicles 21

Sennacherib invaded Judah immediately after the reformation of it and the re-establishment of religion in it. After these things he entered into Judah. It was well ordered by the divine providence that he did not give them this disturbance before the reformation was finished and established as it might then have put a stop to it . . . God ordered it at this time that he might have an opportunity of showing himself strong on the behalf of this returning, reforming people. He brought this trouble upon them that he might have the honour and might put on them the honour of their deliverance. After these things and the establishment thereof one might have expected to hear of nothing but perfect peace and that none durst meddle with a people thus qualified for the divine favour, yet the next news we hear is that a threatening destroying army enters the country and is ready to lay all waste. We may be in the way of our duty and yet meet with trouble and danger. God orders it so for the trial of our confidence in him and the manifestation of his care concerning us.

God, by the power of his almighty grace could have prevented the sin, but he permitted it for wise and holy ends that by this trial and his weakness in it, he might know, that is, it might be known, what was in his heart. That he was not so perfect in grace as he thought he was but had his follies and infirmities as other men.

2 Chronicles 32

Job's friends charged him with hypocrisy because he was greatly afflicted, Satan because he greatly prospered.

Job 1

It is true that we and our children have sinned against God, and we ought to justify him in all he brings upon us and ours; but extraordinary afflictions are not always the punishment of extraordinary sins, but sometimes the trial of extraordinary graces; and, in our judgment of another's case (unless the contrary appears), we ought to take the more favourable side, as our Saviour directs (Luke 13:2—4).

Job 8

He laid the unkindness of his countrymen too much to heart. 'They wearied him', because it was 'in a land of peace wherein he trusted' (v. 5). It was very grievous to him to be thus hated and abused by his own kindred. He was disturbed in his mind by it; his spirit was sunk and overwhelmed with it, so that he was in great agitation and distress about it. Nay, he was discouraged in his work by it, began to be weary of prophesying, and to think of giving it up. He did not consider that this was but the beginning of his sorrow, and that he had sorer trials yet before him; and, whereas he should endeavour by a patient bearing of this trouble to prepare himself for greater, by his uneasiness under this he did but unfit himself for what further lay before him.

God's usual method being to begin with smaller trials, it is our wisdom to expect greater than any we have yet met with. We may be called out to 'contend with horsemen', and the sons of Anak may perhaps be reserved for the last encounter.

In order to our preparation for further and greater trials, we are concerned to approve ourselves well in present smaller trials, to keep up our spirits, keep hold of the promise, keep in our way, with our eye upon the prize, so run that we may obtain it.

Jeremiah 12

It is hard to take comfort from former smiles under present frowns.

Jeremiah 31

Young beginners in religion, like freshwater soldiers, are apt to be discouraged with the little difficulties which they commonly meet with at first in the service of God. They do but run with the footmen, and it wearies them; they faint upon the very dawning of the day of adversity and it is an evidence that their strength is small (Prov. 24:10), that their faith is weak, and that they are yet but babes, who cry for every hurt and every fright.

Jeremiah 45

As long as we are here in this world we must expect 'troublous times', upon some account or other. Even when we have 'joyous times' we must rejoice with trembling; it is but a gleam, it is but a lucid interval of peace and prosperity; the clouds will return after the rain. When the Jews are restored in triumph to their own land, yet there they must expect troublous times, and prepare for them. But this is our comfort, that God will carry on his own work, will build up his Jerusalem, will beautify it, will fortify it, even in troublous times; nay, the troublousness of the times may by the grace of God contribute to the advancement of the church. The more it is afflicted,

the more it multiplies.

Daniel 9

When the terrors of the law set themselves in array against a convinced soul, when the temptations of Satan assault the people of God, and the troubles of the world threaten to rob them of all their comforts, then the 'Assyrian comes into their land' and treads in their palaces.

Micah 5

They were Christ's disciples, and were now in the way of their duty, and Christ was now in the mount praying for them; and yet they were in this distress. The perils and afflictions of this present time may very well consist with our interest in Christ and his intercession. They had lately been feasted at Christ's table; but after the sunshine of comfort expect a storm.

They came to Capernaum, and, for aught that appears, these unsound hypocritical followers of Christ had a calm and pleasant passage, while his sincere disciples had a rough and stormy one. It is not strange if it fare worst with the best men in this evil world.

John 6

The disciples of Christ are apt to be offended at the cross; and the offence of the cross is a dangerous temptation, even to good men, to turn back from the ways of God, or turn aside out of them, or drive on heavily in them; to quit either their integrity or their comfort. It is not for nothing that a suffering time is called 'an hour of temptation'.

Though they were sent to 'proclaim peace on earth, and goodwill towards men', they must expect trouble on earth, and illwill from men. *Note,* It has been the lot of Christ's disciples to have more or less tribulation in this world. Men persecute them because they are so good, and God corrects them because they are no better. Men design to cut them off from the earth, and God designs by affliction to make them meet for heaven; and so between both 'they shall have tribulation'.

John 16

Weak believers often make that the matter of their complaint which is really just ground of hope, and matter of joy. We cry out that this and the other creature comfort are taken away, and we know not how to retrieve them, when indeed the removal of our temporal comforts, which we lament, is in order to the resurrection of our spiritual comforts, which we should rejoice in too.

We often perplex ourselves needlessly with imaginary difficulties, which faith would discover to us as real advantages. Many good people complain of the clouds and darkness they are under, which are the necessary methods of grace for the humbling of their souls, the mortifying of their sins, and the endearing of Christ to them.

John 20

There is no valley so dark but he can find a way through it, no affliction so grievous but he can prevent, or remove, or enable us to support it, and in the end overrule it to our advantage.

1 Corinthians 10

In being called to offer up his Isaac, he seemed to be called to destroy and cut off his own family, to cancel the promises of God, to prevent the coming of Christ, to destroy the whole world, to sacrifice his own soul and his hopes of salvation, and to cut off the church of God at one blow: a most terrible trial!

Hebrews 11

The afflictions of serious Christians are designed for the trial of their faith. God's design in afflicting his people is their probation, not their destruction; their advantage, not their ruin: a 'trial', as the word signifies, is an experiment or search made upon a man, by some affliction, to prove the value and strength of his faith.

1 Peter 1

Trinity

This allusion seems to imply that the Holy Spirit is as much in God as a man's mind is in himself. Now the mind of the man is plainly essential to him. He cannot be without his mind. Nor can God be without his Spirit. He is as much and as intimately one with God as the man's mind is with the man. The man knows his own mind because his mind is one with himself. The Spirit of God knows the things of God because he is one with God.

1 Corinthians 2

There is a consent and co-operation of all the persons of

the Trinity in the affair of man's salvation, and their acts are commensurate one to another: whoever the Father elects, the Spirit sanctifies unto obedience, and the Son redeems and sprinkles with his blood. The doctrine of the Trinity lies at the foundation of all revealed religion. If you deny the proper deity of the Son and Holy Spirit, you invalidate the redemption of the one and the gracious operations of the other, and by this means destroy the foundation of your own safety and comfort.

1 Peter 1

Troubles

Waters and seas in Scripture often signify troubles and afflictions (Ps. 42:7; 69:2, 14, 15). God's own people are not exempt from these in this world; but it is their comfort that they are only waters under the heavens (there are none in Heaven), and that they are all in the place God has appointed them and within the bounds that he has set for them.

Genesis 1

It alludes to a tempestuous sea, such as the wicked are compared to (Isa. 57:20). The 'heathen rage' (Ps. 2:1), and think to ruin the church, to overwhelm it like a deluge, to sink it like a ship at sea. The church is said to 'be tossed with tempests' (Isa. 54:11), and the 'floods of ungodly men make the saints afraid' (Ps. 18:4). We may apply it to the tumults that are sometimes in our own bosoms, through prevailing

passions and frights which put the soul in disorder, and are ready to overthrow its graces and comforts; but, if the Lord reign there, even the winds and seas shall obey him.

Psalm 93

True Happiness

They shall be my people. He will make them his by working in them all the characters and dispositions of his people, and then he will protect, and guide, and govern them as his people. 'And, to make them truly, completely, and eternally happy, I will be their God.' They shall serve and worship God as theirs and cleave to him only and he will approve himself theirs. All he is, all he has, shall be engaged and employed for their good.

Jeremiah 32

True Religion

To be religious is to fear God and to keep his commandments. The root of religion is the fear of God reigning in the heart, a reverence of his majesty, a deference to his authority, and a dread of his wrath. Fear God, that is, worship God, give him the honour due to his name, in all the instances of true devotion, inward and outward. See (Rev. 14:7).

Ecclesiastes 12

It will not be asked at the great day, 'Who ate flesh, and who ate herbs?' 'Who kept holy days, and who did not?' Nor will it be asked, 'Who was conformist and who was nonconformist?' But it will be asked, 'Who feared God and worked righteousness, and who did not?' Nothing more destructive to true Christianity than placing it in modes, and forms, and circumstantials, which eat out the essentials.

Romans 14

True Worth

We never read of giants among the Israelites as we do of giants among the Philistines. Giants of Gath but not giants of Jerusalem. The growth of God's plants is in usefulness, not in bulk. Those who covet to have cubits added to their stature do not consider that it will but make them more unwieldy. In the balance of the sanctuary, David far outweighs Goliath.

1 Chronicles 20

Heavenly wisdom is better than worldly wealth, and to be preferred before it. Grace is more valuable than gold. Grace is the gift of God's peculiar favour; gold only of common providence. Grace is for ourselves; gold for others. Grace is for the soul and eternity; gold only for the body and time. Grace will stand us in stead in a dying hour, when gold will do us no good.

Proverbs 16

Trust

We reproach our Leader if we follow him trembling.

Deuteronomy 3

We may be sure of the righteousness when we cannot see the reasons, of God's proceedings.

Judges 20

How helpless do Saul and all his forces lie, all, in effect, disarmed and chained and yet nothing is done to them. They are only rocked asleep. How easily can God weaken the strongest, befool the wisest and baffle the most watchful. Let all his friends, therefore, trust him and all his enemies fear him.

1 Samuel 26

Truthfulness

Though we must be harmless as doves, so as never to tell a wilful lie, yet we must be wise as serpents, so as not needlessly to expose ourselves to danger by telling all we know.

Jeremiah 38

Types

It is observable that those creatures were chosen for sacrifice which were most mild and gentle, harmless and inoffensive to typify the innocence and meekness that were in Christ and to teach the innocence and meekness that should be in Christians.

Leviticus 1

Aaron must not enter Canaan to show that the Levitical priesthood could make nothing perfect. That must be done by the bringing in of a better hope. Those priests could not continue by reason of sin and death but the priesthood of Christ, being undefiled, is unchangeable and to this, which abides for ever, Aaron must resign all his honour (Heb. 7: 23—25).

Numbers 20

When Moses was dead, God buried him. When Christ was dead, God raised him, for the law of Moses was to have an end but not the gospel of Christ.

Deuteronomy 34

Great destruction had been made both in city and country but in both there was a remnant that escaped which typified the saved Israelites indeed (as appears by comparing Isa. 10: 22, 23 which speaks of this very event with Rom. 9:27, 28) and they shall go forth into the glorious liberty of the children of God.

2 Kings 19

As the tabernacle was built of the spoils of the Egyptians so the temple of the spoils of other Gentile nations. A happy presage of the interest the Gentiles should have in the church.

1 Chronicles 18

Zion must be here looked upon as a type of the gospel church, which is called 'Mount Zion' (Heb. 12:22), and in it what is here said of Zion has its full accomplishment. Zion was long since ploughed as a field, but the church of Christ is the 'house of the living God' (1 Tim. 3:15), and it is his 'rest for ever', and shall be blessed with his presence always, even to the end of the world. The delight God takes

in his church, and the continuance of his presence with his church, are the comfort and joy of all its members.

Psalm 132

The words have a double aspect, speaking historically of the calling of Israel out of Egypt and prophetically of the bringing of Christ thence; and the former was a type of the latter, and a pledge and earnest of the many and great favours God had in reserve for that people, especially the sending of his Son into the world, and the bringing him again into the land of Israel when they had unkindly driven him out, and he might justly never have returned. The calling of Christ out of Egypt was a figure of the calling of all that are his, through him, out of spiritual slavery.

Hosea 11

The temple was in a special manner sanctified to be a house of prayer, for it was not only the place of that worship, but the medium of it, so that the prayers made in or toward that house had a particular promise of acceptance (2 Chron. 6:21), as it was a type of Christ; therefore Daniel looked that way in prayer; and in this sense no house or place is now, or can be, a house of prayer, for Christ is our Temple; yet in some sense the appointed places of our religious assemblies may be so called, as places where prayer is wont to be made (Acts 16:13).

Matthew 21

The doctrines of the gospel concerning Christ —that he is

the Mediator between God and man, that he is our peace, our righteousness, our Redeemer; by these things do men live. Our bodies could better live without food than our souls without Christ. Bread-corn is bruised (Isa. 28:28), so was Christ; he was born at Bethlehem, the house of bread, and typified by the show-bread.

John 6

Christ comes to do that which the law could not do. Moses brought the children of Israel to the borders of Canaan, and then died, and left them there; but Joshua did that which Moses could not do, and put them in possession of Canaan.

Romans 8

Judaism was Christianity under a veil, wrapt up in types and dark hints. The gospel was preached to them, in their legal rites and sacrifices. And the providence of God towards them, and what happened to them notwithstanding these privileges, may and ought to be warnings to us.

They were miraculously conducted through the Red Sea, where the pursuing Egyptians were drowned: it was a lane to them, but a grave to these: a proper type of our redemption by Christ, who saves us by conquering and destroying his enemies and ours.

Not only the laws and ordinances of the Jews, but the providences of God towards them, were typical. Their sins against God, and backslidings from him, were typical of the infidelity of many under the gospel. God's judgments on them were types of spiritual judgments now. Their exclusion from the earthly Canaan typified the exclusion of many under the gospel out of the heavenly Canaan, for their unbelief. Their history was written, to be a standing monitor to the church, even under the last and most perfect dispensation.

1 Corinthians 10

Now of this tabernacle it is said that it was divided into two parts, called a first and a second tabernacle, an inner and an outer part, representing the two states of the church militant and triumphant, and the two natures of Christ, human and divine.

In entering into the holiest, the high priest must first go through the outer sanctuary, and through the veil, signifying that Christ went to heaven through a holy life and a violent death; the veil of his flesh was rent asunder.

Hebrews 9

Tyranny

Those that willingly walk after the commandment, even when it walks contrary to the command of God, will find the commandment an encroaching thing, and that the more power is given it the more it will claim. Note, nothing gives greater advantage to a mastiff-like tyranny, that is fierce and furious, than a spaniel-like submission, that is fawning and flattering. Thus is 'Ephraim oppressed and broken in judgment', that is, he is wronged under a face and colour of right. Note, it is a sad and sore judgment upon any people to be oppressed under pretence of having justice done them.

Hosea 5

Unbelief

Like foolish froward children they fall acrying yet know not what they cry for. It would have been time enough to cry out when the enemy had beaten up their quarters and they had seen the sons of Anak at the gate of their camp.

Unbelief, or distrust of God, is a sin that is its own punishment. Those that do not trust God are continually vexing themselves.

Disbelief of the promise is a forfeiture of the benefit of it.

Numbers 14

It was not the breach of any of the commandments of the law that shut them out of Canaan, no, not the golden calf, but their disbelief of that promise which was typical of Gospel grace, to signify that no sin will ruin us but unbelief which is a sin against the remedy.

Deuteronomy 1

The same thing that kept their fathers forty years out of Canaan kept them now out of the full possession of it, and that was unbelief. Distrust of the power and promise of God lost them their advantages and ran them into a thousand mischiefs.

Judges 1

Nothing is more offensive to

God than disbelief of his promise and despair of the performance of it because of some difficulties that seem to lie in the way.

Psalm 96

The unbelief of the deceived, with all the falsehood of the deceivers, shall not make the divine threatenings of no effect; sword and famine will come, whatever they say to the contrary; and those will be least safe that are most secure. Impenitent sinners will not escape the damnation of hell by saying that they can never believe there is such a thing, but will feel what they will not fear.

Jeremiah 14

There are many things in Christ which they who are ignorant and unthinking are apt to be offended at, some circumstances for the sake of which they reject the substance of his Gospel. The meanness of his appearance, his education at Nazareth, the poverty of his life, the despicableness of his followers, the slights which the great men put upon him, the strictness of his doctrine, the contradiction it gives to flesh and blood, and the sufferings that attend the profession of his name; these are things that keep many from him, who otherwise cannot but see much of God in him.

Matthew 11

Unbelief is the great obstruction to Christ's favours. All things are in general possible to God (ch. 19:26), but then it is to him that believes as to the particulars (Mark 9:23). The gospel is the power of God unto salvation, but then it is to every one that believes (Rom. 1:16). So that if mighty works be not wrought in us, it is not for want of power or grace in Christ, but for want of faith in us.

Matthew 13

Unbelief is apt to mistake recruits for enemies, and to draw dismal conclusions even from comfortable premises (Judges 13:22, 23); but faith can find encouragement even in that which is discouraging, and get nearer to God by taking hold on that hand which is stretched out to push it away. So good a thing it is to be of 'quick understanding in the fear of the Lord' (Isa. 11:3).

Matthew 15

'They showed to the chief priests all the things that were done'; told them of the earthquake, the descent of the angel, the rolling of the stone away, and the coming of the body of Jesus alive out of the grave. Thus the sign of the prophet Jonas was brought to the chief priests with the most clear and incontestable evidence that could be; and so the utmost means of conviction were afforded them; we may well imagine what a mortification it was to them, and that, like the enemies of the Jews, they were much cast down in their own eyes (Neh. 6:16). It might justly have been expected that they should now have believed in Christ, and repented their putting him to death; but they were obstinate in their infidelity, and therefore sealed up under it.

Matthew 28

They acknowledged the two great proofs of the divine original of his gospel — the divine wisdom that appeared in the contrivance of it, and the divine power that was exerted for the ratifying and recommending of it; and yet, though they could not deny the premises, they would not admit the conclusion.

May we think that if they had not known his pedigree, but he had dropped among them from the clouds, without father, without mother, and without descent, they would have entertained him with any more respect? Truly, no; for in Judea, where this was not known, that was made an objection against him (John 9:29); 'As for this fellow, we know not from whence he is'. Obstinate unbelief will never want excuses.

Mark 6

Afterward, when he was nailed to the cross, they prescribed a new sign; 'Let him come down from the cross, and we will believe him'; thus obstinate infidelity will still have something to say, though ever so unreasonable. They demanded this sign, tempting him; not in hopes that he would give it them, that they might be satisfied, but in hopes that he would not; that they might imagine themselves to have a pretence for their infidelity.

Mark 8

Unbelief may truly be called the great damning sin, because it leaves us under the guilt of all our other sins; it is a sin against the remedy, against our appeal.

He that believeth not the Son is undone. The word includes both incredulity and disobedience. An unbeliever is one that gives not credit to the doctrine of Christ, nor is in subjection to the government of Christ.

John 3

But there are those who will trust Christ no further than they can see him, and will not believe his promise, unless the means of the performance of it be visible; as if he were tied to our methods, and could not draw water without our buckets.

John 4

The ambition and affectation of worldly honour are a great hindrance to faith in Christ. How can they believe who make the praise and applause of men their idol? When the profession and practice of serious godliness are unfashionable, are everywhere spoken against — when Christ and his followers are men wondered at, and to be a Christian is to be like a 'speckled bird' (and this is the common case) — how can they believe the summit of whose ambition is to make a fair show in the flesh?

John 5

It is certain that they might have known whence he was, might not only have known, by searching the register, that he was born in Bethlehem; but by enquiring into his doctrine, miracles, and conversation, they might have known that he was sent of God, and had better orders, a better commission, and far better instructions, than any they could give him. See

the absurdity of infidelity. Men will not know the doctrine of Christ because they are resolved they will not believe it, and then pretend they do not believe it because they do not know it. Such ignorance and unbelief, which support one another, aggravate one another.

John 9

The Spirit, in conviction, fastens especially upon the sin of unbelief, their not believing in Christ . . . as the great ruining sin. Every sin is so in its own nature; no sin is so to them that believe in Christ; so that it is unbelief that damns sinners. . . It is a sin against the remedy.

John 16

As when they resolved not to believe the finger of the Spirit in Christ's miracles, they turned it off with this, 'He casteth out devils by compact with the prince of devils'; so, when they resolved not to believe the voice of the Spirit in the apostles' preaching, they turned it off with this, 'These men are full of new wine'.

Acts 2

They held the truth as a captive or prisoner, that it should not influence them, as otherwise it would. An unrighteous wicked heart is the dungeon in which many a good truth is detained and buried. 'Holding fast the form of sound words in faith and love' is the root of all religion (2 Tim. 1:13), but holding it fast in unrighteousness is the root of all sin.

Romans 1

Unction

They went to meet him to congratulate him on his safe passage through fire and water and the honour God had put upon him and they bowed themselves to the ground before him. They were trained up in the schools but Elisha was taken from the plough, yet when they perceived that God was with him and that this was the man whom he delighted to honour, they readily submitted to him as their head and father, as the people to Joshua when Moses was dead.

2 Kings 2

Unequally Yoked

Joseph was a just man, she a virtuous woman. Those who are believers should not be unequally yoked with unbelievers: but let those who are religious choose to marry with those who are so, as they expect the comfort of the relation, and God's blessing upon them in it.

Matthew 1

Union with Christ

Believers dwell in Christ as their stronghold or city of refuge; Christ dwells in them as the master of the house, to rule it and provide for it. Such is the union between Christ and believers that he shares in their griefs, and they share in his graces and joys; he sups with them upon their bitter herbs and they with him upon his rich dainties. It is an inseparable union, like that between the body and digested food (Rom. 8:35; 1 John 4:13).

John 6

'He is crucified with Christ', and yet 'Christ lives in him'; this results from his mystical union with Christ, by means of which he is interested in the death of Christ, so as by virtue of that to live unto God.

Galatians 2

Unity

O that Israel would learn this of Canaanites to sacrifice private interests to the public welfare and to lay aside all animosities among themselves that they may cordially unite against the common enemies of God's kingdom among men.

Joshua 9

It was strange that none of their brethren of their own tribe, much less of any other, came in to their assistance, but it was long after Israel came to Canaan before there appeared among them anything of a public spirit or concern for a common interest which was the reason why they seldom united in a common head and this kept them low and inconsiderable.

Judges 18

All the prophets agreed as one man that Ahab should return from this expedition a conqueror. Unity is not always the mark of a true church and a true ministry. Here were 400 men that prophesied with one mind and one mouth and yet all in error.

1 Kings 22

How much more considerable might Israel have been than they were in the time of the judges if all the tribes had acted in conjunction.

1 Chronicles 5

When they acted as workmen, it was requisite they should be dispersed wherever there was work to do; but when as soldiers it was requisite they should come into close order, and be found in a body. Thus should the labourers in Christ's building be ready to unite against a common foe.

Nehemiah 4

Do the enemies of the church act with one consent to destroy it? Are the kings of the earth of one mind to give their power and honour to the beast? And shall not the church's friends be unanimous in serving her interests?

Psalm 83

Peter talked of making three distinct tabernacles for Moses, Elias, and Christ, which was not well-contrived; for such a perfect harmony there is between the law, the prophets, and the gospel, that one tabernacle will hold them all; they dwell together in unity.

Thus apt are we to imagine that those do not follow Christ at all, who do not follow him with us, and that those do nothing well, who do not just as we do. But the Lord knows them that are his, however they are dispersed; and this instance gives us a needful caution, to take heed lest we be carried, by an excess of zeal for the unity of the

church, and for that which we are sure is right and good, to oppose that which yet may tend to the enlargement of the church, and the advancement of its true interests another way.

Mark 9

He saw that his father had taken him in, and yet he would not go in to him. Note, we think too well of ourselves, if we cannot find in our hearts to receive those whom God hath received, and to admit those into favour, and friendship, and fellowship with us, whom we have reason to think God has a favour for, and who are taken into friendship and fellowship with him.

Luke 15

That is a conspiracy, not a union, which doth not centre in God as the end, and Christ as the way. . . Those words, 'I in them, and thou in me', show what that union is which is so necessary, not only to the beauty, but to the very being, of his church. First, union with Christ: 'I in them'. Christ dwelling in the hearts of believers is the life and soul of the new man. Secondly, union with God through him: 'Thou in me', so as by me to be in them. Thirdly, union with each other, resulting from these: 'that they' hereby 'may be made perfect in one.' We are complete in him.

John 17

Would we have the Spirit 'poured out upon us from on high?' Let us be all of one accord, and, notwithstanding variety of sentiments and interests, as no doubt there was among those disciples, let us agree to love one another; for, where 'brethren dwell together in unity', there it is that 'the Lord commands his blessing.'

Acts 2

A Christian, though not in every thing of our mind, should be loved and respected for his sake whose name he bears, because he belongs to Christ.

Acts 11

We ought not to make any conditions of our brethren's acceptance with us but such as God has made the conditions of their acceptance with him (Rom. 14:3).

Those that have their hearts purified by faith are therein made so nearly to resemble one another, that, whatever difference there may be between them, no account is to be made of it; for the faith of all the saints is alike precious, and has like precious effects (2 Peter 1:1), and those that by it are united to Christ are so to look upon themselves as joined to one another as that all distinctions, even that between Jew and Gentile, are merged and swallowed up in it.

Acts 15

Believers lie not in the world as a confused disorderly heap, but are organised and knit together, as they are united to one common head, and actuated and animated by one common Spirit.

Romans 12

Those that agree in Christ, who

is the Alpha and the Omega, the first and the last, and the great centre of unity, may well afford to agree among themselves.

Jews and Gentiles being thus united in Christ's love, why should they not be united in one another's love?

Romans 15

If you have any regard to that dear and worthy name by which you are called, be unanimous. 'Speak all the same thing'; avoid divisions or schisms (as the original is), that is, all alienation of affection from each other. 'Be perfectly joined together in the same mind', as far as you can. In the great things of religion be of a mind: but, when there is not a unity of sentiment, let there be a union of affections. The consideration of being agreed in greater things should extinguish all feuds and divisions about minor ones.

1 Corinthians 1

To be of one mind, which would greatly tend to their comfort; for the more easy we are with our brethren the more ease we shall have in our own souls. The apostle would have them, as far as was possible, to be of the same opinion and judgment; however, if this could not be attained, yet, he exhorts them to live in peace, that difference in opinion should not cause an alienation of affections — that they should be at peace among themselves. He would have all the schisms that were among them healed, that there should be no more contention and wrath found among them, to prevent which they should avoid 'debates, envyings, backbitings, whisperings,' and such like enemies to peace.

2 Corinthians 13

He showed his charitable and catholic disposition, how ready he was to own the Jewish converts as brethren, though many of them could scarcely allow the like favour to the converted Gentiles, and that mere difference of opinion was no reason with him why he should not endeavour to relieve and help them. Herein he has given us an excellent pattern of Christian charity, and has taught us that we should by no means confine it to those who are just of the same sentiments with us, but be ready to extend it to all whom we have reason to look upon as the disciples of Christ.

Galatians 2

The first step towards unity is humility; without this there will be no meekness, no patience, or forbearance; and without these no unity. Pride and passion break the peace, and make all the mischief. Humility and meekness restore the peace, and keep it.

The seat of Christian unity is in the heart or spirit: it does not lie in one set of thoughts, nor in one form and mode of worship, but in one heart and one soul.

As in a bundle of rods, they may be of different lengths and different strength; but, when they are tied together by one bond, they are stronger than any, even than the thickest and strongest was of itself.

There should be one heart; for 'there is one body, and one Spirit', (v. 4). Two hearts in one body would be monstrous. If there be but one body, all that belong to that body should have one heart.

Ephesians 4

Urgency

If he neglected thus to surrender himself, it was at his peril. If the avenger of blood met him elsewhere or overtook him loitering in his way to the city of refuge and slew him, his blood was upon his own head because he did not make use of the security which God provided for him.

Numbers 35

They ran to the tent not only to show their readiness to obey Joshua's orders but to show how uneasy they were till the camp was cleared of the accursed thing that they might regain the divine favour. Those that feel themselves under wrath find themselves concerned not to defer the putting away of sin; delays are dangerous and it is no time to trifle.

Joshua 7

Usefulness

There was serving work, abundance of service to be done in the tabernacle of the House of God, to provide water and fuel, to wash and sweep and carry out ashes, to kill and flay and boil the sacrifices and to all such services there were Levites appointed. Those of other families, or perhaps those that were not fit to be singers that had either no good voice or no good ear. As every one has received the gift so let him minister. Those who could not sing must not, therefore, be laid aside as good for nothing; though they were not fit for that service, there was other service they might be useful in.

1 Chronicles 6

God was and still is the God of order and not of confusion particularly in the things of his worship. Number without order is but a clog and an occasion of tumult but when everyone has and knows and keeps his place and work, the more the better. In the mystical body every member has its use for the good of the whole.

1 Chronicles 24

Here are no officers for state, none for sport, no master of the wardrobe, no master of the ceremonies, no master of the horse, no master of the hounds but all for service agreeable to the simplicity and plainness of those times.

1 Chronicles 27

Some have maintained that the joys of the saints in heaven are more desirable, infinitely more so, than the comforts of saints on earth; yet the services of saints on earth, especially such eminent ones as David was, are more laudable, and redound more to the glory of the divine grace, than the services of the saints in heaven, who are not employed in maintaining the war against sin and Satan, nor in edifying the body of Christ.

Psalm 6

Here is a promise to him that has, that has true grace, pursuant to the election of grace, that has, and uses what he has; he shall have more abundance: God's favours are earnests of further favours; where he lays the foundation, he will build upon it. Christ's disciples used the knowledge they now had, and they had more abundance at the pouring out of the Spirit (Acts 2). They who have the truth of grace, shall have the increase of grace, even to an abundance in glory (Prov. 4:18). Joseph he will add (Gen. 30:24).

Matthew 13

Vanity

The prophet expressly vouches God's authority for what he said, lest it should be thought it was unbecoming in him to take notice of such things, and should be resented by the ladies: the Lord saith it. 'Whether they will hear, or whether they will forbear, let them know that God takes notice of, and is much displeased with, the folly and vanity of proud women, and his law takes cognizance even of their dress.'

From all this let us learn: 1. Not to be nice and curious about our apparel, not to affect that which is gay and costly, nor to be proud of it. 2. Not to be secure in the enjoyment of any of the delights of sense, because we know not how soon we may be stripped of them, nor what straits we may be reduced to.

Isaiah 3

Vengeance

Though they cried for quarter and begged ever so earnestly for their lives there was no room for compassion. Pity must be forgotten; they utterly destroyed all. If they had not had a divine warrant under the seal of miracles for this execution it could not have been justified nor can it justify the like now when we are sure no such warrant can be produced . . . but the spirit of the gospel is very different for Christ came not to destroy men's lives but to save them (Luke 9:56). Christ's victories were of another nature.

Joshua 6

Victorious Christians

Be they ever so great and strong, ever so many, ever so mighty, ever so malicious, what can they do? While God is for us, and we keep in his love, we may with a holy boldness defy all the powers of darkness. Let Satan do his worst, he is chained; let the world do its worst, it is conquered: principalities and powers are spoiled and disarmed, and triumphed over, in the cross of Christ. Who then dares fight against us, while God himself is fighting for us?

Romans 8

Vindication of God's Ways

Solomon says 'Better is the end of a thing than the beginning thereof' (Eccles. 7:8). It was so here in the story of Job; at eveningtime it was light. Three things we have met with in this book, which, I confess, have troubled me very much; but we find all the three grievances redressed, thoroughly redressed, in this chapter, everything set to rights.

1. It has been a great trouble to us to see such a holy man as Job was, so fretful, and peevish, and uneasy to himself, and especially to hear him quarrel with God and speak indecently to him; but, 'though he thus fall, he is not utterly cast down, for here he recovers his temper, comes to himself and to his right mind again by repentance, is sorry for what he has said amiss, unsays it, and humbles himself before God (v. 1—6).

2. It has been likewise a great trouble to us to see Job and his friends so much at variance, not only differing in their opinions, but giving one another a great many hard words, and passing severe censures one upon another, 'though they were all very wise and good men'; but here we have this grievance redressed likewise, the differences between them happily adjusted, the quarrel taken up, all the peevish reflections they had cast upon one another forgiven and forgotten, and all joining in sacrifices and prayers, mutually accepted of God (v. 7—9).

3. It has troubled us to see a man of such eminent piety and usefulness as Job was, so grievously afflicted, so pained, so

sick, so poor, so reproached, so slighted, and made the very centre of all the calamities of human life; but here we have this grievance redressed too, Job healed of all his ailments, more honoured and beloved than ever, enriched with an estate double to what he had before, surrounded with all the comforts of life, and as great an instance of prosperity as ever he had been of affliction and patience (v. 10—17). All this is written for our learning, that we, under these and the like discouragements that we meet with, through patience and comfort of this scripture may have hope.

Job 42

Warnings

God plagued the Egyptians with flies but the Canaanites with hornets. Those who take no warning by less judgments on others may expect greater on themselves.

Deuteronomy 7

The accomplishment of these predictions upon the Jewish nation shows that Moses spoke by the Spirit of God, who certainly foresees the ruin of sinners and gives them a warning of it, that they may prevent it by a true and timely repentance or else be left inexcusable.

Deuteronomy 28

How strange, 1. That Solomon, in his old age should be ensnared with fleshly lusts, youthful lusts . . . 2. That so wise a man as Solomon was, so famed for a quick understanding and sound judgment should suffer himself to be made such a fool of by these foolish women . . . 3. That one who had so often and so plainly warned others of the danger of the love of women should himself be so wretchedly bewitched with it; it is easier to see a mischief, and to show it to others, than to shun it ourselves . . . 4. That so good a man, so zealous for the worship of God . . . who prayed that excellent prayer at the dedication of the temple, should do these sinful things . . . never was gallant ship so wrecked . . . we see how weak we are of ourselves without the grace of God. Let us, therefore, live in a constant dependence on that grace . . . it is the evening that commends the day.

1 Kings 11

It is a great advantage to us to be warned of our danger, that we may stand upon our guard against it. The work of God's prophets is to give us warning. If, being warned, we do not save ourselves, it is our own fault and our blood will be upon our own head. The king of Israel would regard the warnings Elisha gave him of his danger by the Syrians but not the warnings he gave him of his danger by his sins. Such warnings are little heeded by the most. They will save themselves from death but not from hell.

2 Kings 6

The treachery of those who pretend to cleave to God will be reckoned for, as well as the apostasy of those who openly revolt from him.

Judah saw what Israel did, and what came of it, and should have taken warning. Israel's captivity was intended for Judah's admonition; but it had not the designed effect. Judah feared not, but thought herself safe because she had Levites to be her priests and sons of David to be her kings.

It is an evidence of great stupidity and security when we are not awakened to a holy fear by the judgments of God upon others.

Jeremiah 3

Sinners are commonly hardened in their security by the intermissions of judgments and the slow proceedings of them; and those who will not be awakened by the word of God may justly be lulled asleep by the providence of God.

Satan himself, though he is the great deceiver, could not deceive us if we did not deceive ourselves; and thus sinners are their own destroyers by being their own deceivers, of which this is an aggravation that they are so frequently warned of it and cautioned not to deceive themselves, and they have the word of God, the great design of which is to undeceive them.

Jeremiah 37

Jerusalem should have taught her neighbours the fear of God by her piety and virtue, but, she not doing that, God will teach it to them by her ruin; for they have reason to say, 'If this be done in the green tree, what shall be done in the dry?' If judgment begin at the house

of God, where will it end? If those be thus punished who only had some idolaters among them, what will become of us who are all idolaters? Note, the destruction of some is designed for the instruction of others. Malefactors are publicly punished *'in terrorem'* — that others may take warning.

Ezekiel 5

Christ knew that they were of the elect, who could not possibly be seduced, and yet he said to them, 'Take heed'. An assurance of persevering, and cautions against apostasy, will very well consist with each other. Though Christ said to them 'Take heed', it doth not therefore follow that their perseverance was doubtful, for they were kept by the power of God; and though their perseverance was secured, yet it doth not therefore follow that this caution was needless, because they must be kept in the use of proper means. God will keep them, but they must keep themselves.

Mark 13

Watchfulness

The best of men have their failings, even in those graces for which they are most eminent for. The man Moses was very meek and yet here he sinned in passion. Wherefore, 'let him that thinketh he stands take heed lest he fall.'

Numbers 20

Though Solomon was a man of great learning and knowledge, yet he spent his days, not in contemplation but in action, not in his study but in his country, in building cities and fortifying them; in a time of peace preparing for a time of war which is as much a man's business as it is in summer to provide food for winter . . . The men of Laish who had no business were an easy prey to the invaders (Judges 18:7).

2 Chronicles 8

There are many ways of keeping things — by care, by strength, by calling in help, and we must use them all in keeping our hearts.

Proverbs 4

Being told, before, that there will be seducers, tempters, persecutors, and many bad examples, let us stand upon our guard (Matt. 24:24; Acts 20: 29, 30).

Matthew 18

Weaker Brethren

Our own humour and appetite must not determine our practice, but the honour of God and the good and edification of the church. We should not so much consult our own pleasure and interest as the advancement of the kingdom of God among men. Note, a Christian should be a man devoted to God, and of a public spirit.

1 Corinthians 10

Wealth

Riches and honour in abundance prove to many a clog and a hindrance in the ways of the

Lord. An occasion of pride, security and sensuality but they had a quite contrary effect upon Jehoshaphat. His abundance was oil to the wheels of his obedience and the more he had of the wealth of this world, the more was his heart lifted up in the ways of the Lord.

2 Chronicles 17

It was generously done of the king and the princes, thus plentifully to entertain the whole congregation, but what is a great estate good for but that it puts men into a capacity for doing so much the more good.

2 Chronicles 30

It is the interest of princes and great men to use their wealth and power for the support and encouragement of religion. What else are great revenues good for but that they enable men to do much good of this kind if they have but hearts to do it?

Ezra 7

Riches are called *substance*, in conformity to the common form of speaking; otherwise to the soul and another world, they are but shadows, *things that are not* (Prov. 23:5). It is only in heavenly wisdom that we *inherit substance* (Prov. 8:21).

Job 1

He *shall be thy gold*; so it is in the margin, and it is the same word that is used (v. 24) for gold, but signifies also a stronghold, because *money is a defence* (Eccles. 7:12). Worldlings make gold their god, saints make God their gold; and those that are enriched with his favour and grace may truly be said to *have abundance of the best gold* . . . Those must needs be safe that have omnipotence itself for their defence (Ps. 91:1—3).

Job 22

He reckons his wealth, not by his silver and gold, which were for hoarding, but by his butter and oil, which were for use; for what is an estate good for unless we take the good of it ourselves and do good with it to others?

Job 29

The wealth of the world is so dispensed by the divine providence that it is often the lot of good people to have but a little of it, and of wicked people to have abundance of it; for thus God would show us that the things of this world are not the best things, for, if they were, those would have most that are best and dearest to God.

Psalm 37

Poor people are as much in danger from an inordinate desire towards the wealth of the world as rich people from an inordinate delight in it.

Psalm 49

The things of this world are things that are not. They have a real existence in nature and are the real gifts of providence, but in the kingdom of grace they are things that are not; they are not a happiness and portion for a soul, are not what they promise to be; they are a show, a shadow, a sham upon the soul that trusts to them. They are not, for in a

little while they will not be; they will not be ours.

The covetous man sits hatching upon his wealth, and brooding over it, till it is fledged, as the young ones under the hen, and then it is gone. Or, as if a man should be fond of a flight of wild-fowl that light in his field, and call them his own because they are upon his ground, whereas, if he offer to come near them, they take wing immediately and are gone to another man's field.

Snow will last awhile, and look pretty, if it be left to lie on the ground where it fell, but, if gathered up and laid in the bosom, it is dissolved and gone immediately. They go irresistibly and irrecoverably, as an eagle towards heaven, that flies strongly (there is no stopping her), and flies out of sight and out of call (there is no bringing her back); thus do riches leave men, and leave them in grief and vexation if they set their hearts upon them.

Proverbs 23

Does the estate thrive? And does not the family at the same time grow more numerous and the children grow up to need more? The more men have, the better house they must keep, the more servants they must employ, the more guests they must entertain, the more they must give to the poor, and the more they will have hanging on them, for where the carcase is the eagles will be. What we have more than food and raiment we have for others; and then what good is there to the owners themselves, but the pleasure of beholding it with their eyes? And a poor pleasure it is. An empty speculation is all the difference between the owners and the sharers; the owner sees that as his own which those about him enjoy as much of the real benefit of as he; only he has the satisfaction of doing good to others, which is indeed a satisfaction to one who believes what Christ said, that it is more blessed to give than to receive; but to a covetous man, who thinks all lost that goes beside himself, it is a constant vexation to see others eat of his increase.

Ecclesiastes 5

There are many whose wealth is their snare and ruin. The gaining of the world is the losing of their souls; it makes them proud, secure, covetous, oppressive, voluptuous; and that which, if well used, might have been the servant of their piety, being abused, becomes the stumbling-block of their iniquity.

What the better was the rich man for his full barns when his soul was required of him, or that other rich man for his purple, and scarlet, and sumptuous fare, when in hell he could not procure a drop of water to cool his tongue? Money is no defence against the arrests of death, nor any alleviation to the miseries of the damned.

Ezekiel 7

They shall make a prey of the merchandise. It was in hope of the plunder that the city was set upon with so much vigour. See the vanity of riches, that they are kept for the owners to their hurt; they entice and recompense thieves, and not only cease to benefit those who took pains for them and were duly entitled to them but are made to serve their enemies, who are thereby put into a capacity of doing them so much the more mischief.

Ezekiel 26

It is folly to think that riches are things to be gloried in, and to say with exultation, 'I have become rich'. Riches are not the honours of the soul, are not peculiar to the best men, nor sure to us; and therefore 'let not the rich man glory in his riches' (James 1:9, 10).

Hosea 12

We must reckon ourselves truly enriched by the conversion of our neighbours to the fear of God and the faith of Christ, and their coming to join with us in the worship of God. Such an accession to our Christian communion we must reckon to be more our wealth and strength than an accession to our estates.

Obadiah

See the vanity of worldly wealth, and the uncertainty of its continuance with us. Riches make themselves wings and fly away; nay, and the case may be such that we may be under a necessity of making wings for them, and driving them away, as here, when they could not be kept for the owners thereof but to their hurt, so that they themselves are glad to be rid of them, and sink that which otherwise would sink them, though they have no prospect of ever recovering it. Oh that men would be thus wise for their souls, and would be willing to part with that wealth, pleasure, and honour which they cannot keep without making shipwreck of faith and a good conscience and ruining their souls for ever!

Jonah 1

Riches are but clay, thick clay; what are gold and silver but white and yellow earth? Those that travel through thick clay are both retarded and dirtied in their journey; so are those that go through the world in the midst of an abundance of the wealth of it; but, as if that were not enough, what fools are those that 'load themselves with it', as if this trash would be their treasure!

Habakkuk 2

Riches profit not in the day of wrath (Prov. 11:4). Nay, riches expose to the wrath of men (Eccles. 5:13), and riches abused to the wrath of God.

Zephaniah 1

It is very rare for a man to be rich, and not to set his heart upon his riches; and it is utterly impossible for a man that sets his heart upon his riches, to get to heaven; for 'if any man love the world, the love of the Father is not in him' (1 John 2:15; James 4:4).

Matthew 19

They that have ever so much riches, but do not trust in them, that see the vanity of them, and their utter insufficiency to make

a soul happy, have got over the difficulty, and can easily part with them for Christ: but they that have ever so little, if they set their hearts upon that little, and place their happiness in it, it will keep them from Christ.

Mark 10

It is natural for men to be jealous for that, whether right or wrong, by which they get their wealth; and many have, for this reason alone, set themselves against the gospel of Christ, because it calls men off from those crafts which are unlawful, how much wealth soever is to be obtained by them.

Acts 19

Any man will rather make shipwreck of his goods than of his life; but many will rather make 'shipwreck of faith and a good conscience' than of their goods.

Acts 27

God gives us our worldly possessions that we may honour him and do good with them; but if, instead of this, we sinfully hoard them up, through an undue affection towards them, or a distrust of the providence of God for the future, this is a very heinous crime.

James 5

Weather

There is no sort of weather but what furnishes us with a proof and instance of the wisdom and power of the great Creator.

Jeremiah 10

Wholeheartedness

Those that think to serve both
God and mammon will soon
come entirely to forsake God
and serve mammon only. If
God have not all the heart he
will soon have none of it.

Judges 10

Willingness

A people of willingness, alluding
to servants that choose their
service and are not coerced to
it (they love their masters and
would not go out free), to
soldiers that are volunteers and
not pressed men 'Here am
I, send me', to sacrifices that
are freewill offerings and not
offered of necessity; we 'present
ourselves living sacrifices'. Note,
Christ's people are a willing
people. The conversion of a
soul consists in its being willing
to be Christ's, coming under
his yoke and into his interests,
with an entire compliancy and
satisfaction.

Psalm 110

Wisdom

Solomon's wisdom was given
him not merely for speculation
to entertain himself (though it
is indeed a princely entertainment) not merely for conversation to entertain his friends,
but for action and, therefore, to
action he immediately applies
himself. . . He determined to
build . . . Those are the wisest
men that lay out themselves
most for the honour of the
name of the Lord and the
welfare of communities. We

are not born for ourselves but
for God and our country.

2 Chronicles 2

It is that which recommends us
to God, which beautifies the
soul, which enables us to answer
the end of our creation, to live
to some good purpose in the
world, and to get to heaven at
last; and therefore it is the
principal thing.

Proverbs 4

Wisdom here is Christ, 'in whom
are hidden all the treasures of
wisdom and knowledge'; it is
Christ in the word and Christ in
the heart, not only Christ
revealed to us, but Christ
revealed in us. It is the Word
of God, the whole compass of
divine revelation; it is God the
Word, in whom all divine revelation centres; it is the soul
formed by the Word; it is Christ
formed in the soul; it is religion
in the purity and power of it.
Glorious things are here spoken
of this excellent person, this
excellent thing.

Proverbs 8

A wise man will reckon those
his friends who deal faithfully
with him: 'Rebuke such a one,
and he will love thee for thy
plain dealing, will thank thee,
and desire thee to do him the
same good turn another time,
if there be occasion.' It is as
great an instance of wisdom to
take a reproof well as to give it
well.

Proverbs 9

There is need of a great deal of
wisdom in our adherence to
good truths, and good duties,
and good people, lest in any

of these we be imposed upon and deluded. 'Be ye therefore wise as serpents' (Matt. 10:16), wise to discern that which is really good and that which is counterfeit; wise to distinguish things that differ, to improve opportunities. While we are in the midst of so many deceivers, we have great need of that wisdom of the prudent which is to understand his way (Prov. 14:8).

Romans 16

The person who resigns his own understanding, that he may follow the instruction of God, is in the way to true and everlasting wisdom. 'The meek will he guide in judgment, the meek will he teach his way,' (Ps. 25:9). He that has a low opinion of his own knowledge and powers will submit to better information; such a person may be informed and improved by revelation: but the proud man, conceited of his own wisdom and understanding, will undertake to correct even divine wisdom itself, and prefer his own shallow reasonings to the revelations of infallible truth and wisdom.

1 Corinthians 3

The proper office of wisdom is to apply what we know to ourselves, for our own direction. The word of Christ must dwell in us, not in all notion and speculation, to make us doctors, but in all wisdom, to make us good Christians, and enable us to conduct ourselves in everything as becomes wisdom's children.

Colossians 3

He will not set up for the reputation of being wise without laying in a good stock of knowledge; *and he will not value himself merely upon knowing things.*

Words that *inform,* and *heal,* and *do good,* are the marks of wisdom.

It is a great instance of wisdom prudently to bridle our own anger, *and* patiently to bear the anger of others. And as wisdom will evidence itself in meekness, so meekness will be a great friend to wisdom; for nothing hinders the regular apprehension, the solid judgment, and impartiality of thought, necessary to our acting wisely, so much as passion. When we are mild and calm, we are best able to hear reason, and best able to speak it. Wisdom produces meekness, and meekness increases wisdom.

James 3

Wishful Christians

He shows his opinion of religion to be better than his resolution. There are many who desire to die the death of the righteous but do not endeavour to live the life of the righteous. Gladly would they have their end like theirs but not their way. They would be saints in heaven but not saints on earth.

Numbers 23

Worldliness

The world's smiles are more dangerous than its frowns.
2 Samuel 16

They lay upon the borders and conversed most with the neighbouring nations by which means they learned their idolatrous usages and transmitted the infection to the other tribes. . . These tribes were first placed and they were first displaced. They would have the best land, not considering that it lay most exposed but those who are governed more by sense than by reason or faith in their choices may expect to fare accordingly.
1 Chronicles 5

But he that loves these, that sets his heart upon them, covets them earnestly, is solicitous to have all the delights of sense wound up to the height of pleasureableness, is impatient of everything that crosses him in his pleasures, relishes these as the best pleasures, and has his mouth by them put out of taste for spiritual delights, he is an epicure (2 Tim. 3:4).
Proverbs 21

Let the house of Israel hear and receive this word from the God of Israel: 'Learn not the way of the heathen', do not approve of it, no, nor think indifferently concerning it, much less imitate it or accustom yourselves to it. Let not any of their customs steal in among you (as they are apt to do insensibly) nor mingle themselves with your religion. Note, it ill becomes those that are taught of God to 'learn the way of the heathen', and to think of worshipping the true God with such rites and ceremonies as they used in the worship of their false gods. See (Deut. 12: 29–31).
Jeremiah 10

Worldly-mindedness is as common and as fatal a symptom of hypocrisy as any other, for by no sin can Satan have a surer and faster hold of the soul, under the cloak of a visible and passable profession of religion, than by this; and therefore Christ, having warned us against coveting the praise of men, proceeds next to warn us against coveting the wealth of the world; in this also we must take heed, lest we be as the hypocrites are, and do as they do: the fundamental error that they are guilty of is, that they choose the world for their reward; we must therefore take heed of hypocrisy and worldly-mindedness, in the choice we make of our treasure, our end, and our masters.
Matthew 6

The description of a worldly man: He 'lays up treasure for himself', for the body, for the world, for himself in opposition to God, for that self that is to be denied.
Luke 12

Had they come to take him by force and make him a prisoner, he could not have been more industrious to abscond than he was when they would make him a king. Let us not then covet to be the idols of the crowd, nor be desirous of vainglory.
John 6

The world may be used, but must not be abused. It is abused when it is not used to those purposes for which it is given, to honour God and do good to men — when, instead of being oil to the wheels of our obedience, it is made fuel to lust — when, instead of being a servant, it is made our master, our idol, and has that room in our affections which should be reserved for God. And there is great danger of abusing it in all these respects, if our hearts are too much set upon it. We must keep the world as much as may be out of our hearts, that we may not abuse it when we have it in our hands.

Possess what you must shortly leave without suffering yourselves to be possessed by it. Why should your hearts be much set on what you must quickly resign?

1 Corinthians 7

Those that are forgiven of God are strongly obliged to relinquish this world, which so interferes with 'the love of God'.

If they be not too hard for the devil, he will be too hard for them. *Let vigorous Christians show their strength in conquering the world.*

Their love should be reserved for God; throw it not away upon the world.

The inconsistency of this love with the love of God: 'If any man love the world, the love of the Father is not in him' (v. 15). The heart of man is narrow, and cannot contain both loves. The world draws down the heart from God; and so the more the love of the world prevails the more the love of God dwindles and decays.

1 John 2

Worship

When we are going to worship God, we should seriously consider whether we have everything ready, especially the lamb for a burnt offering. The fire is ready, the Spirit's assistance and God's acceptance; the wood is ready, the instituted ordinances designed to kindle our affections (which indeed, without the Spirit, are but like wood without fire, but the Spirit works by them). All things are now ready but where is the lamb? Where is the heart? Is that ready to be offered up to God to ascend to him as a burnt offering?

Genesis 22

As secret worship is better the more secret it is, so public worship is better the more public it is.

2 Samuel 6

It is not time lost which is spent in composing ourselves for the work of God and disentangling ourselves from everything which might distract or divert us . . . we are truly serving God when we are preparing for his service and furnishing ourselves for it.

1 Kings 6

Crowned heads must bow before the King of kings. What is here said to the mighty is said to all:

Worship God, it is the sum and substance of the everlasting Gospel (Rev. 14:6, 7).

The glorious majesty of God is called the beauty of holiness (2 Chron. 20:21). In the worship of God we must have an eye to his beauty, and adore him, not only as infinitely awful and therefore to be feared above all, but as infinitely amiable and therefore to be loved and delighted in above all; especially we must have an eye to the beauty of his holiness; this the angels fasten upon in their praises (Rev. 4:8).

Psalm 29

The pleasantness of the harp and the awfulness of the trumpet intimate to us that God is to be worshipped with cheerfulness and holy joy, with reverence and godly fear. Singing aloud and making a noise intimate that we must be warm and affectionate in praising God, that we must with a hearty goodwill show forth his praise, as those that are not ashamed to own our dependence on him and obligations to him.

Psalm 81

In all the acts of religious worship, this is that which we must aim at, to pay him some of that reverence which we owe him as the best of beings and the fountain of our being.

Psalm 96

We must praise God with fervency of affection, and must stir up ourselves to do it, that it may be done in a lively

manner and not carelessly (v. 2): 'Awake psaltery and harp', let it not be done with a dull and sleepy tune, but let the airs be all lively. 'I myself will awake early' to do it, with all that is within me, and all little enough. *Warm devotions honour God.*

Psalm 108

His lying prostrate was a posture of greater reverence, but his standing up would be a posture of greater readiness and fitness for business. Our adorings of God must not hinder, but rather quicken and excite, our actings for God. He fell on his face in a holy fear and awe of God, but he was quickly raised up again; for those that humble themselves shall be exalted. God delights not in the dejections of his servants, but the same that brings them low will raise them up.

Ezekiel 2

Gospel-worship is here represented by the 'keeping of the feast of tabernacles', for the sake of those two great graces which were in a special manner 'acted' and 'signified' in that feast — contempt of the world, and joy in God (Neh. 8:17). The life of a good Christian is a constant 'feast of tabernacles', and, in all acts of devotion, we must retire from the world and rejoice in the Lord, must worship as in that feast.

Zechariah 14

If we worship God ignorantly, and without understanding, we bring the blind for sacrifice; if we do it carelessly, and without consideration, if we are cold, and dull, and dead, in it, we bring the sick; if we rest in the bodily exercise, and do not make heart-work of it, we bring the lame; and, if we suffer vain thoughts and distractions to lodge within us, we bring the torn, and 'is not this evil?' Is it not a great affront to God and a great wrong and injury to our own souls? Do not our books tell us, nay, do not our own hearts tell us, that 'this is evil?' For God, who is the best, ought to be served with the best we have.

Malachi 1

Yoke of God

They complained it may be of the strictness of their religion and forsook the law of the Lord because they thought it a yoke too hard, too heavy upon them. 'Well', saith God, 'let them better themselves if they can; let the neighbouring princes rule them awhile since they are not willing that I should rule them and let them try how they like that'. They might have served God with joyfulness and gladness of heart and would not. Let them serve their enemies then in hunger and thirst (Deut. 28: 47, 48) till they think of returning to their first Master for then it was better with them (Hosea 2:7). . . The more God's service is compared with other services, the more reasonable and easy it will appear. Whatever difficulties or hardships we may imagine there are in the way of obedience, it is better a thousand times to go through them than to expose ourselves to the punishment of disobedience. Are the laws of temperance thought hard? The effects of intemperance will be much harder. The service of virtue is perfect liberty, the service of lust is perfect slavery.

2 Chronicles 12

Young people are apt to be impatient of check and control, to vex and fret at anything that is humbling and mortifying to them, and their proud hearts rise against everything that crosses and contradicts them. They are so set upon that which is pleasing to sense that they cannot bear anything that is displeasing, but it goes with sorrow to their heart. Their pride often disquiets them, and makes them uneasy. Put that away, and the love of the world, and lay thy expectations low from the creature, and then disappointments will not be occasions of sorrow and anger to thee.

Ecclesiastes 11

Young People

Young people should be told of their faults as soon as it is perceived that they begin to be extravagant, lest their hearts be hardened . . . those that allow and countenance their children in any evil way and do not use their authority to restrain and punish them, do, in effect, honour them more than God, being more tender of their reputation than of his glory and more desirous to humour them than honour him.

1 Samuel 2

Zeal

It is hereby intimated that we must not seek occasions to abate our zeal in God's service nor be glad of an excuse to omit a good duty but rather rejoice in an opportunity of accumulating and doing more than ordinary in religion. If we perform family worship we must not think that this will excuse us from our secret devotions; nor that on the days we go to church we need not worship God alone and with our families; but we should always abound in the work of the Lord. . . No extraordinary services should jostle out our stated devotions.

Numbers 29

Jerusalem is said to continue in the hands of the Jebusites for the children of Judah could not drive them out through their sluggishness, stupidity and unbelief. Had they attempted it with vigour and resolution, we have reason to think that God would not have been wanting to them to give them success but they could not do it because they would not.

Joshua 15

A brand is put upon the Ephraimites that they did not drive out the Canaanites from Gezer either through carelessness or cowardice, either for want of faith in the promise of God that he would give them success if they would make a vigorous effort or for want of zeal for the command of God which obliged them utterly to drive out the Canaanites and make no peace with them.

Joshua 16

When their sincerity was made to appear, we do not find that they were blamed for their rashness. God does, and men should, overlook the weakness of an honest zeal.

Joshua 22

He did it with all his heart, and all his soul and all his might, with vigour and courage and resolution. He could not otherwise have broken through the difficulties he had to grapple with. What great things may we bring to pass in the service of God if we be but lively and hearty in it. He did this according to all the law of Moses in exact observance of that law and with an actual regard to it. His zeal did not transport him into any irregularities but in all he did he walked by rule.

2 Kings 23

He did that which was right like David. Of several of his predecessors it had been said that they did that which was right but not like David; not with David's integrity and zeal, but here was one that had as hearty an affection for the ark and law of God as ever David had.

2 Chronicles 29

Many of them were a great way from home and had business in the country to look after for this, being the second month, they were in the midst of their harvest, yet they were in no haste to return. The zeal of God's house made them forget their secular affairs.

2 Chronicles 30

By this it appears they were not averse to go, but were slothful and inattentive, and only wanted to be called upon and excited to go. What a pity it is that good men should omit a good work, merely for want of being spoken to! What a pity that they should need it, but, if they do, what a pity that they should be left without it!

Ezra 8

The flame of their zeal in the worship of false gods may shame us for our coldness and indifference in the worship of the true God. They strove to inflame themselves, but we distract and deaden ourselves.

Isaiah 57

The evening drawing on, the disciples moved it to Christ to send the multitude away; they thought there was a good days work done, and it was time to disperse. Note, Christ's disciples are often more careful to show their discretion, than to show their zeal; and their abundant consideration, rather than their abundant affection in the things of God.

Matthew 14

These Pharisees and scribes with whom he had this argument, are said to come from Jerusalem down to Galilee — fourscore or a hundred miles, to pick quarrels with our Saviour there, where they supposed him to have the greatest interest and reputation. Had they come so far to be

taught by him, their zeal had been commendable; but to come so far to oppose him, and to check the progress of his gospel, was great wickedness.

Mark 7

True zeal makes nothing of hardships in the way of duty. They that have a full feast for their souls may be content with slender provision for their bodies. It was an old saying among the Puritans, 'Brown bread and the gospel are good fare.'

Mark 8

He went into every city to preach; so they, one would think, should have contented themselves to hear him when he came to their own city (we know those that would); but there were those here that came to him out of every city, would not stay till he came to them, nor think that they had enough when he left them, but met him when he was coming towards them, and followed him when he was going from them.

Luke 8

They were somewhat surprised at first to see him to whom they were directed as the Lamb of God in such a heat, and him whom they believed to be the King of Israel take so little state upon him as to do this himself; but one scripture came to their thoughts, which taught them to reconcile this action both with the meekness of the Lamb of God and with the majesty of the King of Israel; for David, speaking of the Messiah, takes notice of his zeal for God's house, as so great that it even ate him up, it made him forget himself (Ps. 69:9).

John 2

Those who are newly acquainted with the things of God must be excused, if at first they be so taken up with the new world into which they are brought that the things of this world seem to be for a time wholly neglected.

He resolved never to quit it, nor to lay it down, till he could say, 'It is finished'. Many have zeal to carry them out at first, but not zeal to carry them on to the last; but our Lord Jesus was intent upon finishing his work.

John 4

They did not defer, in hopes to see him again on this side the water; but their convictions being strong, and their desires warm, they followed him presently. Good motions are often crushed, and come to nothing, for want of being prosecuted in time.

John 6

Let us see then that we do good, and have zeal in it; only looking that zeal be guided by knowledge and spirited with love, directed to the glory of God, and always in some good thing.

Titus 2

The origin of their wars and fightings was not (as they pretended) a true zeal for their country, and *for the honour of God*, but that their prevailing lusts were the cause of all. Observe hence: *What is sheltered and shrouded under a specious pretence of zeal for God and religion often comes from men's pride, malice, covetousness, ambition, and revenge.*

James 4

Index to Scripture References